www.wadsworth.com

wadsworth.com is the World Wide Web site for Wadsworth and is your direct source to dozens of online resources.

At *wadsworth.com* you can find out about supplements, demonstration software, and student resources. You can also send email to many of our authors and preview new publications and exciting new technologies.

wadsworth.com
Changing the way the world learns®

Contemporary Political Ideologies

A Comparative Analysis

12th Edition

LYMAN TOWER SARGENT
University of Missouri–St. Louis

THOMSON
———✦———™
WADSWORTH

Australia • Canada • Mexico • Singapore • Spain
United Kingdom • United States

Executive Editor: David Tatom
Development Editor: Drake Bush
Editorial Assistant: Dianna Long
Technology Project Manager: Melinda Newfarmer
Marketing Manager: Caroline Croley
Project Manager, Editorial Production: Katy German
Print/Media Buyer: Kris Waller

Permissions Editor: Elizabeth Zuber
Production Service: G & S Typesetters, Inc.
Photo Researcher: Terri Wright
Copy Editor: John Mulvihill
Printer: Transcontinental Louiseville

Printed in Canada
  2 3 4 5 6 7 06 05 04 03

For more information about our products,
contact us at:
Thomson Learning Academic Resource Center
1-800-423-0563

For permission to use material from this text,
contact us by: **Phone:** 1-800-730-2214
Fax: 1-800-730-2215
Web: http://www.thomsonrights.com

Library of Congress Control Number: 2002107778

ISBN 0-15-506063-5

Wadsworth / Thomson Learning
10 Davis Drive
Belmont, CA 94002-3098
USA

Asia
Thomson Learning
5 Shenton Way #01-01
UIC Building
Singapore 068808

Australia
Nelson Thomson Learning
102 Dodds Street
South Melbourne, Victoria 3205
Australia

Canada
Nelson Thomson Learning
1120 Birchmount Road
Toronto, Ontario M1K 5G4
Canada

Europe / Middle East / Africa
Thomson Learning
High Holborn House
50/51 Bedford Row
London WC1R 4LR
United Kingdom

Latin America
Thomson Learning
Seneca, 53
Colonia Polanco
11560 Mexico D.F.
Mexico

Spain
Paraninfo Thomson Learning
Calle/Magallanes, 25
28015 Madrid, Spain

To Evan

Contents

II NATIONALISM

2 NATIONALISM   21

IV FEMINISM

V IDEOLOGIES THAT ORIGINATED IN THE NINETEENTH CENTURY

About the Author

Lyman Tower Sargent is professor of political science at the University of Missouri—St. Louis. He has been a fellow at the Institute for Advanced Study, Princeton; a visiting professor at the University of Exeter, England, and the University of East Anglia, England; an academic visitor at the London School of Economics and Political Science; and an associate of the Stout Research Centre for the Study of New Zealand Society, History, and Culture, Victoria University of Wellington, New Zealand.

Sargent is the author of *New Left Thought: An Introduction* (Dorsey, 1972); *Techniques of Political Analysis* (with Thomas A. Zant, Wadsworth, 1970); *British and American Utopian Literature, 1516–1985: An Annotated, Chronological Bibliography* (Garland, 1988); *New Zealand Utopian Literature: An Annotated Bibliography* (Stout Research Centre, 1997); *New Zealand Intentional Communities: A Research Guide* (Stout Research Centre, 1997); and numerous articles in political theory. He is the editor of *Consent: Concept, Capacity, Conditions, Constraints* (Franz Steiner Verlag, 1979); *Extremism in America: A Reader* (New York University Press, 1995); *Political Thought in the United States: A Documentary History* (New York University Press, 1997); *The Utopia Reader* (with Gregory Claeys, New York University Press, 1999); and *Utopia: The Quest for the Ideal Society in the Western World* (with Roland Schaer and Gregory Claeys, Oxford University Press, 2000).

Preface

According to Feliks Gross, political ideologies have replaced religion as the focus of both human liberation and human fanaticism.[1] Ideologies such as *nationalism, democracy,* and *feminism* are the focus of this book. The essential features of a wide range of ideologies are presented so that they can be easily understood. To the extent possible, they are described as they are understood by their believers, together with some of the criticisms made by their opponents. In addition, each ideology is shown in the context of contemporary political and social issues and institutions. My goal is to help readers draw their own conclusions about each ideology based on a reasonably balanced presentation of that ideology and the way it functions today.

This book was first published in the period known as the Sixties (in the United States, roughly 1965–75) when Americans were first becoming aware of ideological debate in the United States. Americans had taken pride in being free of ideological conflicts, and compromise was thought to be the essential component of U.S. politics. While many outside the United States saw this very belief as identifying a dominant U.S. ideology, from the Sixties on Americans have generally been aware that political debate in this country is also ideological.

Therefore, to understand what is happening both in the United States and the rest of the world, it is important to understand the ideologies that inform the thought and actions of both politicians and average citizens. Understanding

---

1. Feliks Gross, *Ideologies, Goals, and Values* (Westport, Conn.: Greenwood Press, 1985), xxiii.

ideologies can also help us understand ourselves, what we believe. Self-identity, who we are and how we came to be who we are, is a question that most of us face at various times in our lives. When we are students we are finding out who we are or creating ourselves, and part of that process of identity-building is achieved through identification with like-minded others. Along with that identification often comes a set of beliefs, which sometimes constitutes an ideology. Later in life, we may reaffirm or change whom we identify with, and that change may bring a change in beliefs.

At the same time, many people are unaware of what different groups of people believe. I have heard many women say, "I am not a feminist, but . . . ," finishing the sentence with a statement that comes straight from feminism. The person is rejecting the stereotype of feminism, not understanding the actual beliefs of feminism. When I have asked women who have used the phrase "I am not a feminist" about specific positions taken by most feminists, they have most often agreed with the feminist position. Since stereotypes are used as part of political debate to distort the position of an opponent, it is important to know the actual positions.

Ideologies are reflected in political institutions and policies and are often used as tools, both consciously and unconsciously, by political actors. Ideologies change over time, reflecting both reconsideration of the principles or core beliefs found in the ideologies and the way practical political issues influence these beliefs. Thus, the reader will find here much discussion of current political debates throughout the world to illustrate how ideologies affect politics and are affected by it.

Since the first edition of *Contemporary Political Ideologies: A Comparative Analysis* was published about thirty-five years ago, it has been the leading text in the field. The book has undergone dramatic changes over the years. In this latest incarnation, the structure of the book is very similar to that of the previous edition, but the content has changed significantly because the lived experience of ideologies has changed. Over the past five years or so most ideologies have more clearly become constellations, with core beliefs/values but also with huge disagreements over how those beliefs/values fit together and how peripheral beliefs/values fit with the core. The book has been extensively rewritten to reflect this change. One sign of that change is that a number of topics that previously appeared in only one chapter now occur in more than one chapter, so that a topic is viewed from differing perspectives.

The most obvious changes are in the chapters on nationalism and Islam, reflecting the changed status of those beliefs in today's world. In addition, the separate chapter on Third World ideologies has been eliminated and the material in that chapter moved to other chapters as appropriate. Also, the chapter on Liberation Theology has been significantly changed because Liberation Theology has emerged in Africa, Asia, and the United States and in Protestant denominations. In fact, it had existed in these places in parallel with its development in Latin America, but the links between Roman Catholic Latin America and Protestant Africa, Asia, and the United States were initially hard to see and the ties difficult to forge. I have also added a brief note on terrorism to the introductory chapter.

I have maintained the essential character of the book as a comparative introduction to the dominant and some minor ideologies found in the world today. As always, I have included extensive lists of suggested readings so that readers can explore further questions that interest them. I have added a few Web sites to the suggested readings. Anyone familiar with the Web will know that some of these addresses will not be valid throughout the life of the book, but I have tried to choose ones that seem likely to have a substantial life.

1

◎

Ideologies

What Are They
and Why Study Them?

On September 11, 2001 terrorists attacked the World Trade Center in New York and the Pentagon in Washington, D.C., killing thousands of people. How could anyone justify such an act? On June 11, 2001 Timothy McVeigh (1968–2001) was executed for blowing up the Alfred P. Murrah Federal Office Building in Oklahoma City and killing 168 people. To his death, McVeigh said that his action was justified. Why? A few Americans agree with him, whereas most see him as a mass murderer. How can there be such fundamental differences within one country? In July 2001 a young man was killed in Genoa, Italy while protesting at the so-called G-8 (Group of 8) meeting.[1] Although only a few hundred of the protestors used violence, thousands more opposed the actions of these world leaders. The leaders are certain that they are right and the protestors wrong; the protestors are certain that they are right and the leaders wrong. Why?

The answer to these questions is ideology. The attacks on the World Trade Center and the Pentagon seem to have arisen from conflicts in the Middle East, all of which have strong ideological components. In the penalty phase of McVeigh's trial, his attorney called McVeigh's act an "ideological crime," and those

---

1. The G-7, or Group of Seven, is composed of the seven leading industrialized nations in the world. The G-8 is composed of those countries plus Russia. Industrialized here is defined as having the resources to have the ability to guide the world. The next meeting of the G-8 was held June 26–28, 2002 in Kananaskis Park, 2,400 square miles in the Canadian Rockies, forty miles west of Calgary, Alberta. The location was deliberately chosen to make it difficult for demonstrators to reach.

who believe that his act was justified see it that way. The majority sees it as murder and believe that ideology is irrelevant.[2] The protestors in Genoa came from many different groups, with varying agendas, but they did all agree that the assembled world leaders were damaging or destroying something they held dear (the environment, poor countries, poor people, and so forth). Most of the leaders believed that their actions were actually good for the environment, poor countries, poor people, and so forth. Since it is unlikely that both groups are right, it is necessary to look further at these beliefs. That is the purpose of this book.

Understanding the way ideology works and the content of various significant ideologies is important if we are to understand what happens in the world. In addition, because we are influenced by ideology whether we are aware of it or not, understanding these ideologies will help us understand our own beliefs as well as those of our friends and associates.

We are surrounded by expressions of ideology. Our parents try to influence the way we think, as do our friends, teachers, religious leaders, politicians, and so forth. When we read newspapers or magazines, listen to the radio, or watch TV, we are getting partial views that are consciously or unconsciously distorted. Since these sources of information often disagree, we are exposed to a range of ideologies, and, in the development of our own set of beliefs, we may be influenced by a variety of ideologies.

As we grow older, we also make conscious choices among beliefs and attitudes, either because we weigh one position against another and conclude that one is preferable according to some standard, or because we simply respect or dislike someone who holds that belief. Through this process of influence and choice, we gradually come to the set of beliefs and attitudes with which we will live. This set of beliefs may change, but it changes less as we age. This happens because the experiences of a lifetime have led us to these views, and it is extraordinarily difficult to set aside what we have come to believe to be the truth and accept that we have been wrong. Some people do come to such conclusions, usually because they encounter someone whose life experiences have led to different conclusions, thus forcing a reevaluation of their beliefs.

How do we identify an ideology? The most obvious way is through particular words that are associated with the ideology. For example, someone influenced by capitalism will usually speak favorably of the free market, and someone influenced by Marxism will use the word *class* in specific ways.

IDEOLOGY DEFINED

Scholars disagree over the meaning and importance of ideology. One has even written, "ideology is the most elusive concept in the whole of social science."[3] As a result, today ideology is itself what we have come to call an *essentially con-*

---

2. For a discussion of McVeigh's ideology, see Chapter 5.

3. David McLellan, *Ideology*, 2d ed. (Minneapolis: University of Minnesota Press, 1995), 1.

tested concept, or a concept about which there is truly fundamental disagreement.[4] (One study of ideology from the early 1990s listed sixteen definitions as currently in use, some of which are mutually exclusive.[5]) Most political debate swirls around such contested concepts, and all the ideologies discussed here contain one or more of them.

This section constructs a definition of ideology, distinguishes political ideologies from other ideologies, and shows how political ideology relates to political theory and political philosophy. Finally, a few of the most important theorists of ideology are presented, and some current controversies among theorists are described.

An ideology is a system of values and beliefs regarding the various institutions and processes of society that is accepted as fact or truth by a group of people. An ideology provides the believer with a picture of the world both as it is and as it should be, and, in doing so, organizes the tremendous complexity of the world into something fairly simple and understandable. Ideologies are organized or patterned beliefs. The degree of organization and the simplicity of the resulting picture vary considerably from ideology to ideology, and the ever-increasing complexity of the world tends to blur the pictures. At the same time, however, the fundamental pattern of each ideology remains fairly constant.

Ideologies are stories about the world we live in and our place in it. When we tell a story we structure information to communicate our understanding of something to someone else. Stories can, of course, be "tall tales" or lies, but they are still trying to present a pattern that can be accepted as true. The obvious "tall tale" depends on our recognizing it as such; the lie only works if the hearer believes it to be true.

As in traditional stories, ideologies present a coherent, understandable picture of that world. Believers, telling the story of their beliefs, are, they think, telling the truth; it is up to the reader, viewer, or listener to sort out truth from falsehood. When we read a story, we often suspend our disbelief in it and, at least while we are still reading, watching the film or video, or playing the computer game, the story becomes real. Some people have been known to want the story to be real so much that they lose themselves in it and try to change their world to be like the story rather than to accept its untruth. Although the best-known cases of this are connected with sophisticated computer games, the political stories we are taught that become ideologies have the same effect on many people.

A *political ideology* is, in its simplest formulation, an ideology that focuses on the political. The political system is the way that societies make decisions about their most important values; one scholar defines the political system as "the authoritative allocation of values" for a society.[6] Another scholar entitled a famous

---

4. See W. B. Gallie, "Essentially Contested Concepts," *Proceedings of the Aristotelian Society,* n.s., 56 (1955–56): 167–98; and William E. Connolly, *The Terms of Political Discourse,* 3d ed. (Princeton, N.J.: Princeton University Press, 1993).

5. Terry Eagleton, *Ideology: An Introduction* (London: Verso, 1991), 10–30.

6. David Easton, *The Political System: An Inquiry into the State of Political Science* (New York: Knopf, 1953), 129.

book *Politics: Who Gets What, When, How* (1936);[7] the definitions are much the same. Thus, it would be possible simply to insert the word *political* in front of the word *ideology* in the definition three paragraphs earlier, and the result would be a perfectly acceptable definition of *political ideology.*

And this book deals only with *political* ideologies, or, as in the case of Islam, with the *political* aspects of the religion, together with enough information about the religion to make it understood. There are many belief systems that are not political or in which the political plays a very small role. These belief systems can appropriately be called ideologies, but not *political* ideologies; therefore, they are not discussed here.

Political Philosophy, Political Theory, and Political Ideology

The terms *political ideology, political theory,* and *political philosophy* are frequently used to refer to different ways of thinking about political ideas. The first term, *political ideology,* relates, as we have seen, to the beliefs of a group. That term should never be used in place of either of the other two. The other two terms are often used interchangeably, with nothing lost. But at other times, it is important to distinguish between them.

When narrowly defined, political theory refers to theories or generalizations about politics and society that are based on data, just like any generalization in any science. Political philosophy, on the other hand, is explicitly evaluative or normative. It is a set of ideas about how governments and people should behave.

All three terms are connected. Every political philosophy is based in part on a political theory. In other words, every statement about how people and governments should behave contains a statement about how they do behave. In addition, every political ideology contains both political theory and political philosophy or generalizations about how people and governments do behave and how they should behave. But in a political ideology, these generalizations become belief systems rather than empirical or normative analyses of behavior.

Whatever words are used, the important thing to remember is that there are both differences and connections among generalizations about how social and political institutions and the people making them up behave, how they should behave, and the various belief systems that emerge from such generalizations.

SOCIAL MOVEMENTS AND IDEOLOGIES

Most ideologies initially developed in association with the growth and maturation of a social movement. This is obviously the case with the initial development of democracy in the seventeenth century, Marxism and anarchism in the nineteenth century, and fascism and National Socialism, feminism, Liberation

---

7. Harold Lasswell, *Politics: Who Gets What, When, How* (New York: McGraw-Hill, 1936).

Theology, and environmentalism in the twentieth century. But also, in all cases both scholars and believers have looked back before the emergence of the movement and found precedents and precursors. In the case of nationalism there is a fundamental dispute over whether it has been around for many centuries or just a few. As we shall see in the next chapter, the answers lead to very different interpretations of nationalism.

Today, when no social movement is completely unified, one of the most hotly contested areas is the ideology of the movement. Every faction vying for power says that it has the truth and that to really be part of the movement, believers must accept this as the truth. Thus, in addition to conflicts between ideologies, there are, today, deep divisions within ideologies; probably only an ideology that has lost its vitality could be free from such differences.

Some people may not even notice the differences between the various sets of beliefs that influence them, but others will be so torn apart by the conflict that they develop serious mental problems. Most of us muddle through, aware that we are not really consistent in our beliefs and behavior but not terribly bothered by that fact.

Similar situations occur within countries. In most open societies where many ideologies are recognized and accepted, conflict within the individual is unlikely to become important. But conflicts among ideologies may become obvious, and, if the numbers of adherents of conflicting ideologies are large enough and close enough in size, a country's stability can be affected. On the other hand, in a closed system with only one official ideology, an individual who holds beliefs counter to that ideology will probably be intensely aware of the difference and be affected by it. The same thing is true for the country as a whole. Ideological differences, particularly differences *within* the official ideology, become more important and can cause serious conflict.

In any society, different segments of the population will hold different ideologies. For example, within the United States today, the overwhelming majority, if asked, would call themselves believers in democracy. But some would call themselves anarchists, National Socialists, and so forth. Every society exhibits a variety of ideologies. In no case will a given society be so completely dominated by a single ideology as to have no ideological alternatives available within the system, even though alternatives may be actively suppressed by the regime.

Many of those willing to label themselves as democrats or as adherents of some other ideology do not act in the ways the ideology predicts. But most people build up a pattern of behavior, some aspects of which come directly from the dominant political ideology of the country in which they live. For example, it is a bit surprising that people accept the outcome of elections rather than fighting for their side when they lose. But most people in countries with established democracies are so conditioned to accept loss in elections that they do so without ever thinking about revolt. Just think about the reaction to the 2000 U.S. presidential election. Even though the person who won the most votes lost the election and many people were and are convinced that electoral procedures in a number of states were somewhere between inefficient and corrupt, the result was accepted with very little dissent.

This acceptance is not always the rule, though. There are countries in most parts of the world in which elections produce violent attempts, sometimes successful, to change the results. Such violence occurs even in democratic countries.

IDEOLOGY AND PRACTICE

A central concern of all students of ideology is the extent to which and the ways in which ideology affects practice. Political leaders use the language of the dominant ideology of their country to justify their actions. But are their actions based on ideology or expediency? In addition, contradictions are often apparent between the actions of adherents of some ideologies when out of power and their actions when in power. At the same time, ideological language came to permeate politics in the last quarter of the twentieth century; it is not all facade with no reality behind it.

The most likely effect of ideology is in limiting options. Except in extraordinary circumstances, political leaders will not perceive as options policies that fall outside their ideology. In this way ideology limits but does not determine practice. However, we have had the opportunity to witness just such an extraordinary breakout from ideology in Eastern Europe and the former Soviet Union. Political leaders in various countries have been struggling to free themselves from the preconceptions of communism. Some have simply accepted an alternative ideology, while others have not changed significantly.

THEORIES OF IDEOLOGY

The word *ideology* was first used in the early 1800s by a group of French thinkers called the Ideologues to describe an approach to understanding how ideas are formed. The word was picked up by others and used mostly as a label for ways in which people block out messages that threaten them. For all these thinkers, ideologies keep people from understanding the truth about their situations. It is only recently that theories of ideology generally have ceased to treat ideology negatively, as an escape from or a way to hide reality. Today both social scientists and political theorists are searching for neutral definitions. The following section briefly discusses how some theorists have discussed ideology and a debate over the end of ideology in the West.

Karl Marx

Karl Marx (1818–83) argued that ideologies blind people to facts about their place in society. He described as ideological any set of political *illusions* produced by the social experiences of a *class* (that is, a social group defined by its economic role; for example, owners or workers). Marx called ideology *false consciousness*. For Marx, a person's membership in a particular class produced a picture of the world shaped by the experiences of that class. Thus it would be al-most impossible for an individual class member to form an accurate conception of the world. Marx argued that *socialization* (that is, the process by which an individual comes to learn about and accept the values of the society) is strongly shaped by that person's place in the class system of that society. In other words, he contended that the social setting in which each of us lives determines the broad outlines of the way we think. The members of different classes are both directly and indirectly taught to think and behave in ways "appropriate" for their own class. This pattern is often called the *social construction of reality*. In other words, what we perceive as reality is created by the social world we inhabit; living in a different society, we would perceive a different reality. Other Marxists, like Louis Althusser (1918–90), refined Marx's analysis without changing it fundamentally.

Georges Sorel

Georges Sorel (1847–1922) proposed a different approach to ideology, using the word *myth* rather than *ideology*. Sorel argued that mass movements develop visions of the future in which their members don't quite believe, but that are an essential part of what motivates them. He called these visions myths. Sorel focused on fairly specific myths, like the belief in the general strike prevalent among syndicalists, rather than the broader belief systems that this text calls *ideologies*. Also, as the word *myth* implies, the depth of belief in a myth is not the same as for an ideology. But myths can galvanize people and are clearly part of all ideologies.

Sigmund Freud

Sigmund Freud (1856–1939) made one point that must be noted about beliefs such as ideologies. Freud was specifically concerned with religious belief, but his comments apply equally well to political ideologies. Freud argued that although belief systems are illusions based on the distortion or repression of our psychological needs, they still provide an organized framework for explaining the world and its ills. An accepted explanation, even one that is wrong, can be comforting. Thus, Freud, like Marx, saw ideologies as illusions that keep us deluded and content with a difficult, if not intolerable, condition. Freud prescribed psychoanalysis if the illusion becomes sufficiently pathological; Marx prescribed revolution.

Antonio Gramsci

A political activist and social theorist influenced by Marx and Georges Sorel, Antonio Gramsci (1891–1937) developed most of his contributions while imprisoned by the Italian Fascists during the last eleven years of his life. Gramsci argued that the ruling classes did not need to dominate the lower classes by force because they used the institutions of socialization (schools, churches, families, and so on) to create a social *hegemony*. This means that people are socialized into viewing the world in the same way that those in the ruling class view it. Being socialized to view the world this way means that the view is accepted subconsciously, as common sense or normal.

Karl Mannheim

Karl Mannheim (1893–1947) gave a description of ideology close to Marx's, except Mannheim attempted to avoid the negative connotations that Marx intended in his definition. For Marx, ideologies were illusions that kept members of a class from understanding their true place in society. Mannheim attempted to deal with the same phenomenon scientifically. He argued that ideology should be treated from two perspectives, which he labeled the "total conception" and the "particular conception" of ideology.[8]

The "total conception" is a general description of the beliefs held in common by a group, such as a social class or an age group. These beliefs are similar to the blinders on a horse, limiting the believer's view of the world to what is acceptable to the ideology. A person whose mind has been sufficiently formed by his or her membership in a group either simply does not perceive information that conflicts with the belief system or is provided by that belief system with a convenient explanation that allows the contradiction to be shunted aside without being recognized as a threat. For Mannheim, an ideology is produced by a failing ruling class to protect itself from the realization of its coming extinction.

The "particular conception" is a description of the situation in which people recognize the beliefs of opponents as "more or less conscious disguises of the real nature of a situation, a true recognition of which would not be in accord with his interest."[9] This is the belief that the other person's ideas, but not our own, are false representations of the world, illusions or masks that hide the truth from the believer.

Mannheim believed that intellectuals who were not frozen into a class would be capable of recognizing ideologies and of providing a synthesis of perspectives that would help to overcome ideology. For individual believers he recommended education and psychoanalysis.

Clifford Geertz

In 1964 the anthropologist and social theorist Clifford Geertz (b. 1926) published an article on "Ideology as a Cultural System"[10] in which he outlined a definition of ideology as a system of symbols. Geertz, like Mannheim, was searching for a relatively neutral definition of the term that would be useful to social scientists. As an anthropologist, Geertz sees ideology deriving from culture, which produces a set of psychologically satisfying symbols that bring order to the world by providing a mechanism through which it can be understood.

---

8. Karl Mannheim, *Ideology and Utopia: An Introduction to the Sociology of Knowledge,* trans. Louis Wirth and Edward Shils (1936; London: Routledge, 1991), 50.

9. Mannheim, *Ideology and Utopia,* 49.

10. See Clifford Geertz, "Ideology as a Cultural System," in *Ideology and Discontent,* ed. David E. Apter (New York: Free Press of Glencoe, 1964), 46–76.

Michael Freeden

The most influential scholar writing on ideology today is Michael Freeden (b. 1944), author of *Ideologies and Political Theory* (1996) and editor of the *Journal of Political Ideologies* (founded 1996). Freeden argues that ideologies are "a distinguishable and unique genre of employing and combining political concepts."[11] They are "distinctive configurations of political concepts."[12]

Each ideology has a set of core concepts, some of which may vary over time and others of which tend to remain unchanged. They tell us, as Freeden puts it, what the concepts mean. Through ideologies we come to know the right meaning of justice, liberty, equality, and so forth, and we "know" that other meanings given to these concepts are wrong.

The "End of Ideology" Debate

In the 1950s and 1960s a debate started, particularly in the United States, about whether or not ideological politics had ended in the West.[13] In a few cases this argument went so far so to suggest that ideological politics had never existed in the United States. However, even if this were once true, it no longer is, and the roots of the contemporary situation, in which ideological politics is common, go back precisely to the time when the debate over the end of ideology was raging.

Today we see ideological politics throughout the world. How could anyone believe that ideology was ending thirty to forty years ago? Part of the answer is definitional. For some people the word *ideological* simply meant extremist, and U.S. politics were perceived as based on compromises that assumed a fundamental agreement. This perception of the U.S. political system was possible only if the focus was on the political center, where such agreement used to exist. But even in the 1950s the agreement was unraveling.

The end of ideology, to the extent it existed at all, is better labeled the *exhaustion with ideology*. By the late 1950s, the twentieth century had seen two world wars; numerous minor wars; the full development of two major new ideologies, communism and fascism; and, in the United States, two major anti-left campaigns (in the 1920s and 1950s) and a major antifascist campaign during World War II. One of the responses to all this was an attempt to escape from ideology into objectivity. Particularly in the social sciences, attempts were made to eliminate value judgments from research. Although the social sciences are more objective than they were prior to World War II, scholars rapidly discovered that there are limits to objectivity where human beings are concerned.

---

11. Michael Freeden, *Ideologies and Political Theory: A Conceptual Approach* (Oxford: Clarendon Press, 1996), 48.

12. Ibid., 4.

13. For the debate, see Mostafa Rejai, ed., *Decline of Ideology?* (Chicago: Aldine-Atherton, 1971), and Chaim I. Waxman, ed., *The End of Ideology Debate* (New York: Funk & Wagnalls, 1968). The book that gave rise to the debate in the United States was Daniel Bell, *The End of Ideology: On the Exhaustion of Political Ideas in the Fifties* (Glencoe, Ill.: Free Press, 1960).

Also, the development of important political movements—such as the civil rights movement in the United States, which demanded that people take a stand —taught us that understanding a situation as objectively and thoroughly as possible and taking a position about it can be complementary actions rather than contradictory ones. And then came the conflict over the war in Vietnam, and the need to take a position shattered whatever remained of objectivity.

Some writers argued that not only had ideology ended in the West, but that its demise was a good thing because ideology was a bad thing. Ideological politics were seen as divisive politics—politics that made compromise impossible, that drove people apart. Ideology also hindered Western progress toward the "good society." Had ideology not gotten in the way, a better society might have been possible in the near future through the usual practices of compromise politics.

The participants in the debate differed both over what they were talking about and to some extent over whether the end of ideology was a good thing. Some people suggested ideology was ending in communist as well as Western countries. Again, this was generally seen as favorable. The single point on which the debaters came closest to agreeing was that ideology is bad for us and if it hadn't ended, it should.

In the years since the 1960s, thinking has moved a long way in the opposite direction, back toward objectivity but with a much greater recognition of the difficulties involved. With the collapse of communist regimes, the end of ideology debate was revived, but what is actually happening is that the adherents of one ideology—democratic capitalism—are celebrating what is perceived as victory over that ideology's main opponent. Ideology has certainly not come to an end.

A redevelopment of the end of ideology theory greeted the publication in 1989 of "Have We Reached the End of History?" by Francis Fukuyama (b. 1952).[14] In this essay, Fukuyama argued that liberalism—his name for democratic capitalism—had obviously won the day and that no other ideology was a serious contender for dominance. For Fukuyama, fundamental contradictions no longer exist in the world, either in ideology or practice.

In his most recent reflections on his 1960 book *The End of Ideology,* Daniel Bell argues that he was right to say that ideology had ended, but says, "But I conclude: the 'end of ideology,' as the great historic crossover of beliefs, has run its course, I think. It is now the resumption of history that has begun," by which he appears to mean that the nations or "ethnies" of the world are clamoring for recognition of their unique identities.[15] Even the title of this essay is a direct challenge to Fukuyama's analysis.

---

14. Francis Fukuyama, *The End of History and the Last Man* (New York: Free Press, 1992). The essay was originally published as "Have We Reached the End of History?" (Santa Monica, Calif.: RAND Corporation, February 1989).

15. Daniel Bell, "The Resumption of History in the New Century," in Bell, *The End of Ideology: On the Exhaustion of Political Ideas in the Fifties with "The Resumption of History in the New Century"* (Cambridge: Harvard University Press, 2000), xxviii.

The Situation Today

The overwhelming tradition has been that ideology hides truth. Thus it has been considered dangerous by most commentators. Today, influenced by post-modernism, scholars focus on competing ideologies and their "truths" without worrying too much about whether or not these ideologies are hiding a truth. To each set of believers, the other ideologies are hiding the truth.

In the recent past we have witnessed the emergence of numerous new or, more accurately, newly labeled views of the world that are sometimes called ideologies. We have also seen the advocates of certain well-established ideologies, such as capitalism, gain an intellectual self-confidence that was not apparent earlier, while adherents of other ideologies, most notably communism, have lost confidence. In addition, as groups have become aware of themselves as having ideological ties, they seem also to have become more aware of the roots of their beliefs, and forerunners who were hitherto not considered very important have become more significant.

The competition among ideologies has become more clearly both political and intellectual. The battle is for the hearts and the minds of adherents and for political converts, and within ideologies there is a quest for coherence and grounding that contradicts many of the theories we use to understand ideology, which suggest that any coherence is necessarily false. The result is that the ideological map is more complex than ever, and it is even more necessary to understand the theoretical roots of ideologies than it was in the past.

DO I (YOU) HAVE AN IDEOLOGY?

While I like to think that I select my beliefs, I am also very aware of how I am influenced by different ideologies. Of course, as the author of this book I am likely to be particularly aware of such influences. And I have always thought that one purpose of this book should be to encourage readers to examine their own beliefs, and perhaps even critically evaluate them.

As a teacher I have had relatively few students who saw the world wholly through the viewpoint of an ideology, but I have had students who take the position of each of the ideologies in this book. Marxists, fundamentalist Muslims, anarchists, fascists, capitalists, socialists, feminists, quite a few nationalists, and a growing number of environmentalists, all of whom knew the answer to certain questions without needing to do any thinking about them. Thus, it is clear that some of the people that we meet throughout life will have an ideology in the most complete sense of that term—will be an ideologue. Most of us, though, hold beliefs that are influenced by more than one ideology. One person is influenced by feminism, environmentalism, and Liberation Theology; another is influenced by Marxism and environmentalism; and so on.

In this sense, it is more accurate to say that we have beliefs rather than ideologies while recognizing that those beliefs come, in part, from ideologies.

Since these beliefs are often drawn from more than one ideology, there is a potential for conflict among beliefs.

POSTMODERNISM

A new approach to thinking about the world, which some call an ideology, is postmodernism, a term coined by Jean-François Lyotard (1924–98). Since postmodernism is not primarily political, it will not be discussed here as a separate ideology, but since it both influences most of the ideologies under discussion and challenges the way we think about ideologies, it needs to be considered briefly.

If accepted, postmodernism has the potential for undermining belief in any ideology because ideologies have traditionally claimed to have and have been accepted by believers as having the, singular truth. The postmodern position is that truth depends on where you stand. Ideologies claim to be universal; today, influenced by postmodernism, we in the twenty-first century are much more aware of the local and contingent. As noted earlier, each ideology is now probably best thought of as composed of subsets of closely related ways of viewing the world.

A complication for most of us is that we stand in more than one place. We view the world through eyes provided by ideology, gender, race, nationality, ethnicity, religion, and so forth. For many people, one of these will dominate, but others look through different eyes at different times regarding different issues. Most of us manage to go through these shifts in perspective without conflict, often without even being aware that we are doing so. We see ourselves as a whole rather than as multiple selves.

A NOTE ON TERRORISM

On September 11, 2001 the reality of world terrorism was brought home to the United States in the destruction of the World Trade Center and the attack on the Pentagon. Although there had been a prior attack on the World Trade Center on February 26, 1993, numerous attacks on American individuals and institutions abroad, and the destruction of the Alfred P. Murrah Federal Office Building in Oklahoma City in 1995, the impact of the September 2001 attacks has been of a much greater magnitude.[16]

Terrorism is a form of killing for political ends. It differs from assassination in that it is frequently directed at nonpolitical targets and groups of people rather

---

16. On contemporary terrorism, see Mark Juergensmeyer, *Terror in the Mind of God: The Global Rise of Religious Violence* (Berkeley: University of California Press, 2000); and Walter Laqueur, *The New Terrorism: Fanaticism and the Arms of Mass Destruction* (New York: Oxford University Press, 1999).

than individuals. Its purpose, as implied by the word, is to terrorize the people in a country. Advocates of political murder can be traced far back in history, and in the Middle Ages there was a debate over the justification of tyrannicide, the murder of a tyrant. But these actions were aimed at individuals perceived to have earned attack by their personal actions and do not constitute terrorism as we now know it.[17]

Since the nineteenth century, adherents of various ideologies have resorted to terrorism to attack their opponents and publicize their beliefs. Anarchists in the second half of the nineteenth century called these actions "propaganda by the deed." Around the same time a group of Russian terrorists earned the name "nihilist," which indicated that their aim was the destruction of current social institutions with no concern for what might replace them. The best-known statement of this position is *Catechism of the Revolutionist* (1869) usually attributed to Sergei Nechaev (1847–82) and Mikhail Bakunin (1814–76), although Bakunin's role was very limited.[18] In this pamphlet, Nechaev uses the word "revolutionist" where we would use the word "terrorist"; even most supporters of violent revolution have rejected Nechaev. Typical of the statements in the *Catechism,* and one in which the connection to contemporary terrorism is obvious, is "He [the terrorist] despises public opinion. He despises and hates the present day code of morals with all its motivations and manifestations. To him whatever aids the triumph of the revolution is ethical; all that which hinders it is unethical and criminal."[19]

During the antiwar movement, there were a small number of bombings in the United States. Most of these were directed at institutions like banks and did not target individuals. Later the so-called Unabomber, on the other hand, targeted individuals, sending them mail bombs, some of which seriously injured their recipients.

Today terrorism is obviously most closely connected with the events of September 11, 2001, Osama bin Laden (b. 1957), and his peculiar brand of Islam. But terrorism is also connected with ethnic nationalism (certain Basques in Spain, for example), the American right wing (Timothy McVeigh and various militia groups, for example), and religious conflict (the continuing conflicts between the Protestants and Roman Catholics in Northern Ireland, for example).

---

17. On the history of terrorism, see Walter Laqueur, *A History of Terrorism* (New Brunswick, N.J.: Transaction Books, 2001). Originally published as *Terrorism* (Boston: Little, Brown, 1977). The new edition has a new introduction by the author. See also Walter Laqueur and Yohan Alexander, eds., *The Terrorism Reader: An Historical Anthology,* rev. ed. (New York: NAL Penguin, 1987). On the motivations of terrorists, see Walter Reich, ed., *Origins of Terrorism: Psychologies, Ideologies, Theologies, States of Mind* (Cambridge: Woodrow Wilson International Center for Scholars and Cambridge University Press, 1990).

18. On the relationship, see Paul Avrich, *Bakunin & Nechaev* (London: Freedom Press, 1974).

19. The text of the *Catechism* can be found in Max Nomad, *Apostles of Revolution,* rev. ed. (New York: Collier Books, 1961), 230–35, with the quoted passage on 230.

We tend to identify terrorism with the acts of individuals and small groups, but *state terrorism* describes a situation in which a state uses terrorist acts against its enemies (Iraq and Libya have often been identified as doing this) or against its own citizens (Argentina and Peru did this in the recent past).[20] Thus, terrorism is a complex phenomenon driven by a multiplicity of motives and ideologies. It has existed in isolated acts occurring irregularly since the mid–nineteenth century, but has occurred with increasing frequency in the past twenty-five years.

IDEOLOGIES TO BE CONSIDERED

The ideologies considered in this book have been chosen on the basis of two main criteria: their importance in the world today and the author's desire to present a broad range of political beliefs. Nationalism; democracy and its two major forms, democratic capitalism and democratic socialism; Marxism; and Islam clearly fall into the first category. Each must be understood before the news of the day can be intelligently grasped. Anarchism clearly belongs in the second category. Although anarchism never has been dominant in any area for long, it still has many adherents and a continuing popularity. A survey of political ideology would be incomplete without anarchism. The other ideologies included fall somewhere between these two categories. Each is important for an understanding of recent history and current events but not to the same degree as nationalism, democracy, Marxism, and Islam. In addition, each represents a point on the spectrum of political beliefs that is not clearly occupied by any of the others.

One belief system, nationalism, is different from all the others because it is part of the other ideologies. Therefore, it will be discussed first to clarify its effects on the other ideologies. The placement and order of the other ideologies are not arbitrary, but other arrangements are possible. Feminism is placed in its own section, between democracy and Marxism, because it has developed so much internationally that it no longer fits anywhere else.

METHOD OF ANALYSIS

The wide variety of ideologies raises a problem for the analyst. Since each ideology differs significantly from the others, no single approach is appropriate to all of them. Each ideology emphasizes different aspects of society and ignores other aspects that are stressed by another ideology. Therefore, it is not possible to treat each ideology in exactly the same way. It is necessary to present ideol-

---

20. On contemporary terrorism in general, see Walter Laqueur, *The New Terrorism: Fanaticism and the Arms of Mass Destruction* (New York: Oxford University Press, 1999). On state terrorism, see Jeffrey A. Sluka, ed., *Death Squad: The Anthropology of State Terror* (Philadelphia: University of Pennsylvania Press, 2000).

ogies as they exist in the world rather than on the basis of a formal model. Thus each one will be analyzed as its nature dictates.

Reasons for Comparing Ideologies

It is nevertheless desirable to compare ideologies. Why compare? Political scientists compare political systems and political ideologies for a number of reasons. At the simplest level, we compare in order to remind ourselves and others that there are different ways of doing things; in the context of ideologies, differing beliefs exist in the world. It is important to realize that people who hold these beliefs are as sure that they are right as we are that we are right. On a more complicated level, we compare things because it helps us better understand other people and ourselves—to see what both they and we do and believe. Understanding is important because we can't change anything unless we understand it and because we need to recognize that there are other ways of doing things and of believing that might be useful to us.

Through comparison we discover both great differences and great similarities; we discover that differences often hide similarities. We find, for example, that most belief systems have a means of ranking people in some sort of hierarchy, but we also find that the bases for those rankings differ. Thus we conclude that there is disagreement over what is most important about the differences among people, but that there is agreement that some basis for making distinctions exists. In other words, we find that a difference is the result of a similarity.

Questions

Any analysis of any part of society, including the value system, is an attempt to answer a series of questions regarding the various institutions and processes mentioned above. This series of questions can be divided into two parts: (1) How should society function? and (2) How does society actually function? The answers to the first question give us a picture of the value system. The answers to the second question give us an image of the social system in operation.

The following is a set of questions designed to provide a fairly complete analysis of the assumptions of an ideology. Using questions like these, it is possible to compare ideologies.

1. Human nature
   a. What are the basic characteristics of human beings as human beings?
   b. What effect does human nature have on the political system?
2. The origin of society and government or the state
   a. What is the origin of society? Why does it develop?
   b. What is the origin of government or the state? Why does it develop?
3. Political obligation (duty, responsibility, law)
   a. Why do people obey the government?
   b. Why should people obey the government, or should they obey it at all?

    c. Is disobedience ever justifiable?

    d. Is revolution ever justifiable?

4. Law

    a. What are the nature and function(s) of law?

    b. Should the regulation of society depend on the immediate decisions of individuals or on sets of rules and regulations that place limitations on all members of society, including political leaders—in other words, the rule of law?

    c. Should there be sets of fundamental laws or constitutions that cannot be changed by the ordinary processes of legislation?

5. Freedom and liberty (rights—substantive and procedural)

    a. Are men and women free in any way vis-à-vis the government?

    b. Should they be free vis-à-vis the government?

    c. Assuming that some type or types of freedom are both possible and desirable, what should these be? Should they be limited or unlimited? Who places the limits?

6. Equality

    a. Are individuals in any way "naturally" equal?

    b. Should they be in any way equal?

    c. Assuming that some type or types of equality are both possible and desirable, what should these be? Should they be absolute or relative? If relative, what criteria should be used to establish them? Who establishes them? Who establishes the criteria? Who enforces the criteria?

7. Community (fraternity)

    a. Should ties among individuals composing a group form a bond that takes precedence over the needs and wishes of the individual members of the group?

    b. If this is desirable, how can it be encouraged? If this is undesirable, how can it be discouraged? Who decides?

8. Power (authority)

    a. Should any individual or group of individuals be able to control, determine, or direct the actions of others?

    b. If this is desirable, what form or forms should it take? Should it be limited or unlimited? Who limits it and how?

9. Justice

    a. It is usually assumed that justice is desirable, but what is it? Is it individual or social?

    b. Who decides the characteristics of justice? Who enforces these characteristics?

10. The end of society or government

    a. For what purpose or purposes does society or government exist?

    b. Who decides what these purposes are, or are they consciously chosen?

11. Structural characteristics of government

    a. What is the best or best possible form of government? Why?

    b. Are there alternative forms of government that are equally good?

The Social System

To compare differing ideologies, similar information must be made available for each ideology. In order to achieve some sort of comparability, the complex of interactions among individuals, groups, and institutions that we call society has been divided into five segments:

1. value system
2. socialization system
3. social stratification and social mobility systems
4. economic system
5. political system

This breakdown is simply a very loose set of categories designed to provide some minimal order to the analysis. These categories allow the attitudes found in the various ideologies to be described.

Is there, as Mannheim thought, some way of standing completely outside all ideologies, thus making it possible to evaluate them from the standpoint of something at least approaching objectivity? There is a growing consensus that this may not be possible or, at the minimum, is extremely difficult. At the same time it is essential that we evaluate ideologies and differentiate among them, and that evaluation needs to be based on something reliable. Evaluation cannot be based simply on belief or the lack of belief, although some people find that sufficient. For other people the answer is found in trying, as objectively as possible, to measure the effects of ideologies on human beings or, to include the most radical environmentalists, on the natural order as a whole.

Each chapter will attempt to explain the attitudes found in each ideology toward the various institutions and processes of society. As a result, it will be possible to see what questions are important within each ideology and therefore to establish a basis for comparing them. Before this can be done, it is necessary to understand a bit more about each of these institutions and processes.

Values The value system is determined by the answers given to the above questions, which show the hierarchy of values in each society and each ideology. The value system provides us with the basis for evaluating each ideology from within that ideology. To what extent are the expressed values of the ideology compatible with one another? Do the adherents of the ideology live up to the values expressed in the ideology or at least try to? Do followers of the ideology adhere to its values when in power?

Socialization The socialization system is the process by which individuals accept the values of the society as their own. The most important institutions affecting the ways in which and the degree to which individuals gain these values are (1) the family system, (2) the educational system, (3) the religious system, and (4) a variety of other influences, such as the mass media and the peer group. We are not always sure of the mechanisms by which the various institutions of socialization operate. It is obvious that a child is strongly influenced in her or his whole outlook on life by family environment and by early school years. It is, perhaps, less clear how the other institutions of socialization influence an individual's outlook on life. We can assume that the same messages repeated over and over again in institutions that the individual has been taught to respect, such as the religious and educational systems, have a cumulative effect and thereby become part of the individual's value system. The mass media operate in the same way.

Social Stratification The social stratification system is the way in which a society ranks groups within it. This ranking may be a very clearly defined class system or it may be very loose, with the lines between classes or status groups somewhat hazy. Social stratification is usually summed up within a political ideology by the question of equality. Some ideologies contain the idea that everyone within the society should be equal in specified ways. For example, some people talk about equality of opportunity and political equality; others believe in economic and social equality. Only if there were no economic, social, political, or any other inequalities would there be no social stratification system. Almost no one has ever suggested such complete equality, but each of these more limited types of equality has been suggested or tried at various times.

Social Mobility One of these types of equality—equality of opportunity—is particularly important in any society. Equality of opportunity means that no artificial obstacles or barriers keep any individual or group from moving from one class to another. Equality of opportunity defines certain parts of the social mobility system within a society. Every society has a social mobility system determining the ease or difficulty with which an individual can move among classes or other strata in the society. The system also determines the basis for such movement. For example, in traditional China an individual could move into the upper classes of society by successfully completing a series of examinations. Many contemporary societies have no such formal system but base mobility on standards such as wealth.

The Economic System The economic system is concerned with the production, distribution, and consumption of wealth. The major parts of the economic system that will concern us relate to (1) production, (2) distribution and consumption, and (3) the relationship of the economic system to the political system. We shall be particularly concerned with questions about the desired degree of economic equality and the means for achieving this goal. Most ideologies reject extremes of wealth and poverty; therefore, each contains means of correcting the imbalance, such as the graduated income tax or the nationalization of industries. But each ideology also differs from others as to what constitute extremes of wealth and poverty.

These days it is generally accepted that the economic and political systems are closely intertwined. This has not always been the case, and some ideologies still stress the separation of the two systems. Therefore, it is particularly important to understand each ideology's position on the appropriate relationship between the economic system and the political system.

The Political System The political system is that segment of society that draws together or integrates all the others. Within the political system decisions are made that are binding on the whole society; thus the political system holds the key to any understanding of the whole ideological and social system. A political ideology does not concern itself only with narrowly defined governmental activity, but rather touches on all aspects of the social system; therefore, a political ideology provides answers, in one form or another, to all of the questions outlined earlier.

SUGGESTED READINGS

Some Classic Works

Bell, Daniel. *The End of Ideology: On the Exhaustion of Political Ideas in the Fifties with "The Resumption of History in the New Century."* Cambridge: Harvard University Press, 2000.

Mannheim, Karl. *Ideology and Utopia: An Introduction to the Sociology of Knowledge.* Translated by Louis Wirth and Edward Shils. New York: Harcourt, Brace & Co., 1936; London: Routledge, 1991. The English edition brings together *Ideologie und Utopie* (Bonn, Germany: Cohen, 1929) and other essays by Mannheim.

Marx, Karl, and Friedrich Engels. *The German Ideology.* Vol. 5 of Karl Marx and Frederick Engels, *Collected Works.* 50 vols. New York: International Publishers, 1976.

Books and Articles

Adams, Ian. *The Logic of Political Belief: A Philosophical Analysis of Ideology.* Savage, Md.: Barnes & Noble Books, 1989.

Althusser, Louis. "Ideology and Ideological State Apparatuses (Notes towards an Investigation)." In Althusser, *Lenin and Philosophy and Other Essays,* 121–73. Translated by Ben Brewster. London: NLB, 1971.

Barrett, Michéle. *The Politics of Truth: From Marx to Foucault.* London: Polity Press, 1991.

Boudon, Raymond. *The Analysis of Ideology.* Translated by Malcolm Slater. Chicago: University of Chicago Press, 1989.

Cranston, Maurice, and Sanford A. Lakoff, eds. *A Glossary of Political Ideas.* New York: Basic Books, 1969.

Crick, Bernard. *In Defense of Politics.* 5th ed. London: Continuum, 2000.

Donskis, Leonidas. *The End of Ideology & Utopia: Moral Imagination and Cultural Criticism in the Twentieth Century.* New York: Peter Lang, 2000.

Eagleton, Terry. *Ideology: An Introduction.* London: Verso, 1991.

———, ed. *Ideology.* London: Longman, 1994.

Freeden, Michael. *Ideologies and Political Theory: A Conceptual Approach.* Oxford: Clarendon Press, 1996.

Gabel, Joseph. "Political Ideologies." In Gabel, *Ideologies and the Corruption of Thought,* 129–43. Edited by Alan Sica. New Brunswick, N.J.: Transaction, 1997.

Geertz, Clifford. "Ideology as a Cultural System." In *Ideology and Discontent,* 47–76. Edited by David E. Apter (New York: Free Press of Glencoe, 1964).

Gerring, John. "Ideology: A Definitional Analysis." *Political Research Quarterly* 50, no. 4 (December 1997): 957–94.

Gramsci, Antonio. *Pre-Prison Writings.* Edited by Richard Bellamy. Cambridge: Cambridge University Press, 1994.

Hamilton, Malcolm B. "The Elements of a Concept of Ideology." *Political Studies* 35, no. 1 (March 1987): 18–38.

Journal of Political Ideologies 1, no. 1–present (founded February 1996).

Manning, D. J., and T. J. Robinson. *The Place of Ideology in Political Life.* London: Croom Helm, 1985.

McLellan, David. *Ideology.* 2d ed. Minneapolis: University of Minnesota Press, 1995.

Mészáros, István. *The Power of Ideology.* New York: New York University Press, 1989.

Mullins, Willard A. "On the Concept of Ideology in Political Science." *American Political Science Review* 66 (June 1972): 498–510.

Parenti, Michael. *Land of Idols: Political Mythology in America.* New York: St. Martin's Press, 1994.

Rejai, Mostafa. "Ideology." In *Dictionary of the History of Ideas.* Edited by Philip P. Wiener. 5 vols. New York: Scribner's, 1973.

Schwartzmandel, John. *The Age of Ideology: Political Ideologies from the American Revolution to Postmodern Times.* New York: New York University Press, 1998.

Scott, Alan. *Ideology and the New Social Movements.* London: Unwin Hyman, 1990.

Sim, Stuart, ed. *The Routledge Critical Dictionary of Postmodern Thought.* New York: Routledge, 1999. Also published as *The Icon Critical Dictionary of Postmodern Thought.* Cambridge, England: Icon Books, 1998.

Spivak, Gayatri Chakravorty. *A Critique of Postcolonial Reason: Toward a History of the Vanishing Present.* Cambridge: Harvard University Press, 1999.

Susser, Bernard. *The Grammar of Modern Ideology.* London: Routledge, 1988.

Thompson, Simon. "Postmodernism." In *New Political Thought: An Introduction,* 143–62. Edited by Adam Lent. London: Lawrence & Wishart, 1998.

Tourish, Dennis, and Tim Wohlforth. *On the Edge: Political Cults Right and Left.* New York: M.E. Sharpe, 2000.

Van Dijk, Teun A. *Ideology: A Multidisciplinary Approach.* London: Sage, 1998.

Williams, Raymond. *Keywords: A Vocabulary of Culture and Society.* Rev. ed. New York: Oxford University Press, 1983.

Žižek, Slavoj. *The Sublime Object of Ideology.* London: Verso, 1989.

———, ed. *Mapping Ideology.* London: Verso, 1994.

Terrorism

Laqueur, Walter. *A History of Terrorism.* New Brunswick, N.J.: Transaction Books, 2001. Originally published as *Terrorism.* Boston: Little, Brown, 1977. (The new edition has a new introduction by the author.)

Laqueur, Walter, and Yohan Alexander, eds. *The Terrorism Reader: An Historical Anthology.* Rev. ed. New York: NAL Penguin, 1987.

Reich, Walter, ed. *Origins of Terrorism: Psychologies, Ideologies, Theologies, States of Mind.* Cambridge: Woodrow Wilson International Center for Scholars and Cambridge University Press, 1990.

Sluka, Jeffrey A., ed. *Death Squad: The Anthropology of State Terror.* Philadelphia: University of Pennsylvania Press, 2000.

Wilkinson, Paul. *Terrorism Versus Democracy: The Liberal State Response.* London: Frank Cass, 2001.

Web Sites

http://polisci.nelson.com/ideologies.html

http://www.geocities.com/sysideo/ Systematic Ideology

http://www.sosig.ac.uk/roads/subject-listing/World-cat/polideol.htm

2

@

Nationalism

Is nationalism an ideology? Scholars flatly disagree. On the one hand, Michael Freeden writes that nationalism is not a distinct ideology.[1] On the other hand, one of the most common topics of the *Journal of Political Ideologies,* which Freeden edits, is nationalism. And many of the articles there explicitly refer to nationalism as an ideology. Both positions can be defended. Each actually existing nationalism differs, and nationalism can be found affecting (some would say infecting) the other ideologies. Thus, many, like Freeden, say that nationalism cannot be called an ideology. But nationalism also has a set of core attributes that parallel the core attributes of other ideologies. Thus, many, like the authors of the articles in the *Journal of Political Ideologies,* say that clearly nationalism is an ideology. Some even use Freeden's definition of ideology in doing so. My position is simply that it is impossible to understand the world of the twenty-first century without understanding nationalism, and the similarities to other ideologies mean that it is plausible to treat nationalism as an ideology.

The importance of nationalism is underscored by the statement of Robert Coles (b. 1929), an authority on the political beliefs of children, that, "Nowhere on the five continents I've visited in this study has nationalism failed to

---

1. Michael Freeden, "Is Nationalism a Distinct Ideology?" *Political Studies* 46 (1998): 748–65. Another recent argument that nationalism is not an ideology can be found in Mark N. Hagopian, "Ideology," in *Encyclopedia of Nationalism,* ed. Alexander J. Motyl (San Diego, Calif.: Academic Press, 2001), 1:385–403.

become an important element in the developing conscience of young people."[2] And a recent scholar has argued, "No single political doctrine has played a more prominent role in shaping the face of the modern world than nationalism."[3]

Or as the editors of a recent anthology put it: "It is incontestable that the resurgence of nationalist sentiment in many areas of the world is one of the most important and least anticipated phenomena of contemporary international politics. People are increasingly conscious of their national identities; they are rediscovering their national histories, pressing for recognition of their distinctness, and making various demands under the banner of national self-determination."[4]

Because nationalism affects and infects the other ideologies, it must be discussed first. Of course, as will be clear throughout the text, ideologies also affect nationalism. This interchange is a clue to one of the greatest difficulties in dealing with nationalism. For many, there is "good" and "bad" nationalism, often meaning "ours" and "theirs" but equally often reflecting a considered analysis of the types of nationalism or the differential impacts of nationalism. The tradition, both popular and scholarly, has been to view nationalism as mostly bad, but a number of recent scholars have pointed out that nationalism has many positive factors. In the United States, we have always had this dual position without recognizing it because we use "patriotism" for a "good" nationalism and reserve nationalism for a "bad" nationalism. Part of the reason that we have tended to see nationalism as primarily "bad" is the connection it has to National Socialism, which is discussed in Chapter 9.

This chapter presents nationalism as a coherent set of beliefs that produces a wildly divergent set of actually existing nationalisms. It illustrates how important nationalism is today, for good and ill, and deals with a number of countervailing forces that may, in time, diminish the importance of nationalism, for good or ill. These forces include globalization, internationalism or cosmopolitanism, and regionalism. None of these are, at present, ideologies, but it is possible to conceive a future in which one or more of them have become ideologies, perhaps even among the more important ones.

The root of the word *nationalism* is *nation;* it means a people with a common culture and history that produce an identity. Nations can have the same geographical boundaries as countries, can occur as small, identifiable units within the political boundaries of a country, or, at times, cross over those boundaries. Most countries, often called nation-states, are examples of the first sort. The French Canadians in Canada are an example of the second sort. The Romany, or Gypsies, are an example of the third sort. They exist in many countries while having certain traditions in common, and many of them share a common language. A fourth type might be represented by Black Nationalism within the United States because, while Black Nationalists perceive themselves to be a

---

2. Robert Coles, *The Political Life of Children* (Boston: Atlantic Monthly Press, 1986), 66.

3. Umut Özkirimli, *Theories of Nationalism: A Critical Introduction* (New York: St. Martin's Press, 2000), 1.

4. Robert McKim and Jeff McMahon, introduction to *The Morality of Nationalism,* ed. Robert McKim and Jeff McMahon (Oxford: Oxford University Press, 1997), 3.

people with a common culture and history and call for some form of cultural, economic, or political separation from the United States, they live in many places throughout the country rather than as a small, identifiable unit.[5]

DEFINING NATIONALISM

Most definitions of *nationalism* include the following:

1. national consciousness or awareness of oneself as part of a group
2. national identity or identification with the group
3. geographical identification or identification with a place (there are exceptions, such as the Romany, or Gypsies)
4. patriotism or love of the group
5. demands for action to enhance the group

The neutral term "group" is used because there are serious differences among commentators over who or what constitutes the national group.

There is a difference between consciousness and identity. I can be aware of my membership in a group without identifying myself with it. In fact, there may well be groups that I am aware I belong to, for example, by birth or upbringing, but that I do not identify with, that I actually reject.

Most of us are born in a nation, but we are not aware of that until later. We have to be taught about all the communities of which we are members. In the language of Benedict Anderson (b. 1936), nations are "imagined communities" because they, like most other communities, are created by the actions of those who, over time, identify certain myths and symbols that have a powerful effect on those who identify with the community.[6] Symbols of nationality such as the flag and the national anthem evoke such feelings of identification, at times even in those who do not think of themselves as having a strong identification with the country. But, as noted above, identification is also an active process in which the various symbols are molded into something that affects the way we live and the way we interact with others, both those who are members of our nation and those who exist legally or physically outside its boundaries.

One of the most common identifying characteristics of a nation is language. In the United States, Native American children once were punished for speaking their national languages (some of which have been lost altogether or are now endangered), and some states have passed laws mandating the use of English.

---

5. See, for example, Wilson Jeremiah Moses, ed., *Classical Black Nationalism: From the American Revolution to Marcus Garvey* (New York: New York University Press, 1996); William L. Van Deburg, ed., *Modern Black Nationalism: From Marcus Garvey to Louis Farrakhan* (New York: New York University Press, 1997); and Dean E. Robinson, *Black Nationalism in American Politics and Thought* (Cambridge: Cambridge University Press, 2001).

6. Benedict Anderson, *Imagined Communities: Reflections on the Origin and Spread of Nationalism,* rev. and ext. ed. (London: Verso, 1991).

When people in a country speak different languages, that usually means different groups of people existed or still exist who have separate identities. For example, the country that was known as Czechoslovakia was formed after World War I from two ethnic groups, the Czechs and the Slovaks. After the overthrow of communism, Czechoslovakia became the Czech and Slovak Federative Republic, which, in 1993, became two separate countries, the Czech Republic and Slovakia. Likewise, Yugoslavia was formed after World War I from five ethnic groups and has fragmented into at least that number of countries.

I become most conscious of being an American when I am out of the country. Partially this is because others identify me as American, but mostly it is the contrast between what I am used to and what I am surrounded by when elsewhere. But before I ever left the country, I was aware of my membership in this group because I grew up surrounded by the symbols of group identity like the flag and the national anthem, July 4th and Thanksgiving. And my parents and others made the connection between the symbols and the nation explicit. For most of us, this is how national consciousness develops.

National identity is a much more conscious act. It means that I identify myself as an American both to myself and to others. For those of us born in this country, there is no universal rite of passage in which we become officially American like the naturalization (note the word meaning to become natural) process in which someone born in another country becomes a citizen of this one; so identification either takes place gradually or occurs during some rite of passage such as joining the military.

One of the earliest theorists of nationalism, Johann Gottfried von Herder (1744–1803), argued that it is a basic human need to belong to a group, and that being part of a nation gives us a part of our identity. We have a history, ancestors—"roots"—that place us in a tradition. We are born in a "stream of tradition" that helps define us as individuals.[7]

In a small country, the geographical dimension of one's nationalism is clear. In the United States, it is not as clear, except, perhaps, when out of the country. I have visited forty-six of the fifty U.S. states, but, even though I have a picture of the United States in my head, I cannot say that I have a real sense of the country as a unit, a whole.

For most Americans, the geographic identification is with a region, but with the awareness that the region is part of a whole. In smaller countries, there may also be a regional identification, but the national boundaries are much clearer. And boundaries and their maintenance are central to the nation and nationalism. Of course, boundaries are clearer the closer you are to them. I was much more aware of the boundary between the United States and Canada when I lived in Minnesota than now when I live in Missouri.

Patriotism, or love of the nation, like most of our loves, depicts the loved one as better than it actually is because we have created an image of the loved one for ourselves. Remember Benedict Anderson's idea of the nation as an imag-

---

7. Isaiah Berlin, "The Bent Twig: A Note on Nationalism," *Foreign Affairs* 51, no. 1 (October 1972): 16.

ined community. We create an image of the nation in a form that fits our needs. This image will have certain core elements like symbols of nationhood (flag, anthem, Statue of Liberty), fundamental documents (the Declaration of Independence, the Constitution), institutions (democracy, electing our leaders), and events (the American Revolution). But other things will be added to this list, such as the Civil War/War between the States, World War II, or the civil rights movement. It is how we create our image of the nation through the mix of images that characterizes the nation we love.[8]

The demands for action are what generally provoke opposition to nationalism. These demands are of a number of sorts ranging from the demand for self-government, to demand for recognition of the nation within the borders of an existing country (often a request of indigenous populations), to the demand to change borders to enlarge the nation. They may include dismembering a currently existing country to create one or more new political entities. For example, at the time of independence from Great Britain in 1947, India included what is now Pakistan and Bangladesh, which was a part of Pakistan (called East Pakistan) until 1971. Thus, in this case, three countries were created from one, and India and Pakistan have been at war over Kashmir, a region claimed by both, since 1948.

As the last example indicates, nationalist demands often lead to conflict, and that is what has given nationalism a bad name. The current list of examples where nationalism has produced violence includes the Basques in Spain, Israel and the Palestinians, the Albanians in Macedonia, Bosnia, Northern Ireland, and Chechnya.

Nationalism: Ancient or Modern?

One of the central debates today over the nature of nationalism is whether it is an ancient or modern phenomenon. This dispute has connections with the two ways most scholars categorize nationalism today, ethnic or cultural and civic or liberal. Clearly some ethnicities have ancient roots, although the awareness of that ethnicity may be more recent. Thus, whether nationalism is ancient or recent has no simple answer.

One of the classic statements regarding the nation, Ernest Renan's (1823–92) "What Is a Nation?" says that "Nations . . . are fairly new in history,"[9] and Homi K. Bhabha (b. 1949) writes, "The nation's claim to modernity, as an autonomous or sovereign form of political rationality, is particularly questionable. . . ."[10] Until recently, most scholars treated nations and nationalism as a modern phenomenon. The major parts of the mix of ideas that came together

---

8. For a discussion of patriotism in the United States, see John Bodnar, ed., *Bonds of Affection: Americans Define Their Patriotism* (Princeton, N.J.: Princeton University Press, 1996).

9. Ernest Renan, "What Is a Nation?" trans. Martin Thom, in *Nation and Narration,* ed. Homi K. Bhabha (London: Routledge, 1990), 9. Originally given as a lecture entitled "Qu'est-ce qu'une nation?" March 11, 1882.

10. Homi K. Bhabha, "DissemiNation: time, narrative, and the margins of the modern nation," in *Nation and Narration,* 293.

to become nationalism were seen as originating in the fourteenth through the sixteenth centuries.[11] As Isaiah Berlin (1909–97) wrote, "consciousness of national identity may be as old as consciousness itself. But nationalism, unlike tribal feeling or xenophobia, to which it is related but with which it is not identical, seems scarcely to have existed in ancient or classical times."[12] Those emphasizing the modernity of nationalism argue that a coherent *doctrine* of nationalism came into existence only in the eighteenth century, first in Germany and later in France.

   Those arguing for ancient roots to nationalism contend that the argument for modernity rests entirely on the experience of western Europe and ignores, for example, China, which existed as a nation centuries before any western European nation. Also, and more important to the current debate over nationalism, those arguing for ancient roots are saying that the source of the nation is the ethnic group and that those arguing for a modern nationalism are confusing nation and state, which is why I have carefully avoided using the word "state."

   John J. Breuilly says that nationalism "is intimately linked to the development of the modern state [defined in terms of legitimacy, sovereignty, and territoriality], which both shapes nationalism and which nationalists claim for themselves."[13] But Margaret Moore says, as I noted above, that nations and states are not identical. My example was the Romany, or Gypsies, as a nation with no state; she notes the Kurds and the Palestinians as nations with no states.[14] And, of course, the desire for a state by both the Kurds and the Palestinians have caused years of bloodshed in the Middle East.

Nationalism: Ethnic and Civic

The division between ancient and modern versions of nationalism is reflected in the other current conflict between scholars of nationalism, between cultural or ethnic nationalism and civic or liberal nationalism. Roughly speaking, the former are based on ancient roots and the latter on modern ones, and for most people the distinction is between "bad" (ethnic) and "good" (civic) nationalism.

   Civic nationalism reflects positive versions of nationalism or patriotism; having shared identity and purpose counteracts apathy and atomization, currently considered a major problem in the United States.[15] "Civic nationalism maintains that the nation should be composed of all those—regardless of race, colour, creed, gender, language, or ethnicity—who subscribe to the nation's political creed. This nationalism is called civic because it envisages the nation as a community of equal, rights-bearing citizens, united in patriotic attachment to

---

11. The best discussion is Quentin Skinner, *The Foundations of Modern Political Thought,* (Cambridge: Cambridge University Press, 1978).

12. Berlin, "Bent Twig," 15.

13. John J. Breuilly, "The State," in *Encyclopedia of Nationalism,* 1:796.

14. Margaret Moore, *The Ethics of Nationalism* (Oxford: Oxford University Press, 2001), 6.

15. See Robert D. Putnam, *Bowling Alone: The Collapse and Revival of American Community* (New York: Simon & Schuster, 2000).

a shared set of political practices and values." [16] And Margaret Canovan says, "To make sense, democracy requires a 'people,' and social justice a political community within which redistribution can take place, while the liberal discourse of rights and the rule of law demands a strong and impartial polity." [17] To her this means that nations and people identifying with nations are necessary for democracy.

One author has noted that "Nations have called forth heroism and sacrifice as well as murder and torture. People have risked their lives to restore democracy and civil rights in their own country, when they could easily have chosen comfortable exile elsewhere. Programmes of health reform, social welfare and environmental repair have gained political support because they appeal to a sense of national identity." [18]

On September 11, 2001 and the days following, Americans could readily see these two faces of nationalism. The terrorists were ethnic nationalists, and much of the response within the United States reflected civic nationalism. The fact that there were many attacks (from verbal to violent) on Arab Americans, anyone wearing a turban, Muslims, and others thought to be (rightly or wrongly) from the Arab world demonstrates that ethnic nationalism is not just a phenomenon found outside U.S. borders.

COUNTERVAILING TENDENCIES

Regionalism

At various times two or more countries have established ties that have raised questions about the continuing identity of the parts, but turning such agreements into long-term successes has proved difficult. For example, in 1964 Tanganyika and Zanzibar established a new country, the United Republic of Tanzania. And while Tanzania still exists, many Zanzibaris have never been entirely happy with the arrangement and, even after almost forty years, there is a strong movement for greater autonomy.

The single most successful effort at regionalism is among developed nations. The European Union, or EU, originated as the European Coal and Steel Community (ECSC); became the European Economic Community (EEC), popularly known as the Common Market; and then became the European Community (EC). In 1993 the name was changed again to European Union. The ECSC began with six countries; the EU is made up of fifteen countries, and there are negotiations under way to add up to thirteen more, but some current members, particularly Denmark and Ireland, have expressed reservations regarding

---

16. Michael Ignatieff, *Blood and Belonging: Journeys into the New Nationalism* (New York: Farrar, Straus & Giroux, 1993), 261.

17. Margaret Canovan, *Nationhood and Political Theory* (Cheltenham, England: Edward Elgar, 1996), 2.

18. Ross Poole, *Nation and Identity* (London: Routledge, 1999), 1.

expansion. In an Irish referendum on the Treaty of Nice, which was designed to ease expansion, 53.87 percent of those voting (albeit with a low turnout) voted against the treaty. Ireland is generally considered one of the countries to have benefited the most from EU membership; it was once one of the poorest countries in Europe but is now considered to be among the better off as a direct result of European Union support.

As the EU has grown, it has changed from an almost purely economic union to an economic and political one. The European Court of Justice acts as an appeals court for cases brought against national laws, and the European Parliament, composed of directly elected members, has begun to act as an independent political body, and has even managed to force the EU bureaucracy to become more responsive to it.

The European Parliament has 626 members chosen by proportional representation, which ensures that a wide range of parties across the political spectrum will win seats. But in the 1999 election only 50 percent of the eligible voters cast a vote, indicating that the parliament has not yet convinced voters of its importance.

The EU is a very powerful economic bloc, and its expansion into Central Europe will make it even stronger. Officially all interior barriers to trade were dropped in 1992. In 2001 a single currency, the Euro, was instituted and became the only legal currency for most of the countries during the first months of 2002.[19] And in 1998 a European Central Bank was established to set monetary policy for the EU.

Africa may be at the beginning of forming a union similar to the European Union. The Organization of African Unity has voted to disband, and an African Union, modeled on the European Union, is being established. It is much too early to do more than note the attempt, but the attempt is important in that it is explicitly designed to counteract the nationalism that has divided African countries against themselves.

Cosmopolitanism

The emphasis on there being a whole within which differing peoples and cultures can be accepted is the heart of internationalism or cosmopolitanism. In Western thought this goes back to ancient Greek and Roman philosophers who saw themselves as "citizens of the world." And during the same period that gave rise to the nation-state, Dante (1265–1321) wrote *Monarchia* (1310–11?), arguing for a worldwide monarchy. But even though there have been significant areas of world cooperation like the Universal Postal Union (founded 1874), the International Civil Aviation Organization (founded 1944), and the Food and Agricultural Organization (founded 1945), there have also been a number of international organizations that have either failed or been perceived as failures. Even the United Nations, which has been extremely successful in many of its

---

19. Three countries in the European Union, Denmark, Sweden, and the United Kingdom, chose not to adopt the Euro.

activities, is thought of by many, mostly in the United States, as both a failure and a serious threat to national sovereignty. How a failed organization can constitute a threat is rarely discussed.

Space exploration has produced pictures of earth hanging in space surrounded by absolutely nothing. The realization that we human beings live together with no place else to go has led many to believe that some way must be found for all of us to get along peacefully.

Cosmopolitanism, or thinking of oneself as a citizen of the world, or at least as a member of the human race who together inhabit a fragile earth, is a growing phenomenon. Most people have simply come to see themselves as having much in common with others around the world. This usually comes about as a result of contact with people from different backgrounds through travel, business or professional contacts, interaction with immigrants, or education.

Internationalists believe that the world should be united in some way. They do not all agree on what this way should be. Some, for example, argue for a world government with very strong powers. Others argue for some sort of loose confederation. Still others argue for a federal system of government similar to that of the United States, with powers divided between a world government and the government of each country belonging to the federation. Others are unsure what form unity might take but believe strongly that unity is essential.

In a general sense, internationalism is similar to nationalism. It requires recognition of ties among all individuals in the world just as nationalism requires recognition of ties among those living in a country. We noted the symbols that can help give rise to the feeling of nationalism. Internationalism does not have many such symbols, and it is likely that an individual will have less of an emotional identification with the world as a whole than with a nation or region, even though he or she may intellectually recognize ties to others around the world. Thus internationalism is not likely to be as strong a force as nationalism unless some crisis produces the need for these ties to be recognized and the emotional fervor that would bring about an identification of the individual with a world community. A science fiction cliché has an invasion from outer space acting as the crisis that produces the recognition that we are all human beings living together.

Today, recognition that actions in one country affect the health and safety of people in another country—through pollution such as acid rain, the destruction of the ozone layer, changes in weather patterns, and other impacts on the global environment—have brought a new urgency and prominence to internationalism. Although there have been few specific policy changes, there is a growing sense that nations must find ways of cooperating on environmental issues.

In addition, the world now seems to recognize that conflict in one place is dangerous for other places, and the United Nations is involved in a number of "peacekeeping" missions. Part of the reason for internationalizing peacekeeping through the United Nations is that nationalism produces resentment at the involvement of powerful countries like the United States; the use of troops from small countries, particularly countries from the same general area of the world, helps reduce this resentment. Thus nationalism is helping the creation of at least one instance of internationalism.

But one author notes that "cosmopolitanism is the privilege of those who can take a secure nation-state for granted,"[20] which implies that cosmopolitanism is not in opposition to nationalism, but instead something that can be built on nationalism.

Globalization

Undoubtedly the most widely discussed of the forces working against nationalism today is globalization. It attracts the same "good" and "bad" labels as nationalism. As often happens, the problem is that globalization is defined through ideological spectacles. Is it a positive force bringing people together, creating jobs, and diminishing the likelihood of war? Or, is it a negative force shifting power from individuals and legislatures to unelected corporate leaders and bureaucrats; destroying the environment in the name of profit; shifting jobs from developed countries to Third World countries where wages are low, working conditions poor, and environmental regulations nonexistent; and reinforcing the dominance of the industrialized countries of the North over the rest of the world? These differences are reflected in the different views of the demonstrations at the World Trade Organization (WTO) meetings in Seattle, November 30 to December 3, 1999, at the Summit of the Americas (thirty-four countries from the Americas; only Cuba is excluded) meeting in Québec, Canada, in April 2001, and at the G-8 meeting in Genoa, Italy in July 2001.

From the point of view of the Third World, globalization equals Americanization and is about power—it means a new colonization in which the Western countries support those who support them. One positive result of globalization, from the point of view of Third World workers, is that corporate codes of behavior developed within the First World have sometimes, usually because of protests within the First World, been applied in the Third World to help oppressed workers there. The best known example is the international campaign against the wages and working conditions found in Third World companies acting as suppliers to Nike. Protests and boycotts in North America and Europe helped change conditions in Third World factories. Protests by Third World workers alone, without First World support, generally have little effect.

Whether for good or ill, globalization is taking place and has been for some years. The protests may modify the process, but they are unlikely to stop it. As a result, some thinkers have begun to consider how globalization might be changed to reduce the perceived negative impact on the Third World. An obvious proposal, made by protestors and analysts alike, is the cancellation of Third World debt. Other proposals are directed at encouraging growth for domestic consumption, to counter the tendency of globalization to encourage export-led growth rather than production for use in the home countries.[21]

20. Ignatieff, *Blood and Belonging*, 13.

21. For a consideration of various such proposals, see, for example, Robert Went, *Globalization: Neoliberal Challenge, Radical Responses*, trans. Peter Drucker (London: Pluto Press with the International Institute for Research and Education, 2000), 122–26.

Empire A recent book that has quickly become unusually influential, at least among scholars, *Empire* (2000) by Michael Hardt and Antonio Negri, argues that "over the past several decades, as colonial regimes were overthrown and then precipitously after the Soviet barriers to the capitalist world market finally collapsed, we have witnessed an irresistible and irreversible globalization of economic and cultural exchanges."[22] Their contention is that a new form of socio-political-economic-cultural organization has emerged that they label "Empire." It is "composed of a series of national and supranational organisms united under a single logic of rule"[23] and has neither spatial or temporal boundaries. Thus, nations, states, and nationalism are already outmoded and in the process of being supplanted. We are, to Hardt and Negri, already beginning to live in a postnational era dominated by institutions that may be based in currently existing states but reach throughout the world. Obviously it is too early to know to what extent they are right, but they have clearly tapped into what many believe is the next great social change.

NATIONALISM IN THE THIRD WORLD

Until the breakup of the former Soviet Union, we were most aware of nationalism in the Third World. In the terminology in use then, the First World was the United States and those countries aligned with it, the Second World was the Soviet Union and those countries aligned with it, and the Third World was everything else but specifically those developing countries that tried to avoid being aligned with either. While the Second World is gone, Third World is now the most common term in use to describe the underdeveloped or developing countries of the world.[24] Other "worlds" have been added to the list. Fourth World is used by some to refer to the poorest of the poor countries and by others to refer to the indigenous or native peoples of the world. Recently others have begun to use Fifth World to refer to those who have lost status through immigration.

Movements for National Liberation

Most Third World countries have gone through a series of stages in the process of development from the colonial period to independence. The colonial experience was the first stage, followed, not necessarily in this order, by the development of a movement for independence, the revitalization of the indigenous culture, political independence, neocolonialism, one-party rule with internal conflict, and, often, a military takeover.

---

22. Michael Hardt and Antonio Negri, *Empire* (Cambridge: Harvard University Press, 2000), xi.

23. Ibid.

24. "Third World" was first used in 1952 by Albert Sauvy (1898–1990), a French demographer, to refer to those countries trying to find a "third" way between capitalism and communism.

The Colonial Experience The one experience that all Third World countries share is having been colonies. Although Western countries like the United States, Canada, Australia, and New Zealand were also colonies (of Britain) at one time, generally the experience is sufficiently in the past so there is little awareness of what it means politically, economically, and psychologically. For most countries of the Third World the colonial experience is still part of the recent past.

Being a colony meant that others made all decisions for their own benefit. Major decisions were not even made in the colony but in Europe; a colonial bureaucracy composed of people sent from Europe made other decisions. In political terms, a colony was just a minor concern in the overall policy of the European power.

Economically, the colony was there to provide raw materials for the "home" country, a market for its goods, and cheap labor. Most colonies were required to limit their economies to one or two cash crops or other raw materials and were not allowed to diversify. Little more than minimal processing was done in the colony; that would have required trained workers, and training workers might raise their expectations and pose problems. Ultimately, such predictions proved correct; training workers for skilled jobs did raise expectations and produced leaders of the independence movements.

Even more dangerous was education. Most colonial powers did not educate the indigenous population, although Christian missionaries provided schools and, in fact, educated many of the leaders of the later independence movements. The fact that most of the education was provided by Christian missionaries illustrates another fact about the colonial experience—the attack on the indigenous culture. This process of deculturation proved traumatic for many people, but it also provided the tools that made independence possible. On the one hand, the imposition of an alien culture stripped many people of their sense of self. Their religions were suppressed; their languages were replaced; their customs were denigrated; even their clothes and hairstyles were replaced by Western styles. Everything indigenous was treated as inferior, and this attitude was taught in schools.

On the other hand, the acceptance, at least temporarily, of Western culture provided both the intellectual and physical tools needed for independence. The Western traditions of liberty and equality provided the vocabulary needed for an independence movement. Technical training provided the ability to replace the colonial rulers in running the government and the economy. And at least some colonial rulers found it more difficult to treat as inferior someone who dressed and spoke as they did and who had been educated at the same schools and universities.

The Independence Movement The most common scenario for an independence movement was years of covert and overt opposition. Most, if not all, independence leaders spent time in prison for their activities; in fact, in many countries some years in prison became a requirement for gaining acceptance, respect, and credibility.

In most cases independence was actually won through violent revolution or long years of a war for independence. India was the major exception; although there were violent incidents, its independence leaders, Mohandas K. Gandhi (1869–1948) and Jawaharlal Nehru (1889–1964), used nonviolent techniques to win independence.

The struggle for independence provided a focus for the development or re-development of a national identity. It also became the basis for a national culture. In almost all cases, the independence movements attempted to ensure that their supporters worked solely for the benefit of the people as a whole rather than for their own benefit. A good example of this approach is found in the "Rules of Discipline" announced by Kwame Nkrumah (1909–72), the leader of the independence movement in what was the British colony of Gold Coast, which became Ghana on independence in 1957. In his "Rules of Discipline," Nkrumah says that those involved in the revolution should "not take a single needle or piece of thread from the masses," "not take liberties with women," "always guide and protect the children," and "always be the servant of the people."[25] Julius K. Nyerere (1922–99), the leader of the independence move-ment in Tanganyika (later Tanzania), went even further in the Arusha Decla-ration, declaring that no member of government or leader in a political party should "hold shares in any company," "hold directorships in any privately owned enterprise," "receive two or more salaries," or "own houses which he rents to others." He states explicitly that the prohibition extends to spouses.[26] Until independence and for a while afterward, such programs usually worked, but after a time, many leaders of liberation movements used their new power to line their own pockets rather than to help develop the country as a whole. There were, of course, exceptions. Nyerere was one.

The Revitalization of Indigenous Cultures Despite colonization, indige-nous cultures were only damaged but not destroyed, and national identity re-quired that the culture be revived.[27] Language, literature, and the arts, together with religion and music, were all rediscovered, encouraged, and, with indepen-dence, taught in a refashioned educational system. In places where the tradi-tional culture had been most nearly destroyed, notably sub-Saharan Africa, the process of revitalization has been slow, but it is still taking place and provides more and more people a recovered sense of self. Still, the continued Western-ization and urbanization that have followed independence have added to the

---

25. Kwame Nkrumah, *Handbook of Revolutionary Warfare: A Guide to the Armed Phase of the African Revolution* (New York: International Publishers, 1969), vii.

26. Julius K. Nyerere, *Ujamaa—Essays on Socialism* (Dar es Salaam, Tanzania: Oxford University Press, 1968), 36.

27. See, for example, Sékou Touré, "A Dialectical Approach to Culture," in *Pan-Africanism*, ed. Robert Chrisman and Nathan Hare (Indianapolis: Bobbs-Merrill, 1974), 52–73; Amilcar Cabral, "National Liberation and Culture," trans. Maureen Webster, in Cabral, *Return to the Source: Selected Speeches* (New York: Monthly Review Press, 1973), 39–56; and Cabral, "The Role of Culture in the Battle for Indepen-dence," *UNESCO Courier* (November 1973): 12–16, 20.

Courtesy of the Embassy of Tanzania

Julius K. Nyerere (1922–99) was president of the United Republic of Tanzania (formed by uniting Tanganyika and Zanzibar) from 1964 to 1985. He is one of the few leaders of an African independence movement not to be overthrown (a few attempts were made) and to retire from office. He was president of the Tanganyika African National Union (TANU), the political party active in bringing independence to Tanganyika, from 1954 on. He was known for his advocacy of African socialism and what he called *ujamaa* (a Swahili word that he translates as "familyhood") as the basis for developing Third World economies.

difficulty of establishing a national culture. Independence is not the solution to all problems that it had seemed to many.

For most Third World countries, political independence, which had been the sole goal, suddenly became a step to the goals of economic independence, political stability, and decent lives for their citizens. The first action needed to achieve these goals was to take effective control of the economy, but this proved difficult.

Neocolonialism After formal independence is achieved, economic ties with the former colonial power may resemble continued control. This is known as neocolonialism. Most of the new countries develop some sort of rapprochement with former colonists, usually to mutual advantage. The problem of neocolonialism is a complex one. It is essential for rapid economic development that the new nation be able to trade with older, more established nations. Often the only thing the new nation has to trade is raw materials. In return it gets manufactured goods or even industries. The problem stems from the fact that raw materials sell on the world market at a much lower price than do manufactured goods. Therefore, the new nation feels it is being exploited by selling a commodity that is relatively inexpensive in order to purchase one that is relatively expensive.

Such problems make neocolonialism an extremely important and difficult issue for the new nation. It must deal with older, more developed countries, often including its previous colonial ruler, in order to survive, but it feels it is being exploited in virtually the same way it was while still a colony. Therefore, many new countries have insisted that the processing of the raw materials take place at home, thus producing an industry, employing people, and giving them some sense that they are not being exploited.

Political Instability After independence, usually one political party dominated, and it often allowed no significant opposition to develop. One-party rule, it was argued, was necessary to provide the unity and stability needed to forge a new nation. Frequently one-party rule has resulted in military coups because the military was the only alternative center of power. This pattern has left many Third World countries struggling for political and economic survival and searching for an identity that allows them independence from the former colonial powers.

NEW NATIONS

Throughout the twentieth century new nations were created, but national consciousness and identity cannot be created overnight. In most new twentieth-century nations the experience of being a colony and the movement to overthrow the colonial power helped the citizens develop a sense of themselves as a people. But these experiences are not enough to maintain the identity for long.

The ancient/modern, ethnic/civic splits can be seen in the process of creating a nation or *nation-building,* as it used to be called.[28] Identification is easiest if it is based on a single ethnic group, which has to have a consciousness of itself that long precedes the creation of the new nation. It is relatively easy to proclaim a new nation with agreed-on boundaries and a government; it is much harder to imagine that nation into existence in the minds of its inhabitants. Flags, national anthems, and other symbols of nationhood must be accepted by the people and move into their personal identities before more than an outer shell of a nation can be said to exist.

The first new nation that succeeded in developing a national consciousness and identity was the United States.[29] It was a difficult process even though some of the states that became united had histories going back 150 years. These states had the initial advantage of an enemy, Britain, but they also had separate iden-

---

28. See Karl Deutsch and William J. Foltz, eds., *Nation-Building* (New York: Atherton Press, 1963).

29. See Seymour Martin Lipset, *First New Nation: The United States in Historical and Comparative Perspective* (New York: Basic Books, 1963).

tities in the minds of many of their citizens, and the process of creating an identification with the new nation was long and arduous. The United States went through a civil war before it was clear that a nation had been established, and the United States reached its current geographic dimensions only in 1959 when Alaska and Hawaii were admitted as the 49th and 50th states.

CURRENT TRENDS

Contemporary scholarship indicates that past studies of nationalism neglected three subjects: minorities, women, and postcolonial societies. Postcolonialism has become a major theme of contemporary scholarship, but the other two, while attracting some attention, are still generally neglected.

These neglected subjects are important for different reasons. Minorities are important because they complicate the imagining of the nation. As noted above, it is fairly easy to imagine a nation composed of one ethnic group but much harder if there are minorities. Assimilation or the belief in assimilation (the melting pot) has been the traditional strategy to deal with the problem. This approach suggests that there are no important minorities, just people who are in the process of becoming part of the nation. But today we realize both that the process takes much longer than was previously thought and that assimilation is almost always partial. In other words, minorities remain who identify with both the nation they live in and the one they emigrated from.

Women play particularly important roles in both bearing the future citizens of the nation and in socializing those future citizens. In the latter case, they are likely to give their children the first sense of the nation to which they belong and their future role in it. Thus, if women do not identify with the nation, their children are less likely to do so.

In addition, in a world of multiple identities and as feminism becomes more global, with whom should women identify: other women wherever they reside, or just those men and women—or just other women—residing in the same country? In other words, which of their (and our) identities should take precedence? In a world half female, this is obviously an important question for each nation.[30]

Postmodernism/Postcolonialism

Nationalism, since it is based on "imagined" or "created" communities, can easily be read from the perspective of postmodernism. Specifically, as postmodernism undermines the idea of universalism, particularly a universalism seen

---

30. For various perspectives on women and nationalism, see Cynthia Cockburn, *The Space Between Us: Negotiating Gender and National Identities in Conflict* (London: Zed Books, 1998); Caren Kaplan, Norma Alarcón, and Minoo Moallem, eds., *Between Woman and Nation: Nationalism, Transnational Feminisms, and the State* (Durham, N.C.: Duke University Press, 1999); and Tamar Mayer, ed., *Gender Ironies of Nationalism: Sexing the Nation* (New York: Routledge, 2000).

through Western eyes, nationalism becomes extremely important, especially from the postcolonial perspective.[31] While those of us who are born and stay within the bounds of country are likely to see the nation as a given, it is not. In the United States we used to use the metaphor of the "melting pot" to suggest that in some way those who immigrated to the United States from other places melted together into one whole. (The term originated with a play of that name that was performed on Broadway in 1908.)[32] What we forgot was that each melting changed the whole, and today we are more likely to use a metaphor like "tossed salad" to suggest that while a whole is created, the parts of that whole remain recognizable.

And this perspective shows how nationalism today reflects postcolonialism, although postcolonialism is itself a contested concept.[33] As Homi K. Bhabha put it, "the founding dictum of the political society of the modern nation" is "out of many one."[34] But it is clear that the multicultural, multiethnic modern state remains multiple.

Immigration

The United States is a nation of immigrants, the only difference being when our ancestors arrived. Even the ancestors of the Native Americans appear to have immigrated here, just at a much earlier stage in history. Thus, the famous poem "The New Colossus" by Emma Lazarus (1849–87) that appears on the Statue of Liberty:

> Give me your tired, your poor,
> Your huddled masses yearning to breathe free,
> The wretched refuse of your teeming shore.
> Send these, the homeless, tempest-tost to me,
> I lift my lamp beside the golden door.[35]

For various reasons, immigration is today a major issue throughout the developed world. Immigrants are being divided roughly into "political" immigrants, or those fleeing their homelands in fear of their lives, and "economic" immigrants, or those hoping to improve their lives. Of course, the categories overlap, but economic immigrants have always been the vast majority of immigrants. Today countries are much more welcoming to political than economic immigrants.

One reason for the concern with immigration is that contemporary economies are less able to absorb large numbers of new workers than they once were. Countries are worried that the new immigrants will be unable to find work and will become an economic burden as well as providing a dissatisfied minor-

---

31. See Rachel Walker, "Postmodernism," in *Encyclopedia of Nationalism*, 1:611–30.

32. Israel Zangwill, *The Melting Pot: Drama in Four Acts* (New York: Macmillan, 1909).

33. See Leela Gandhi, *Postcolonial Theory: A Critical Introduction* (New York: Columbia University Press, 1998), for a discussion of the conflicted nature of postcolonial studies.

34. Bhabha, "DissemiNation," 294. Emphasis in the original.

35. http://www.libertystatepark.com/emma.htm

ity ripe for exploitation by extremist elements. This concern is related to the problem of ethnic nationalism because it reflects the worry that ethnic enclaves will develop within countries and resist integration into the national culture. It is related to civic nationalism because civic nationalism depends on the growing identification with the new nation by immigrant groups. While we now recognize that it can take years for a new immigrant to become fully identified with the new nation (the melting pot), civic nationalism depends on there being sufficient identification with the new nation to clearly become part of it (the tossed salad).

Many theorists of civic nationalism are aware of this problem. For example, in *Citizenship and National Identity* (2000), David Miller argues against multiculturalism and suggests positive steps to incorporate immigrants into their new country. Will Kymlicka, a major theorist of multiculturalism, argues, in his *Politics in the Vernacular* (2001), in favor of multiculturalism but also in favor of education for citizenship.

The entire question looks different from the point of view of the immigrant. Some people have even begun to use the phrase Fifth World to refer to immigrants and those who lose status through immigration. For others the whole concept of immigration no longer applies and they prefer the word *diaspora,* which suggests the scattering of a people. Homi K. Bhabha writes, "I have lived that moment of the scattering of the people that in other times and other places, in the nations of others, becomes a time of gathering."[36]

Secession

Many ethnic groups argue for positions ranging from the recognition of some degree of autonomy for their group within the larger political unit to secession from that unit to establish a new unit. Today such movements exist among the Kurds in Iraq and Turkey, French Canadians in the Province of Québec in Canada, the Basques in Spain, Tibetans in China, and, most notably, the Palestinians in Israel. Although not based on ethnicity, a secessionist movement occurred in the United States during the period of the Civil War (known in the South as the War between the States). Abraham Lincoln (1809–65) is remembered as one of the greatest U.S. presidents because of his dedication to saving the Union, for which he was assassinated. Proponents of secession argue for it as national self-determination, asking: Shouldn't a people who want their own state be able to have it? Opponents, like Lincoln, argue that the maintenance of the current state takes precedence over the desires of a minority within it.[37]

Nationalist Conflicts

Many conflicts in the world today reflect nationalism. Some are of very long standing, such as the Basque nationalist movement in northern Spain and southern France, the conflict in Northern Ireland, and the conflict between Israel and

---

36. Bhabha, "DissemiNation," 291.

37. On secession movements, see Percy Lehning, ed., *Theories of Secession* (London: Routledge, 1998); and Margaret Moore, *The Ethics of Nationalism* (Oxford: Oxford University Press, 2001).

the Palestinians. The terrorist attacks on the United States have led both the Basques and the Irish Republican Army (IRA) to make conciliatory gestures so as to not be targets of the world campaign against terrorism. In a major concession, the IRA has begun to make some of their weapons unusable. They had long declared that they would never allow themselves to be in a position where they could not defend themselves. The Basques have suggested that they might be willing to enter negotiations with the Spanish government. But since they also murdered a Spanish official after September 11, 2001, the response from the government has not been particularly favorable.

As of 2002, the situation between Israel and the Palestinians is generally worse than it was a few years ago. There are a number of reasons for this. Most importantly, the present Israeli government is less inclined to negotiate than were some of the previous governments, and a growing number of Palestinians have used terror tactics within Israel. As a result, violence on both sides has escalated and resulted in many deaths, mostly of Palestinians. Yasir Arafat (b. 1929), the leader of the Palestinian Authority, is not in control of many of the factions into which the Palestinians are divided. It is difficult to know whether he would succeed if he tried to assert his authority over the other factions, as both Israel and other countries have urged, but he does not appear to have tried very hard.

In particular, Hamas (Harakat al-Muqawama al-Islamiyya, or the Islamic Resistance Movement), which opposes Arafat and has solidly established itself within the Palestinian territories by providing services to the people, is the source of most of the violent acts that take place within Israel. Hamas's goal is the establishment of an Islamic Palestinian state and so far has shown little interest in negotiations. As a result, they are in a position to constantly undermine Arafat.[38]

Other nationalist conflicts are more recent in origin. One of these stands out, the one in the Chiapas region of Mexico. Although it has deeper roots, the Zapatista rebellion began on the day that Mexico and the United States signed the North American Free Trade Agreement. It has been called "the first postmodern revolution,"[39] and represents an unusual coalition between the so-called two Mexicos, the indigenous people of the region and the white elite. Subcomandante Marcos and the others identified as "leaders" of the rebellion always appear masked and say that they do so to stress that there are in fact no leaders, but only a collective of elected village representatives who are bound by the decision of each village they represent. Subcomandante Marcos is described as a university-educated poet, and his writings include stories and poems as well as manifestos and political tracts. In the January 1, 1996 "Fourth Declaration of the Lancandon Jungle," Marcos writes:

---

38. For different views of Hamas, see Shaul Mishal and Avraham Sela, *The Palestinian Hamas: Vision, Violence, and Coexistence* (New York: Columbia University Press, 2000); and Andrea Nüsse, *Muslim Palestine: The Ideology of Hamas* (Amsterdam: Harwood Academic Publishers, 1998).

39. Ana Corrigan, "Afterword: Chiapas, The First Postmodern Revolution," in Subcomandante Marcos, *Our Word Is Our Weapon: Selected Writings,* ed. Juana Ponce de León (New York: Seven Stories, 2001), 417–43.

Our fight has been to make ourselves heard, and the bad government creates arrogance and closes its ears with its cannons.

Our fight is caused by hunger, and the gifts of the bad government are lead and paper for our children's stomachs.

Our fight is for a worthy roof over our heads, and the bad government destroys our homes and our history.

Our fight is for knowledge, and the bad government distributes ignorance and disdain.

Our fight is for land, and the bad government gives us cemeteries.

Our fight is for a job that is just and dignified, and the bad government buys and sells our bodies and our shame.

Our fight is for life, and the bad government offers death as our future.

Our fight is for respect, for our right to sovereignty and self-government, and the bad government imposes the laws of the few on the majority of the people.

Our fight is for freedom of thought and movement, and the bad government builds jails and erects graves.

Our fight is for justice, and the bad government is made up of criminals and assassins.

Our fight is for history, and the bad government proposes to erase history.

Our fight is for the homeland, and the bad government dreams with a foreign flag and language.

Our fight is for peace, and the bad government announces war and destruction.[40]

Although there have been many setbacks, the rebellion in Chiapas has succeeded in forcing the Mexican government to negotiate with representatives of local communities.

Nationalism in the United States

Nationalism in the United States mirrors nationalism elsewhere. For the most part, Americans have responded to the attacks on the World Trade Center and the Pentagon with the sort of positive identification with the country that represents the best of civic nationalism. Patriotism, the positive support for and identification with the country, has been widespread. "Good" nationalism clearly predominates. On the other hand, a small minority has exhibited the "bad" nationalism sometimes called jingoism that we condemn as ethnic nationalism when we see it elsewhere. The murder of Muslims and Sikhs (a religion originating in India that is unrelated to Islam but requires its men to wear turbans and beards) illustrates that this sort of nationalism exists in the United States also. And the treatment during World War II of Japanese-American U.S. citizens, who were interned in prison camps, shows that it is not a new phenomenon.

---

40. "Fourth Declaration of the Lancandon Jungle," in ibid., 87.

Indigenous Peoples

In addition to the activities of Native Americans in the United States and First Nations in Canada, which take place largely within the political realm, there are indigenous peoples movements throughout the Americas. In the Amazon River basin in Brazil, native peoples are struggling for recognition and against the oil and other companies that have been given access to the natural resources in the area. Since few South American countries have strict environmental laws or choose not to enforce those that exist, a number of indigenous people have become involved with environmental activists in attempting to protect the environment that is central to their way of life. They have generally been ignored, have failed even when their efforts were recognized as just, or been murdered.

The problem with nationalism is that it both unites and divides. Renan eloquently describes the nation as "a soul, a spiritual principle. Two things, which in truth are but one, constitute this soul or spiritual principle. One lies in the past, one in the present. One is the possession of a rich legacy of memories; the other is present-day consent, the desire to live together, the will to perpetuate the value of the heritage that one has received in an undivided form."[41] At the same time nationalism defines any non-national as "other," "alien," with the implication of fundamental difference, often leading to fear. The alien may be "naturalized" and assimilated, but even these characteristics do not necessarily eliminate the fear of the outsiders, which often leads to violence against them.

Thus, nationalism is both a positive and a negative force in the world today, pulling people together and pushing them apart. And in one aspect or another it is a force in all other ideologies.

SUGGESTED READINGS

Some Classic Works

Anderson, Benedict. *Imagined Communities: Reflections on the Origin and Spread of Nationalism*. Rev. and ext. ed. London: Verso, 1991.

Deutsch, Karl W. *Nationalism and Its Alternatives*. New York: Knopf, 1969.

————. *Nationalism and Social Communication: An Inquiry into the Foundations of Nationality*. 2d ed. Cambridge: MIT Press, 1966.

Hayes, Carlton J. H. *The Historical Evolution of Modern Nationalism*. New York: Macmillan, 1931.

————. *Nationalism: A Religion*. New York: Macmillan, 1960.

Kohn, Hans. *The Age of Nationalism: The First Era of Global History*. New York: Harper & Row, 1962.

————. *American Nationalism: An Interpretive Essay*. New York: St. Martin's Press, 1957.

————. *The Idea of Nationalism: A Study in Its Origins and Background*. New York: Macmillan, 1944.

Smith, Anthony D. *Nationalism in the Twentieth Century*. Oxford, England: Martin Robertson, 1979.

Snyder, Louis L. *The Meaning of Nationalism*. New Brunswick, N.J.: Rutgers University Press, 1954.

41. Renan, "What Is a Nation?" 19.

———. *New Nationalism*. Ithaca, N.Y.: Cornell University Press, 1968.

Tagore, Sir Rabindranath. *Nationalism*. New York: Macmillan, 1917.

Books and Articles

Alter, Peter. *Nationalism*. Translated by Stuart McKinnon-Evans. 2d ed. London: Edward Arnold, 1994.

Anderson, Sarah, ed. *Views from the South: The Effects of Globalization and the WTO on Third World Countries*. [Oakland, Calif.]: Food First Books and the International Forum on Globalization, 2000.

Beiner, Ronald, ed. *Theorizing Nationalism*. Albany: State University of New York Press, 1999.

Bello, Walden. *The Future in the Balance: Essays on Globalization and Resistance*. Edited by Anuradha Mittal. Oakland, Calif.: Food First Books; Focus on the Global South, 2001.

Berlin, Isaiah. "The Bent Twig: A Note on Nationalism." *Foreign Affairs* 51, no. 1 (October 1972): 11–30.

———. "Nationalism: Past Neglect and Present Power." *Partisan Review* 46, no. 3 (1979): 337–58.

Bhabha, Homi K., ed. *Nation and Narration*. London: Routledge, 1990.

Billig, Michael. *Banal Nationalism*. London: Sage, 1995.

Bragança, Aquino de, and Immanuel Wallerstein, eds. *The African Liberation Reader*. 3 vols. London: Zed Press, 1982.

Breuilly, John. *Nationalism and the State*. Manchester, England: Manchester University Press, 1982.

Brown, David. *Contemporary Nationalism: Civic, Ethnocultural, and Multicultural Politics*. New York: Routledge, 2000.

Calhoun, Craig. *Nationalism*. Minneapolis: University of Minnesota Press, 1997.

Canovan, Margaret. *Nationhood and Political Theory*. Cheltenham, England: Edward Elgar, 1996.

Castle, Gregory, ed. *Postcolonial Discourses: An Anthology*. Oxford: Blackwell, 2001.

Cockburn, Cynthia. *The Space between Us: Negotiating Gender and National Identities in Conflict*. London: Zed Books, 1998.

Cohen, Joshua, ed. *For Love of Country: Debating the Limits of Patriotism*. Boston: Beacon Press, 1996.

Connor, Walker. *Ethnonationalism: The Quest for Understanding*. Princeton, N.J.: Princeton University Press, 1994.

Dallmayr, Fred. *Alternative Visions: Paths in the Global Village*. Lanham, Md.: Rowman & Littlefield, 1998.

———. *Beyond Orientalism: Essays on Cross-Cultural Encounter*. Albany: State University of New York Press, 1996.

Eley, Geoff, and Ronald Grigor Suny, eds. *Becoming National: A Reader*. New York: Oxford University Press, 1996.

Fanon, Frantz. *Black Skin, White Masks*. Translated by Charles Lam Markmann. New York: Grove Press, 1967. Originally published as *Peau noire, masques blancs* (Paris: Éditions du Seuil, 1952).

———. *The Wretched of the Earth*. Translated by Constance Farrington. New York: Grove Press, 1963. Originally published as *Les Damnés de la terre* (Paris: F. Maspero, 1961).

Fawcett, Louise, and Yezid Sayigh. *The Third World beyond the Cold War: Continuity and Change*. Oxford: Oxford University Press, 1999.

Gandhi, Leela. *Postcolonial Theory: A Critical Introduction*. New York: Columbia University Press, 1998.

Gandhi, M[ohandas] K[aramchand]. *Hind Swaraj and Other Writings*. Edited by Anthony J. Parel. Cambridge: Cambridge University Press, 1997.

Gellner, Ernest. *Nations and Nationalism*. Oxford: Oxford University Press, 1983.

Gordon, David C. *Images of the West: Third World Perspectives*. [Savage, Md.]: Rowman & Littlefield, 1989.

Gould, Carol C., and Pasquale Pasquino, eds. *Cultural Identity and the Nation-State*. Lanham, Md.: Rowman & Littlefield, 2001.

Greenfield, Liah. *Nationalism: Five Roads to Modernity*. Cambridge: Harvard University Press, 1992.

Guibernau, Montserrat, and John Hutchinson, eds. *Understanding Nationalism*. Cambridge, England: Polity, 2001.

Haas, Ernst B. *Nationalism, Liberalism, and Progress*. 2 vols. Ithaca, N.Y.: Cornell University Press, 1997–2000.

Hall, John A., ed. *The State of the Nation*. Cambridge: Cambridge University Press, 1998.

Hardt, Michael, and Antonio Negri. *Empire*. Cambridge: Harvard University Press, 2000.

Harvey, Neil. *The Chiapas Rebellion: The Struggle for Land and Democracy*. Durham, N.C.: Duke University Press, 1998.

Hastings, Adrian. *The Construction of Nationhood: Ethnicity, Religion, and Nationalism*. Cambridge: Cambridge University Press, 1997.

Hechter, Michael. *Containing Nationalism*. Oxford: Oxford University Press, 2000.

Hughey, Michael W., ed. *New Tribalisms: The Resurgence of Race and Ethnicity*. New York: New York University Press, 1998.

Ignatieff, Michael. *Blood and Belonging: Journeys into the New Nationalism*. New York: Farrar, Straus & Giroux, 1993.

Isbister, John. *Promises Not Kept: The Betrayal of Social Change in the Third World*. 4th ed. West Hartford, Conn.: Kumarian Press, 1998.

Iyob, Ruth. *The Eritrean Struggle for Independence: Domination, Resistance, Nationalism, 1941–1993*. Cambridge: Cambridge University Press, 1995.

Kaplan, Caren, Norma Alarcón, and Minoo Moallem, eds. *Between Woman and Nation: Nationalism, Transnational Feminisms, and the State*. Durham, N.C.: Duke University Press, 1999.

Katzenberger, Elaine, ed. *First World, Ha Ha Ha! The Zapatista Challenge*. San Francisco: City Lights, 1995.

Kymlicka, Will. *Politics in the Vernacular: Nationalism, Multiculturalism, and Citizenship*. New York: Oxford University Press, 2001.

Langley, J. Ayo. *Ideologies of Liberation in Black Africa 1856–1970: Documents of Modern African Political Thought from Colonial Times to the Present*. London: Rex Collings, 1979.

Lazarus, Neil. *Nationalism and Cultural Practice in the Postcolonial World*. Cambridge: Cambridge University Press, 1999.

Lehning, Percy, ed. *Theories of Secession*. London: Routledge, 1998.

Levy, Jacob T. *The Multiculturalism of Fear*. Oxford: Oxford University Press, 2000.

Mandela, Nelson. *Long Walk to Freedom*. Boston: Little, Brown, 1994.

Marcos, Subcomandante. *Our Word Is Our Weapon: Selected Writings*. Edited by Juana Ponce de León. New York: Seven Stories, 2001.

———. *Shadows of Tender Fury: The Letters and Communiqués of Subcomandante Marcos and the Zapatista Army of Liberation*. Translated by Frank Bardacke, Leslie López, and the Watsonville, California, Human Rights Committee. New York: Monthly Review Press, 1995.

Mayer, Tamar, ed. *Gender Ironies of Nationalism: Sexing the Nation*. New York: Routledge, 2000.

McCrone, David. *The Sociology of Nationalism*. New York: Routledge, 1998.

McGarry, John. "Explaining Ethnonationalism: The Flaws in Western Thinking." *Nationalism and Ethnic Politics* 1, no. 4 (winter 1995): 121–42.

McKim, Robert, and Jeff McMahon, eds. *The Morality of Nationalism*. Oxford: Oxford University Press, 1997.

Miller, David. *Citizenship and National Identity*. Cambridge, England: Polity Press, 2000.

———. *On Nationality*. Oxford: Oxford University Press, 1995.

Mishal, Shaul, and Avraham Sela. *The Palestinian Hamas: Vision, Violence, and Coexistence*. New York: Columbia University Press, 2000.

Moore, Margaret. *The Ethics of National-ism*. Oxford: Oxford University Press, 2001.

————, ed. *National Self-Determination and Secession*. Oxford: Oxford University Press, 1998.

Motyl, Alexander J., ed. *Encyclopedia of Nationalism*. 2 vols. San Diego, Calif.: Academic Press, 2001.

Nasser, Gamal Abdel. *The Philosophy of the Revolution*. Buffalo, N.Y.: Smith, Keynes & Marshall, 1959.

Nkrumah, Kwame. *The Autobiography of Kwame Nkrumah*. Edinburgh: Thomas Nelson & Sons, 1957.

————. *I Speak of Freedom: A Statement of African Ideology*. New York: Praeger, 1970.

Nüsse, Andrea. *Muslim Palestine: The Ideol-ogy of Hamas*. Amsterdam: Harwood Academic Publishers, 1998.

Nyerere, Julius K. *Freedom and Develop-ment: Uhuru na Maendelo. A Selection from Writings and Speeches 1968–1973*. Dar es Salaam, Tanzania: Oxford Uni-versity Press, 1973.

————. *Freedom and Socialism: Uhuru na Ujamaa. A Selection from Writings and Speeches 1965–1970*. Dar es Salaam, Tanzania: Oxford University Press, 1968.

————. *Ujamaa—Essays on Socialism*. Dar es Salaam, Tanzania: Oxford Univer-sity Press, 1968.

Özkirimli, Umut. *Theories of Nationalism: A Critical Introduction*. New York: St. Martin's Press, 2000.

Pecora, Vincent P., ed. *Nations and Identi-ties: Classic Readings*. Oxford: Black-well, 2001.

Poole, Ross. *Nation and Identity*. London: Routledge, 1999.

Punter, David. *Postcolonial Imaginings: Fic-tions of a New World Order*. Lanham, Md.: Rowman & Littlefield, 2000.

Robinson, Dean E. *Black Nationalism in American Politics and Thought*. Cam-bridge: Cambridge University Press, 2001.

Said, Edward W. *Orientalism*. New York: Pantheon Books, 1978.

Sandoval, Chela. *Methodology of the Op-pressed*. Minneapolis: University of Minnesota Press, 2000.

San Juan, E[pifanio], Jr. *Beyond Postcolonial Theory*. New York: St. Martin's Press, 1998.

Schöpflin, George. *Nations, Identity, Power*. New York: New York University Press, 2000.

Schwarz, Henry, and Sangeeta Ray, eds. *A Companion to Postcolonial Studies*. Malden, Mass.: Blackwell, 2000.

Sen, Amartya. *Development as Freedom*. New York: Knopf, 1999.

Shapiro, Ian, and Lea Brilmayer, eds. *Global Justice*. New York: New York University Press, 1999.

Smith, Anthony D. *Myths and Memories of the Nation*. Oxford: Oxford University Press, 1999.

————. *Nationalism and Modernism: A Critical Survey of Recent Theories of Na-tions and Nationalism*. London: Rout-ledge, 1998.

Spencer, Philip, and Howard Wollman. "Good and Bad Nationalisms: A Cri-tique of Dualism." *Journal of Political Ideologies* 3, no. 3 (October 1998): 255–74.

Spivak, Gayatri Chakravorty. *A Critique of Postcolonial Reason: Toward a History of the Vanishing Present*. Cambridge: Harvard University Press, 1999.

Tamir, Yael. *Liberal Nationalism*. 2d ed. Princeton, N.J.: Princeton University Press, 1995.

Viroli, Maurizio. *For Love of Country: An Essay on Patriotism and Nationalism*. Oxford: Clarendon Press, 1995.

Went, Robert. *Globalization: Neoliberal Challenge, Radical Responses*. Translated by Peter Drucker. London: Pluto Press with the International Institute for Research and Education, 2000.

Wicker, Hans-Rudolf, ed. *Rethinking Na-tionalism and Ethnicity: The Struggle for Meaning and Order in Europe*. Oxford: Berg, 1997.

¡Zapatistas! Documents of the New Mexi-can Revolution (December 31, 1993–June 12, 1994. Brooklyn: Autono-media, 1994.

Web Sites

http://www.nationalismproject.org/

Third World

http://www.twnside.org.sg/ Third World Network

Indigenous Peoples

http://www.cwis.org/ Center for World Indigenous Studies

http://www.cwis.org/drft9329.html Draft Declaration on the Rights of Indigenous Peoples

http://www.cwis.org/fwj/ Fourth World Journal

http://www.ipcb.org Indigenous Peoples Council on Biocolonialism

http://www1.umn.edu/humanrts/instree/r1citp.htm Convention concerning Indigenous and Tribal Peoples in Independent Countries

3

☷

The Principles of Democracy

The word *democracy* comes from two Greek words: *demos* = people and *kratos* = rule. Therefore, the word means "rule by the people," sometimes called "popular sovereignty," and can refer to direct, participatory, and representative forms of rule by the people. Today the word has a positive meaning throughout most of the world, so much so that, to connect themselves with this positive image, even some political systems with very little or no rule by the people are called democratic.

The following analysis uses a simple model of the key elements of democracy as it exists today. They are

1. citizen involvement in decision making
2. a system of representation
3. the rule of law
4. an electoral system—majority rule
5. some degree of equality among citizens
6. some degree of liberty or freedom granted to or retained by citizens
7. education

CITIZEN INVOLVEMENT

The most fundamental characteristic of any democratic system, truly its defining characteristic, is the idea that citizens should be involved in the making of political decisions, either directly or through representatives of their choosing. These two approaches can be characterized as

1. *Direct democracy*—Citizens take part personally in deliberations and vote on issues. Citizens debate and vote on all laws.
2. *Representative democracy*—Citizens choose (elect) other citizens to debate and pass on laws.

Voting on issues personally is the defining activity of a citizen in a direct democracy. Direct democracy has only rarely been practiced as a means of governing a country, but most people have experienced such involvement at a lower level. Almost everyone in the West has, at some time, had a chance to discuss and vote on an issue. This may have taken place at a school or university, in a church or synagogue, in a union meeting or at a club, or in one of the hundreds of other groups that allow voting members to decide at least some of the questions that concern the membership.

In addition, most people have voted in an election in some such organization, thereby taking part in one of the basic steps of choosing a representative; fewer people, but still a substantial number, have cast their vote in the election of a public official. These are the defining activities of a citizen in a representative democracy.

Other forms of citizen involvement in a democratic system include actively participating in a political party or interest group, attending and participating in political meetings or public hearings, simply discussing politics, or contacting a public official about an issue. A growing area of involvement is for citizens to work for or against issues that will be voted on during an election. This area is growing because interest groups or groups of citizens are bringing more issues directly to the electorate through initiative petitions or referenda.

In a representative system, citizen involvement helps to ensure that public officials are accountable and responsive to the people. Candidates for public office must convince voters that there are good reasons to vote for them rather than their opponents. In particular, elected officials are expected to show that they are responsive to the changing needs and demands of their constituents. Of course, no system can guarantee responsive public officials, but having to run for reelection helps.

In addition, involvement is thought to be good for the citizen. Defenders of democracy believe that being involved in decision making (even if this means simply casting a vote at an election) expands the horizons of voters and makes them more aware of issues. Involvement brings about a feeling of responsibility, a sense of belonging to a community, and knowledge. Involved citizens become better, more complete people.

This is particularly true for those whose involvement goes beyond the vote to more active participation. Citizens who choose to get directly involved in the political life of their community will benefit more than more passive citizens who limit their participation to the vote.

Defenders of democracy ask a simple question: Who else should make political decisions? A monarch? A political boss? Bureaucrats? The rich? Who better knows the interests of the average citizen than the average citizen?

In some countries, including the United States, many people—sometimes even the majority—do not bother to vote. In the 2000 presidential election in the United States, just 51 percent of the eligible voters participated.

Not voting does not mean that decisions won't be made; someone will still make them. Do high levels of not voting undermine democracy? Does it matter? These questions have produced a number of approaches to either justify the system that exists or propose changes in it. These approaches include elitism, pluralism, corporatism or neo-corporatism, and participatory theories of democracy. The first three all assume that democracy is working fairly well with low levels of participation. Participatory theories argue that democracy is not working and that ways must be found to increase participation.

Elitism

The elitist approach asserts that democracy is "a method of making decisions which ensures efficiency in administration and policy making and yet requires some measure of responsiveness to popular opinion on the part of the ruling elites."[1] In this view, citizen involvement is primarily a check on political leaders while maintaining competition among rival elites. The arguments for elitist theories center on efficiency and the perceived inability of the voter to make informed decisions. The citizen casting his or her vote is, in this view, simply a mechanism for deciding among competing elites. Given the complexity of the modern world and the issues involved, so the argument goes, it is impossible for the average citizen to know enough to participate intelligently in decision making. But since competition is still thought desirable, the vote is used to choose the group that will be given temporary power.

The classic response to elitist theories is to argue that efficiency is not as important as the positive influence of participation on the citizen and that the average citizen is probably capable of understanding most issues. The elitist theorists argue, in effect, that classical representative democracy does not—even cannot—work in the modern world. Their opponents argue that a truly informed citizenry is even more important than in the past and that representative democracy can work even though new problems make it more difficult to achieve.

---

1. Jack L. Walker, "A Critique of the Elitist Theory of Democracy," *American Political Science Review* 60 (June 1966): 286.

Pluralism

Closely related to the elitist argument is pluralism, in which the political system is composed of interest groups competing for power with none strong enough to dominate. As long as competition exists and is fair, no single interest can gain too much power; one interest will always be held in check by the other interests. Advocates contend that pluralism is the best system for a representative democracy, because pluralism protects citizens from too great a centralization of power and allows all the diverse interests within a society to be expressed. In the United States today, pluralism connects neatly to the growth of interest in multiculturalism, or structuring society around competing and cooperating cultures. But it is important to note that pluralism is about the distribution of power and multiculturalism is about toleration of difference.

Most modern societies are pluralistic in that they are composed of a variety of groups based on characteristics such as wealth, race, gender, ethnic or national origin, profession, and religion. Defenders of pluralism argue that this diversity should be recognized and protected. Thus pluralism includes both a positive awareness of the group basis of most contemporary societies and an attitude toward democracy. Pluralists in the United States argue that pluralism supplements the system of checks and balances enshrined in the U.S. Constitution with additional checks on power. Outside the United States, pluralists argue that the competition among groups is often the major means of limiting centralized power.

Critics of pluralism make two major points. First, according to the antipluralists, the only thing of interest to the competing elites is staying in office; all values are secondary to this overriding goal. Thus the suggestion that pluralism protects freedom is false. Pluralism is a protection for freedom, or any other value, only as long as that value is to the political benefit of the competing groups. Second, antipluralists note that the supposedly competing groups cooperate to maintain the present system and their positions of power within it. Thus pluralism and the groups that compete within it are obstacles to change, particularly in trying to avoid the emergence of new groups that might successfully compete for power.

Corporatism

Corporatism (or neo-corporatism, as some of its proponents prefer to call it to distinguish it from a similar idea found in fascism) contends that interest groups both compete and cooperate with each other and share power with government bureaucracies. Interest groups do not merely consult with government but are fully integrated into the process of policy making and implementation. As one writer put it, corporatism means the "negotiation of policy between state agencies and interest organisations arising from the division of labour in society, where policy agreements are implemented through the collaboration of the interest organisations and their willingness and ability to secure the compliance of their members."[2]

The theory of corporatism has had a great impact on the way in which interest organizations perceive their relations with one another and with government. Although corporatism has not significantly reduced competition among interest groups, it has provided the theoretical basis for their taking a more active role in the actual development of policy in cooperation with government bureaucracies.

Critics of corporatism argue that it simply justifies greater power on the part of unelected people, that the similarity of the concept in fascism is no accident, and that corporatism constitutes an explicit denial of the power of citizens to control their own lives in a democracy. Critics of elitism, pluralism, and corporatism often suggest that more, not less, direct participation on the part of the citizens is the best approach to democracy.

Participatory Democracy

The most direct challenge to previous approaches is found among those who argue that the low level of citizen involvement is a problem that should not be rationalized away but solved. Advocates of participatory democracy regard elitism, pluralism, and corporatism as disregarding the most fundamental principle of democracy, and they contend that shifting power away from elected officials to citizens can save the principle. In other words, they propose moving the system away from representative democracy in the direction of direct democracy.[3]

The participatory democrat argues that laws they did not help make or participate in making should not bind individuals. In other words, the individual, all individuals, must be consulted in the making of laws that will affect them. If they are not consulted, the law is invalid.

In addition to asserting that a more participatory democracy can work, advocates of this position argue that only with greater participation can the other principles of democracy be fulfilled. According to this argument, people will never be politically equal or free unless they become active and involved citizens committed to making the system work by making representative democracy more like direct democracy. At the same time, contemporary defenders of participatory democracy are not opponents of representation; they just believe that voters should keep their representatives on a shorter leash.

Opponents of participatory democracy argue that it simply goes too far and as a result is impractical; it would be fine if it were possible, but they contend that it cannot be achieved in our complex world, and the fact that many choose not to vote raises questions about any participatory theory. These critics assert that contemporary political decisions require both an expertise and an amount

---

2. Wyn Grant, introduction to *The Political Economy of Corporatism,* ed. Wyn Grant (London: Macmillan, 1985), 3–4.

3. See, for example, Carole Pateman, *Participation and Democratic Theory* (Cambridge: Cambridge University Press, 1970); and Benjamin R. Barber, *Strong Democracy: Participatory Politics for a New Age* (Berkeley: University of California Press, 1984).

of time not available to the average citizen. As a result, they argue, a system of representative democracy is necessary.

REPRESENTATION

If direct participation is difficult to achieve or not a good idea, then it is necessary to develop a way for people to participate indirectly. The primary means has been through representatives, or people chosen by citizens to act for them. In other words, citizens delegate to one of their number the responsibility for making certain decisions. The person chosen may be a delegate from a geographical area or of a certain number of people (representation by area or population). The citizens represented are called the *constituents,* or the representative's *constituency.*

The word *represent* is used in a number of different ways that help provide an understanding of the situation:

1. Something *represents* something else when it is a faithful reproduction or exact copy of the original.
2. Something that symbolizes something else is said to *represent* it.
3. A lawyer *represents* a client when he or she acts in place of or for the client.

Clearly, the third is closest to the way we think of a representative in democracy, but it isn't that simple because no constituency is composed of citizens whose interests are identical. As a result, there are two main approaches to the relationship between the representative and her or his constituency, with most actual representatives fitting somewhere between the two extremes.

Some representatives do try to reflect the varied interests of their constituents as precisely as possible, while others take the position that they were elected to make the best decisions they can for the nation as a whole. The latter position was first put forth by Edmund Burke (1729–97), who said,

> To deliver an opinion is the right of all men; that of constituents is a weighty and respectable opinion, which a representative ought always rejoice to hear, and which he ought always most seriously to consider. But *authoritative* instructions, *mandates* issued, which the member is bound blindly and implicitly to obey, to vote for, and to argue for, though contrary to the dearest conviction of his judgment and conscience—these are things utterly unknown to the laws of this land, and which arise from a fundamental mistake of the whole order and tenor of our Constitution.
>
> Parliament is not a *congress* of ambassadors from different and hostile interests, which each must maintain, as an agent and advocate, against other agents and advocates; but Parliament is a *deliberative* assembly of *one* nation, with one interest, that of the whole; where, not local purposes, not local prejudices, ought to guide, but the general good, resulting from the general reason of the whole. You choose a member, indeed; but when you have chosen him, he is not a member of Bristol, he is a member of *Parlia-*

ment. If the local constituent should form a hasty opinion evidently opposite to the real good of the rest of the community, the member for that place ought to be as far as any other from an endeavor to give it effect.[4]

Here Burke presents a case for the representative as an independent agent who is a representative solely in the sense that she or he is elected by the people in a particular area. In doing this, Burke specifically rejects representation in the third sense outlined above, the representative as agent for some individual or group.

Seldom, if ever, will an elected official fit exactly one and only one of the roles assigned by the theories of representation. Even the most Burkean representative will act as a constituency agent at times or on certain issues. The typical representative is likely to act as a constituency agent whenever constituents are actively concerned with a particular issue or to assist individuals or groups of constituents when they are dealing with the bureaucracy and need assistance. At the same time, the typical representative is likely to act as the Burkean representative on issues that do not directly concern the constituency (and thus about which little or no pressure is received from the constituency).

As we have already seen in the discussion of participatory theories, an issue that concerns some theorists is how to give representative democracy some of the attributes of direct democracy. In the United States such practices as the initiative, referendum, and recall were developed as devices to allow the people as a whole to play a direct role in political decision making, and they are again being used extensively.

This issue can be seen most clearly in the thinking of Jean-Jacques Rousseau (1712–78). At one point he said, "Thus deputies of the people are not, and cannot be, its representatives; they are merely its agents, and can make no final decisions. Any law which the people have not ratified in person is null, it is not a law."[5] Here Rousseau has used two of our definitions of *represent.* For him a representative is not an independent agent but one who acts only with constituent approval. Rousseau realized that within a large country direct democracy was impractical, even impossible, and although he maintained the ideal of direct democracy, he did discuss representation in a more favorable light. He said:

> I have just shown that government weakens as the number of magistrates [elected officials] increases; and I have already shown that the more numerous the people [are], the more repressive force is needed. From which it follows that the ratio of magistrates to government should be in inverse proportions to the ratio of subjects to sovereign; which means that the more the state expands, the more the government ought to contract; and thus that the number of rulers should diminish in proportion to the increases of the population.[6]

---

4. Speech to the Electors of Bristol (1774), in *The Works of the Right Honorable Edmund Burke,* 7th ed. (Boston: Little, Brown, 1881), 11:96 (emphasis in the original).

5. Jean-Jacques Rousseau, *Du contrat social* (Paris: Le Renaissance de Livre, 1762), 86.

6. Rousseau, *Du contrat social,* 59.

Jean-Jacques Rousseau (1712–78) is best known as a political philosopher. His works *Discours sur les sciences et les arts* (*Discourse on the Arts and Sciences,* 1750), *Discours sur l'origine et les fondements de l'inégalité* (*Discourse on the Origin and Foundations of Inequality,* 1755), *Émile* (1762), a treatise on education, *Du contract social* (*The Social Contract,* 1762), and others placed him in the fore-front among critics of contemporary soci-ety. He argued that civilization was cor-rupting and that a return to a simpler society in which each individual could fully participate was the remedy for the current social ills. His arguments were used as justifications for the French Revo-lution. The meaning, intent, and effect of Rousseau's ideas are still widely de-bated; interpretations of his thought range from the belief that he was one of the founders of modern totalitarianism to the belief that he was an important defender of democracy.

Rousseau would have liked to see a country small enough so every per-son could be his[7] own representative, but as a population rises this becomes more and more difficult. Thus the number of rulers must of necessity dimin-ish through the establishment of some type of representative system, and the larger the country the more powerful those representatives must be. But Rous-seau strongly believed that the closer a system can come to a direct democracy through an increase in the number of magistrates, the better the system will be, but this is only possible in a very small country. Rousseau's approach to repre-sentation has gained favor in recent years in movements in support of partici-patory democracy.

THE RULE OF LAW

In a democracy an elected representative participates in the making of laws but is still bound by the law. Once passed, the law is supreme, not those who made the law. Representatives can participate in changing a law, but until it is changed they, along with everyone else, must obey it.

This apparently simple notion came about only after a long struggle. It was one of the basic principles demanded in the early conflicts that led to the es-

---

7. In Rousseau's case it is fairly clear that he would not extend direct political involvement to women. On Rousseau's treatment of women, see Susan Moller Okin, "Rousseau," in Okin, *Women in Western Political Thought* (Princeton, N.J.: Princeton University Press, 1979), 99–194.

tablishment of democratic institutions. Before that, monarchs claimed that they had been appointed by God to rule (the divine right of kings) and were, therefore, above the law. The principle involved is that a society should be able to bind itself to the rules it collectively has chosen and that no individual or institution should be outside the rules so chosen.

Of course, the apparently simple rule of law can end up being quite complex. For example, not all, perhaps even few, laws are so clear that everyone agrees on their meaning. Therefore, every country has procedures for interpreting the meaning of laws, and those interpretations can change over time. In the United States, for example, the Supreme Court ruled in *Plessy v. Ferguson* (163 US 537 [1896]) that racially segregated facilities were legal under the U.S. Constitution. In *Brown v. Board of Education of Topeka* (347 US 483 [1954]), it ruled that they were not.

Another way in which the rule of law is not so simple is that some laws conflict or at least appear to conflict with other laws. And again countries have to rely on some mechanism for deciding which law takes precedence and must be obeyed. In the United States the Supreme Court has the role of deciding which laws conflict with the U.S. Constitution and is the ultimate arbiter of all disputes over conflicting laws.

THE ELECTORAL SYSTEM

The means of choosing representatives is central to making democracy work, and there has been considerable conflict over procedures to do this.

As we learned during the vote count in Florida in the 2000 presidential election, the details of electoral procedures can be a significant part of determining the outcome of an election. What might appear to be simple questions prove to raise serious issues. Consider the following examples.

1. For what period of time should someone be elected?

2. Should elected representatives be allowed to be reelected to the same office? If yes, how many times? If no, can they be elected again after not holding the office for a period of time? How long?

3. What percentage of the vote does a person need to be chosen? Fifty percent + 1 works nicely if there are only two candidates, but poses problems if there are more than two.

4. If there are more than two candidates, should there be a second election (called a runoff) to choose between the two highest vote getters in the first election?

5. Are there any circumstances where more than a majority (more than 50 percent + 1) should be required?

6. How large should a representative assembly be?

7. How many representatives should be chosen from each area or for what population size?

All of these questions have been in dispute at times and most still are. Also, many countries are currently going through what is being called *democratization* in which these questions *must* be answered in the process of establishing representative institutions where none had existed.

The electoral process begins with the selection of candidates. The means by which this takes place varies from country to country and even within countries. In some cases, the system is entirely under the control of political parties, and a citizen must become active in a party to influence the choice of candidates. In other cases, although the political party is still important, an election (in the United States called a primary) is held to reduce the number of candidates. In this situation citizens can influence the final list of candidates by voting. Obviously, donating money to or working actively for a candidate can also influence the outcome.

For a citizen who simply wants to vote intelligently, deciding whom to vote for will depend largely on the available information. For many offices a high percentage of voters vote on the basis of party identification alone; others depend on information provided by the candidate's campaign and the media. Reliable information is not always easy to come by, and voters often feel they are forced to make choices without the information necessary to make a fully informed decision. This may be one of the reasons for the low voter turnout in some countries. Getting adequate information can take more effort than some voters are willing to expend. And sometimes simply making a decision that reflects your own beliefs is hard. For example, recently there was a local election in my area. Both candidates took positions I liked and both took positions I disliked, and it was a fairly dirty campaign. In these circumstances, the temptation to not vote is strong, and it is hardly surprising that many people choose not to. But not voting is giving the decision on who holds power to others.

With a few exceptions, specific institutional arrangements for elections are not of much importance, but the exceptions are noteworthy. The normal rule of elections is that the side with the most votes wins, but it is always important to remember that this does not mean that those with the most votes are right; it just means that because more people voted for A rather than B, A must be accepted until the next election gives people the chance to change to B if they wish.

Majority rule tends to be based on the assumption that any issue has only two sides. If, for example, there are three candidates in an election, majority rule becomes more complicated, since it is harder to determine what the majority wants. In addition, in many elections relatively few potential voters actually cast their ballots; therefore, the majority may not be represented in the result. (Some countries, therefore, *require* their citizens to vote.) This objection can, of course, be answered by saying that those who do not vote do not care, but what if some of the people who do not vote do not feel that any candidate sufficiently reflects their position? This difficulty indicates the advantage of having more than two candidates in an election, but we have already seen the disadvantage of such an arrangement—if no one receives a clear majority, does this constitute majority rule?

To avoid these problems, various governments have made it difficult or impossible for more than two sides to be represented on the ballot, and other governments have used a system called *proportional representation* (PR), which allocates seats in the legislature on the basis of the percentage of the votes cast for an individual or party. In a very simple example of PR, using a 100-seat legislature like the U.S. Senate, if a minor party got 10 percent of the vote it would get 10 seats, whereas in the usual system where only the party that gets the majority of votes in a district is seated, the minor party would almost certainly get no seats.

Another way to make the representative system more representative is to change from single-member to multiple-member districts. In the usual system, one person is elected from each district, but some places elect two or more people from a district. In most, but not all, cases, this results in more women and minorities being elected.

A final institutional arrangement designed to protect minorities is the common practice in the United States of requiring more than a simple majority on certain issues, such as money issues and amending basic sets of rules like constitutions. The purpose is to protect the rights of the minority, it being felt that at least on some issues a minority with strongly held opinions should not be dictated to by the majority.

The electoral system, although seemingly only a mechanism for determining the composition of the government over the next few years, actually provides the major and sometimes the sole means of political participation for individuals living in a large, complex, modern society. The electoral system, therefore, takes on peculiar importance for democratic theory. Since it often provides a significant or the only means of political participation, the electoral system is the key to whether or not the system is democratic. Individuals, when entering the voting booth, must be sure that their vote will be counted; that the election provides some choice; and that the choice is meaningful in that voters are actually free to vote for any of the options. It is also important to remember the most obvious point—that is, that an individual is allowed to vote in the first place. Finally, each vote should be equal to any other vote, although in the nineteenth century proposals for plural votes based on some criterion like education were fairly common.[8]

These questions of electoral procedure bring into focus other important problems. The electoral system, in addition to providing a means of political participation, is designed to guarantee the peaceful change of political power from one individual or group to another. This in turn raises the whole problem of leadership within a democracy, a question confronting democratic theorists since ancient Athens. The importance of leadership in democratic theory is particularly significant in representative democracy. Whatever theory of representation is accepted, the elected official is given some political power not directly held by constituents. This power can be removed through the electoral

---

8. See, for example, John Stuart Mill, *Considerations on Representative Government,* ed. Currin V. Shields (New York: Liberal Arts Press, 1958), 136–43.

Library of Congress

James Madison (1751–1836) was secretary of state (1801–1809) during the presidency of Thomas Jefferson and then was the fourth president of the United States (1809–17). Madison is now mostly remembered as one of the authors of *The Federalist Papers* (1787–88) and as a major contributor to the drafting of the U.S. Constitution. Madison was concerned with the problem of minority rights and argued that the Constitution as written would provide adequate protection for minorities.

process, but in the meantime it is held by an individual who can directly participate in political decision making to the extent of the power vested in the office. In addition, the official may exercise political leadership by helping form or inform the opinions of constituents and others by defining the political issues he or she believes significant and by propagandizing for particular positions.

Historically, most democratic theorists have been concerned with limiting the political power held by any one individual or group within the society while at the same time providing intelligent and capable leadership. For example, James Madison (1751–1836), an important figure in the framing of the U.S. Constitution and fourth president of the United States, was greatly worried about the possibility of some faction, including a "majority faction," gaining political power and exercising it in its own interest.

In the tenth number of the Federalist Papers (1787–88), Madison suggested that the best protectors of freedom are the division of powers between the states and the national government; the separation of powers among the executive, legislative, and judicial branches of government found in the U.S. Constitution;[9] and the diversity of a large country. Others involved in the writing and defense of the Constitution advocated an enlightened aristocracy exercising political power but periodically checked through election, rather than rule by the people. In other words, they accepted Burke's theory of representation and made it the essence of their theory of government.

A central problem with majority rule and the purpose of all these proposals to limit it is the tendency of majorities to suppress minorities. Systems like

---

9. The idea of the separation of powers came mostly through the writings of the French political theorist Montesquieu (1689–1755), particularly his *De l'esprit des lois* (*The Spirit of the Laws*) (1748).

proportional representation, requirements for a higher percentage than 50 percent of the vote, and Madison's proposals regarding the U.S. Constitution are
attempts to ensure that minorities are protected from the majority.

EQUALITY

Although equality has been discussed for centuries, it became of central importance in the twentieth century. Today equality is one of those concepts, called
essentially contested concepts, that produce fundamental disagreement.[10] For some
people the achievement of some form of equality is absolutely essential; for others the achievement of any form of equality is impossible; for still others, even
if some form of equality were possible, it would not be desirable. Part of this
disagreement comes from lumping together very different types of equality in
one concept. Equality as a general concept includes five separate types of equality: political equality, equality before the law, equality of opportunity, economic
equality, and equality of respect or social equality.

   If there is a strict sense of equality applicable to human beings, it is sameness in relevant aspects.[11] But the phrase "in relevant aspects" modifying "sameness" shows that we have to define carefully what is relevant and what is not
relevant in talking about equality; failure to do this is another reason for the disagreements over the meaning and importance of equality.

Political Equality

The importance of defining *relevant aspects* can be seen even in what would appear to be the simplest form of equality, political equality. If we assume the
existence of some form of representative democracy, political equality refers to
equality at the ballot box, equality in the ability to be elected to public office,
and equality of political influence.

Voting   Equality at the ballot box entails the following:

1. Each individual must have reasonably easy access to the place of voting.

2. Each person must be free to cast his or her own vote as he or she wishes.

3. Each vote must be given exactly the same weight when counted.

These conditions constitute an ideal and are much harder to fulfill than they at
first appear.

---

10. A number of concepts produce such fundamental disagreement. See W. B. Gallie,
    "Essentially Contested Concepts," *Proceedings of the Aristotelian Society,* n.s., 56
    (1956), 167–98; and William E. Connolly, "Essentially Contested Concepts in
    Politics," in Connolly, *The Terms of Political Discourse,* 3d ed. (Princeton, N.J.:
    Princeton University Press, 1993), 10–44.

11. See the discussion in *Nomos IX: Equality,* ed. J. Roland Pennock and John W. Chap-
    man (New York: Atherton Press, 1967), particularly the article "Egalitarianism and
    the Idea of Equality," by Hugo Adam Bedau, 3–27.

There are a number of reasons for this difficulty. First, there is the question of *citizenship*. To vote one must be a citizen. Each country has its own regulations about who is a citizen and how citizenship is acquired. For example, in most countries, if you are born in that country you are a citizen. But if your parents are citizens of another country, you will probably have the right to be a citizen of their country. Some countries also allow their citizens to be simultaneously citizens of another country; others do not. Citizenship also can be gained by being *naturalized,* or granted citizenship by a country. Naturalization usually requires a formal process culminating in a ceremony in which allegiance is sworn to the new country.

Citizenship can also be lost. In many, though not all, countries, swearing allegiance to another country will result in the loss of citizenship. In the United States, serving in the military of another country is supposed to result in the loss of U.S. citizenship. Each country has its own rules on the loss of citizenship; in some countries it is virtually impossible to lose citizenship, whereas in others many different actions can result in such loss.

Second, there is an age requirement for voting. Each country has an established age at which citizens are first allowed to vote. At present the most common voting age is eighteen, although there are exceptions (for example, the voting age in Indonesia is seventeen and in India, twenty-one). No one under that age can vote.

Third, various people may have had the right to vote taken away from them. In the United States, for example, people convicted of certain crimes lose the right to vote. Also, at times and in various countries other formal limitations have been placed on the right to vote. Examples of such limitations are requirements that a voter own a specified amount of property or belong to a particular religion; race and gender have also served as limitations and in some places still do.

In addition, there are many informal avenues of inequality. First, and perhaps most obvious, are racial and sexual discrimination. Even with legal limitations on voting removed, women and minorities in most countries have been so discouraged from political participation that they vote at a much lower rate than males of the racial majority. Second, some older and many disabled voters may have difficulty getting to the polling place. For example, the polling place in my area requires voters to negotiate two sets of stairs, and although arrangements can be made to vote without having to use the stairs, some voters didn't know this or felt that the effort required was too great and chose not to vote. This example illustrates that the right to vote can be taken away simply by not thinking through what is required to actually vote.

Also, a person who cannot influence what names are printed on the ballot —that is, choose the candidates—is not equal to those who can. There are two ways to influence the choice of who becomes a candidate: money and active participation in the political system. For many people the lack of money makes it very difficult to participate actively, but most people who don't participate simply choose not to.

Finally, each voter votes in a district, which should be roughly equal in population to other districts. If one district has a much larger population than another district, each vote is diluted in that it does not have the same strength in determining the outcome as a vote in a smaller district. The closer the districts are in population size, the closer the votes will be in strength. For example, to take an extreme case, if voter A lives in a district of 50,000 voters and voter B lives in one with only 10,000, B's vote will be worth five of A's. Some countries, such as the United States, require that district boundaries be changed regularly (usually after each census) to achieve this form of equality. The process is called *reapportionment*.

Running for Office   Equality in the ability to be elected to public office means that everyone who has the vote can be elected to public office, although particular offices usually have age qualifications and other specific requirements, such as residence in a specified area. In many countries it has become very expensive to run for public office; hence, equality in the ability to be elected to public office has been seriously eroded. Most countries have seen attempts to limit the effect of wealth by legally controlling campaign spending. Some countries, such as Great Britain, place very strict limitations on the amount that candidates can spend. It has been estimated that an average campaign for the U.S. Senate in 1996 cost $4.5 million, meaning that the average senator had to raise $14,000 during every week of his or her six years in office. In the United Kingdom, by contrast, no candidate can spend more than £8000 or about U.S. $13,000 in a campaign.

In addition, there are social constraints on running for office. Traditionally in the United States, it has been difficult or even impossible for African Americans, women, Hispanics, and other ethnic minorities, to name just a few groups, to become serious candidates for office. Similar situations, although with different groups, exist in most countries. Although members of such groups may have the legal right to run for office, that right has frequently been meaningless because there was no chance they could be elected. To avoid this, in New Zealand four seats in Parliament were set aside for Maori representation. The situation is slowly improving in most countries.

Political Influence   Political equality also refers to an equality of political influence among citizens. Such equality means that all who choose to participate can do so without any formal limitations based on their membership in any religious, racial, ethnic, gender, or economic category. Of course, all these categories have at times both formally affected political influence and informally affected people's ability to participate and the likelihood that they will choose to participate. In much of the world, most of these limitations still exist.

Equality before the Law

Equality before the law resembles the definition of equality as sameness in relevant aspects because it means that all people will be treated in the same way by the legal system, and it is not hedged about by so many formal definitions of relevant aspects. Depictions of justice usually show a blindfolded woman hold-ing a scale. The scale is an indication that the issues will be weighed; the blind-fold indicates that they will be weighed fairly, taking into account nothing be-yond the issues of the case.

Since a major function of law and legal procedures is to establish general rules that all people are expected to accept, law, by its very nature, is an equal-izing force in society if it is enforced fairly. Clearly, equality before the law in practice is undermined by the socioeconomic inequalities that exist in all soci-eties. But equality before the law is one of democracy's clearest goals.

Equality of Opportunity

The third type of equality is related to social stratification and mobility systems. Equality of opportunity means, first, that every individual in society will be able to move up or down within the class or status system depending on that individual's ability and application of that ability. Second, it means that no arti-ficial barrier will keep any person from achieving what she or he can through ability and hard work. The key problem in the definition of equality of op-portunity is the word *artificial,* which refers to individual characteristics that do not affect inherent abilities. Race, gender, religion, ethnic or national origin, and sexual orientation are most often cited as such artificial barriers.

Social stratification and mobility systems vary greatly from society to soci-ety. We tend to think of social status and mobility as easy to measure because we link them to an easily quantifiable object—money. In most Western soci-eties today, that measure is a fairly accurate guide to status (except at the level of the traditional aristocracy) and the major means of gaining or losing status. But even in the West it is not quite that simple because status depends on the respect a position in society is given as well as the income that goes with the position. For example, clergy are not generally very well paid but are accorded a status higher than their income. In a society that accords status on the basis of some other value (such as education), money would not automatically bring status. Equality of opportunity depends on the value accorded status.

Economic Equality

The fourth aspect of equality, economic equality, is rarely used to refer to eco-nomic sameness, but a complete discussion of the subject cannot ignore this definition. Economic equality could mean that every individual within a soci-ety should have the same income, and Edward Bellamy (1850–98) in his popu-lar novel *Looking Backward* (1888) proposed such a definition. This definition is normally avoided because most advocates of economic equality are more con-cerned with the political and legal aspects of equality and with equality of op-portunity than with strict financial equality. In addition, complete equality of income could be unfair to everyone because it would not take into account the differing needs of different individuals. Of course, if income levels were suf-ficiently high, differences in need would be irrelevant, because all individuals would have enough no matter what their needs were. But very few exponents of economic equality expect such high income levels; therefore, what constitutes basic or fundamental human needs is a matter of considerable concern.

The usual argument for economic equality is that every individual within society must be guaranteed a minimum level of economic *security*. The stress is on security, not equality. Such security will allow the individual the scope to become a fully active citizen. The major contention, the key to the argument, is that without some degree of security citizens will not be in a position to participate effectively even in the limited role of voter.

Extreme levels of poverty effectively bar an individual from participation in the life of the community and can create continuing inequalities. This effect is particularly significant in education. A child in a typical middle-class or lower middle-class home has had toys and other objects that help teach many of the skills essential to learning. A simple thing such as having a book read aloud a number of times shows the child the turning of the pages and will indicate that the English language is read from left to right and, thus, will set up a pattern the eyes will follow. The child who has not had any of this preparation will start out a year or two, or even more, behind the child who has. There are also certain skills essential even for relatively unskilled jobs that a child learns by playing with toys. A child who has simple toys to play with is learning these skills; a child who does not have such toys will not gain these skills and will have to find a way of learning them later or be barred from even those unskilled jobs. The effect of such deprivation on a child's life can be profound, and we are unsure whether some of these effects can be reversed for children who are already in our school systems. Thus children at age five or six may already have handicaps they will never be able to overcome. There are exceptions: Some children brought up in families that have suffered generations of extreme poverty do make it. However, the overwhelming majority do not.

Does a great inequality in income eliminate equality of opportunity? How great an inequality is permissible? How can the extremes be brought closer together? We shall look at these problems in greater detail as we discuss the differences between democratic capitalism and democratic socialism.

Equality of Respect or Social Equality

The fifth type of equality, equality of respect or social equality, is in some ways the most difficult to define. At its base is the belief that all human beings are due equal respect just because they are human; we are all equal in our fundamental humanity. Social equality is derived from this belief. Equality of respect refers to a level of individual interpersonal relations not covered by any of the other aspects of equality. The civil rights movement in the United States once developed a slogan, "Black is Beautiful," which illustrates the point. In Western society, the color black has had connotations of evil, as in the black clothes of the villain in early movies about the Old West. Advertising on television and in magazines used to reinforce this connotation by never using black models. The slogan "Black is Beautiful" was directed particularly at African American children to give them the idea that it could be good, not bad, to be black, and that they could be black and still respect themselves and be respected by others.

In a narrow sense, social equality means that no public or private association may erect artificial barriers to activity within the association. Again, there is the problem of defining *artificial,* but generally we use it in the same sense described earlier, that is, denoting characteristics, such as gender, sexual orientation, race, ethnic or national origin, or religion, that do not affect an individual's inherent abilities. Examples of this type of equality might be the lack of such barriers to membership in a country club or in the use of a public park. Thus social equality refers to the absence of the class and status distinctions that raise such barriers. In this sense, it includes aspects of equality of opportunity.

Education is believed to be one of the main mechanisms for overcoming inequality, but in many countries education is also a means of preserving inequalities. For example, in Britain large numbers of students are educated privately in what are called public schools. These students then proceed to the best universities and generally into the best jobs. (The same process takes place in most countries but on a smaller scale.) In the process, these students are cut off from the broader society, and thus privilege, antagonism, and ignorance establish the basis for significant social inequality. In some countries efforts have been made to overcome such patterns by establishing schools that bring together people from a wide variety of backgrounds in an attempt to eliminate class or racial ignorance and animosity.

FREEDOM, LIBERTY, AND RIGHTS

Historically, the desire for equality has often been expressed as an aspect of liberty. When Thomas Jefferson (1743–1826), drafting the Declaration of Independence, spoke of equality, he meant that people were equal in the rights they had. Equality of opportunity is often thought of as a right. On the other hand, many people believe attempts to achieve a degree of economic equality are directly in conflict with attempts to maintain economic liberty.

The words *liberty, freedom,* and *right* are most often used interchangeably. Although some prefer to make careful distinctions among the meanings, it is not necessary to do so. All three refer to the ability to act without restrictions or with restrictions that are themselves limited in specified or specifiable ways. *Freedom* is the most general term. *Liberty* usually refers to social and political freedom. *Right* usually refers to specific legally guaranteed freedoms. Also, *right* has been broadened to include basic human or natural rights. Finally, rights have become the focus of those in the United States who wish to expand constitutional guarantees and protections. As a result such questions as "Does the U.S. Constitution provide for a right of privacy?" or, more recently, "Is there a right to die?" have become the center of legal, political, and philosophic debate.

There is no such thing as complete freedom. In the first place, one must maintain life and perform a number of essential bodily functions. It is possible to choose the times one eats, drinks, sleeps, and so on, but one cannot choose not to eat, drink, sleep, and so forth for very long. In the second place, there are other people. Although they are essential for a complete life, they are re-

Thomas Jefferson (1743–1826), the third president of the United States, was involved in almost all the issues that dominated American political life during his lifetime. Of all the things he accomplished, Jefferson thought his three most important actions were writing the Declaration of Independence, writing the Virginia Act for Establishing Religious Freedom, and founding the University of Virginia.

Library of Congress

stricting. An old adage states, "Your freedom to swing your arm stops at my nose." Although superficial, it does point out that the existence of others must be taken into account and that other people can be a limit on free action.

A democratic society should be fairly free and open rather than controlled. It is the general assumption of democratic theory that whatever does no damage to the society as a whole or to the individuals within it should be the concern of no one but the individual or individuals involved.

Natural Rights and Civil Rights

The most influential approach to liberty is found in the distinction between the rights a person has or should have as a human being and the rights derived from government. The former are often called *natural rights;* the latter are called *civil rights.* Although the trend today is either to reject the concept of natural rights altogether and call all rights civil rights or to replace the word *natural* with *human,* the traditional distinction is still useful.

Many democratic theorists, such as John Locke, have argued that human beings, separate from all government or society, have certain rights that should never be given up or taken away. People do not give up these rights on joining a society or government, and the society or government should not attempt to take these rights away. If a government does try to take them away, the people are justified in revolting to change the government. Not all theorists make this last argument. The point is that natural rights establish limits. The Bill of Rights in the U.S. Constitution is a good example. Many of the amendments in the Bill of Rights begin, "Congress shall make no law regarding. . . ." The wording clearly indicates a limit on governmental activity. Isaiah Berlin calls this approach *negative liberty.* By this term he describes the area of life within which

John Locke (1632–1704) was an important British philosopher and political thinker of the seventeenth century. His most important works were *Essay Concerning Human Understanding* (1689) and, in political thought, *Two Treatises of Government* (published in 1690 but written earlier). The first of the two treatises is an attack on the divine right of kings as put forth by Robert Filmer (1588–1653). The second treatise is an argument for rule by consent of the governed, a defense of private property and majority rule, and a justification for revolution. The U.S. Declaration of Independence was based on the second treatise, and Locke was a major influence on a number of thinkers in the United States at the time of the revolution and the drafting of the U.S. Constitution.

one "is or should be left to do or be what he is able to do or be, without interference by other persons."[12]

In the United States, tradition emphasizes the danger of possible interference from government. Certain areas of life, such as speech, religion, press, and assembly, have been defined as areas of "negative liberty" where each person is left to do, on the whole, what she or he wants. Negative liberty as practiced illustrates the complexity of democracy. Government is seen as the most likely agent to attempt to restrict liberty. Government is also the major protector of liberty, and it must protect people even against itself. This is one reason many Western democracies have established what we call a system of checks and balances within the government. No segment of government should be able to rule unchecked by any other segment; as a result, the rights of citizens are protected.

Berlin also developed a concept that he called *positive liberty*. As used by Berlin, this refers to the possibility of individuals controlling their own destiny or their ability to choose among options. For Berlin, positive liberty is the area of rational self-control or "self-mastery." For others, positive liberty means that the government should ensure conditions in which the full development of each individual is possible.[13] On the whole, as will be seen in the next chapter,

---

12. Isaiah Berlin, "Two Concepts of Liberty," in Berlin, *Four Essays on Liberty* (London: Oxford University Press, 1969), 121–22.

13. See, for example, the argument in Christian Bay, *The Structure of Freedom* (Stanford, Calif.: Stanford University Press, 1958); and Bay, *Strategies of Political Emancipation* (Notre Dame, Ind.: University of Notre Dame Press, 1981).

democratic capitalists stress negative liberty and democratic socialists stress positive liberty while trying to maintain most of the negative liberties.

The most important natural right—the right to self-preservation—is basic to this understanding of positive liberty. This right can be interpreted to mean that every person has a right to the necessary minimum of food, clothing, and shelter needed to live in a given society. Since standards vary considerably from society to society, the necessary minimum might vary a great deal.

From this perspective, positive liberty might include the right to an education equal to one's ability and the right to a job. This approach to positive liberty logically extends to establishing as a right anything that can be shown to be essential to the development, and perhaps even the expression, of each person's potential as a human being.

Thus, positive liberty can include as rights a wide variety of economic and social practices in addition to the political rights that usually come to mind when speaking of rights. The Universal Declaration of Human Rights[14] adopted by the United Nations includes such rights in its definition of human rights. For example, Article 22 states that "everyone, as a member of society, has the right to social security and is entitled to realization, through national effort and in accordance with the organization and resources of each State, of the economic, social and cultural rights indispensable for his dignity and the free development of his personality." Positive liberty is not usually extended this far, but these examples illustrate the complexity of the questions involved.

Other so-called natural rights have also been widely debated. One of the most controversial is the right to property. Some contend that there must be a nearly absolute right to acquire and accumulate private property because ownership of property is an avenue to the full development and expression of the human personality. Others argue that private property must be limited because the control of such property gives additional power to those who own it. (Additional arguments for and against the institution of private property will be considered in Chapter 4.)

Although there is widespread disagreement on the specific natural rights, it is generally agreed that after the formation of government, these rights must become civil rights or rights specifically guaranteed and protected by the government, even—or particularly—against itself. This formulation of liberty raises many difficulties. The most basic difficulty is the assumption that a government will be willing to guarantee rights against itself. Many thinkers have assumed that representative democracy with fairly frequent elections will solve the problem. Any such government should recognize that an infringement of people's civil rights would ensure its defeat in the next election. Experience has shown this is not necessarily true, and the result has been apathy, civil disobedience, and revolution, with apathy currently the greatest concern in most developed democracies. At the same time, the protection of liberties is still considered one

---

14. "The Universal Declaration of Human Rights" was adopted by the United Nations in
    1948. The text can be found at http://www.un.org/Overview/rights.html.

of the primary duties of a democratic political system and a central part of democratic theory.

Types of Liberty

It is more difficult to define types of liberty than types of equality but, loosely, civil rights include the following specific liberties or freedoms:

1. the right to vote
2. freedom of speech
3. freedom of the press
4. freedom of assembly
5. freedom of religion
6. freedom of movement
7. freedom from arbitrary treatment by the political and legal system

The first six of these are areas of life that the democratic argument says should be left, within very broad limits, to the discretion of the individual. Of these six, freedom of movement is the least commonly discussed among theorists of democracy. The seventh item, freedom from arbitrary treatment, is simply a way of stating positively the belief that government must protect the citizen from government. The various freedoms—particularly those of speech, press, assembly, and religion—are closely related.

The Right to Vote The right to vote without interference is, of course, the key to the ability to change the system. It is the ultimate check on government and the true guarantor of any freedom.

Freedom of Speech With some minimal disagreement, most thinkers consider freedom of speech the most important freedom. Within democracy freedom of speech has a special place. The right to vote does not mean much if it is impossible to hear opposing points of view and to express one's own opinion. The same reasoning is behind the freedoms of press and assembly. The rights to publish opinion and to meet together to discuss political issues are fundamental rights if people are to vote intelligently. The right to vote implies, even requires, a right to information and the free expression of opinion both orally and in writing. Freedom of speech requires freedom of assembly; freedom to speak is meaningless without the possibility of an audience.

John Stuart Mill (1806–73) explained the importance of freedom of speech and press in a slightly different way in his classic *On Liberty* (1859).

> This, then, is the appropriate region of human liberty. It comprises, first, the inward domain of consciousness; demanding liberty of conscience in the most comprehensive sense; liberty of thought and feeling; absolute freedom of opinion and sentiment on all subjects, practical or speculative, scientific, moral, or theological. The liberty of expressing and publishing

opinions may seem to fall under a different principle, since it belongs to that part of the conduct of an individual which concerns other people; but, being almost of as much importance as the liberty of thought itself and resting in great part on the same reasons, is practically inseparable from it.[15]

For Mill, thought requires the freedom to express oneself orally and in writing. The search for truth requires that challenge, debate, and disagreement be possible. Mill argued this from four different perspectives.

First, if any opinion is compelled to silence, that opinion may, for aught we can certainly know, be true. To deny this is to assume our own infallibility.

Secondly, though the silenced opinion be an error, it may, and very commonly does, contain a portion of truth; and since the general or prevailing opinion on any subject is rarely or never the whole truth, it is only by the collision of adverse opinions that the remainder of the truth has any chance of being supplied.

Thirdly, even if the received opinion be not only true, but the whole truth; unless it is suffered to be, and actually is, vigorously and earnestly contested, it will, by most of those who receive it, be held in the manner of a prejudice, with little comprehension or feeling of its rational grounds. And not only this, but, fourthly, the meaning of the doctrine itself will be in danger of being lost or enfeebled, and deprived of its vital effect on the character and conduct; the dogma becoming a mere formal profession, inefficacious for good, but cumbering the ground and preventing the growth of any real and heartfelt conviction, from reason or personal experience.[16]

Without freedom of expression truth is lost, is never found, becomes mere prejudice, or is enfeebled. Assuming that there is truth to be found, freedom of expression is essential; if there is no truth to be found, freedom of expression is even more important as the only device available to sort out the better opinion from the worse.

Freedom of the Press   Mill joined speech and press closely together and, for political concerns, the argument that a generally free press is essential in a democracy is almost noncontroversial. But there are areas of concern outside the strictly political realm, most obviously related to the publication of pornography, and there are even concerns about some more narrowly political issues.

If freedom of the press is taken to be an absolute, there should be no restrictions on the publication of pornography. With some exceptions, much pornography depicts individuals of one of two groups—women or children—as objects to be used, often violently, by another group—men. Viewed this way

---

15. John Stuart Mill, *On Liberty,* 4th ed. (London: Longman, Reader & Dyer, 1869), 26.

16. Mill, *On Liberty,* 95.

pornography is an issue with strong political overtones and illustrates a central concern of contemporary students of democracy, the conflict of rights. Whose rights should be protected, the publishers and consumers of pornography or the women and children who are turned into consumer goods?

A more narrowly political issue involves the publication of material designed to incite the overthrow of a government by violence. An absolute version of freedom of the press would require the government to ensure that those trying to overthrow it have the right to publish calls for its overthrow and even manuals on how to produce bombs and directions on where and how to place them. Many people find such a position ludicrous; many find it perfectly reasonable.

A third issue is governmental secrecy. Some, particularly those working for the press, contend that the press should have free access to the whole government decision-making process. Others, particularly those working in government, argue that government should be free to choose what the press is allowed to know and publish. Most people fall somewhere in between, believing that some governmental actions must be secret and that other actions, ranging from a few to most, should not be secret. The problem is that governments decide what must be secret, and this leads to distrust. There is no way around this problem, and the press and government will inevitably be at odds about the extent of permissible secrecy.

A related issue is self-censorship by the press. Media that are privately owned (most of them in the developed world) must attract and keep readers/viewers/listeners to make a profit. Some media sensationalize material to attract a larger audience; others limit what they report or the language that is used to avoid upsetting their owners, corporate sponsors, or the audience they have already attracted. Both tendencies distort the information available and undermine the value of a free press.

Tension between the press and government is unavoidable and probably healthy. Western democracies criticize countries with a controlled press while trying to keep their own press from publishing things they want kept secret. The degree of press freedom varies among democracies; there is no such thing as a completely free press, but a fairly high degree of such freedom is essential in a democracy since in the modern world the communication of political ideas requires the right to publish those ideas.

Freedom of Assembly The freedom to speak requires the freedom to have an audience. Although broadcasting means that the audience need not be gathered in one place, the ability to meet together to discuss political issues, make decisions on those issues, and choose candidates is clearly still fundamental to a functioning democracy.

The political issues related to the freedom of assembly are issues of public order. Should parades and demonstrations that may produce violence be allowed? What limitations on assembly should be permissible to keep traffic moving or to prevent violence? All governments, from the local to the national, in all democracies are constantly faced with the problem of how to regulate assembly without making it politically ineffective.

Freedom of Religion   Freedom of religion is usually supported on precisely the same grounds Mill used to defend freedom of speech and press, and worshipping together requires the freedom of assembly. Even if we are certain that we have the whole truth—perhaps particularly if we are certain—we should always distrust our own presumed infallibility and welcome the continuation of the search. Freedom of religion has, particularly in North America, come to be identified with the separation of church and state. The search for religious truth, in this view, requires that government be a neutral bystander neither favoring nor suppressing any aspect of that search.

In many countries this issue takes a more complex form. In the first place, many countries have an established church or a church that is officially recognized by the government and may receive financial and other public support. Secondly, many countries have political parties that are tied (directly or indirectly) to religious bodies. In Europe most of these parties are labeled Christian Democrats or some variant thereof. These parties are most often conservative. In such circumstances the quest for freedom of religion becomes more problematic. But every religion has had at some time or other to face the question of its relationship to political power. This issue is particularly important today in the Third World, and it deeply divides the Roman Catholic Church.

Freedom of Movement   Freedom of movement is less commonly included among the basic freedoms, but it is as important as the others because the ability to move freely is a major protection for other freedoms. Some restrictions are already in effect. Many democratic countries, particularly in Europe, require their citizens to carry identity papers and, for example, require hotels to record the number on these papers when someone registers. All countries require passports for travel to some foreign countries. And the growth of government programs means that most countries have records of the location of and changes of permanent address for a growing number of citizens. But in no democracy is it necessary to get prior approval from a government to travel within its borders, and, most important, within a democracy people can freely move from place to place for political activity.

Freedom from Arbitrary Treatment   The last freedom, freedom from arbitrary treatment by the political and legal system, is also a major protection for the other freedoms. All democratic societies have clearly established procedural rights designed to guarantee that every individual will be treated fairly by the system. Without these procedural rights, the substantive rights of freedom of speech, press, and so on would not be as secure.

Basic guarantees include those found in the U.S. Bill of Rights, such as freedom from cruel and unusual punishment (designed to prohibit torture; now an issue in the debate over capital punishment); the right to a writ of habeas corpus (Latin meaning "[that] you have the body"), or the right to demand that a prisoner be brought before an officer of the court so that the lawfulness of the imprisonment can be determined; and the right to a trial by a jury of one's peers.

Among the other means by which freedom has been expressed are toleration, the silence of the law, and unenforceability.

Toleration   Toleration means that one accepts another person believing or doing something that one believes to be wrong. Religious toleration is the most obvious case, and in some ways it is the most difficult. If I am certain that my way is the only one that leads to salvation, I am unlikely to tolerate an opposing belief that I am convinced is dangerous to my and your salvation. Religious tolerance is, in fact, a relatively recent phenomenon; as late as the seventeenth century the word *tolerance* had a negative meaning and *intolerance* a positive one. Within a relatively short time, though, the connotation of the words shifted: tolerance became a virtue and intolerance a vice, although even today there are many who do not believe in tolerating beliefs or behaviors they are convinced are wrong. Today most people accept toleration and extend it beyond religion to other beliefs and ways of life. In this way, freedom comes to include a large area in which we accept other people even though we disagree with them.

Politically, tolerance is basic to modern democracy because one of the keys to democracy is the recognition and acceptance of even very basic disagreements among citizens. The diversity of the population and the protection of that diversity through tolerance are extremely important. Tolerance must exist or democracy cannot work.

The Silence of the Law and Unenforceability   Two other areas of freedom should be noted briefly: the silence of the law and unenforceability. It is part of the Anglo-American tradition that if there is no law prohibiting an action, that action is within the area of individual discretion until such a law is written. In the United States, when the law is written, it cannot affect actions that preceded it. In many other countries, newly passed laws can be used to find past acts illegal. Also, the experience of Prohibition in the United States indicated that there are unenforceable laws, laws that people simply won't accept. Thus, unenforceability can also be seen as aspect of freedom.

EDUCATION

Liberty is limited to some extent by all political systems. The democratic system has built into it certain safeguards that tend to protect individuals from having their freedoms too severely restricted. Of course, these safeguards do not always work. The most fundamental of these safeguards is the basic characteristic of a democracy—the people have some control over their government. Democratic theorists have never adequately dealt with the problem of severe restrictions of rights that are desired or acquiesced in by the majority. Thus a problem for democracy is how to achieve sufficient tolerance of differences so that the majority is willing to protect the rights of the minority. For many the answer is education.

Education as a fundamental principle of democracy may be mildly controversial, but it should not be. Democratic theorists such as John Locke, Jean-Jacques Rousseau, and John Stuart Mill wrote treatises on education that tied their political theories loosely or tightly to the need for an educated populace. In the United States the founders of the democracy believed in the essential role of education in making an effective democracy possible. In fact, the statement that an educated citizenry is necessary in a democracy is commonplace. What might make it appear controversial is the argument over the nature of the education needed.

The argument regarding the need for education is fairly simple. Citizens are required to make choices among candidates and issues. In order to do so they must have the basic skills of reading, writing, and arithmetic (rather illiterately known as the three Rs), because the information provided is often communicated in print, because it may be necessary for citizens to communicate in writing, and because numbers are used extensively. Equally important, the citizen must be able to evaluate the information, weigh pros and cons, and decide what positions best correspond to their interests. Of course, the citizen must also be able to correctly identify those interests.

A democracy can operate without an educated populace. India is a functioning democracy with a very high level of illiteracy. But a democracy of illiterates is limited unless the culture actively encourages oral dissemination of information and discussion of issues. The elitist model of democracy would have no trouble with a high level of illiteracy, but every other approach to democracy would find it an issue requiring solution. Thus it is fair to say that an educated populace is one of the prerequisites of a fully functioning democracy.

One central concern today is how to educate citizens. This applies both to children as they grow up and immigrants hoping to become citizens of their new country. Given the apparent level of apathy in the United States, many people feel that it has become essential to educate for citizenship, to help people realize the advantages of active, involved citizenship.

In the modern world the knowledge and evaluative skills necessary to judge the issues might appear to require considerable formal education, and that is where part of the current controversy lies. What constitutes an educated populace? On this question there are basic divisions. Some people believe that knowledge of how the government functions is sufficient. Others believe that formal education in the principles of democracy and how to evaluate arguments is necessary. Many positions between these are taken, with about the only agreement in most democracies being that the educational system isn't doing what it should. (See also the discussion of civil society, below.)

The principles of democracy all relate to one another and all stem from the most fundamental democratic principle: citizen involvement. Politically, equality and freedom both characterize and protect citizen involvement. They characterize citizen involvement in that democracy demands the freedom to vote and equality of the vote; they protect citizen involvement because a free and equal electorate can insist on the maintenance of that freedom and equality. A free and equal electorate needs education to ensure that freedom and equality are meaningful and to make informed choices as citizens. Today the electoral system is the major avenue for the expression of citizen involvement, and of course the system of representation is the purpose and result of the electoral system and the way in which citizens are involved.

CURRENT TRENDS

The principles of democracy do not change, but how they are interpreted does. The most obvious current trend is that many countries are trying to reestablish democracy or establish it for the first time, but there are also other significant trends.

Democratization

If any ideology is dominant today, it is democracy. Most countries put forth the pretense of being democratic in the most minimal sense, holding elections. And many countries are going through a process called democratization. Thus, it is particularly important today to understand what range of meanings can be applied to democracy. Does it mean merely holding elections, even though the electoral process is corrupt? If the elections are honestly run, is that enough? If more is required, what is necessary? What constitutes a full democracy, and do any exist?

Since 1989 and the fall of the Berlin Wall, *democratization*, or the process by which countries establish democratic institutions and procedures and, even more importantly, a culture of democracy, has been a major topic of discussion. Putting such institutions and procedures in place is fairly easy; making them work is often quite difficult.

Democratization continues in the Third World where elections are commonplace but the development of a democratic culture lags far behind. And the countries of Central Europe and the former Soviet Union face similar problems. Some of the countries in Central Europe had democratic institutions in place prior to World War II, but few current citizens have any experience with democracy. Few of the countries that emerged from the former Soviet Union have ever had any experience with democracy. And in the Third World, democratic institutions borrowed from the previous colonial rulers were put in place, but again, citizens have little or no previous experience with these institutions. In a few cases, the Czech Republic and India for example, democracy has taken root, but in most of these countries, it is very fragile. As a result, dictators of various sorts exist throughout the Third World, in many of the countries of the former Soviet Union, and in a few countries in Central Europe.

Myanmar (formerly Burma) is an interesting case that has gained publicity primarily though the house arrest since 1989 of the main democratic leader, Daw Aung San Suu Kyi (b. 1945), who won the Nobel Peace Prize in 1991 for her efforts to restore democracy to Myanmar. Myanmar has had brief periods of democracy since it gained its independence from Britain in 1947, but most of the time it has been ruled by the military, a common phenomenon throughout the Third World. In its most recent free election in 1990, the National League for Democracy, led by Aung San Suu Kyi, who was already under house arrest, won a large majority of seats in the legislative assembly, but the military simply ruled the election invalid and has continued in power. Aung San Suu Kyi has continued to agitate for the restoration of democracy, and, from time to time, the military rulers have made gestures to conciliate her. So far, the military is still in power, but Aung San Suu Kyi was released in May 2002.

Myanmar is a good example of the central problem faced by countries struggling with democracy, the weakness or nonexistence of a culture that supports democratic culture, procedures, and institutions. And, given the extreme poverty of many of these countries, particularly those in the Third World, many have argued that development must come first and then democracy will follow.

But Amartya Sen (b. 1933), who won the Nobel Prize in economics in 1998, has recently argued that development and at least some features of democracy are inseparable. He argues

> Development requires the removal of major sources of unfreedom: poverty as well as tyranny, poor economic opportunities as well as systematic social deprivation, neglect of public facilities as well as intolerance or overactivity of repressive states. Despite unprecedented increases in overall opulence, the contemporary world denies elementary freedoms to vast numbers—perhaps even a majority—of people.[17]

Sen contends that the establishment of such freedoms will spur economic development.

Civil Society

The culture that supports democracy includes a concept, *civil society,* that has a long history but had largely been forgotten. Civil society refers to the set of largely voluntary associations and interactions found in the family, clubs, neighborhood associations, religious organizations, and so forth that operate outside the formal political system and thus outside its control in which people learn tolerance, the process of winning and losing elections, living with rules determined by the group, and all the other key democratic values.

Civil society also refers to economic relationships and institutions that are outside direct political control, such as private banking and the free market. Just as democratic values must be learned, so must the attitudes and behaviors appropriate to private economic life, such as profit and loss, the ability of enterprise to both succeed and fail, and the need to be responsible for one's own future economic health. Many argue that a healthy civil society is essential to the existence of both democracy and private economic institutions.

In Central Europe and the former Soviet Union the problem is how to create a civil society where there were few to no associations that were not con-

17. Amartya Sen, *Development as Freedom* (New York: Knopf, 1999), 3–4.

trolled by the state. In the Third World the problem is how to create a specifically democratic civil society where private institutions have been based on
hierarchical relationships of clans, ethnic groups, religions, tribes, and so forth.

The United States used to be described as a country based on voluntary
associations, but recently, as popularly explained in *Bowling Alone* (2000) by
Robert D. Putnam, Americans are much less likely to be members of such associations. For many, this suggests that even in the United States, civil society
is less vital than it needs to be to provide the support needed for a vibrant democratic culture.

Group Rights

A major focus of attention that relates to many of the other contemporary points
of contention is the issue of group rights. When we think of legally enforceable rights we tend to think solely in terms of individuals, although the fact that
in the United States corporations are legally classified as individuals complicates
the issue. Today many are arguing that they are deprived of rights solely based
on their membership in a group and that, therefore, the rights of groups should
be protected.

The assumption has been that individuals make up groups and, as a result,
there is no need to have rights for groups. But the issue today is the belief that in
practice only some individuals are in fact protected and that those whose rights
are not protected are in that situation because they are members of a group.

Some of the claims are based on the American myth of the "melting pot"
in which ethnic, religious, and other differences are supposed to disappear. But
of course racial and gender differences have never disappeared, and many have
contended that without group rights the pressure to conform to the majority
is a violation of people's ability to practice the religion of their choice, particularly if that choice is not Christian, to maintain their ethnic identity, to speak
their native language, to have a sexual orientation other than heterosexual, and
so forth, putting them at risk of prosecution and persecution, or, at minimum,
threatening their cultural identity.

Of course, the obvious problem is, what groups need their rights protected?
Most of us are members of multiple groups. Some are more important to us
than others, and most of us might easily be able to say that we most identify with
our ethnic group, our religious group, or some other easily identifiable group,
but others might not find it so easy. And are all groups worthy of legal protection? And what if the culture of one group includes discrimination against
members of another group? As a result of these problems, a number of approaches to groups have developed.

Multiculturalism One of the growing concerns with democratic pluralism is
multiculturalism, particularly in education. To what extent should a society
with a dominant culture or cultures teach children about the dominant cultures
rather than the minority cultures? Put another way, don't children have a right
to learn about their heritage rather than being forced to learn about the dominant culture? These two ways of putting what is essentially the same question

illustrate the problem. Those in the dominant culture have as much a right to value their culture as those in the minority cultures, but do they have a right to impose it? In the past this right was never questioned. Today people in minority cultures are demanding that their cultures be taught as well as the majority culture. Multiculturalism raises questions of majority versus minority rights and how to make a plural society genuinely pluralistic.

As noted in the previous chapter, the issues raised by multiculturalism are also part of the current debate around immigration. In a recent book, *Democracy and the Foreigner* (2001), Bonnie Honig illustrates how immigration enriches a democratic society while raising issues of autonomy, citizenship, and rights, among others that the foreigner poses for democracy.

Difference   How can individual and group difference be recognized and valued in a society that believes in equality. Or should they? In a development that has changed the focus of debate, a shift has occurred, stemming primarily from debates within feminism, from a concern with the *sameness* component of equality to the recognition that *difference* is important and valuable and should be protected, even fostered. The argument does not depend on whether the differences are based on biology or are socially constructed.

While the definition of equality as "sameness in relevant aspects" does not prohibit a focus on difference, the emphasis since the beginning of the civil rights movement has been on sameness. The change is to move the focus to what is a *relevant* difference. Thirty years ago such an emphasis was used as an excuse to take rights from minorities; the assumption now is that such rights are so well established that it is now safe to again recognize relevant differences.

The issue comes back to one of the fundamental questions of democracy: How do we balance the interests of the majority and the minority? Or, what may be a more accurate reflection of the current situation in the United States: How do we balance the interests of various minorities given that there is no longer an overall or general minority—only temporary majorities and minorities on specific issues?

For example, what does equality mean to someone who is disabled? Immediately after World War II various European countries tried to compensate for war injuries by providing those physically disabled in the war easier access to certain jobs and transportation, and they established other programs that clearly recognized that society needed to act to integrate the physically disabled as much as possible into the postwar society. The United States had much more limited programs. With time these programs gradually disappeared, but recently, and now beginning in the United States, people with disabilities have been gaining recognition by stressing that they must be compensated for their disabilities so they are able to fully participate in society. Establishing legally protected rights that will provide them with equal opportunity has done this. Again, it is important to note the connection between rights and equality.

Groups advocating for people with disabilities have also attempted to change the language used to describe them. The earlier usage was "handicapped." Later usage has included "disabled," "people with disabilities," and "differently abled."

I teach at a public university that happens to be located on fairly hilly terrain. Some years ago, well before there were advocacy groups for the disabled, some faculty and students decided to demonstrate the difficulties faced by students in wheelchairs by spending a few days trying to get around the campus in wheelchairs. In many places it was virtually impossible to get between buildings, into buildings, or from parking lots to buildings. On the whole, the university responded positively by removing certain barriers, replacing steps with ramps, and providing a parking area that was close to and on the same level as the center of the campus. But it was not until laws requiring access were passed that other barriers disappeared. Problems remain.

Most efforts to bring about equality of opportunity for the disabled have focused on those with observable physical disabilities; those with less obvious problems have had difficulty getting the help they need. For example, a student with severe heart problems that restricted the distance she could walk was regularly chastised by other disabled students for using handicapped parking because she had no outward signs of a disability.

How does democracy deal with subjects when those on one side are absolutely convinced that they are right and the other side is wrong? How does democracy deal with a situation where a temporary majority is willing to impose its version of the truth on a sizable minority? How does democracy deal with a situation in which "informing" voters becomes "manipulating" voters with half-truths and outright lies?

Consociational Democracy An approach to all these issues that redefines some of the usual organizational structures is consociational democracy, which is, in essence, a system of formal power sharing. Each significant group in a country is guaranteed a place in the governing bodies and has a veto on some issues. In addition, representation is based on proportionality and each group is able to control its own affairs.[18] The central problem in such a system is getting the groups to agree in the first place. Disagreements on who is to be included and what issues will be covered by the veto system are other problems, but it is designed to avoid the division of countries into separate nations and is working in countries like Lebanon.

SUGGESTED READINGS

Classic Works

Bentham, Jeremy. *An Introduction to the Principles of Morals and Legislation* (printed 1780 but not published until 1789).

Burke, Edmund. *Reflections on the Revolution in France* (1790).

The Constitution of the United States of America (1787).

Declaration of Independence of the United States (1776).

Hamilton, Alexander, John Jay, and James Madison. *The Federalist Papers* (1787–88).

---

18. On consociational democracy, see Arend Lijphart, *Democracy in Plural Societies: A Comparative Exploration* (New Haven, Conn.: Yale University Press, 1977), 25–52.

Locke, John. *Two Treatises of Government* (first edition dated 1690; probably written sometime between 1679 and 1682).

Mill, John Stuart. *On Liberty* (1859).

Montesquieu, Charles-Louis de Secondat. *De l'esprit des lois (The Spirit of the Laws)* (1748).

Rousseau, Jean-Jacques. *Du contrat social (The Social Contract)* (1762).

Wollstonecraft, Mary. *A Vindication of the Rights of Woman* (1792).

Books and Articles

Ackerman, Bruce, and Anne Alstott. *The Stakeholder Society.* New Haven, Conn.: Yale University Press, 1999.

Ackerman, Peter, and Jack DuVall. *A Force More Powerful: A Century of Nonviolent Conflict.* New York: St. Martin's Press, 2000.

Allen, Anita L., and Milton C. Regan, Jr., eds. *Debating Democracy's Discontent: Essays on American Politics, Law, and Public Philosophy.* Oxford: Oxford University Press, 1998.

Amy, Douglas J. *Real Choices/New Voices: The Case for Proportional Representation Elections in the United States.* New York: Columbia University Press, 1993.

Barber, Benjamin R. *A Passion for Democracy: American Essays.* Princeton, N.J.: Princeton University Press, 1998.

―――. *Strong Democracy: Participatory Politics for a New Age.* Berkeley: University of California Press, 1984.

Barker, Paul, ed. *Living as Equals.* Oxford: Oxford University Press, 1996.

Barnett, Randy E. *The Structure of Liberty: Justice and the Rule of Law.* Oxford: Clarendon Press, 1998

Barry, Brian. *Culture and Equality: An Egalitarian Critique of Multiculturalism.* Cambridge: Harvard University Press, 2001.

Barry, John, and Marcel Wissenburg, eds. *Sustaining Liberal Democracy: Ecological Challenges and Opportunities.* Basingstoke, England: Palgrave, 2001.

Batstone, David, and Eduardo Mendieta, eds. *The Good Citizen.* New York: Routledge, 1999.

Bauer, Joanne R., and Daniel A. Bell, eds. *The East Asian Challenge for Human Rights.* Cambridge: Cambridge University Press, 1999.

Bay, Christian. *The Structure of Freedom.* Stanford, Calif.: Stanford University Press, 1958.

Beiner, Ronald, ed. *Theorizing Citizenship.* Albany: State University of New York Press, 1995.

Bowles, Samuel, and Herbert Gintis. *Recasting Egalitarianism: New Rules for Communities, States, and Markets.* Vol. 3 of The Real Utopias Project, edited by Erik Olin Wright. London: Verso, 1998.

Braithwaite, Valerie, and Margaret Levi, eds. *Trust and Governance.* New York: Russell Sage Foundation, 1998.

Callan, Eamonn. *Creating Citizens: Political Education and Liberal Democracy.* Oxford: Clarendon Press, 1997.

Callinicos, Alex. *Equality.* Cambridge, England: Polity, 2000.

Carens, Joseph H. *Culture, Citizenship, and Community: A Contextual Exploration of Justice as Evenhandedness.* Oxford: Oxford University Press, 2000.

Carter, April. *The Political Theory of Global Citizenship.* London: Routledge, 2001.

Carter, April, and Geoffrey Stokes. *Liberal Democracy and Its Critics: Perspectives in Contemporary Political Thought.* Cambridge, England: Polity Press, 1998.

Carter, Ian. *A Measure of Freedom.* Oxford: Oxford University Press, 1999.

Cohen, Joshua, and Joel Rogers. *Associations and Democracy.* Vol. 1 of The Real Utopias Project, edited by Erik Olin Wright. London: Verso, 1995.

Crick, Bernard. *Essays on Citizenship.* London: Continuum, 2000.

Dahl, Robert A. *Democracy and Its Critics.* New Haven, Conn.: Yale University Press, 1989.

―――. *On Democracy.* New Haven, Conn.: Yale University Press, 1998.

Delanty, Gerard. *Citizenship in a Global Age: Society, Culture, Politics*. Buckingham, England: Open University Press, 2000.

Dunn, John, ed. *Democracy: The Unfinished Journey, 508 B.C. to A.D. 1993*. Oxford: Oxford University Press, 1992.

Dworkin, Ronald. *Sovereign Virtue: The Theory and Practice of Equality*. Cambridge: Harvard University Press, 2000.

Elkin, Stephen L., and Karol Edward Soltan, eds. *Citizen Competence and Democratic Institutions*. University Park: Pennsylvania State University Press, 1999.

Elster, Jon, ed. *Deliberative Democracy*. Cambridge: Cambridge University Press, 1998.

Faulks, Keith. *Citizenship*. London: Routledge, 2000.

Gewirth, Alan. *The Community of Rights*. Chicago: University of Chicago Press, 1996.

Gould, Carol C., and Pasquale Pasquino, eds. *Cultural Identity and the Nation-State*. Lanham, Md.: Rowman & Littlefield, 2001.

Green, Judith M. *Deep Democracy: Community, Diversity, and Transformation*. Lanham, Md.: Rowman & Littlefield, 1999.

Green, Philip. *Equality and Democracy*. New York: New Press, 1998.

Guinier, Lani. *The Tyranny of the Majority: Fundamental Fairness in Representative Democracy*. New York: Free Press, 1994.

Gutmann, Amy, ed. *Freedom of Association*. Princeton, N.J.: Princeton University Press, 1998.

Hollis, Martin. *Trust within Reason*. Cambridge: Cambridge University Press, 1998.

Honig, Bonnie. *Democracy and the Foreigner*. Princeton, N.J.: Princeton University Press, 2001.

Hueglin, Thomas O. *Early Modern Concepts for a Late Modern World: Althusius on Community and Federalism*. Waterloo, Ontario: Wilfrid Laurier University Press, 1999.

Ivison, Duncan. *The Self at Liberty: Political Argument and the Arts of Government*. Ithaca, N.Y.: Cornell University Press, 1997.

Katkin, Wendy F., Ned Landsman, and Andrea Tyree, eds. *Beyond Pluralism: The Conception of Groups and Group Identities in America*. Urbana: University of Illinois Press, 1998.

Katz, Richard S. *Democracy and Elections*. New York: Oxford University Press, 1997.

Kelly, David, and Anthony Reed, eds. *Asian Freedoms: The Idea of Freedom in East and Southeast Asia*. Cambridge: Cambridge University Press, 1998.

Kymlicka, Will, and Wayne Norman, eds. *Citizenship in Diverse Societies*. New York: Oxford University Press, 2000.

Lakoff, Sanford. *Democracy: History, Theory, Practice*. Boulder, Colo.: Westview Press, 1996.

Lauren, Paul Gordon. *The Evolution of International Human Rights*. Philadelphia: University of Pennsylvania Press, 1998.

Lijphart, Arend. *Democracy in Plural Societies: A Comparative Exploration*. New Haven, Conn.: Yale University Press, 1977.

————. *Patterns of Democracy: Government Forms and Performance in Thirty-Six Countries*. New Haven, Conn.: Yale University Press, 1999.

Lipset, Seymour Martin, ed. *The Encyclopedia of Democracy*. 4 vols. Washington, D.C.: Congressional Quarterly, 1995.

Lummis, C. Douglas. *Radical Democracy*. Ithaca, N.Y.: Cornell University Press, 1996.

Macpherson, C. B. *The Real World of Democracy*. Oxford: Clarendon Press, 1966.

Manin, Bernard. *The Principles of Representative Government*. Cambridge: Cambridge University Press, 1997.

Mansbridge, Jane J. *Beyond Adversary Democracy*. New York: Basic Books, 1980.

McKinnon, Catriona, and Iain Hampsher-Monk, eds. *The Demands of Citizenship*. London: Continuum, 2000.

Miller, David. *The Principles of Social Justice*. Cambridge: Harvard University Press, 1999.

Miller, David, and Michael Walzer, eds. *Pluralism, Justice, and Equality*. Oxford: Oxford University Press, 1995.

Morsink, Johannes. *The Universal Declaration of Human Rights: Origins, Drafting, Intent*. Philadelphia: University of Pennsylvania Press, 1999.

Mouffe, Chantal. *The Democratic Paradox*. London: Verso, 2000.

Patman, Robert G., ed. *Universal Human Rights?* New York: St. Martin's Press, 2000.

Paul, Ellen Frankel, Fred D. Miller, Jr., and Jeffrey Paul, eds. *The Welfare State*. Cambridge: Cambridge University Press, 1997.

Powell, G. Bingham. *Elections as Instruments of Democracy: Majoritarian and Proportional Visions*. New Haven, Conn.: Yale University Press, 2000.

Putnam, Robert D. *Bowling Alone: The Collapse and Revival of American Community*. New York: Simon & Schuster, 2000.

Robinson, Mark, and Gordon White, eds. *The Democratic Development State: Politics and Institutional Design*. Oxford: Oxford University Press, 1998.

Roemer, John E. *Equality of Opportunity*. Cambridge: Harvard University Press, 1998.

————. *Theories of Distributive Justice*. Cambridge: Harvard University Press. 1996.

Rosenblum, Nancy L. *Membership and Morals: The Personal Uses of Pluralism in America*. Princeton, N.J.: Princeton University Press, 1998.

————, ed. *Obligations of Citizenship and Demands of Faith: Religious Accommodation in Pluralist Democracies*. Princeton, N.J.: Princeton University Press, 2000.

Saward, Michael. *The Terms of Democracy*. Cambridge, England: Polity Press, 1998.

Shapiro, Ian, and Stephen Macedo, ed. *Nomos XLII: Designing Democratic Institutions*. New York: New York University Press, 2000.

Siedentorp, Larry. *Democracy in Europe*. New York: Columbia University Press, 2001.

Smith, Rogers M. *Civic Ideals: Conflicting Visions of Citizenship in U.S. History*. New Haven, Conn.: Yale University Press, 1997

Sunstein, Cass. *Republic.com*. Princeton, N.J.: Princeton University Press, 2001.

Van Gunsteren, Herman. *A Theory of Citizenship*. Boulder, Colo.: Westview Press, 1998.

Walzer, Michael. *On Toleration*. New Haven, Conn.: Yale University Press, 1997.

————. *Spheres of Justice*. New York: Basic Books, 1983.

Warren, Mark E. *Democracy and Association*. Princeton, N.J.: Princeton University Press, 2001.

————, ed. *Democracy and Trust*. Cambridge: Cambridge University Press, 1999.

Weale, Albert. *Democracy*. New York: St. Martin's Press, 1999.

Whitehead, Laurence. "The Vexed Issue of the Meaning of 'Democracy.'" *Journal of Political Ideologies* 2, no. 2 (June 1997): 121–35.

Young, Iris Marion. *Inclusion and Democracy*. Oxford: Oxford University Press, 2000.

Civil Society

Barber, Benjamin R. *A Place for Us: How to Make Society Civil and Democracy Strong*. New York: Hill & Wang, 1998.

Chambers, Simone, and Jeffrey Kopstein. "Bad Civil Society." *Political Theory* 29.6 (December 2001): 837–65

Cohen, Jean L., and Andrew Arato. *Civil Society and Political Theory*. Cambridge: MIT Press, 1992.

Ehrenberg, John. *Civil Society: The Critical History of an Idea*. New York: New York University Press, 1999.

Gellner, Ernest. *Conditions of Liberty: Civil Society and Its Rivals*. New York: Allen Lane/Penguin Press, 1994.

Hall, John A., ed. *Civil Society: History, Comparison*. London: Polity Press, 1995.

Hefner, Robert W., ed. *Democratic Civility: The History and Cross-Cultural Possibility of a Modern Political Ideal*. New Brunswick, N.J.: Transaction, 1998.

Janoski, Thomas. *Citizenship and Civil Society: A Framework of Rights and Obligations in Liberal, Traditional, and Social Democratic Regimes*. Cambridge: Cambridge University Press, 1998.

Keane, John. *Civil Society: Old Images, New Visions*. Stanford, Calif.: Stanford University Press, 1998.

Kleinberg, Remonda Bensabat, and Janine A. Clark. *Economic Liberalization, Democratization, and Civil Society in the Developing World*. New York: St. Martin's Press, 2000.

Mohanty, Manoranjian, and Paratha Nath Mukherji, with Olle Törnquist, eds. *People's Rights: Social Movements and the State in the Third World*. New Delhi: Sage, 1998.

Morales, Isidro, Guillermo De Los Reyes, and Paul Rich, eds. *Civil Society and Democratization*. Vol. 565 of *The Annals of the American Academy of Political and Social Science* (September 1999).

Norton, Augustus Richard, ed. *Civil Society in the Middle East*. 2 vols. Leiden: E. J. Brill, 1995–96.

Democracy in the Third World

Arat, Zehra F. *Democracy and Human Rights in Developing Countries*. Boulder, Colo.: Lynne Rienner, 1991.

Bauzon, Kenneth E., ed. *Development and Democratization in the Third World: Myths, Hopes, and Realities*. Washington, D.C.: Crane Russak, 1992.

Dannreuther, Roland. "The Political Dimension: Authoritarianism and Democratization." In *The Third World beyond the Cold War: Continuity and Change*, [edited by] Louise Fawcett and Yezid Sayigh, 34–55. Oxford: Oxford University Press, 1989.

Diamond, Larry, Juan J. Linez, and Seymour Martin Lipset, eds. *Democracy in Developing Countries*. 4 vols. Boulder, Colo.: Lynne Rienner, 1988.

Nyerere, Julius K. *Freedom and Development: Uhuru na Maendelo. A Selection from Writings and Speeches 1968–1973*. Dar es Salaam, Tanzania: Oxford University Press, 1973.

———. *Freedom and Unity: Uhuru na Umoja. A Selection from Writings and Speeches, 1952–1965*. Nairobi, Kenya: Oxford University Press, 1967.

Pinkney, Robert. *Democracy in the Third World*. Boulder, Colo.: Lynne Rienner, 1994.

Web Sites

http://democracyonline.org/ The Democracy Online Project

http://www.access.gpo.gov/su_docs/locators/coredocs/ Core Documents of U.S. Democracy

http://www.fairvote.org/ The Center for Voting and Democracy

http://www.idea.int/ The International Institute for Democracy and Electoral Assistance

http://www.internetdemocracyproject.org/ The Internet Democracy Project

http://www.ned.org/ The National Endowment for Democracy

http://www.nypl.org/utopia/I_meta.html New York Public Library. Includes a discussion on the Internet as democratic space.

4

Capitalism, Socialism, and Democracy

To most citizens of North America, democracy and capitalism are so closely tied that the idea there might be an alternative seems foolish; to many citizens of some countries in other parts of the world, it is self-evident that democracy and socialism are the only possible partners. In the United States the word *socialist* is so negative that using the word produces rejection of an idea without further discussion; in many countries the word *capitalist* has the same effect. To put it mildly, there is a lot of disagreement and misunderstanding concerning these two economic systems.

The discussion that follows is intended to clarify the meaning of capitalism and socialism and show why adherents of each claim to be the only true democrats. Thus the emphasis will be on the arguments for and against capitalism and socialism as supportive of democracy. Both positive and the negative arguments are presented, because in each case much of the argument for one alternative is based on the argument against the other. Both capitalism and socialism can be found combined with democratic and authoritarian political systems;[1] therefore, it is particularly important to understand how both advocates and critics see their relationship to democracy.

---

1. There have been many studies of authoritarianism, going back to Theodor W. Adorno et al., *The Authoritarian Personality* (New York: Harper & Row, 1950).

DEMOCRATIC CAPITALISM

Today democratic capitalism is perceived as having won the argument with socialism. With the collapse of the authoritarian socialism that we call communism, capitalists have a renewed confidence. Capitalism has returned to its roots in the free market, and many of its defenders contend that the problems capitalism encountered were due to a loss of faith in the free market rather than any inherent problem with the system. This resurrected belief in the free market makes the whole argument much simpler than it was when most capitalists supported something they called the mixed economy, but it also simplifies and focuses the attack on capitalism because the operations of the free market are the traditional point of attack.

The Principles of Democratic Capitalism

Traditional capitalism, often called *free market capitalism* or *laissez-faire capitalism,* is characterized by

1. private ownership of property
2. no legal limit on the accumulation of property
3. the free market—no government intervention in the economy
4. the profit motive as the driving force
5. profit as the measure of efficiency

The fundamental position as stated by Adam Smith (1723–1790), the Scottish economist and moral philosopher who is generally thought of as the intellectual father of capitalism, is that human beings are most effectively motivated by self-interest.[2] In economic terms, this means that individuals should be free (the free market) to pursue their interests (profit). The result should be the most efficient economic system, and, therefore, everyone will benefit. Goods will be produced that sell as cheaply as possible since, if they aren't, someone else will step in and replace the current manufacturer. Jobs will be created by entrepreneurs searching for a way to make a profit. The entire economy will be stimulated and grow, thus producing a higher standard of living for everyone, as long as the entrepreneur is free to operate and can make a sufficient profit. Workers can choose to spend their money on consumer goods or, by saving, enter the competition by going into business for themselves. Some will fail, some will succeed, and some will succeed beyond all expectations.

The Mixed Economy   In this century some changes were made in capitalism. First, in the culmination of a trend that had begun in the late nineteenth century, government regulation of the economy was accepted. Regulation came about because the English economist John Maynard Keynes (1883–1946) had

---

2. For an extensive history of the development of capitalism, see Fernand Braudel, *Civilization and Capitalism, 15th–18th Century,* 3 vols. (New York: Harper & Row, 1982–1984).

Adam Smith (1723–90) is best known as the author of *An Inquiry into the Nature and Causes of the Wealth of Nations* (1776), better known under the short title *The Wealth of Nations*. In *The Wealth of Nations* he presented a history of economics in Europe, a description of manufacturing in his day, and, most important, a set of recommendations. The key argument is that individuals, each pursuing his or her own self-interest, will produce the greatest benefits for everyone. He applied this idea to the operations of the economic system and thereby became famous for providing the moral justification for and part of the intellectual foundation of capitalism.

Library of Congress

argued, and generally convinced other economists, that depressions could be avoided by regulating the economy, specifically by using public expenditures to pump money into the economy and soak up excess unemployment. By doing this, prosperity for all without serious fluctuations—the so-called boom-and-bust cycle—could be virtually guaranteed.

Second, during the Great Depression banks closed, causing the loss of people's life savings, and pensions disappeared along with the companies that had provided them. These events left many people without the financial support they had counted on for their old age. As a direct result, government-administered retirement systems were established in most Western countries. In the United States this was the beginning of the social security system, which was initially designed to be self-supporting (monies paid in by employees and employers would accumulate and be paid out on retirement). The expansion of the program to most of the population, the expansion of benefits, and the rapid increase in the number of persons who not only lived long enough to retire but then lived a long time after retirement combined to undermine the financial base of the system.

On the same principle—that people should be protected from radical shifts in economic fortune—other programs were added. Countries varied in the speed and extent of expansion of such governmental intervention in the economy; the United States was probably the slowest of the economically developed democracies to add programs, and it added far fewer than most. In the United States most of the programs were established during the so-called War on Poverty of the presidency (1963–69) of Lyndon Johnson (1908–73). These programs were then greatly expanded during the presidency (1969–74) of Richard Nixon (1913–94).

The argument for regulation goes as follows: The amount of property and money held by individuals directly affects the amount of money they spend; the amount individuals spend directly affects the amount any industry can produce; the amount industry can produce affects the number of people it can hire; the number of people industry can hire again affects the amount of money available to be spent by individuals for the products of industry; the number of products industry can produce then affects its profit. In this way, some limitation on the amount of property or money that can be held by any individual helps rather than deters the entire capitalist system because it forces the money to circulate more widely. Thus, even some strong supporters of capitalism argue for some regulation.

Democratic capitalism originated in the West, and that area has provided the model for many countries, but alternative models are available. The best-known alternative occurs in Japan. In Japan an attempt was made to avoid the continual conflict between owners or managers and workers that has characterized the West and that still exists in some countries. The largest Japanese corporations used to provide what were, in essence, lifetime contracts for workers. In return they expected the workers to have a real identification with the corporation. Some such contracts still exist, but the practice is no longer the standard.

A number of Western countries are trying to replace the conflict or adversary model of industrial relations that has dominated democratic capitalism with a model that sees management and labor as dependent on each other for success. Germany, the most successful Western industrial democratic capitalist country, has a system that gives a great deal of power to unions as a means of avoiding conflict, but it should be noted that both Japan and Germany are currently having economic problems. In both cases, free market capitalists argue that at least some of the problems are the result of their practices modifying the free market.

Avoiding conflict is also one goal of the corporatist or neo-corporatist theory of democracy described in the previous chapter. Corporatists want workers and employers to join with government in ensuring the smooth running of the economy.

The Return to the Free Market As has already been mentioned, capitalists have turned against the mixed-economy model and reasserted the primacy of the free market. During the 1980s and 1990s, most Western countries dismantled at least some government regulation, cut back assistance and pension programs, and privatized parts of the economy that had been publicly owned or operated. But many programs have proven immensely popular with citizens and politically difficult or impossible to eliminate.

Capitalism and Democracy

For capitalists, democracy requires capitalism because, they believe, it supports the central democratic value of freedom. Capitalists believe that freedom is based on private property, and capitalism, by stressing private property, makes economic freedom central. Capitalists also believe that economic freedom is a primary support for political liberty. Economic freedom means that everyone is free to enter the marketplace, accumulate property without limit, and use that property as they choose. Capitalists see two potential sources of control that must be blocked—monopolies and government. Monopolies, they believe, will always be temporary if the free market is allowed to operate; therefore, the real problem is government.

Free market capitalists argue that any government regulation destroys the basis for the capitalist system and, hence, individualism and liberty. The defenders of some government regulation (but not control) of the economy say that the absence of government regulation itself destroys the democratic capitalistic system because a few people can control the economy, and even the government, through monopolies. Other bad effects of a lack of government regulation are sometimes mentioned, but the development of monopolies is the most important politically.

Monopolies   The problem of monopolies was illustrated in the United States during the period of the first growth of industrialism and particularly the great expansion of the railroads. Such men as J. P. Morgan (1839–1937) virtually controlled the American economy and thereby the American government. This monopolistic tendency, some capitalists argue, destroys the capitalist system by radically limiting competition. The system is not competitive when only a few companies can set prices. Under such circumstances few people with new ideas or approaches are able to try them out; it is not talent that succeeds in such a system but the monopolist's will. This situation does not fit the traditional myth of the capitalist system in which the clerk becomes corporation president by hard work. The clerk of a monopolist might become a business president someday, but not necessarily by hard work. The key to success would be the whim of the monopolist.

The most important effect of monopoly, viewed from the perspective of democracy, is that the monopolist can control the government. Such control severely restricts the degree to which democracy can exist because it might even negate the effect of popular participation in political decision making.[3]

President Dwight D. Eisenhower (1890–1969, president 1953–61), in his farewell address, warned the American people about a military-industrial complex that he contended was close to ruling the United States through informal channels. Eisenhower was concerned about the close relationship between the military and the large industries that produced military goods under contract to the Pentagon. He was also concerned with the fact that many high-ranking officers "retired" after twenty years in the military to take jobs with the industries with which they had negotiated contracts and with whom their former colleagues would be negotiating future contracts. He believed that these rela-

---

3. For a different view, see Gabriel Kolko, *The Triumph of Conservatism: A Reinterpretation of American History, 1900–1916* (New York: Free Press, 1963).

tionships and the growth of the sector of the economy providing goods to the military were leading to a dangerous concentration of economic and political power. This could happen even more readily under a monopolistic system.[4]

Many capitalists believe that the competitive pressures of a truly free market will prevent the development of monopolies. They also believe that any monopoly that does develop will not last long because of the same pressures.

One of the main reasons that monopolies are expected to collapse is that their dominance of the market will reduce their incentive to innovate or take risks. In these circumstances, new people with new ideas and the risk-taking capitalist mentality will bring new goods onto the market and undermine the power of the monopoly. Much of the court case regarding whether or not Microsoft is to be classified as a monopoly has had to do with whether it used its market dominance to keep innovative risk takers out of the market.

Economic Freedom   Thus even within capitalism the desired extent of economic freedom is the subject of debate. The basic premise is that capitalism allows more freedom for the individual than does any other economic system. Any individual with sufficient interest and funds can buy stock in any number of companies. Stockholders become part owners of a company or companies and can, if time and money permit, participate in some decisions of the company at the annual meetings, although this opportunity is limited for the small shareholder.

In addition, there are those like Milton Friedman (b. 1912) who argue that capitalism provides greater political freedom than any other system. "The kind of economic organization that provides economic freedom directly, namely, competitive capitalism, also promotes political freedom because it separates economic power from political power and in this way enables the one to offset the other."[5] This separation can be compared to a checks-and-balances system such as that in the U.S. Constitution. Government power is limited by centers of economic power that also limit one another. These centers of economic power are in turn limited by government, which is also subject to regular elections. If both economic and political power are centralized in government, there is no check on the activities of government except through the vote.

The individual is free to enter the economic system subject to some government regulation and some limitation due to the existence of many large corporations. The individual succeeds or fails depending on his or her willingness to work hard and the desire of the consumer, manipulated to some extent by advertising, to buy the product. This is economic freedom and shows the relationship of capitalism to equality of opportunity. Every person should be able to become a capitalist and have the potential to get rich.

---

4   Some critics argue that this happened some time ago. See, for example, Paul A. Baran and Paul M. Sweezy, *Monopoly Capital: An Essay on the American Economic and Social Order* (New York: Monthly Review Press, 1966).

5. Milton Friedman, *Capitalism and Freedom* (Chicago: University of Chicago Press, 1962), 9.

Equality of Opportunity This concern with equality of opportunity was one of the motivations behind the development of a welfare system designed to ensure that everyone within the society has such opportunity. This concern is not based solely on humanitarian ends but also on the recognition that people who cannot provide for themselves can be a burden on society and a waste of potential human resources. In addition, welfare programs have been concerned with the aged, who have contributed to society but who need help to provide for retirement when many costs, such as medical bills, tend to rise while incomes decline.

Criticisms of Democratic Capitalism

Critics of capitalism focus on the extremes of wealth and poverty, the power over the political process that such wealth gives its owners, and the extreme inequality between employer and employee that exists under capitalism. Some of these points have also bothered defenders of capitalism. Other criticisms attack the institution of private property, the free market, and the profit motive.

Results There are two related issues in the criticism of capitalism's results—power and poverty. The power issue can be framed generally by asking how much power one person should have in a democratic society. Great wealth gives potential power in a political system, and critics argue that such wealth makes rule by the people impossible. Defenders of capitalism argue either that this is a non-issue (the rich are a minority, and the majority can always defeat them) or that limited regulation can solve the problem. But the essence of the argument is that the benefits of capitalism outweigh any danger.

Great wealth appears to go hand in hand with extreme poverty. Critics of capitalism argue that such extremes are inevitable in a capitalist system and are wrong. No one should be condemned to a life of poverty so that a few individuals can be rich. Defenders of capitalism argue either that poverty is the fault of the poor (they have not worked hard enough) or that poverty will be overcome through the economic growth that capitalism makes possible.

Most defenders of capitalism, and in the United States most people, believe the power of an employer over an employee to be simply in the nature of things. But critics of capitalism see this exercise of power as undemocratic and demeaning to the worker. In addition, many people believe that the power relationship between employer and worker fosters undemocratic attitudes, leading to authoritarianism in the employer and servility in the worker. This was clearly the case in Britain in the nineteenth and early twentieth centuries.

Private Property Critics of capitalism argue that the private control of property used in the manufacture and distribution of goods is wrong because it gives a great deal of power to a few people. Today, the power of private property is obvious as many companies relocate their operations for various reasons. Critics contend that such factors as the effect on a community, the well-being of the employees, and the economic strength of a country should be taken into account in economic decision making. They usually argue that the creation of the value of property is social, not private—that is, it is created by groups of people working together, including those who invest, those who manage, and those who labor, all working within a structure of legal rules. Therefore social effects should outweigh other factors in decision making. Capitalists respond that if wealth is to be produced, they must consider their competitive situation first and foremost in any decision. Giving social factors precedence would make capitalists uncompetitive and ultimately force them out of business to the detriment of all concerned.

The Profit Motive   Capitalists believe that the profit motive drives people to succeed and create wealth; their critics argue that even if that idea is true, it is wrong. They argue that the competition fostered is personally and socially unhealthy. Capitalists argue that competition is natural and healthy, both personally and socially, and that it is the major source of effort and excellence.

The Free Market   Critics of capitalism argue that there is no such thing as a free market and that the whole point of business activity is to control or dominate the market, not compete freely in it. They also argue that the free market, to the extent there is one, is inefficient. Capitalists, of course, argue that there either is a free market or could be one in most circumstances and that it is the only truly efficient mechanism for producing and distributing goods.

As can be seen, the disagreements are fundamental. They will come up frequently in succeeding pages, particularly because the same issues are often involved in the discussion of socialism.

The Problem of Welfare

In the mid-1990s, politicians in most developed democracies came to the conclusion that the systems put in place to provide assistance to the poor had developed fundamental problems and were keeping people out of jobs rather than helping them until they were in a position to enter or reenter the job market. Helped by a strong economy and a very low unemployment rate, so-called welfare-to-work programs were put in place to force people to enter the job market by setting dates at which their welfare payments would be stopped. In the United States the states came up with a wide variety of such programs with different dates for the cutoff, different job training programs, and a wide variety of incentives to get a job and disincentives to stay on welfare. Initially these programs were huge successes, with large numbers of welfare recipients entering or reentering the workforce and welfare rolls dropping dramatically. Two problems have emerged recently, one expected, the other not planned for. The first is that there are people on welfare with serious health problems (both mental and physical) or other problems that make it very difficult to get or keep a job. States have varied on how they planned to deal with this issue, and it is too soon to know what will work. The second problem is that the economy is no longer strong and many people recently hired off the welfare rolls are being fired, not through any fault in their job performance but because companies are cutting back. Again, it is too soon to know how much of a problem this will be.

DEMOCRATIC SOCIALISM

Socialism in all forms is currently under attack, and many democratic socialists are dropping the label because many communists are now calling themselves democratic socialists. Particularly in Eastern Europe, it is difficult to know what a current political label really means. Democratic socialists are in this position because communism, which they criticized, is a form of socialism and has failed. Thus, democratic socialists, while not giving up their beliefs, do not want to be falsely identified with communism and are unsure what to call themselves. *Social democracy* is the most common new label and allows for the incorporation of some elements of the market into democratic socialist theory.

The Principles of Democratic Socialism

Democratic socialism can be characterized as follows:

1. much property held by the public through the democratically elected government, including most major industries, utilities, and the transportation system
2. a limit on the accumulation of private property
3. governmental regulation of the economy
4. extensive publicly financed assistance and pension programs
5. social costs and the provision of services added to purely financial considerations as the measure of efficiency

Socialism has a long history, which some advocates like to trace back to biblical sources. It is more accurate to see socialism as originating as a response to the excesses of early industrial capitalism, but it should also be recognized that many socialists, particularly those calling themselves Christian socialists, found their inspiration in the New Testament.

Still, the origins of contemporary democratic socialism are best located in the early to mid-nineteenth century in the writings of the so-called utopian socialists, Robert Owen (1771–1858), Charles Fourier (1772–1837), Claude-Henri Saint-Simon (1760–1825), and Étienne Cabet (1788–1856). All these writers proposed village communities combining industrial and agricultural production and owned, in varying ways, by the inhabitants themselves. Thus, the essence of early socialism was the public ownership of the means of production. These theorists all also included varying forms of democratic political decision making, but they all distrusted the ability of people raised under capitalism to understand what was in their own best interest.

Karl Marx, discussed in detail in Chapter 7, rejected these early socialists and developed his own version of socialism, which he called communism. There is considerable controversy among scholars regarding Marx's own attitude toward democracy, but two lines of thought developed from Marx, one emphasizing democracy and one, the dominant line, rejecting it. But other socialists rejected Marx, and later in the century two American writers, Edward Bellamy (1850 – 98) and Henry George (1839–97), produced versions of public ownership with what they saw as democratic control, although again both placed some limitations on democracy. In his last work, *Equality* (1897), Bellamy dropped most of those limitations.

In Britain a form of socialism developed, called Fabian Socialism (now embodied in the Fabian Society), that emphasizes the democratic elements of democratic socialism: electoral success, the rational presentation of their position (in innumerable publications), careful study of the current social situation, and gradualism.

Since that time many democratic socialist political parties, such as the Labour Party in the United Kingdom and the Social Democratic Party in Sweden, have been elected to office, been defeated and left office, and later been returned to office or remained in opposition. In Europe today democratic socialists often call themselves social democrats. This label is intended to stress the democratic nature of democratic socialism and to deemphasize links with other forms of socialism, particularly Marxian socialism or communism. The best known adherents of this position have been Willy Brandt (1913 – 92) of Germany, Olof Palme (1927 – 86) of Sweden, and Michael Harrington (1928 – 89) of the United States.

If one assumes citizens should control their political lives and contribute to political decision making, it is only a short step to the democratic socialist argument that citizens should have some say in economic decision making. There is no question that economic decisions in connection with, for example, an automobile manufacturing industry have a tremendous impact on an entire country. Therefore, democratic socialists argue, there must be some means for the people to oversee such economic decisions through their elected representatives. However, what economic decisions are significant? What industries are key industries for a national economy? Democratic socialists argue that the elected representatives of the people should answer these questions and that the answers are likely to vary from country to country. In addition, the forms of governmental control and regulation and the extent of the public ownership of industry will vary depending on the decisions made by the elected representatives of the people, checked at the polls by the people themselves.

Another argument for democratic socialism, perhaps the most appealing one, is what might be called the humanitarian argument. Democratic socialists argue that only when the people control the economic system will solutions to basic social problems, like hunger and disease, be possible. Only under democratic socialism can the people demand solutions; therefore, democratic socialism is essential to overcome the most basic problems of society.

In practice democratic socialist systems vary considerably from country to country, particularly in the degree to which such things as industries, utilities, and transportation systems are directly owned by the government. In some

Michael Harrington (1928–89) was cochair of the Democratic Socialists of America, a professor of political science at Queens College of the City University of New York, a public speaker, a commentator for National Public Radio, and a writer. He described himself as an "organizer, agitator, and activist." Harrington is best known for the book *The Other America: Poverty in the United States* (1962), which provided the basis for President Lyndon Johnson's War on Poverty. Harrington argued in *The New American Poverty* (1984) that the war on poverty had failed because politicians had never devoted the needed resources to it. Harrington's personal odyssey carried him through most of the major left-wing groups in the United States, and at his death he was respected as a critic of American policy by people from all parts of the political spectrum.

Gretchen Donart/DSA

countries most of these are governmentally owned, but in most countries the government owns only specific parts of industrial complexes. For example, in Sweden, which most Americans think of as a socialist country, very few of the major industries are governmentally owned.

When we say the public holds much property, this refers to property crucial to the functioning of the economic system. It does not mean there is no private property. Private property is still held by the individual in personal belongings, housing, most small businesses, and, in some cases, large corporations. Some democratic socialists, theorists, and systems do not limit the amount of private property that can be held by an individual, but most do. There is no necessity within democratic socialist theory for such limitations. On the other hand, most approaches suggest some degree of redistribution of income and thereby justify limited private property.

Socialism and Democracy

The fundamental assumption underlying democratic socialism is that participation in political decision making should be extended to include economic decision making. Democratic socialists argue that since the economy and politics are so closely intertwined, voters should be in a position to control their economic futures through the government they elect. Such voter control presupposes government's ability to control much of the economy through ownership and/or regulation of the most important parts of the economy.

The government of a democratic socialist system regulates that part of the economy it does not own directly. This regulation is designed to ensure that the privately owned businesses are operated in the best interest of the society as a whole rather than simply for private profit. This point illuminates the ethos of democratic socialism. The word *socialism* refers to *social* theories rather than to theories oriented to the individual.

In addition to the democratic proposition proclaimed in the basic assumption outlined earlier, democratic socialism suggests that liberty cannot be maintained without economic security. This argument resembles the democratic capitalist argument for welfare as a means of attaining equality of opportunity, but it is broader in that it demands more than equality of opportunity. The democratic socialist says neither the right to vote nor any other form of liberty is possible unless every person within the society is economically secure. If insecure, citizens will be incapable of exercising personal liberty. Such economic security is possible, it is argued, only with an extensive welfare system.

Welfare   The typical democratic socialist welfare system includes an extensive medical care system, which is provided either free or at minimal cost, usually including prenatal care for expectant mothers, dental care, and eye examinations, in addition to the more typical health services. An obvious practical rationale for such a system is that a healthy individual can contribute more to society than a sick one. Therefore, it is to the advantage of society to ensure the health of all. This is the fundamental rationale of any welfare system—an individual who is maintained at the minimum level of life can contribute to society. The welfare system is also designed to take care of those who have already made a contribution to society and are now incapable of caring for themselves. Thus the welfare system provides money for food, housing, and the other minimum necessities.

The Problem of Bureaucracy   Bureaucracy presents one of the greatest problems for democratic socialism. Whether in business or government, it is difficult for a bureaucracy to be as well informed or as responsive to the needs of the people or industry it serves as would be ideal. Since bureaucracies are not directly responsible to the people, many argue that a large bureaucracy threatens the public control that the democratic socialist is trying to preserve. In democratic capitalism the economy is controlled privately; therefore, there are powerful people who aren't directly accountable to the electorate. In democratic socialism bureaucrats who are not directly accountable to the electorate replace these people. In addition, because bureaucrats remain while politicians and governments change, it is not unusual for the bureaucrats to follow their own policies rather than those of the political leaders.

The problem is fundamental to the nature of a bureaucracy. Bureaucracies are established to administer laws (rules) established by the normal processes of legislation. These rules are applied equally (in the same way) to people even though people differ. Attempts to allow flexibility generally produce charges of favoritism, corruption, discrimination, and other forms of illegality. Quite simply, flexibility seems to undermine the equal application of rules even though that equal application may seem unfair. Thus, bureaucracy raises a problem: How can rules be applied unequally but fairly? Laws are rules, and rules by their very nature are supposed to apply to everyone in the same way. People are different, and they have different needs. How can a bureaucracy ever do its job in these circumstances?

Therefore, at times democratic socialism faces the same problems for which it criticizes democratic capitalism. Still, the democratic socialist argues that people do have control over the bureaucracy through their elected representatives and that the government can immediately change the operations of the bureaucracy when it becomes cumbersome or ineffective. Democratic capitalists argue that under capitalism the people control the economic system through the market.

Many countries, both democratic socialist and democratic capitalist, have instituted an *ombudsman* (the word derives from a Swedish term for deputy or representative) who hears and investigates complaints about the bureaucracy. Sometimes the ombudsman is empowered to make sure the causes of the complaints are corrected. Such a person fills an obvious need because most bureaucracies are unwieldy, operate inefficiently, and find it hard to take individual differences into account. Of course, elected representatives, particularly in the United States, also play this role.

Democratic countries have begun to recognize the problem of bureaucracy and have attempted to correct it. At the same time, the relatively independent nature of the bureaucracy may provide some protection for liberty. One agency may force another to respond better than it would on its own. Thus conflicts among parts of the bureaucracy may have a positive result.

Criticisms of Democratic Socialism

Critics of democratic socialism have two basic arguments focusing on the destruction of the free market and the centralization of power. Although many socialists now accept "market socialism," critics contend that the free market of competitive capitalism is essential for the efficient production and distribution of goods. Socialists have found that a limited market is more efficient and better able to respond to consumer demands than completely centralized regulation and, they argue, much more fair than a completely unregulated market.

In a related criticism, opponents of socialism argue that interference with the free market through government ownership and regulation puts too much power in the hands of government. This, they contend, leads inevitably to even greater centralization of power and the destruction of democracy. A more limited version of the same argument suggests that even if democracy is not destroyed, freedom will necessarily be limited in a democratic socialist regime. Democratic socialists respond that the electoral process is capable of checking any such tendency if it does occur, but they see no reason that it should occur.

Related to both criticisms is the question, what motivates the socialist bureaucrat? As we saw, the capitalist believes that human beings are motivated by self-interest—the profit motive. Self-interest, capitalists argue, will always make socialism unworkable. The socialist argues that the bureaucrat is motivated by the desire to serve. The capitalist laughs. The socialist responds that while the profit motive—the socialist might call it "greed"—may be necessary under capitalism, socialism makes it possible to be motivated by a desire to serve the public.

There is as much distance between socialism and its critics as between capitalism and its critics. But both socialists and capitalists are making the same claim—each group contends that it is the best for democracy.

Market Socialism

Market socialism, a phrase that democratic capitalists see as a contradiction in terms, is the most significant addition to the vocabulary of democratic socialism in many years. Supporters of market socialism accept the democratic capitalist argument that centralized economic power is inefficient, and they argue, along with democratic capitalists, that markets promote greater freedom. But market socialists contend that democratic capitalism places power in the hands of the rich and that large corporations are as inefficient as large government. They contend that such large corporations can function only by controlling the market, and, therefore, that regulated markets protect the weak, avoid monopolies, and produce markets at least as free as those under unregulated democratic capitalism.

In addition, market socialists insist that it is essential to have a functioning welfare system to protect people from the inevitable shifts of a market economy. Thus, market socialists have not abandoned the principles of democratic socialism but have moved in the direction of a mixed economy with variously owned enterprises (private, public, worker, and cooperative) competing within a regulated market.[6]

Developmental Socialism

Economic systems have been developed that are neither capitalist nor communist. The most original such creation has been called African socialism and communitarian socialism but is best known as developmental socialism. It was developed by Julius Nyerere; Léopold Senghor (1906–2001) of Senegal; U Nu (1907–95) of Myanmar, formerly Burma; and India's Vinoba Bhave (1895–1982), and it stresses social solidarity and cooperation as the means of developing the economy. Developmental socialism has also emphasized the establishment of a network of close social and economic ties to help form national identity. World economic and political realities have brought failure to developmental socialism.

A good illustration of the basic idea of developmental socialism is found in the Swahili word Nyerere uses for socialism, *ujamaa*—familyhood. As he put it, "The foundation, and the objective, of African socialism is the extended fam-

---

6. The classic studies of market socialism, predating the current interest in it, are Oscar Lange and Fred M. Taylor, *On the Economic Theory of Socialism,* ed. Benjamin E. Lippincott (Minneapolis: University of Minnesota Press, 1938; New York: McGraw-Hill, 1964); and Alec Nove, *Efficiency Criteria for Nationalised Industries* (London: George Allen & Unwin, 1974).

ily."[7] The extended family—consisting of a wide range of relatives who work cooperatively and share all family resources—is the model for village and tribal socialism. All members of the village are fed, clothed, and housed as well as the group can afford. The aged and the ill are supported. Developmental socialism explicitly rejects the class divisions of communism. All are workers; there is little or no tradition of an indigenous exploiting class.

In Nyerere's socialism all people must recognize that they are part of a single group working together to achieve a common end. This end is designed to achieve economic security and human dignity by changing the distribution system. "There must be something wrong in a society where one man, however hardworking or clever he may be, can acquire as great a 'reward' as a thousand of his fellows can acquire between them."[8] A cardinal principle in Nyerere's socialism reflects the fact that in traditional African society, as in Native American societies, land could not be owned, only used.

These lofty goals remain unmet or only partially met, with a future that looks grim at best. External forces produced conditions that might have made success impossible even if everything had gone perfectly within the countries.

Internally, all Third World countries face a multitude of problems. Among the worst problems are rampant corruption, extreme differences of wealth, the threat of military takeover, and tribal and religious conflict. As a result, no Third World country has been in a position to put developmental socialism into practice.

CURRENT TRENDS

The Third Way

Just as the phrase "Third World" was coined to refer to countries trying to find a position between capitalist and communist countries, the phrase "Third Way" has been coined to refer to the attempt to find a place between capitalism and socialism.[9]

Generally, socialists condemn the Third Way as capitalism and capitalists condemn it as socialism, but what it tries to suggest is that the economy cannot operate effectively under either the free market or under state control, however democratically those state controllers have been elected. Thus, it has affinities with market socialism, but it is often not socialist enough for the supporters of market socialism. It also has affinities with the mixed economy of capitalism, but it is often not capitalist enough for the supporters of the mixed economy. As these comments suggest, the Third Way is still rather undefined, but po-

---

7. Julius K. Nyerere, Ujamaa: *Essays on Socialism* (Dar Es Salaam, Tanzania: Oxford University Press, 1968), 11

8. Ibid., 3.

9. The phrase is most associated with Anthony Giddens (b. 1938). See his *The Third Way: The Renewal of Social Democracy* (London: Polity Press, 1998); and *The Third Way and Its Critics* (London: Polity Press, 2000).

litical leaders in both Germany and the United Kingdom say that they are bas-
ing their policies on the Third Way. Perhaps it is best thought of as taking the
position that policy should be based on what works to achieve the desired goal,
and that it simply does not matter whether that policy is capitalist or socialist.

Economic Democracy

Many people from different ideological perspectives have consistently raised the
question of the degree to which democratic approaches can be applied to various aspects of the economy. For example, there have been many experiments
—some successful, some not—in which companies have been owned and democratically operated by the workers in the company. This means that the workers set policy and hire and fire management. Such businesses are operating successfully in many Western countries, including, most notably, Spain and the
United States.

A growing trend is for workers in a company to own a substantial share of
the stock, with the company run by a board of directors and managers in the
same way as any other company. This is not an example of economic democracy unless the workers are actively involved in decision making that gives them
significant authority.

The argument for economic democracy is the same as that for political democracy outlined in the previous chapter. Robert A. Dahl (b. 1915) has weighed
the theoretical arguments for and against economic democracy in *A Preface to
Economic Democracy* (1985). He concludes, "A system of self-governing enterprises would be one part of a system of equalities and liberties in which both
would, I believe, be stronger, on balance, than they can be in a system of corporate capitalism." [10]

Cooperation

Cooperation, a significant economic movement of long-standing that many
adherents relate to democratic socialism, seems to be having something of a recent revival after a temporary decline in interest. Cooperation takes two forms
—producer cooperatives and consumer cooperatives (some include both); both
are generally well known and exist throughout the world, although today they
are probably most common in the Third World. In all forms of cooperation,
decision making within the cooperative is democratic, usually as direct involvement based on majority rule, although some cooperatives use consensual
systems. Larger operations have representative systems, with the representatives
checked by regular meetings of the entire membership.

The consumer cooperative is a group of people who form a nonprofit organization to purchase goods in large quantities. Thus, they can pass on the savings from the bulk purchase, eliminate some levels of distribution, and not add
a profit to the price. If goods are sold to nonmembers, any profit made by the
cooperative is distributed to the members.

---

10. Robert A. Dahl, *A Preface to Economic Democracy* (Berkeley: University of California
    Press, 1985).

The producer cooperative is a group of people who form an organization to produce and distribute goods, usually under the management of the workers. Profits are then distributed among the workers. Agricultural cooperatives usually involve the processing and distribution of goods together with the joint purchase of expensive equipment but do not normally involve the joint ownership of land. Producer cooperatives frequently establish cooperative financial institutions such as banks, credit unions, and insurance agencies.

Consumer cooperation originated in 1844 with the Rochdale Society of Equitable Pioneers in England. The Rochdale Pioneers, as they are known, established a series of basic principles that cooperatives, with some updating, still follow. These principles include open membership; one member, one vote; limited rate of return on equity capital; surplus returned to the members or reinvested into the business; continuous education; and cooperation among cooperatives.

Communal Living

Communes, now known as intentional communities, are generally thought of as a phenomenon of the sixties, but they have experienced a major revival in the last decade. Many communities founded in the sixties are thirty years old or older, and others are being founded regularly. Many are religious communities in which people join together to practice a particular religious way of life, but there are many secular communities in which the appeal is the communal life itself. A subset of these communities that bridges the gap between democratic capitalism and democratic socialism is cohousing. The rapidly growing cohousing movement establishes communities in which the dwellings are individually owned but in which there is much community-owned land and buildings, where communal interaction is encouraged architecturally and culturally, and where decision making is democratic.

SUGGESTED READINGS

Democratic Capitalism

Some Classic Works

Friedman, Milton. *Capitalism and Freedom.* Chicago: University of Chicago Press, 1962.

Keynes, John Maynard. *The Economic Consequences of the Peace.* New York: Harcourt, Brace & Howe, 1920.

————. *The General Theory of Employment, Interest, and Money.* New York: Harcourt Brace, 1936.

Smith, Adam. *An Inquiry into the Nature and Causes of the Wealth of Nations.* 2 vols. Oxford: Clarendon Press, 1976.

Books and Articles

Berger, Peter L., ed. *Capitalism and Equality in the Third World.* Lanham, Md.: Hamilton Press and the Institute for Educational Affairs, 1987.

Boswell, Terry, and Christopher Chase-Dunn. *The Spiral of Capitalism and Socialism: Toward Global Democracy.* Boulder, Colo.: Lynne Rienner, 2000.

Braudel, Fernand. *Civilization and Capitalism, 15th–18th Century.* 3 vols. New York: Harper & Row, 1982–84.

Chapman, John W., and J. Roland Pennock, eds. *Nomos XXXI: Markets and*

Justice. New York: New York University Press, 1989.

Chase, Harold W., and Paul Dolan. *The Case for Democratic Capitalism.* New York: Thomas Y. Crowell, 1964.

Duncan, Graeme, ed. *Democracy and the Capitalist State.* Cambridge: Cambridge University Press, 1989.

Hayek, Friedrich A. *Economic Freedom and Representative Government.* London: Institute of Economic Affairs, 1973.

Iliffe, John. *The Emergence of African Capitalism.* Minneapolis: University of Minnesota Press, 1983.

Kelso, Louis O., and Mortimer J. Adler. *The Capitalist Manifesto.* New York: Random House, 1958.

Kennedy, Paul. *African Capitalism: The Struggle for Ascendancy.* Cambridge: Cambridge University Press, 1988.

Kristol, Irving. *Two Cheers for Capitalism.* New York: Basic Books, 1978.

Mueller, John. *Capitalism, Democracy, and Ralph's Pretty Good Grocery.* Princeton, N.J.: Princeton University Press, 1999.

Novak, Michael. *The American Vision: An Essay on the Future of Democratic Capitalism.* Washington, D.C.: American

Enterprise Institute for Public Policy Research, 1978.

———. *The Spirit of Democratic Capitalism.* New York: American Enterprise Institute for Public Policy Research/Simon & Schuster, 1982.

Saunders, Peter. *Capitalism.* Minneapolis: University of Minnesota Press, 1995.

Silk, Leonard, and Mark Silk, with Robert Heilbroner, Jonas Pontusson, and Bernard Wasow. *Making Capitalism Work.* New York: New York University Press, 1996.

Stepelevich, Lawrence, ed. *The Capitalist Reader.* New Rochelle, N.Y.: Arlington House, 1977.

Von Mises, Ludwig. *The Anti-Capitalist Mentality.* Princeton, N.J.: Van Nostrand, 1956.

———. *Bureaucracy.* New Haven, Conn.: Yale University Press, 1944; New Rochelle, N.Y.: Arlington House, 1969.

Waligorski, Conrad P. *The Political Theory of Conservative Economists.* Lawrence: University Press of Kansas, 1990.

Wright, David McCord. *Capitalism.* Chicago: Henry Regnery, 1962.

Web Sites

http://www.capitalism.org/ The Capitalism Site

http://www.moraldefense.com/ The Center for the Moral Defense of Capitalism

Democratic Socialism

Some Classic Works

Crossman, R. H. S., ed. *New Fabian Essays.* London: Turnstile Press, 1925.

Lange, Oscar, and Fred M. Taylor. *On the Economic Theory of Socialism.* Edited by Benjamin E. Lippincott. Minneapolis: University of Minnesota Press, 1938; New York: McGraw-Hill, 1964.

Nove, Alec. *Efficiency Criteria for Nationalised Industries.* London: George Allen & Unwin, 1974.

Nyerere, Julius K. *Ujamaa: Essays on Socialism.* Dar es Salaam, Tanzania: Oxford University Press, 1968.

Senghor, Léopold Sédar. *On African Socialism.* Translated by Mercer Cook. New York: Praeger, 1964.

Shaw, George Bernard, ed. *Fabian Essays in Socialism.* London: Fabian Society, 1889.

Books and Articles

Archer, Robin. *Economic Democracy: The Politics of Feasible Socialism.* Oxford: Clarendon Press, 1995.

Boggs, Carl. *The Socialist Tradition: From Crisis to Decline.* New York: Routledge, 1995.

Busky, Donald F. *Democratic Socialism: A Global Survey.* Westport, Conn.: Praeger, 2000.

Dahl, Robert A. *A Preface to Economic Democracy.* Berkeley: University of California Press, 1985.

Giddens, Anthony. *The Third Way and Its Critics.* London: Polity Press, 2000.

———. *The Third Way: The Renewal of Social Democracy.* London: Polity Press, 1998.

Gunn, Christopher Eaton. *Workers' Self-Management in the United States.* Ithaca, N.Y.: Cornell University Press, 1984.

Harrington, Michael. *Socialism.* New York: Saturday Review Press, 1972.

Howard, Michael W. *Self-Management and the Crisis of Socialism: The Rose in the Fist of the Present.* Lanham, Md.: Rowman & Littlefield, 2000.

Jordan, Bill. *The New Politics of Welfare: Social Justice in a Global Context.* London: Sage, 1998.

Le Grand, Julian, and Saul Estron, eds. *Market Socialism.* Oxford: Clarendon Press, 1989.

Lipset, Seymour Martin, and Gary Marks. *It Didn't Happen Here: Why Socialism Failed in the United States.* New York: Norton, 2000.

Nyerere, Julius K. *Freedom and Socialism: Uhuru na Ujamaa. A Selection from Writings and Speeches 1965–1967.* Dar es Salaam, Tanzania: Oxford University Press, 1968.

Ollman, Bertell, ed. *Market Socialism: The Debate among Socialists.* New York: Routledge, 1998.

Pierson, Christopher. *Hard Choices: Social Democracy in the Twenty-First Century.* Cambridge, England: Polity, 2001.

———. *Socialism after Communism: The New Market Socialism.* University Park, Pa.: Pennsylvania State University Press, 1995.

Roemer, John E. *Equal Shares: Making Market Socialism Work.* Vol. 2 of *The Real Utopias Project,* edited by Erik Olin Wright. London: Verso, 1996.

Russell, Peter, ed. *The Future of Social Democracy: Views of Leaders from Around the World.* Toronto: University of Toronto Press, 1999.

Townshend, Jules. *C. B. Macpherson and the Problem of Liberal Democracy.* Edinburgh: Edinburgh University Press, 2000.

Unger, Roberto Mangabeira. *Democracy Realized: The Progressive Alternative.* London: Verso, 1998.

Web Sites

http://www.peaceandfreedom.org/mainpage.html California Peace and Freedom Party

http://www.thesocialistparty.org/spo/index.html The Socialist Party of Oregon

http://home.vicnet.net.au/~dmcm/ The Socialism Web Site

http://dir.yahoo.com/Social_Science/Political_Science/Political_Theory/Socialism/ Yahoo Directory—Political Theory—Socialism

5

○

Conservatism, Liberalism, and Democracy

onservatism and liberalism within democracy must be treated in three different ways because they are three different things. First, they are general
sets of attitudes toward change, human nature, and tradition. Second, they are
specific positions taken at different times and places by identifiable groups of
people. Third, they have different histories in different countries, although these
histories are so complex that the same individuals are sometimes included in the
histories of both. Today, we generally trace the histories of Western conservative and liberal traditions back to the seventeenth and eighteenth centuries. For
North Americans, the histories are primarily connected with British political
thought, with limited French and German influence.

The general attitudes linked to the histories will be presented first, followed
by the identifiable groups that exist in the United States in the beginning of the
twenty-first century—the New Right, traditional conservatives, neoconservatives, neoliberals, and traditional liberals. Finally, the extreme right is briefly
discussed. Some of these groups exist in other countries, but not all of them do.
The general attitudes labeled *conservative* and *liberal* have existed at most times,
although not always under these labels. If the labels are made sufficiently vague,
these attitudes exist in most or all countries today.

Some writers choose to treat conservatism and liberalism as separate ideologies rather than as tendencies within democracy, as they are presented here.
Neither approach is perfect, but the approach used here captures the complexity of attitudes toward democracy by showing that, in addition to democrats
who are capitalist and democrats who are socialist, there are democrats who

are liberal and democrats who are conservative. In the United States almost all democrats are capitalists and are either liberal or conservative. In some countries there are liberal and conservative democratic socialists as well as liberal and conservative democratic capitalists.

Conservatism and liberalism also differ from place to place and time to time. For example, a Canadian conservative will emphasize something different from a Japanese or Swedish conservative. And a conservative in the United States at the beginning of the twenty-first century does not believe the same things as a U.S. conservative in 1890. In fact, the position taken by many conservatives today was called liberalism in the late nineteenth century, and many conservatives believe that they are the true liberals.

Even though conservatives often think of liberals as extremists and vice versa, both liberals and conservatives are found in the middle of the political spectrum; they both want to maintain the basic institutions and processes of the society in which they live. Other terms include *reactionary,* or one who wants to move dramatically in the direction of an idealized past society, and *radical,* or one who wants dramatic change in the direction of a vision of a better society that has not yet existed. Today the term *reactionary* has generally disappeared because both extremes are really radical, desiring a society that has never existed.

CONSERVATISM

Conservatives are interested in conserving something. Conservatism within democracy today has the following characteristics:

1. resistance to change

2. reverence for tradition and a distrust of human reason

3. rejection of the use of government to improve the human condition— ambivalence regarding governmental activity for other purposes

4. preference for individual freedom but willingness to limit freedom to maintain traditional values

5. antiegalitarianism—distrust of human nature

Modern Anglo-American conservatism is traceable to Edmund Burke (1729–97), although he had precursors, and a variety of alternative traditions exist in various countries. Burke is most noted for his emphasis on tradition. As he wrote in his most famous book, *Reflections on the Revolution in France* (1790),

> In states there are often more obscure and almost latent causes, things
> which appear at first view of little moment, on which a very great part
> of its prosperity or adversity may most essentially depend. The science
> of government being therefore so practical in itself, and intended for such
> practical purposes, a matter which requires experience, and even more
> experience than any person can gain in his whole life, however sagacious
> and observing he may be, it is with infinite caution that any man ought to

Edmund Burke (1729–97) is best known as the founder of modern conservatism. His most famous work is *Reflections on the French Revolution* (1790), in which he argued that society is a complex web of relationships among the past, present, and future. He contended that social institutions slowly evolve over time to fit needs and conditions and that, therefore, tampering with tradition is likely to bring grief rather than improvement. He was an advocate of slow, gradual change; he did not reject change altogether nor argue for the return to some idealized past.

venture upon pulling down an edifice which has answered in any tolerable degree for ages the common purposes of society, or on building it up again, without models and patterns of approved utility before his eyes.[1]

Here we see both Burke's concern with the wisdom of the past and his concern with the complexity of social and political life. This latter concern leads to the conservative rejection of the liberal emphasis on rational planning;[2] life is too complicated for human beings to comprehend and control. In addition, some factors in society do not lend themselves to rational planning.

Burke also stressed another factor that is part of contemporary conservatism—private property. "Nothing is a due and adequate representation of a state that does not represent its ability, as well as its property."[3] And, Burke notes, both ability and property are inherited unequally.

What is generally called traditional conservatism is much the same as Burke's thinking. Neoconservatism is a reaction to particular conditions that exist today. New Right Theory, while also responding to current issues, is similar to early conservative theories that developed parallel to Burke's conservatism, but there is no evidence that it has been influenced by those theories. Although Burke emphasized the importance of religion, he wanted it completely separate from political life. Many Continental conservatives, on the other hand, did not want such a separation, but believed that religion should be part of political decision making. Some contemporary American conservatives also take this position.

---

1. Edmund Burke, *The Works of the Right Honorable Edmund Burke,* rev. ed. (Boston: Little, Brown, 1865), 3:312.

2. See, for example, Michael Oakeshott, "Rationalism in Politics," in Oakeshott, *Rationalism in Politics and Other Essays* (New York: Basic Books, 1962), 1–36.

3. Burke, *Works,* 3:297–98.

F. A. Hayek (1899–1992) wrote, "Conservatism proper is a legitimate, probably necessary, and certainly widespread attitude of opposition to drastic change."[4] Although his point is correct, it is too specific. Conservatives not only oppose "drastic change," as he says, but are hesitant about any change. As one writer put it, "the conservative does not oppose change, but he does resist it."[5] Conservatives do not unthinkingly oppose change; they resist and question it because they are wary of social experimentation. They believe that something that has worked, even if not very well, is better than something untried and unknown.

The second characteristic of conservatism, a reverence for tradition, is composed of a number of subsidiary points, including traditional moral standards, religion (with very few exceptions), and the assumption that the longer an institution has existed, the more likely it is to be worth preserving. Reverence for tradition springs from the conservative's basic distrust of reason as a means of improving humanity's lot. Conservatives do not reject reason completely, but they would rather trust tradition because they believe that tradition contains the accumulated wisdom of past generations. Note also how closely connected the first and second characteristics are—honoring tradition entails resistance to change.

This point is quite simple and clear-cut. The only really complicating factor is that conservatives (and liberals) change over time regarding the specifics they wish to preserve. The world changes, and conservatives change with it. They do not want to conserve all the past; they want to conserve what they believe is the best of the past.

The third characteristic presents the major dilemma in conservative thought. On the whole, conservatives believe governmental power should be reduced and individuals should make their own way in the world. (Note the similarity to traditional capitalism.) But there is an ambivalence here. Governmental power to support traditional moral standards and limit an individual's freedom regarding them is perfectly acceptable to some conservatives. Conservatives believe "genuinely ordered freedom is the only sort of liberty worth having: freedom made possible by order within the soul and order within the state."[6]

The case must not be overstated, however. Conservatives reject the use of government to improve the human condition. They do so because (1) they are convinced the use of government does not necessarily improve the human condition, and (2) they believe people left alone can do a better job. The first point is the key. It asserts that the use of government for social betterment will actually produce the opposite. People, according to most conservatives, will come to rely on government and lose the ability to help themselves.

---

4. F. A. Hayek, "Why I Am Not a Conservative," in *The Constitution of Liberty* (London: Routledge & Kegan Paul, 1960), 397.

5. Jay A. Sigler, introduction to *The Conservative Tradition in American Thought,* ed. Jay A. Sigler (New York: Capricorn Books, 1969), 13.

6. Russell Kirk, "Prescription, Authority, and Ordered Freedom," in *What Is Conservatism?* ed. Frank S. Meyer (New York: Holt, Rinehart & Winston, 1964), 24.

Conservatives have held this position very consistently. Edmund Burke (1729–97), writing in the eighteenth century, held it; Bernard Bosanquet (1848–1923), writing at the beginning of this century, held it; and modern conservatives, such as Russell Kirk (1918–94), continued to hold it. Governmental help will hurt persons of the better sort; the poorer sort will not be helped.

Conservatives believe some people are better than other people and, therefore, should be honored more by society. "Aye, men are created different; and a government which ignores this law becomes an unjust government, for it sacrifices nobility to mediocrity; it pulls down the aspiring natures to gratify the inferior natures."[7] This is precisely the reason that conservatives are ambivalent about both government and individual freedom.

"The conservative accepts as natural the differences that separate men. Class, intelligence, nationality, and race make men different."[8] This recognition of differences sometimes implies superiority or inferiority, but it does not necessarily do so. The recognition states that inferiority and superiority exist but does not necessarily tie them to race, class, or sex.

These are the defining characteristics of conservatism. These principles do not change much over time, and later in the chapter we will see how they are applied today in the United States.

LIBERALISM

Both liberalism and conservatism have complex histories, and there are fundamental disputes regarding the origins of liberalism. Some scholars purport to find liberalism in ancient Greece and Rome, but most commonly liberalism is traced to the English revolutions of the seventeenth century. Politically, liberalism originated in the revolution of the 1640s and the Levellers, particularly the Putney debates where Colonel Thomas Rainsborough (d. 1648) argued for widening the electoral franchise, saying "I think that the poorest he that is in England hath a life to live, as the greatest he; and therefore truly, sir, I think it's clear, that every man that is to live under government ought first by his own consent to put himself under that government; and I do think that the poorest man in England is not at all bound in a strict sense to that government that he hath not had a voice to put himself under."[9] Intellectually, liberalism stems from the writings of John Locke (1632–1704), who developed the arguments for consent, majority rule, and rights, particularly property rights.

Today, most liberals argue that liberalism is primarily concerned with liberty and trace their roots to John Stuart Mill (1806–73) and his little book *On Liberty* (1869), which stressed freedom of thought and speech. But the liberal

---

7. Kirk, "Prescription," 34.

8. Sigler, introduction to *Conservative Tradition,* 13.

9. From A. S. P. Woodhouse, ed., *Puritanism and Liberty: Being the Army Debates (1647–9) from the Clarke Manuscripts with Supplementary Documents,* 2d ed. (London: Dent, 1974), 59.

John Stuart Mill (1806–73) was the most influential philosopher in the English-speaking world in the nineteenth century. His major political works were *On Liberty* (1859), *Considerations on Representative Government* (1861), *Utilitarianism* (1861), and *The Subjection of Women* (1869). Mill developed and modified the philosophy of utilitarianism of Jeremy Bentham (1748–1832), but is best known today for his defense of freedom in *On Liberty.* With his wife, Harriet Taylor (1807–58), Mill began to explore the subordinate role of women in contemporary society, and he became an advocate of women's rights.

Library of Congress

emphasis on liberty has taken two differing routes from Mill to the present. One approach is really a continuation of Locke's concern with rights, including property rights. The other approach developed in the late nineteenth and early twentieth centuries in the writings of T. H. Green (1836–82) and others, who argued that some people need help in order to be able to exercise their liberty. This argument was the beginning of what became known as *welfare liberalism.*

These varied strands bring us to a liberalism that today can be described as having the following characteristics:

1. a tendency to favor change
2. faith in human reason
3. willingness to use government to improve the human condition
4. preference for individual freedom but ambivalence about economic freedom
5. greater optimism about human nature than conservatives

Hubert H. Humphrey (1911–78) once wrote: "Liberals fully recognize that change is inevitable in the patterns of society and in the challenges which confront man." [10] Liberals generally believe people should keep trying to improve society. Somewhat less optimistic about progress than they once were, liberals still believe beneficial change is possible. Such change can come about through the conscious action of men and women, as unforeseen side effects of decisions,

---

10. Hubert H. Humphrey, introduction to Milton Viorst, *Liberalism: A Guide to Its Past, Present, and Future in American Politics* (New York: Avon Books, 1963), vii.

or through the operation of various social forces. But there will be change, and the liberal is convinced it can be directed and controlled for human benefit.

Liberals do not desire radical change that would do away with the basic structure of the current system. On this point, the difference between liberalism and conservatism is a matter of degree rather than kind. Liberals want more change and tend to favor social experimentation, but they want this only within the framework of the current political, legal, and economic system. Liberals are not radicals.

Change is welcomed because liberals trust human reason to devise solutions to human problems. This faith in the potential of reason is the key to the liberal credo—only with such faith can they accept the use of governmental power to improve the human condition. This faith is not a naive, unquestioning faith, but it assumes that social experimentation is valid and that it is better to use such powers as we have to control change than to allow change to control us.

Liberals contend some people must be helped to live better lives and fulfill their individual potentials, and they believe that such assistance can work. Conservatives believe just the opposite—helping people may make it impossible for them to fulfill their potentials as individuals. Liberals argue that people, though capable of reason and reasoned action, are often caught in situations where self-help, even if possible, is very difficult and that government should help. This assistance, far from injuring people, can (although it may not) give them the impetus to do more for themselves. The liberal assumption is that, although not everyone will respond, it is better to attempt to help than to do nothing. In contemporary society, liberals believe government is in the best position to provide help.

Liberals believe this help through governmental activity will lead to greater individual freedom. They argue that a person, once relieved of some basic problems, can enlarge his or her sphere of activity and improve both life and mind. Still, liberals are somewhat ambivalent about human nature. They contend that most problems derive from impersonal social and economic forces acting on humanity; human reason can solve the problems, but an unaided human being cannot. This is why liberals are ambivalent about economic freedom; they are afraid that one of the results of an unregulated economy would be great differences in individuals' power, which would be used to the detriment of the weaker members of society.

The tradition of liberalism most strongly stresses individual freedom. The term *liberalism* is closely related to liberty, and the emphasis on liberty has been a major thread in all liberal thought. The role of the government is limited— it cannot invade the rights and freedoms of the individual. Human beings will err, but liberals have always believed error is far better than the suppression of error. This belief follows from the belief in the value and inevitability of change. If change is good and will always occur, today's error may be tomorrow's truth.

As general tendencies, liberalism and conservatism are primarily attitudes toward change within the democratic tradition, resting uneasily between reaction and radicalism. Too often attempts are made to transform them into major ideologies with rigidly defined beliefs. Doing this is an error. Liberalism and conservatism do not have clear-cut belief systems except in response to current problems, but in such responses they can be identified.

CONTEMPORARY CONSERVATISM
IN THE UNITED STATES

Three groups of people share the label *conservative* in the United States today: the New Right, traditional conservatives, and neoconservatives. At times they seem to disagree as much among themselves as with the liberals, and at other times the lines between them seem quite blurred. Still, they are defined by their positions on specific issues and therefore can usually be clearly identified.

Three sets of issues can be used to define contemporary conservatives (and liberals): social, fiscal, and foreign policy issues. The mixture of positions on each of these and the emphasis placed on them define the differences among the three types of conservatives. Very briefly these positions can be characterized as follows:

- Social—a belief in traditional values centering on the home, family, and religion. At present this includes the belief that the appropriate place for women is in the home; a strong opposition to abortion; support for required prayer in schools; and opposition to the teaching of sex education and evolution, among other subjects.

- Fiscal—a belief in capitalism, opposition to most government regulation of the economy, and support for a balanced budget.

- Foreign policy—a belief in a strong military, an active opposition to communism (obviously now less important), support for our allies whatever their political position, and opposition to giving authority to international organizations like the United Nations.

The New Right

What was then called the *radical right* developed in the 1950s and emphasized opposition to communism. At that time most radical right programs were negative and oppositional. Today, what is better called the *New Right* is concerned with social issues, such as abortion, busing to integrate schools, pornography (a concern shared with some feminists), prayer in schools, and local control of education, which are all seen as fundamentally moral questions.

The new right is primarily concerned with issues centering on the family, religion, and education. All these issues are, they argue, basically about morals. They generally believe that the proper place for women is in the home caring for and educating their children. They strongly oppose any position that can be seen as supporting nontraditional sexual relations, such as the movement for gay rights. The role of the schools is to teach parentally approved values and "the basics" (reading, writing, and arithmetic). Schools should have required Christian prayer, and creationism rather than evolution should be taught in biology classes (the New Right does not believe in the separation of church and state).

These positions pose an apparent dilemma for the New Right. They oppose government activity that imposes moral positions that they oppose, but they are willing to use government to impose their own moral positions. But for the New Right there is no dilemma because there is a simple division of right and wrong on moral questions, and government has an appropriate role to support the right morality and oppose the wrong morality. To them, tolerance of what they know to be the wrong positions is unacceptable.

The New Right remains strongly conservative on foreign policy, with the conservatism formerly driven by anticommunism now driven by support for a strong military. Patriotism seems to be the motivation behind most new right foreign policy positions. On fiscal policy, the New Right argues for a free market and against government regulation because they see these positions as essential to political freedom.

Traditional Conservatism

What I call *traditional conservatism* is closest to the general characterization of conservatism outlined previously, but has currently rather faded from view under pressure from the New Right and neoconservatism. This does not mean that such conservatives don't exist; they have always been the mainstream of conservative thought, both in numbers and influence, and remain so. They are simply not getting the publicity that the other brands of conservatism are getting.

Traditional conservatives are more likely to support some government regulation of the economy than the New Right is, but they are still fiscal conservatives. They are much less likely to be social conservatives than are members of the New Right. While they support traditional moral values, they are not generally in favor of using government power to enforce them. Traditional conservatives are also foreign policy conservatives, but in all three areas they emphasize gradual change and continuity rather than immediate, radical change.

Neoconservatism

Neoconservatives originated with former liberals who felt that liberalism lost its way in the 1960s and 1970s.[11] They are foreign policy and fiscal conservatives but more liberal than other conservatives on social issues. Neoconservatives are close to traditional conservatives in their respect for religion and the family, and they want less government regulation and a greater reliance on the free market.

---

11. An excellent short statement of the neoconservative position is Richard T. Seager, *American Government and Politics: A Neoconservative Approach* (Glenview, Ill.: Scott, Foresman, 1982), 39–48; also see Peter Steinfels, *The Neoconservatives: The Men Who Are Changing America's Politics* (New York: Simon & Schuster, 1979).

Neoconservatives do not reject the culture of the modern West—something they accuse the New Right of doing. They believe that economic growth will allow more people to share in the benefits of that culture.[12]

The differences in these forms of conservatism are primarily ones of emphasis. The members of the New Right stress social questions, neoconservatives stress the free market, and traditional conservatives take a moderately conservative position on those plus fiscal policy. All conservatives support free market capitalism, want the United States to have a strong defense and foreign policy, and are concerned with traditional values.

CONTEMPORARY LIBERALISM
IN THE UNITED STATES

Liberalism is somewhat in disarray today, and liberals are less sure about their policies than they used to be. There has been a movement away from government regulation of the economy to the acceptance of the position that less regulation (not *no* regulation) might be a good idea. Liberals have also concluded that the welfare system needs to be redesigned but not entirely scrapped. The old liberal faith that the government could help people to help themselves and the belief that recession and depression could be avoided by stimulating the economy have been challenged but not entirely discarded. Liberalism has not yet found a new faith, but it has not yet lost its old faith either. Liberals still stand for expanded personal freedom and therefore find themselves constantly at odds with the radical right. Liberals still believe that greater human equality is a desirable and achievable goal and thus are usually opposed to their traditional opposition, the conservatives, who reject the belief in equality as not reflecting the reality of the human race.

Liberals can be characterized on the same three measures as conservatives, but there is much less agreement on the mix of the three than there is among conservatives. On social, fiscal, and foreign policy, liberals can be characterized very roughly as follows:

- Social—a belief in freedom of choice. Today this tends to mean support for the pro-choice position on abortion and advocacy of the rights of women and minorities.

- Fiscal—a belief in the use of government intervention in the economy to regulate it. Deficit spending was once a fundamental tenet of liberal belief; some liberals still hold to it as a means of regulating the economy.

- Foreign policy—a belief in the need to work within the international community for the peaceful resolution of conflicts. Stress on cooperation and aid with a related reduction in emphasis on defense and the military.

---

12. See Irving Kristol, *Reflections of a Neoconservative: Looking Back, Looking Ahead* (New York: Basic Books, 1983), 75–77.

Neoliberalism

Neoliberals have identified themselves as fiscal conservatives while remaining social and foreign policy liberals, albeit with a slight shift to the conservative side in both cases. Neoliberals stress that they are concerned with getting the system to work rather than with ideology. They want to change the pattern of government spending because it is, they say, too high and inefficiently handled. They want a strong defense but more government oversight of military spending. They want efficient and effective welfare programs. Generally they want what they consider to be a realistic liberalism that faces up to rapid social and economic change. Today, they dominate the Democratic Party.

Traditional Liberalism

Traditional liberalism (in this sense a tradition from the 1930s) is everybody's scapegoat and is usually described as advocating big government, deficit spending, and expensive welfare programs. Traditional liberals see themselves as advocates of working people, the poor, and minorities against big business and as supporters of civil rights for African Americans, women, and ethnic minorities against the repression of government and business. Thus, they see themselves as defenders of freedom and equality. They believe that only government is powerful enough to achieve these goals; therefore, they are in favor of strong government. Liberals are unified on goals but divided on means. All liberals believe in an egalitarian society with protection for civil rights; they are divided on how to achieve it.

John Rawls

The most important contribution to liberalism in the last quarter century was the publication of *A Theory of Justice* (1971) by John Rawls (b. 1921). In this work, Rawls is concerned with establishing the fundamental principles of social justice. To do this he undertakes a thought experiment in which he imagines people in what he calls "the original position," in which people are assumed not to know what talents and abilities they have or what position they hold in society. They do not know their race or gender, whether they are rich or poor, powerful or weak. They are then asked to choose the principles on which to build a society. Rawls argues that the following principles would be chosen in such a situation:

> First: Each person is to have an equal right to the most extensive basic liberty compatible with a similar liberty for others.
> Second: Social and economic inequalities are to be arranged so that they arc both (a) reasonably expected to be to everyone's advantage, and (b) attached to positions that are open to all.[13]

The second principle is intended to ensure equality of opportunity. These principles are intended to be applied in order. Thus, equality of rights has a higher priority than equality of opportunity.

---

13. John Rawls, *A Theory of Justice* (Cambridge: Harvard University Press, 1971), 60.

Rawls contends that these are the fundamental principles of liberalism. The publication of *A Theory of Justice* set off a long debate among political theorists over all aspects of the book, but particularly about the thought experiment and the priorities that Rawls had assigned to the values he believed would result from it. In *Political Liberalism* (1993) Rawls made explicit that he sees his arguments as contributions to contemporary political debate as well as contributions to a general theory of justice. He contends that we must recognize that our societies are composed of peoples with irreconcilable fundamental beliefs. As he puts it, "the problem of political liberalism is: How is it possible that there may exist over time a stable and just society of free and equal citizens profoundly divided by reasonable though incompatible religious, philosophical, and moral doctrines?"[14] To answer the question, Rawls subtly modifies the two principles stated above, which now read as follows:

1. Each person has an equal claim to a fully adequate scheme of basic rights and liberties, which scheme is compatible with the same scheme for all; and in this scheme the equal political liberties, and only those liberties, are to be guaranteed their fair values.

2. Social and economic inequalities are to satisfy two conditions: first, they are to be attached to positions and offices open to all under conditions of fair equality of opportunity; and second, they are to be of the greatest benefit to the least advantaged members of society.[15]

This revision of his argument for "justice as fairness" puts Rawls squarely back in the middle of a recent debate that originated in arguments over *A Theory of Justice* but had moved into new territory, the debate between liberalism and communitarianism.

LIBERALISM AND COMMUNITARIANISM

In the last fifteen years a major debate erupted among democratic theorists between those who call themselves liberals and those who call themselves communitarians. According to the communitarian critique of liberalism, liberalism overemphasizes the individual to the detriment of the community. Put another way, liberalism is said to focus on an individual with no social context. Liberals argue both that communitarians misrepresent liberalism and that the communitarian alternative destroys liberty.

In this debate, liberals focus on the desirability of developing autonomous individuals who are protected from government by universally applicable rights. Liberals believe that there is a substantial area of private life that should be completely outside the concern of government.

Communitarians focus on the community rather than the individual as the basis for personal and political identity and moral decision making. Much of the

---

14. John Rawls, *Political Liberalism* (New York: Columbia University Press, 1993), xviii.

15. Ibid., 5–6.

communitarian argument developed in opposition to Rawlsian liberalism, but the positive content of communitarianism stems from the contention that all individuals are to some extent created by and embedded in specific communities. Our beliefs, moral systems, our senses of self come from the community or communities of which we have been and are a part.

The political conclusions drawn by communitarians from their critique of liberalism and the emergence of the community as a theoretical focus vary across the political spectrum from left to right, although the right has been most clearly identified with communitarianism. Some left-wing communitarians see it as simply an extension of participatory democracy with a greater concern for the community in which the participation takes place. Thus, communitarianism could be seen as a development of the emphasis on community that was found in the New Left,[16] but this is not how most communitarians see it.

Most communitarians are clearly conservatives who believe that the growth of legally enforceable individual rights has gone too far to the detriment of the society as a whole. They believe that there must be a renewed focus on personal, family, and community responsibility. Many liberals do not actually disagree, and many of the differences between liberals and communitarians are fairly technical, but although the desired results are perhaps not very different—fully developed individuals interacting within a healthy society—the differences in the means of getting there are immense. Are individuals responsible to and for themselves? Or, as products of the communities of which they are a part, are they responsible to the community (and the community to them)? Most important from the liberal point of view: Should we accept the dominance of community values if those values include the elimination of minority rights? In a sense, this is asking the question, who constitutes the community? Is it the current majority in some geographic area? Are they to be allowed to simply impose their values on everyone else in that area?

These questions are at the heart of the confused state of liberalism and conservatism in the United States today. People want to live the lives they choose without interference, and they worry about interference from both government and their neighbors, whose vision of the good life may be different than theirs and who might want to impose it on them. This concern is not without justification. There are people who want us all to live their way. We usually call them extremists.

THE EXTREME RIGHT

There are extremists on both ends of the political spectrum, but at present it is the right that most concerns people. The most obvious examples of right-wing extremism in the United States today are the Oklahoma City bombing and the

16. See Lyman Tower Sargent, *New Left Thought: An Introduction* (Homewood, Ill.: Dorsey Press, 1972).

militia movement. One motive for the bombing was clearly to attack a symbol of the federal government. The position taken on the bombing on the extreme right is that it was a government plot, and the bomb was set off by government agents to incriminate those on the right. The militia movement also opposes federal authority, arguing that authority should be held by those in each locality. Generally speaking, those in this part of the extreme right hold that the county is the highest legitimate government. This part of the extreme right also tends to take a strongly anti-international position; while communists have not disappeared as the focus of their concern, the fear of communism has been partially superceded by the perception of a communist-dominated United Nations.

While the extreme right is strongly in favor of property rights, it has no use for large corporations or financial capitalism, symbolized by Wall Street. They believe that there is a conspiracy among wealthy capitalists to control the economy for their own benefit and that the federal government is part of this conspiracy.

A common theme on the extreme right is racism. Anti-Semitism is common, with both Jews and Arabs grouped together; African Americans are defined as America's major problem. The goal is a purely Caucasian country.

One example of a racist and anti-Semitic program can be found in the novel *The Turner Diaries* (2d ed., 1980), which a number of far-right groups in the United States treat as a blueprint for a future race war and which Timothy McVeigh had with him when captured. Probably the best known of the contemporary U.S. groups is the Aryan Nations, which was led by Richard Girnt Butler (b. ca. 1919–20) and which operated from an enclosed compound in Hayden Lake, Idaho. All these groups are very small, but most of them are bigger than Hitler's initial political party.[17]

The extreme racist right is particularly popular with the group of disaffected people generally called "skinheads." There are music festivals that are all white (and overwhelmingly male), featuring bands with names like The Bully Boys; groups like the National Alliance headed by William Pierce receive a lot of their funding through record sales.

Far Right Policy

Many of the issues that bother the far right are the same as those that bother others, like globalism, the difficulty of surviving on small farms and in small businesses, crime, drugs, big government, the power of large corporations, changing patterns of marriage and family life, education, and so forth. The central difference is that they see these problems through different lenses. They see many issues through the lens of race, very broadly defined. Thus, globalization, corporate power, big government, and related issues are often viewed

17. For more on these groups, see Lyman Tower Sargent, ed. *Extremism in America: A Reader* (New York: New York University Press, 1995). For a history, see Michael Barkun, *Religion and the Racist Right: The Origins of the Christian Identity Movement* (Chapel Hill: University of North Carolina Press, 1994.)

through the lens of anti-Semitism as a Jewish conspiracy. Many other problems are blamed on African Americans, Hispanics, and immigrants. Almost always central to their worldview is one or more conspiracies.

As a result, their solutions tend to be fairly simple or simplistic. If all our problems are due to conspiracies, if we get rid of the conspiracy, the problems will go away. But, of course, if the conspiracy is worldwide and centuries old, as they think some are, it is hard to see how to make it go away. Some have taken to violence, but, for all the headlines, that is fairly rare. Most just want to be left alone. Some achieve this by retreating to an isolated part of the country (Idaho and eastern Washington are favorite spots), homeschooling their children, living as much as possible in a cash-only or barter economy so as to avoid the attention of government, and generally cutting as many ties with the outside world as possible.

But there are those who find staying out of sight inadequate, who want to change the world they reject. There are many journals, pamphlets, books, videos, and records published by the extreme right, but today the Internet is a major means of communication.

CURRENT TRENDS

The divisions between conservatism and liberalism are mostly long-standing but, in some cases, are focusing on new issues. One division that is discussed throughout the book is multiculturalism. On the whole conservatives oppose it and liberals support it, but there are liberals who raise doubts about the rights of individual members of groups versus the rights of groups as a whole, fearing that these could conflict with each other.[18]

Another division is over the Internet. Issues range from free speech to the role of the Internet in fostering democracy, with particular concerns over the degree to which the Internet should be regulated.[19] But here there is no clear-cut conservative–liberal split.

At the time of writing, there is one issue that shows a clear conservative–liberal division—how to stimulate the economy. On the whole conservatives want to give money to large corporations and the wealthy on the assumption that that is the most effective way to get the money into the economy productively and create jobs. Liberals, on the other hand, tend to want to give money to the poorest people both to help them directly and because the poor are most likely to spend the money immediately, thus putting it into the economy. Both want the same result but with very different approaches.

---

18. See Brian Barry, *Culture and Equality: An Egalitarian Critique of Multiculturalism* (Cambridge: Harvard University Press, 2001); and Susan Moller Okin, with respondents, *Is Multiculturalism Bad for Women?* eds. Joshua Cohen, Matthew Howard, and Martha C. Nussbaum (Princeton, N.J.: Princeton University Press, 1999).

19. For a discussion, see Cass Sunstein, *Republic.com.* (Princeton, N.J.: Princeton University Press, 2001).

SUGGESTED READINGS

Conservatism

Some Classic Works

Bloom, Allan. *The Closing of the American Mind*. New York: Simon & Schuster, 1987.

Buckley, William F., Jr. *Up from Liberalism*. 25th anniv. ed. New York: Stein & Day, 1984.

Burke, Edmund. *Reflections on the Revolution in France* (1790).

Hayek, Friedrich A. *The Constitution of Liberty*. London: Routledge & Kegan Paul, 1960.

————. *The Road to Serfdom*. Chicago: University of Chicago Press, 1944.

Kendall, Willmoore. *The Conservative Affirmation*. Chicago: Henry Regnery, 1954.

Kirk, Russell. *A Program for Conservatives*. Chicago: Henry Regnery, 1954.

Books and Articles

Bloom, Allan. *The Closing of the American Mind: How Higher Education Has Failed Democracy and Impoverished the Souls of Today's Students*. New York: Simon & Schuster, 1987.

Buchanan, Patrick. *Right from the Start*. Boston: Little, Brown, 1988.

Carey, George W., ed. *Freedom and Virtue: The Conservative/Libertarian Debate*. Rev. and updated ed. Wilmington, Del.: Intercollegiate Studies Institute, 1998.

Dahl, Göran. *Radical Conservatism and the Future of Politics*. London: Sage, 1999.

Dunn, Charles W., and J. David Woodard. *The Conservative Tradition in America*. Lanham, Md.: Rowman & Littlefield, 1996.

Durham, Martin. *The Christian Right and the Boundaries of American Conservatism*. Manchester, England: Manchester University Press, 2000.

Eccleshall, Robert. "The Doing of Conservatism." *Journal of Political Ideologies* 5, no. 3 (October 2000): 275–87.

Falwell, Jerry. *Listen America!* Garden City, N.Y.: Doubleday, 1980.

Feulner, Edwin J., Jr., ed. *The March of Freedom: Modern Classics in Conservative Thought*. Dallas: Spence, 1998.

Huntington, Samuel P. "Conservatism as an Ideology." *American Political Science Review* 51 (June 1957): 454–73.

Kekes, John. *A Case for Conservatism*. Ithaca, N.Y.: Cornell University Press, 1998.

Kendall, Willmoore, and George W. Casey. "Towards a Definition of 'Conservatism.'" *Journal of Politics* 26 (May 1964): 406–22.

Kristol, Irving. *Reflections of a Neoconservative: Looking Back, Looking Ahead*. New York: Basic Books, 1983.

Moen, Matthew C. *The Transformation of the Christian Right*. Tuscaloosa: University of Alabama Press, 1992.

Schoenwald, Jonathan M. *A Time for Choosing: The Rise of Modern American Conservatism*. New York: Oxford University Press, 2001.

Web Sites

http://www.aei.org/ The American Enterprise Institute for Public Policy Research

http://www.cato.org/ The Cato Institute

http://www.compassionateconservative.cc/ The Center for the Study of Compassionate Conservatism

http://www.heritage.org/ The Heritage Foundation

Liberalism

Some Classic Works

Hartz, Louis. *The Liberal Tradition in America.* New York: Harcourt Brace, 1955.

Pateman, Carole. *The Problem of Political Obligation: A Critical Analysis of Liberal Theory.* New York: Wiley, 1979.

Rawls, John. *Justice as Fairness: A Restatement.* Edited by Erin Kelly. Cambridge: Harvard University Press, Belknap Press, 2001.

————. *Political Liberalism.* New York: Columbia University Press, 1993.

————. *A Theory of Justice.* Cambridge: Harvard University Press, Belknap Press, 1971. Rev. ed.: Oxford: Oxford University Press, 1999.

Books and Articles

Ackerman, Bruce A. *Social Justice in the Liberal State.* New Haven, Conn.: Yale University Press, 1980.

Avnon, Dan, and Avner de-Shalit, eds. *Liberalism and Its Practice.* London: Routledge, 1999.

Barber, Benjamin R. *The Concept of Politics: Liberal Philosophy in Democratic Times.* Princeton, N.J.: Princeton University Press, 1988.

Bobbio, Norberto. *Liberalism and Democracy.* Translated by Martin Ryle and Kate Soper. London: Verso, 1990.

Brands, H. W. *The Strange Death of American Liberalism.* New Haven, Conn.: Yale University Press, 2001.

Carens, Joseph H. *Culture, Citizenship, and Community: A Contextual Exploration of Justice as Evenhandedness.* Oxford: Oxford University Press, 2000.

Cummings, Robert Denoon. *Human Nature and History: A Study of the Development of Liberal Thought.* 2 vols. Chicago: University of Chicago Press, 1969.

DeRuggiero, Guido. *The History of European Liberalism.* Translated by R. G. Collingwood. Boston: Beacon Press, 1959.

Flathman, Richard. *Toward a Liberalism. . . .* Ithaca, N.Y.: Cornell University Press, 1989.

Gaus, Gerald F. "Liberalism at the End of the Century." *Journal of Political Ideologies* 5, no. 2 (June 2000): 179–99.

————. *Value and Justification: The Foundations of Liberal Theory.* Cambridge: Cambridge University Press, 1990.

Gray, John. *The Two Faces of Liberalism.* New York: New Press, 2000.

Gunnell, John G. "The Archaeology of American Liberalism." *Journal of Political Ideologies* 6, no. 2 (June 2001): 125–45.

Kymlicka, Will. *Multicultural Citizenship: A Liberal Theory of Minority Rights.* Oxford: Clarendon Press, 1995.

Laski, Harold J. *The Rise of European Liberalism: An Essay in Interpretation.* London: George Allen & Unwin, 1936.

Levy, Jacob T. *The Multiculturalism of Fear.* Oxford: Oxford University Press, 2000.

Lowi, Theodore J. *The End of Liberalism: The Second Republic of the United States.* 2d ed. New York: Norton, 1979.

Rawls, John. *The Law of Peoples with "The Idea of Public Reason Revisited."* Cambridge: Harvard University Press, 1999.

Rosanvallon, Pierre. *The New Social Question: Rethinking the Welfare State.* Translated by Barbara Harshaw. Princeton, N.J.: Princeton University Press, 2000.

Rosenblum, Nancy, ed. *Liberalism and the Moral Life.* Cambridge: Harvard University Press, 1989.

Russell, Conrad. *An Intelligent Person's Guide to Liberalism.* London: Duckworth, 1999.

Ryan, Alan. *Liberal Anxieties and Liberal Education.* New York: Hill & Wang, 1998.

Sandel, Michael J. *Democracy's Discontent: America in Search of a Public Philosophy.*

Cambridge: Harvard University Press, Belknap Press, 1996.

Schmidtz, David, and Robert E. Goodin. *Social Welfare and Individual Responsibility.* Cambridge: Cambridge University Press, 1998.

Unger, Roberto Mangabeira, and Cornel West. *The Future of American Progressivism: An Initiative for Political and Economic Reform.* Boston: Beacon Press, 1998.

Web Site

http://www.brook.edu/ The Brookings Institution

Communitarianism

Books

Bell, Daniel. *Communitarianism and Its Critics.* Oxford: Clarendon Press, 1993.

Etzioni, Amitai. *The Monochrome Society.* Princeton, N.J.: Princeton University Press, 2001.

———. *The New Golden Rule: Community and Morality in a Democratic Society.* New York: Basic Books, 1996.

———. *The Spirit of Community: Rights, Responsibilities, and the Communitarian Agenda.* New York: Crown, 1993.

———, ed. *The Essential Communitarian Reader.* Lanham, Md.: Rowman & Littlefield, 1998.

Tam, Henry [Benedict]. *Communitarianism: A New Agenda for Politics and Citizenship.* New York: New York University Press, 1998.

Web Sites

http://www.gwu.edu/~ccps/ The Communitarian Network

http://www.gwu.edu/~icps/about.html Institute for Communitarian Policy Studies

The Extreme Right

Classic Work

Macdonald, Andrew [William L. Pierce]. *The Turner Diaries.* 2d ed. Washington, D.C.: National Alliance, 1980.

Books and Articles

Barkun, Michael. "Religion, Militias, and Oklahoma City: The Mind of Conspiratorialists." *Terrorism and Political Violence* 8, no. 1 (spring 1996): 50–64.

Kaplan, Jeffrey. "Right Wing Violence in North America." *Terrorism and Political Violence* 7, no. 1 (1995): 44–95.

Mariani, Mack. "The Michigan Militia: Political Engagement or Political Alienation? *Terrorism and Political Violence* 10, no. 4 (winter 1998): 122–48.

Sargent, Lyman Tower, ed. *Extremism in America: A Reader.* New York: New York University Press, 1994.

White, Jonathan R. "Political Eschatology: A Theology of Antigovernment Extremism." *American Behavioral Scientist* 44.6 (February 2001): 937–56.

Whitsel, Brad. "Aryan Visions for the Future in the West Virginia Mountains." *Terrorism and Political Violence* 7, no. 4 (winter 1995): 117–39.

Web Sites

http://www.naawp.com National Association for the Advancement of White People

http://www.natvan.com/ National Alliance

http://www.nordland.net/vinland/ Vinland Records

http://www.panzerfaust.com/ Panzerfaust Records

http://www.resistance.com/ Resistance Records

6

@

Feminism

Today feminism is a well-established ideology with certain core positions and a range of variants that move off in somewhat different directions from those core positions. Feminism is also an international movement that cuts across class, national, and racial barriers even while those same barriers reveal significant differences among the positions taken.

One subject on which feminists agree is the need to replace what they see as the system of male dominance, or *patriarchy,* that affects all social institutions. Clearly, feminism focuses on the position of women in society and the roles they play, but feminists argue that improving the status of women will also benefit men. Not all men agree. At present the most obvious example of the problems women face are the laws that the Taliban imposed in Afghanistan that required most women to stay at home, allowing them to leave only if accompanied by a male relative, prohibited their employment and education, and required them to wear the *burqa,* the traditional head-to-toe covering. The Taliban also restricted men's freedom in many ways but much less severely. Such measures are extremely rare, but women face a wide variety of major and minor restrictions, both customary and legal, throughout the world.

Feminism focuses on the need for both men and women to recognize these restrictions and act to reduce and ultimately eliminate them with the goal of gender equality. Feminism has long realized that the first problem is that women themselves often do not recognize the restrictions within which they live, and the modern women's movement has often focused on *consciousness-raising,* or helping first women and then men to become aware of the limits imposed on women by both law and custom.

THE DEVELOPMENT OF FEMINISM

Debates over the social roles of men and women go back to classical and biblical times. Both the Old and New Testaments contain passages that have been used to argue either that women are inferior or that women are equal. Plato's *Republic* has been interpreted as contending both that women should be treated as equals to men and that they are naturally inferior to men.

Such debates are a constant of Western history. For example, in March 1776 Abigail Adams (1744–1818) wrote to her husband John Adams (1735–1826), who was then involved in the movement for American independence and later was second president of the United States, entreating him to "Remember the Ladies" in the laws drawn up for the newly independent country. John Adams responded, "I cannot but laugh," and continued, "We know better than to repeal our Masculine systems."[1]

At about the same time in England, Mary Wollstonecraft (1759–97) was writing the first major work arguing for rights for women. Her *Vindication of the Rights of Woman* (1792) was part of a European and American movement to develop a theory of individual human rights. Thomas Paine's *The Rights of Man* (1791–92) and the French Declaration of Rights of Man and Citizen (1789) are other expressions of the movement. But in most cases, these rights were only for men. Thus Wollstonecraft's book was an early and generally neglected plea that the radical thinkers of the time should argue for human rights rather than man's rights.

Earlier, writers like Mary Astell (1668–1731) in *A Serious Proposal to the Ladies* (1694) and Sarah Scott (1723–95) in *A Description of Millenium Hall* (1762) had so despaired of being treated as autonomous human beings that they argued that women should separate themselves from men. And, as we shall see, many women still argue today that real freedom for women can come only through separation from men.

In the nineteenth century, the women's movement began as a general movement for sexual equality and ended dominated by a single issue—the campaign for the vote. In the United States this pattern was repeated in the recent past with the attempt to pass the Equal Rights Amendment (ERA), which was temporarily the sole political focus of the women's movement in this country. In both cases the general feminist arguments tended to get lost in the political campaign.

In the first half of the nineteenth century in the United States women like Angelina Grimké (1805–79), Sarah Grimké (1792–1873), Margaret Fuller (1810–50), and Frances Wright (1795–1852) became involved in the abolition-

---

1. *Adams Family Correspondence*, ed. L. H. Butterfield, 4 vols. (Cambridge: Harvard University Press, Belknap Press, 1963), 1:370, 382.

Culver Pictures, Inc.

The campaign to extend the vote to women was one of the longest-running reform movements in Western democracies. In most countries women did not gain the right to vote until well into the twentieth century. The campaign for the vote included activities such as this parade, along with marches, petitions, fasts, violent protests, and demonstrations in which women chained themselves to the doors of public buildings. Their efforts involved virtually all the tactics used in later protest movements. The suffrage movement was a single-issue campaign and, as such, many feminists today believe that it detracted from attempts to bring about more radical changes in the condition of women. At the time, many women felt that women with the vote would be able to bring about greater changes. So far this has not been true.

ist movement and, from there, moved into other areas of reform including the rights of women. As Angelina Grimké put it, "I recognize no rights but human rights—I know nothing of man's rights and women's rights."[2] Later Elizabeth Cady Stanton (1815–1902) argued for a wide-ranging emancipation of women. As she put it in a famous statement to the court on being found guilty of voting, "You have trampled underfoot every vital principle of our government. My natural rights, my civil rights, my political rights, are all alike ignored. Robbed of the fundamental privilege of citizenship, I am degraded from the status of a citizen to that of a subject."[3]

In 1848 a convention in Seneca Falls, New York, was called "to discuss the social, civil, and religious conditions and rights of woman."[4] This convention

2. Angelina E. Grimké, *Letters to Catherine E. Beecher in Reply to an Essay on Slavery and Abolitionism Addressed to A. E. Grimké, Revised by the Author* (Boston: Printed by Isaac Knapp, 1838; reprint, New York: Arno Press & *New York Times,* 1965), 118.

3. *History of Woman Suffrage,* ed. Elizabeth Cady Stanton, Susan B. Anthony, and Martha Joslyn Gage. 3 vols. (New York: Fowler & Wells, 1881; reprint, New York: Arno Press & *New York Times,* 1969), 2:687.

4. Ibid., 1:67.

passed the famous "Declaration of Sentiments" modeled on the U.S. Declaration of Independence. It stated "that it is the duty of the women of this country to secure to themselves their sacred right to the elective franchise."[5] It also stated, much more radically, in words similar to those of Henry David Thoreau's "On the Duty of Civil Disobedience" (1849), that "all laws which prevent women from occupying such a station in society as her conscience shall dictate, or which place her in a position inferior to that of man, are contrary to the great precept of nature, and therefore of no force or authority."[6]

Similar movements existed in most western European countries, and they generally followed the same pattern of radical demands for equality giving way to the sole demand for the vote. In Britain three works in the nineteenth century were particularly important in establishing the early stages of the women's movement. *Appeal of One-Half of the Human Race, Women, Against the Pretensions of Other Half, Men* (1825) by William Thompson (1775–1833), *The Enfranchisement of Women* (1851) by Harriet Taylor (1808–58), and *The Subjection of Women* (1869) by John Stuart Mill (1806–73) all pointed to the mistreatment of women and argued for emancipation. Emmeline Pankhurst (1858–1928) was one of the leaders in the movement for the vote. Her group, the Women's Social and Political Union, used civil disobedience in the campaign. As a result, Pankhurst and many of her followers were repeatedly jailed, thus bringing more attention to the movement. Her daughters Christobel (1880–1958) and Sylvia (1882–1960) were also active feminists. Sylvia attacked the institution of marriage and bore a child out of wedlock.

Before World War I the single most important issue for the women's movement besides the vote was birth control. The most prominent figure in the birth control movement was Margaret Sanger (1883–1966), but others like the anarchist Emma Goldman (1869–1940), whose broad radical agenda included many issues of particular interest to women, supported her. Others who were concerned with more than the vote included Charlotte Perkins Gilman (1860–1935), whose journal *The Forerunner* was a forceful advocate for women, and Jane Addams (1860–1935), who exemplified and argued for an active role for women in improving life in the cities. Gilman's *Women and Economics* (1898) was a widely acclaimed study that argued for the need to restructure social institutions to permit women to work. Her utopian novel *Moving the Mountain* (1911) fictionally shows such a changed society.

When the vote was won there was little noticeable effect on social policy. But with the coming of World War II women were encouraged to join the workforce for the war effort and learned to do things that they had been taught were impossible for women. After the war these same women were told to go back home and give up the money and independence that they had come to expect. The publication in France in 1949 of Simone de Beauvoir's *Le Deuxième Sexe* (published in English in 1952 as *The Second Sex*), a study of the treatment of women by various academic disciplines, helped fan the anger at this loss.

---

5. Ibid., 1:72.

6. Ibid.

Still, it wasn't until the 1960s and the publication of *The Feminine Mystique* (1963) by Betty Friedan (b. 1921), combined with the rejection of women's issues by the New Left, that a renewed feminist movement began. While this early movement was predominantly white, a number of African American women were also active in the burgeoning feminist movement. Today, the women's movement is acutely aware of the importance of speaking to the needs of minority women and of women in the developing nations. And, of course, these women are finding their voices and speaking for themselves.

THE PERSONAL IS THE POLITICAL

In opposing all forms of discrimination against women (and men), feminists have argued that the term *political* needs to be redefined. If, as some would have it, politics is about power, there is politics between men and women both individually and as groups. There are power relations between friends and lovers and within families. For example, in the family, who makes decisions and how they are made are political questions, as are questions about who spends how much and on what, who allocates tasks around the house, and the division of labor reflected in such allocation.

An interesting case is housework. This is an important issue because it includes the traditional sexual division of labor in which men work outside the home for a wage and, if a man's wage is high enough, the woman does not work. But if the man's income is not high enough to hire servants, the woman works at home without a wage. And, of course, if a woman works outside the home, in the traditional division of labor, she still does the housework. Housework is the largest sector of unwaged labor in the economy. Anyone attempting to replace that unpaid labor with paid labor finds that certain aspects of it command substantial wages because, although the work is not well paid, long hours are required. Cooking and child care can be very expensive; regular cleaning is not cheap, and high quality work is hard to find. Housework is also repetitive and not particularly exciting work. Many people—men and women alike—if given a choice, don't do it.

For these reasons, housework illustrates how political work allocation is in a modern household. Generally, although there is much awareness of a change toward men helping more around the house (the word *help* implies assistance freely donated, not required), the traditional pattern remains common, with the added factor that the woman works outside the home for a wage as well as doing the same work in the home as before. In other words, the pattern of sexual division of labor that once applied only to the poor has spread to the middle class. Thus both the economics and the internal dynamics of housework illustrate the maxim that the personal is the political. Similar questions affect all relations between women and men.

Another way of putting the situation in which women find themselves can be seen in an expansion of the notion of the personal as the political. If all human relationships are power relationships, whatever else they may also be, women as individuals and as a group have been and are among the powerless. Some examples can illustrate the point. When men were telephone operators and secretaries, these positions were adequately paid positions with some prestige; when these positions became "women's work," they changed into low-paid positions with little prestige.

The fact that we are aware of power relations where we previously failed to notice them does not mean that such relations are necessarily subject to public policy, but our changed awareness does raise the very complicated question of the relationship between the public and the private and what activities should belong to each sphere. Many things we consider private have entered the public arena. For example, until recently spousal and, to a slightly lesser extent, child abuse were not considered appropriate subjects for public action. In most states in the United States, it was, until the last two decades, legally impossible for a man to rape his wife; he literally owned access to her body, and she had no right to deny him that access. Thus, one of the central debates raised by feminism is what, if anything, remains private and not subject to public/political scrutiny. At present, there is no clear answer, but the boundaries set by both public opinion and the law have clearly moved toward including more life experiences within the public realm.

SEXISM

Sexism is the belief that women are inferior to men. Racism is the belief that one group of people is inferior or superior based on factors such as skin color. But sexism and racism are just examples of the much broader point that people are oppressed both individually and as groups by socially constructed patterns of beliefs, attitudes, and practices. Like racism, but to an even greater extent, sexism is pervasive in our languages, art, literature, and religions. More obviously, sexism pervades politics and the economy. Sexism is part of what feminists oppose and hope to eliminate. Eliminating sexism will be extremely difficult since it is, feminists contend, part of all Western languages and part of many dearly held beliefs, including religious beliefs.

Socialization

Women have been socialized to believe that only certain narrowly defined roles are acceptable for them, and there is considerable debate over how much this has changed. As was seen in the first chapter, socialization is the process by which individuals are given the fundamental values of their society. In the case of women, this means that they internalize the sense of inferiority that has been the dominant image of women. Feminists argue that the process of socialization should not eliminate options for women; women should be allowed to see all the possibilities open to them, not just a few. For example, at one time women could not be secretaries or telephone operators; these jobs were reserved for men, both because women were not thought capable of doing them and because women were not expected to have paid employment. But, of course, poor women have always worked in paid employment, and women on farms have always worked along with other family members. And feminist historians have discovered multitudes of women who refused to be limited by stereotypes of acceptable female behavior. This illustrates how the work of recovering the history of women, African Americans, ethnic minorities, and other groups provides psychological support for individuals living today and a basis for political arguments against discrimination.

In addition, feminists argue that men socialize women to accept both physical and mental mistreatment. Rape has been considered the most underreported crime in the United States, but the "discovery" of the extent of incest and child abuse indicates that there are a number of rarely reported crimes, almost all of which are crimes against women and children. Feminists argue that these crimes are underreported for a number of reasons. First, women who report rape must still generally deal with male police officers who, even if—too rarely—they are sensitive to the woman's trauma, are still men. Second, the legal system has traditionally treated the woman as the responsible party. Third, women have been taught to accept such abuse from men and to consider it almost normal. This socialization process also leads women to accept abuse from husbands or companions.

Feminists note that in addition to physical abuse, women are subject to pervasive mental abuse. It consists, in large part, of treating women as objects or things rather than as individuals or persons. Clearly rape is the most extreme form of treating a person as an object, but many other ways of objectifying women do not involve physical abuse.

Physical and mental abuse are part of the oppression of women, as is the fact that in many jobs women are not paid the same as men for doing the same work and are frequently sexually harassed at work. In addition, although overt political discrimination has been reduced, more subtle forms are still common.

Religion

Orthodox Judaism makes a rigid division between men and women, with women defined as inferior. Liberal Judaism advocates, but does not always practice, equality. Only recently have women been allowed to be rabbis in liberal congregations, and the acceptance of women as rabbis is spreading slowly even where it is the policy to allow them.[7]

Even though in the New Testament Christ is presented as treating men and women equally, the same pattern of gender discrimination holds true in Christianity. Almost as soon as the first Christian churches were organized, women were placed in subordinate roles. In fact, some of the earliest heresies centered on the advocacy of equality for women, and such heresies continued

---

7. See *On Being a Jewish Feminist: A Reader,* ed. Susannah Heschel (New York: Schocken Books, 1983).

to appear from time to time, particularly around the Reformation and again in seventeenth-century England.[8]

Christian churches today are still divided over the role of women. The Episcopalian Church in the United States decided, after a long, intense debate, to admit women to the priesthood, and an African American woman has been consecrated as a bishop in the United States. Some Episcopalian churches and priests have left the denomination as a result. And in 4 of the church's 113 dioceses women are not allowed to serve as priests because the local bishop does not believe in a female priesthood. The Anglican Church has been deeply divided on the same issue. The Roman Catholic Church excludes women from the priesthood. Most Protestant denominations encourage the ordination of women as ministers, but there are still relatively few women ministers in most churches.

These divisions reflect a deep ambivalence about women in Christianity, particularly in the Roman Catholic Church. Two women, Eve the rebel and temptress and Mary the mother of Christ, can symbolize the conflict. Roughly the position has been that to the extent women emulate Mary and remain subordinate to men they are correctly fulfilling their natures; to the extent that they emulate Eve they are dangerous. As a result, many feminists see Eve, the rebel, as a symbol of the real strength of women, but the message that most churches present to women is one of subordination to men.

Language

Feminists have often been both criticized and laughed at for proposing changes in language use to remove the male bias. But taking the argument seriously and looking at the history of language use, we can see the force of their point. For example, a female first-year university student is called a freshman. Why? Well, at one time, not all that long ago, women could not attend a university, and the term implies that. Of course, language use changes, and most people now use freshman to refer to both male and female first-year students, but the word is a relic of a past of greater sexual discrimination.[9]

To take another example, when Thomas Jefferson drafted the Declaration of Independence and wrote, "All men are created equal," did he mean all human beings or just male human beings? We don't really know what Jefferson meant, but we do know that for many people at the time the words referred only to white, male human beings. And when we read major thinkers of the past, we often don't know what the word "man" means; we can read it to mean all human beings, but this may well lead us into simply missing what the author intended us to understand.

---

8. See Elaine Pagels, *The Gnostic Gospels* (New York: Random House, 1979); Norman Cohn, *The Pursuit of the Millennium: Revolutionary Millenarians and Mystical Anarchists of the Middle Ages* (London: Granada, 1970); and Christopher Hill, *The World Turned Upside Down: Radical Ideas during the English Revolution* (London: Temple Smith, 1972).

9. See Dale Spender, *Man Made Language,* 2d ed. (London: Routledge & Kegan Paul, 1985).

A particularly interesting example can be seen in the novel *The Left Hand of Darkness* (1969) by Ursula K. Le Guin (b. 1929). When *The Left Hand of Darkness* was originally published, there was relatively little awareness of the gendered character of language, and Le Guin called her characters, who changed gender at different points in their lives, "he." The twenty-fifth anniversary edition (1994) of *The Left Hand of Darkness* addresses the criticism she received for her lack of awareness by providing sample chapters with four different sets of pronouns, one using invented pronouns and genderless personal nouns and titles, one using feminine pronouns and personal nouns rather than the masculine of the original, one using pronouns that reflect the changes her characters go through—neuter and gendered at different life stages—and one using masculine and feminine pronouns for the same character as that person goes through a transition. One's understanding of the text varies remarkably depending on the set of pronouns and personal nouns used, which makes this exercise by Le Guin a striking contribution to the debate on language.

THE FEMINIST RESPONSES

Feminists agree on some responses to sexism, but they also disagree. Almost all feminists agree that fundamental answers to the problem of women's position in modern society include freedom and equality, but there are disagreements over both the meaning of these terms and how to achieve the desired result. All feminists agree that any changes should not benefit women alone. They oppose racism and homophobia (the belief in the inferiority of homosexuals) as well as sexism, and they argue that discrimination against any human being is an attack on all human beings. And, they agree, men will also benefit from a free and egalitarian society.

There are a number of ways to classify the feminist responses; none is entirely satisfactory because all of them tend to group people who have important disagreements and separate people who agree on significant questions. No set of categories is currently acceptable, and many of the suggested categories are nonpolitical. The categories I use are reform or liberal, Marxist, socialist, integrative or transformative, and separatist or radical. In addition, ecofeminism is discussed in Chapter 12. I have chosen, following Angela Miles (b. 1946),[10] to call the middle group *integrative* or *transformative* feminisms because these feminists generally try to recognize and incorporate the concerns of all feminists while taking a strong political stand.

Reform or Liberal Feminism

Reform feminists argue that the basic pattern of society is generally acceptable but that changes are needed so that women are not put at a disadvantage by their sex. Reform feminists want an equal opportunity to compete with men.

---

10. See Angela Miles, *Integrative Feminisms: Building Global Visions 1960s–1990s* (New York: Routledge, 1996).

Reform feminists propose that means be found, such as improved and expanded day-care facilities and improved parental leave policies, to more readily allow women to combine paid employment and motherhood. Obviously, these proposals also suggest that men must change their attitude to sharing responsibility for child rearing, housework, and all other aspects of women's traditionally unwaged labor.

Reform feminists in the United States were particularly supportive of the Equal Rights Amendment, which read:

> Section 1. Equality of rights under the law shall not be denied by the United States or by any State on account of sex.
>
> Section 2. The Congress shall have the power to enforce, by appropriate legislation, the provisions of this article.
>
> Section 3. This amendment shall take effect two years after the ratification.

Forces that considered the amendment dangerously radical or unnecessary defeated its passage.

Marxist Feminism

In its earliest manifestations, Marxism had a split personality regarding women. On the one hand, Marxists often said that women's issues must wait until after the class revolution. On the other hand, in 1884 Friedrich Engels (1820–95) published *Origins of the Family, Private Property, and the State,* in which he noted the central role of women and the family in the development and maintenance of the social system. Engels thereby put what was called "the woman question" at the forefront of issues Marxists needed to solve, and many women were attracted to Marxism because of this.

In the last quarter of the twentieth century, feminists noted both of these tendencies within Marxism, and, while many believed that Marx's analysis of capitalism was correct and pointed in useful directions, most concluded that Marxists in the twentieth century had generally ignored the insights of Engels and others and adopted the "wait until after the revolution" approach. And since the so-called Marxist revolutions in China, Russia, and other countries did not produce the significant changes in women's roles that had been promised, considerable disillusionment resulted.

Socialist Feminism

Contemporary socialist feminists are perhaps best seen as democratic socialists with a focus. They reject the Marxist tendency to put class before gender, race, sexual identification, ethnicity, and the other ways in which human beings identify and classify themselves. And in doing so, they stress democratic decision making and the acceptance of difference within community. In this they are quite close to what Angela Miles has called integrative feminism.

Integrative Feminism

Integrative feminists have shown the ways in which men have created a male-centered way of understanding the world that severely limits our ability to conceptualize human relations that are not hierarchical and patriarchal. The integrative feminist's goal is to break through those mental barriers as well as the political, economic, and cultural barriers that keep all human beings from becoming fully human. For example, Nancy Hartsock (b. 1943) has noted that feminists have begun to reconceptualize the notion of power. Power as dominance will give way to power as "energy and competence."[11] All our ways of thinking need to undergo a similar revolution.

Hence, integrative feminists are arguing for a fundamental transformation of not only our political and economic lives but our social, cultural, and personal lives as well. As Angela Miles says, "The alternative value core of integrative feminisms in all their variety is the holistic, egalitarian, life-centered rejection of dominant androcentric, dualistic, hierarchical, profit-centered ideology and social structures."[12] The goal is to achieve equality while recognizing difference or specificity.

Separatist or Radical Feminism

Separatist feminism, with some exceptions, argues for lesbianism and a woman-centered culture. Lesbian communes exist in all Western countries. Shulamith Firestone (b. 1944) argues for the abandonment of the biological family in *The Dialectic of Sex* (1970), and the development of a woman's culture can be seen in the works of Judy Chicago (b. 1939) and others.

Feminism is developing a critical apparatus for analyzing contemporary society that is challenging all contemporary ideologies. Feminist philosophers and political philosophers are proposing new ways of understanding the world. Feminist economists are analyzing the economic roles of women and suggesting a transformation of economic life. Specifically, feminists have discovered the central role that women play in the agricultural economies of Third World countries and are arguing that the bias-rooted failure to recognize this fact has undercut all attempts to improve agricultural production in developing countries. Feminist writers and artists are developing a substantial body of literature and art that speaks to different concerns than had been previously addressed.

Feminists are encouraging all human beings to envision the possibility of a society rid of sexism, racism, homophobia, and all the other ways in which human beings have subjugated other human beings. At present feminists are divided over exactly how to go about this transformation, and reform feminists are not convinced that it is either necessary or desirable, but feminism is poten-

---

11. Nancy C. M. Hartsock, *Money, Sex, and Power: Toward a Feminist Historical Materialism* (New York: Longman, 1983), 224–25.

12. Miles, *Integrative Feminisms,* xi.

tially the most radical of ideologies and the most likely to change the way most of us live today.

CURRENT TRENDS

Votes for Women

For much of the twentieth century women were concerned with achieving the right to vote. (The first country to grant women the vote was New Zealand, which did so in 1893; the United States did so in 1920.) But the franchise did not translate into many women being elected to office, and while the number slowly rose in most developed countries in the last quarter of the twentieth century, the number of women elected to office has never come close to the percentage of women of voting age in the electorates. While there are many arguments about both the causes and cures for this situation, one cure that is gaining ground is to set aside a certain number of positions to which only women can be elected. There are precedents for this practice in New Zealand, in which seats are set aside for Maori, and India, where seats are set aside for Untouchables.

In France, where the practice is called "parity," a constitutional amendment has passed that states "the law favors equal access for men and women to electoral mandates and elective offices." [13] This amendment is being put into practice by requiring that in certain circumstances political parties must put forward an equal number of men and women as candidates for office. This does not, of course, guarantee election, but it is believed that more women will be elected under this system than have been previously elected. Anne Phillips has developed proposals for a similar system designed for Britain. [14]

Feminism and Legal Theory

Catherine A. MacKinnon (b. 1946) has developed a legal theory that stresses that male dominance has been accepted in American law. She contends that the male has always been the standard, even if not stated as such, and presents a position generally called *nonsubordination,* which argues for the recognition of the woman's actual lived experience as opposed to the supposed "objective" model, which turned out to be the male perspective.

MacKinnon's initial work was on sexual harassment, which when she began was not considered sexual discrimination but merely what should be expected between men and women. It is easy to see that looking at sexual harassment from the point of view of the harassed is essential to seeing the entire

---

13. Sylviane Agacinski, *Parity of the Sexes,* trans. Lisa Walsh (New York: Columbia University Press, 2001), viii.

14. See Anne Phillips, *Engendering Democracy* (University Park: Pennsylvania State University Press, 1991); and Phillips, *The Politics of Presence* (Oxford: Oxford University Press, 1995).

picture. MacKinnon's analysis provided the basis for changes in case law and legal codes so that today sexual harassment is seen as sexual discrimination.[15]

MacKinnon's work on pornography as discrimination based on sex has been much more controversial. MacKinnon argues that freedom of expression is based on the false assumption of general equality and that the fact of gender inequality invalidates negative liberty, or the right of people to be left alone. Thus, pornography is not, for MacKinnon, a question of civil liberties, but an issue "central to the institutionalization of male dominance."[16] Opponents of MacKinnon's position, which on this issue include many feminists, argue that freedom of the press is too important a negative liberty to be compromised to get rid of pornography, however desirable that might be.

Multiculturalism

Given the emphasis on difference by many feminists, multiculturalism would appear to be an obvious position for feminists to take, and many do. But in a recent essay, Susan Moller Okin has asked the question "Is Multiculturalism Bad for Women?" In her essay she suggests that the acceptance of multiculturalism may lead to the acceptance of cultures with gender divisions that disadvantage women.[17] Okin's argument poses a serious question for both feminists and multiculturalists. The assertion of universal human rights has been central to the arguments feminists have made that such rights belong equally to both women and men. On the other hand, the recognition that there are important differences between and among men and women has become central to the argument that equality of rights can go hand in hand with respect for differences among human beings. The problem is that if difference includes cultural differences, then some of those differences include the rejection of an equality of rights. The valuing of differences can allow differences to be used to undermine gender equality, through the argument that valued differences require differential treatment. Okin contends that the equality of rights must not be sacrificed in the name of multicultural respect.

Women of Color   The multicultural argument reflects a central, long-standing problem for feminists, particularly in the United States—the fact that most feminists are white. African American author bell hooks, in her *Ain't I a Woman? Black Women and Feminism* (1981), and the collection of essays *This Bridge Called My Back: Writings by Radical Women of Color* (1983), edited by Cherríe Moraga and Gloria Anzaldúa, made early statements that the "universal" claims of white

---

15. See Catherine A. MacKinnon, *The Sexual Harassment of Working Women* (New Haven, Conn.: Yale University Press, 1979).

16. Catherine A. MacKinnon, "Pornography," in MacKinnon, *Feminism Unmodified: Discourses on Life and Law* (Cambridge: Harvard University Press, 1987), 146.

17. For the essay and a number of responses, both pro and con, see Susan Moller Okin, with respondents, *Is Multiculturalism Bad for Women?* ed. Joshua Cohen, Matthew Howard, and Martha C. Nussbaum (Princeton, N.J.: Princeton University Press, 1999).

feminists did not necessarily apply to them. The title of the former was taken from the famous speech "Ain't I a Woman" (1851) given by Sojourner Truth (ca. 1797–1883) at a women's rights convention and illustrates that the issue is not a new one.

Third World Feminism The multicultural issue, seen through a different lens, is one that continues to be a problem within feminism—the appropriate approach to take toward Third World women. Many Western feminists such as Okin point to the obvious mistreatment of women in the Third World, the Taliban being only the most obvious case, and argue that the Western model of individual rights is the appropriate solution. On the other hand, both a growing number of Western feminists and many Third World feminists see this as an attempt to impose Western, and particularly American, values where they are not appropriate.[18]

Clearly, as Okin points out, multiculturalism poses a major issue for feminists, but the issue is an important one not just for feminists. As is noted throughout this book, in the past all ideologies posited certain universal values, but, with the advent of postmodernism, universals of all sorts are now being questioned. The problem, acutely stated by Okin, is how can we keep important universals while respecting differences among human beings.[19]

Reproductive Rights

All feminists share a concern with freeing women from the tyranny of unwanted childbearing. This concern has been called *reproductive rights,* the right of a woman to control her own body, or, more recently, *reproductive freedom* in an attempt to separate it from the narrow, legal conception of rights. For most feminists this means that all methods of birth control should be available and either free or very inexpensive and, since no system of birth control is 100 percent effective, that safe and affordable abortions should be available for all women. For a few feminists this means the end of biological motherhood and the development of artificial means of reproduction, but for most feminists it means the transformation of society to allow full participation by women. They envision a remodeling of all institutions of socialization so that all human beings can participate fully in all life activities as they freely and independently choose.

There is a difference among feminists on this issue. Some feminists assume that men are capable of the changes needed; others argue that a much more radical transformation of social institutions, with a resulting change in men, will be necessary before men can participate fully in the raising of children. They

---

18. For a forceful argument against Western feminist hegemony, see Chilla Bulbeck, *Reorienting Western Feminisms: Women's Diversity in a Postcolonial World* (Cambridge: Cambridge University Press, 1998).

19. In her *The Futures of Difference: Truth and Method in Feminist Theory* (Cambridge, England: Polity Press, 1999), Susan J. Hekman argues that it is necessary to find a middle ground between the erasure of difference and the emphasis on difference.

argue that without this change increased male participation in child rearing will only result in the reduction of women's power.

SUGGESTED READINGS

Some Classic Works

Brownmiller, Susan. *Against Our Will: Men, Women and Rape*. New York: Simon & Schuster, 1975.

Daly, Mary. *Beyond God the Father: Toward a Philosophy of Women's Liberation*. Boston: Beacon Press, 1973.

Davis, Angela Y. *Women, Race, & Class*. New York: Random House, 1981.

De Beauvoir, Simone. *The Second Sex*. Translated and edited by H. M. Pashley. New York: Knopf, 1952. Originally published as *Le Deuxième Sexe* (Paris: Gallimard, 1949).

Dworkin, Andrea. *Intercourse*. New York: Free Press, 1987.

Friedan, Betty. *The Feminine Mystique*. New York: Norton, 1963.

Gilligan, Carol. *In a Different Voice: Psychological Theory and Women's Development*. Cambridge: Harvard University Press, 1982.

Greer, Germaine. *Female Eunuch*. London: MacGibbon & Kee, 1970.

hooks, bell [Gloria Watkins]. *Ain't I a Woman: Black Women and Feminism*. Boston: South End Press, 1981.

Millett, Kate. *Sexual Politics*. Garden City, N.Y.: Doubleday, 1970.

Books and Articles

Ackerly, Brooke A. *Political Theory and Feminist Social Criticism*. Cambridge: Cambridge University Press, 2000.

Afshar, Haleh. *Women and Politics in the Third World*. London: Routledge, 1996.

————, ed. *Women, Work, and Ideology in the Third World*. London: Tavistock, 1985.

Agacinski, Sylviane. *Parity of the Sexes*. Translated by Lisa Walsh. New York: Columbia University Press, 2001.

Alaimo, Stacy. *Undomesticated Ground: Recasting Nature as Feminist Space*. Ithaca, N.Y.: Cornell University Press, 2000.

Ali, Suki, Kelly Coate, and Wangui wa Goro, eds. *Global Feminist Politics: Identities in a Changing World*. London: Routledge, 2000.

Andermahr, Sonya, Terry Lovell, and Carol Wolkowitz. *A Concise Glossary of Feminist Theory*. London: Arnold, 1997.

Beasley, Chris. *What Is Feminism? An Introduction to Feminist Theory*. London: Sage, 1999.

Bell, Diane, and Renate Klein, eds. *Radically Speaking: Feminism Reclaimed*. London: Zed Press; Melbourne: Spinifex, 1996.

Benhabid, Seyla, ed. *Democracy and Difference: Contesting the Boundaries of the Political*. Princeton, N.J.: Princeton University Press, 1996.

Boylan, Esther, *Women and Disability*. London: Zed Books, 1991.

Brownmiller, Susan. *In Our Time: Memoir of a Revolution*. New York: Dial Press, 1999.

Bryson, Valerie. *Feminist Debates: Issues of Theory and Political Practice*. New York: New York University Press, 1999.

Bulbeck, Chilla. *Re-orienting Western Feminisms: Women's Diversity in a Postcolonial World*. Cambridge: Cambridge University Press, 1998.

Card, Claudia, ed. *On Feminist Ethics and Politics*. Lawrence: University Press of Kansas, 1999.

Charles, Nickie, and Helen Hintjens, eds. *Gender, Ethnicity, and Political Ideologies*. London: Routledge, 1998.

Code, Lorraine, ed. *Encyclopedia of Feminist Theories*. London: Routledge, 2000.

Cornell, Drucilla. *At the Heart of Freedom: Feminism, Sex, and Equality.* Princeton, N.J.: Princeton University Press, 1998.

Crow, Barbara A., ed. *Radical Feminism: A Documentary Reader.* New York: New York University Press, 2000.

Dalla Costa, Mariarosa, and Giovanna F. Dalla Costa, eds. *Women, Development, and Labor of Reproduction: Struggles and Movements.* Trenton, N.J., Asmara, Eritrea: Africa World Press, 1999.

De Oliveira, Rosiska Darcy. *In Praise of Difference: The Emergence of a Global Feminism.* Translated by Peggy Sharpe. New Brunswick, N.J.: Rutgers University Press, 1998.

Donovan, Josephine. *Feminist Theory: The Intellectual Traditions.* 3d ed. New York: Continuum, 2000.

El Saadawi, Nawal. *The Hidden Face of Eve: Women in the Arab World.* Translated and edited by Sherif Hetata. London: Zed Books, 1980.

Elshtain, Jean Bethke. *Public Man, Private Woman: Women in Social and Political Thought.* Princeton, N.J.: Princeton University Press, 1981.

————, ed. *The Family in Political Thought.* Amherst: University of Massachusetts Press, 1982.

Evans, Sara M. *Feminist Theory Today: An Introduction to Second-Wave Feminism.* London: Sage, 1995.

Firestone, Shulamith. *The Dialectic of Sex: The Case for Feminist Revolution.* New York: Morrow, 1970.

Fricker, Miranda, and Jennifer Hornsby, eds. *The Cambridge Companion to Feminism in Philosophy.* Cambridge: Cambridge University Press, 2000.

García, Brígada, ed. *Women, Poverty, and Demographic Change.* Oxford: Oxford University Press, 2000.

Haraway, Donna. *Simians, Cyborgs, and Women: The Reinvention of Nature.* New York: Routledge; London: Free Association, 1991.

Hartsock, Nancy C. M. *The Feminist Standpoint Revisited and Other Essays.* Boulder, Colo.: Westview Press, 1998.

————. *Money, Sex, and Power: Toward a Feminist Historical Materialism.* New York: Longman, 1983.

Hekman, Susan J. *The Futures of Differences: Truth and Method in Feminist Theory.* Cambridge, England: Polity Press, 1999.

————, ed. *Feminism, Identity, and Difference.* Special issue of *Critical Review of International Social and Political Philosophy* 2, no. 1 (spring 1999). London: Frank Cass, 1999.

hooks, bell [Gloria Watkins]. *Talking Back: Thinking Feminist, Thinking Black.* Boston: South End Press, 1989.

Jackson, Stevi, and Jackie Jones, ed. *Contemporary Feminist Theories.* New York: New York University Press, 1998.

Jaggar, Alison M., and Iris Marion Young, eds. *A Companion to Feminist Philosophy.* Oxford: Blackwell, 1998.

Jaywardena, Kumari. *Feminism and Nationalism in the Third World.* London: Zed Books, 1993.

Kaplan, Caren, Norma Alarcón, and Minoo Moallem, eds. *Between Woman and Nation: Nationalisms, Transnational Feminisms, and the State.* Durham, N.C.: Duke University Press, 1999.

King, Ursula, ed. *Feminist Theology from the Third World: A Reader.* Maryknoll, N.Y.: Orbis Books, 1994.

Lacey, Nicola. *Unspeakable Subjects: Feminist Essays in Legal and Social Theory.* Oxford, England: Hart, 1998.

MacKinnon, Catherine A. *Only Words.* Cambridge: Harvard University Press, 1993.

————. *Toward a Feminist Theory of the State.* Cambridge: Harvard University Press, 1989.

Merchant, Carolyn. *The Death of Nature: Women, Ecology, and the Scientific Revolution.* San Francisco: Harper & Row, 1980.

Miles, Angela. *Integrative Feminism: Building Global Visions, 1960s–1990s.* New York: Routledge, 1996.

Minow, Martha. *Making All the Difference: Inclusion, Exclusion, and America Law.*

Ithaca, N.Y.: Cornell University Press, 1990.

Moghissi, Haideh. *Feminism and Islamic Fundamentalism: The Limits of Postmodern Analysis.* London: Zed Books, 1999.

Moraga, Cherríe, and Gloria Anzaldúa, eds. *This Bridge Called My Back: Writings by Radical Women of Color.* New York: Kitchen Table, Women of Color Press, 1983.

Morgan, Robin, ed. *Sisterhood Is Powerful: An Anthology of Writings from the Women's Liberation Movement.* New York: Random House, 1970.

Nasta, Susheila, ed. *Motherlands: Black Women's Writings from Africa, the Caribbean, and South Asia.* London: The Women's Press, 1991; New Brunswick, N.J.: Rutgers University Press, 1992.

Nussbaum, Martha C. *Sex and Social Justice.* New York: Oxford University Press, 1999.

O'Brien, Mary. *The Politics of Reproduction.* Boston: Routledge & Kegan Paul, 1981.

Okin, Susan Moller, with respondents. *Is Multiculturalism Bad for Women?* Edited by Joshua Cohen, Matthew Howard, and Martha C. Nussbaum. Princeton, N.J.: Princeton University Press, 1999.

Pateman, Carole. *The Sexual Contract.* Stanford, Calif.: Stanford University Press, 1988.

Phillips, Anne. *Engendering Democracy.* University Park: Pennsylvania State University Press, 1991.

———. *The Politics of Presence.* Oxford: Oxford University Press, 1995.

Schiebinger, Londa. *Has Feminism Changed Science?* Cambridge: Harvard University Press, 1999.

Solanas, Valerie. *SCUM Manifesto.* Edinburgh: AK Press, 1996. Originally published by author, New York, 1967.

Spender, Dale. *Narrating the Net: Women, Power, and Cyberspace.* Melbourne: Spinifex, 1995.

Squires, Judith. *Gender in Political Theory.* Cambridge, England: Polity Press, 1999.

Sturgeon, Noël. *Ecofeminist Natures: Race, Gender, Feminist Theory, and Political Action.* New York: Routledge, 1997.

Tobias, Sheila. *Faces of Feminism: An Activist's Reflections on the Women's Movement.* Boulder, Colo.: Westview Press, 1997.

Tong, Rosemarie. *Feminist Thought: A More Comprehensive Introduction.* 2d ed. Boulder, Colo.: Westview Press, 1998.

Voet, Rian. *Feminism and Citizenship.* London: Sage, 1998.

Warren, Karen J. *Ecofeminist Philosophy: A Western Perspective on What It Is and Why It Matters.* Lanham, Md.: Rowman & Littlefield, 2000.

Whelehan, Imelda. *Modern Feminist Thought: From the Second Wave to "Post-Feminism."* New York: New York University Press, 1995.

Young, Iris Marion. *Intersecting Voices: Dilemmas of Gender, Political Philosophy, and Policy.* Princeton, N.J.: Princeton University Press, 1997.

Web Sites

http://dir.yahoo.com/Society_and_Culture/Cultures_and_Groups/Women/Feminism/ Yahoo Directory—Feminism

http://www.cddc.vt.edu/feminism/ Feminist Theory

http://www.feminist.com/ General

http://www.michfest.com Michigan Womyn's Music Festival

http://www.wwwomen.com/category/femini1.html Directory

7

○

Marxism

K arl Marx (1818–83) and his followers produced one of the dominant ideologies from World War I into the early 1990s — communism—and a number
of variants that have been influential in many parts of the world. This chapter
considers the roots of communism in the writings of Marx and Friedrich Engels (1820–95),[1] and the theoretical structure based on these writings, which is
still widely respected. In addition to communism, a number of other Marxist
traditions developed and will be discussed here.

Communism was the result of a line of intellectual and political development from Marx and Engels through V. I. Lenin (original name Vladimir Ilyich
Ulyanov, 1870–1924) and others that emphasized the authoritarian and central-
ist aspects of Marx's thought. An alternative Marxist tradition has always been
available that stressed the decentralist and democratic aspects of Marx's thought,
but it has always been a minority position. It is this latter tradition, together with
what are widely recognized as Marx's fundamental insights into social relations
in general and the effects of capitalism in particular, that explains Marx's continuing importance.

---

1. On the Marx-Engels relationship, see Terrell Carver, "The Engels-Marx Question:
   Interpretation, Identities, Partnership, Politics," in *Engels after Marx*, ed. Manfred B.
   Steger and Terrell Carver (University Park: Pennsylvania State University Press, 1999),
   17–36. On Engels, see J. D. Huntley, *The Life and Thought of Friedrich Engels* (New
   Haven, Conn.: Yale University Press, 1991); and Christopher J. Arthur, ed., *Engels To-
   day: A Centenary Appreciation* (London: Macmillan; New York: St. Martin's Press, 1996).

The partial demise of communism does not mean the end of Marxism. In the first place, the inability of capitalism to rapidly overcome the failures of communist regimes has led many people in former communist countries to regret the passing of communism and to vote for the former communists, now under new names. Although no informed person expected capitalism to quickly correct communism's legacy, the fact is that many people believed it would, and self-serving anticommunists oversold capitalism. The required restructuring of the economies involved means that many people are significantly worse off than they were under communism: jobs have been lost; pensions have been radically reduced by inflation; and social services and health care that people relied on have disappeared. Thus it is no surprise that former communists are being elected to office.

Another reason for the difficulties encountered in the transition from communism is the lack of certain aspects of a civil society in the former communist countries. Such countries have no tradition of meaningful elections, no private banking system, and no nonstate social institutions like the Red Cross / Red Crescent, scouts, the National Organization of Women, and so forth. Thus, people in these countries traditionally turn to the state for most of their social activities, and all these practices and organizations take time to grow.

Second, Marxism remains a powerful tool for understanding social relations and social change, and many thinkers still find the Marxist critique of capitalism to contain considerable truth. Social classes largely based on economic power remain even though Marxist and other theoreticians have been arguing for some time that this class analysis needs to be complicated by adding such factors as gender and race. In this and other ways, Marxist thinkers are still contributing significantly to our understanding of the world around us. In addition, the collapse of communism has not convinced all communists that communism has failed. Thus, it is still important to understand the various parts of the Marxist tradition.

KARL MARX AND FRIEDRICH ENGELS

To understand the parts of the Marxist tradition, it is essential to look first at the philosophic basis found in the thought of Karl Marx and Friedrich Engels and then to turn to the developments and changes made by others.

Alienation—The Young Marx

In his twenties Marx wrote a number of works that are controversial to this day. Most writers now argue that these early writings are central to any understanding of Marx and that the later writings grow out of and develop the themes of the early writings. Those who stress the early writings argue that authoritarian communism lost sight of the human concerns that motivated Marx and that are central to these early writings.

The central concept in these early writings is *alienation,* particularly found in the work known as *The Economic and Philosophic Manuscripts of 1844* (first published in full in 1932). Alienation refers to a relationship between two or more people or parts of oneself in which one is cut off from, a stranger to, or alien to the others. It has been a major theme in modern literature, in works such as Albert Camus's *The Stranger* (1942; *The Outsider* in the United Kingdom), Jean-Paul Sartre's *Nausea* (1938) and *No Exit* (1945), and Samuel Beckett's *Waiting for Godot* (1952), to name four of the best known, depicting various forms of alienation.

For Marx it meant something more specific. He argued that in capitalism, for reasons that will become apparent later, individuals become cut off from — out of tune with—themselves, their families and friends, and their work. They are not and cannot be whole, fully developed human beings in a capitalist society.[2]

For Marx, private property and alienation are intimately linked because the most basic form of alienation is alienated labor, or labor that is sold like an object. Of course, what is being sold is part of a human being. A worker sells her or his strength, effort, skill, and time; so for much of the worker's life someone else has purchased and thus has the use of the worker (and in Marx's time this was usually a minimum of twelve to fourteen hours a day, six or seven days a week). Alienated labor produced an alienation of self; no longer whole human beings, workers could not establish full human relationships with others, who were in the same situation. This is the human meaning of capitalism for Marx: people cut off from self, others, and work. It is this condition that Marx was determined to change; it was the reason for his writings and his revolutionary activity.

Marx's Critique of Capitalism

The Marxian analysis of society and the forces operating in it is a commentary on and condemnation of industrial capitalism. Marx argued both that capitalism was an essential stage in the development to socialism and that capitalism was the most progressive economic system developed so far. Marx also attributed most of the ills of contemporary society to the capitalist system. Many evils were inherent in developing industrialism, and Marx was not the only one to point them out. His comments are interesting, though, because they indicate a great deal about Marx and the way he viewed the world, and much of the appeal of Marxism is found in these criticisms of the industrial system.

For Marx economic relationships are the foundation of the entire social system; therefore, his economic criticisms must be considered first. For Marx, the most fundamental fact of life is that people must produce goods before they can do anything else. They must also reproduce themselves, but they cannot even do that unless they are capable of feeding themselves. Thus material production or economic relationships are basic to all life.

The primary points in Marxian economics are the *labor theory of value,* the doctrine of *subsistence wages,* and the theory of *surplus value.* Marx used *value* in

2. For extended commentaries, see István Mészáros, *Marx's Theory of Alienation* (London: Merlin Press, 1970); Bertell Ollman, *Alienation,* 2d ed. (Cambridge: Cambridge University Press, 1976); and Adam Schaff, "Alienation as a Social and Philosophical Problem," *Social Praxis* 3, nos. 1–2 (1975): 7–26.

the sense of real costs in labor. Nothing else was considered. In other words, the value (not the price) of any manufactured object was based on the amount of labor time consumed in producing it.

Marx argued that nothing had value without labor. Neither capital nor land is of any value until labor is added. This is the *labor theory of value*. An individual has to work a certain number of hours or days to produce enough to provide a living. Marx assumed that the capitalist would pay workers only enough to keep them alive, a *subsistence wage*. Marx made this assumption for the following reasons:

1. There was a surplus of laborers, and there was no need to pay more.

2. He could not conceive of the capitalist paying more than absolutely necessary.

3. He assumed that the capitalist would be faced with a series of economic crises that would make it impossible for the capitalist to pay more.

In addition, Marx believed that the profit of the capitalist was taken from the amount produced over and above the wages paid the worker. This is the theory of *surplus value* and can be used to explain more fully the doctrine of subsistence wages. As capitalists replaced workers with machines (sometimes called dead labor), they would have to reduce wages to keep up their rate of profit because profit came only from surplus value extracted from labor. They would also be able to reduce wages because replacing workers with machines produced a pool of unemployed workers who must compete for whatever wages the capitalists choose to pay. Of course, the real reason that capitalists are constantly pushing down wages is to maximize profits, and Marx was certainly aware of that fact.

Hence Marx's major economic criticism revolved around the exploitation of the majority, the *proletariat* or workers, by the minority, the *bourgeoisie* or capitalists. His concern was not purely economic but also centered on the extent to which the system kept proletarians from ever fulfilling their potentials as individuals. It was impossible for them to improve themselves in any way, and they were denied education and were thereby kept from any real understanding of their deplorable position.

At the same time Marx noted that the growing need for literate workers meant that some workers had to be educated and that education had the potential of teaching some proletarians about their situation, who then might teach others, thus undermining bourgeois dominance. The same thing happened in the Third World when the colonial power started to educate some of the colonized to fill jobs needing literate workers; these same workers became part of the successful overthrow of colonial regimes.

The state was the tool of the dominant class, the bourgeoisie, and was used to suppress, violently if necessary, any attempt by the proletariat to better themselves. To Marx and most other radical theorists of the day, the *state* referred to all those officials, such as the police, the army, bureaucrats, and so forth, who could be, and were, used to suppress the workers. In addition, Marx contended that as long as the bourgeoisie was the dominant class, the government would

Karl Marx (1818–83) was the father of modern communism. His work as a philosopher, political thinker, and economist has made him one of the most influential thinkers of all time. Born in Germany, Marx spent much of his life in England studying contemporary society and actively working for revolution. In association with Friedrich Engels (1820–95), he published their famous call for revolution, *Manifesto of the Communist Party,* in 1848. He published the first volume of his study of contemporary economics, *Capital,* in 1867; Engels undertook the publication of the other volumes. Today, every word that Marx wrote is carefully studied by a wide range of scholars and revolutionists for clues to his thought.

be its tool and could not be made responsive to the needs of other classes. Marx always saw the state or the government as the tool of the dominant class, whatever class that might be, and he believed the state would so remain as long as there was more than one class. For many radicals the state is the epitome of evil, the symbol of all that is bad about society. This is particularly true among the anarchists and will be discussed in detail in the chapter on anarchism (Chapter 8), but it is also true of Marx and some of Marx's followers, particularly those prior to Lenin. This notion probably developed because the state, through the bureaucracy, the police, and the army, represents and controls the forces regularly used to oppose workers' demands. The history of the labor movement in the United States, for example, reveals the frequent use of the police, the army, and the National Guard to put down strikes and break up demonstrations.[3] Thus Marx's ultimate goal, Full Communism, has no state. In this he is similar to the anarchists.

The religious system was also in the hands of the dominant class, the bourgeoisie, and Marx said religion was used to convince the proletariat that if they obeyed the state and their bosses they would be rewarded in another life. This is what Marx meant by his famous statement that religion is the opium of the people. The proletariat is lulled into accepting its way of life by the vision of

3. For studies from differing viewpoints, see John R. Commons et al., *History of Labor in the United States,* 4th ed. (New York: Kelly, 1955); and Louis Adamic, *Dynamite: The Story of Class Violence in America,* rev. ed. (New York: Viking Press, 1934).

heaven. This life might well be harsh, but, if the workers stand it for a brief time, they will be rewarded in the next life. Marx believed this kept the workers from actively seeking to change the system. In this way, the religious system was a major focus of Marx's criticisms of contemporary society. He saw religion used by the dominant class, the bourgeoisie, to hold the proletariat in its downtrodden position. As a result, Marx made many scathing attacks on religion and argued that the future society in which the proletariat would rule would have no need for religion. At the same time, Marx argued that religion contains the highest expression of the human ethical sense. The fact that the institution of the church and the beliefs of the masses were used to control people did not mean that Marx rejected all aspects of religious belief.

The state and the religious system were both part of what Marx called the *superstructure*. They were not fundamental economic structures of society; they were a reflection of economic relations and would change as these relations changed. Thus, as class antagonism was overcome, both the state and religion would begin to disappear.

The capitalist system degraded workers in all of their relationships. Since they had to fight against others of their own class for bare subsistence, they could never hope to establish any sort of valid relationship with another person. For example, Engels wrote bitterly of the effect capitalism had on marriage and the family. To him, the family system of his day was a repetition of the class struggle. The husband symbolized the bourgeoisie and the wife the proletariat. The contemporary marriage system under capitalism was monogamy supplemented by adultery and prostitution, and it could not change until capitalism ceased to exist. The contemporary marriage system had originated as an institution of private property at about the same time private property in land and goods had originated. It developed in order to ensure that a man's property would be handed on to his sons. The only way this could be done was to endow the sons of one woman with a particular legal status. This did not limit the man's relationships with other women; it supposedly limited the wife's relationships with other men. In practice, as shown by the incidence of adultery, this latter proscription did not work. It failed because of "individual sex-love." Sometime after the development of monogamous marriage, there developed the tendency to find one sex-love partner and no other. This could, of course, occur after marriage, and it explained the existence of adultery. But, as will be seen later, it also provided the basis for the true monogamous marriage, which Marx believed would develop after the revolution.[4]

It is easy to see how many of Marx's criticisms of capitalism stemmed from the concerns found in his early writings. He was also impressed by Engels's description of the position of industrial workers in *The Condition of the Working Class in England* (1845), which depicted the extreme poverty in which the workers lived and the dehumanizing lives they led as mere extensions of the

---

4. Engels discussed the family at length in *The Origin of the Family, Private Property, and the State* (Harmondsworth, England: Penguin, 1985). For a modern Marxist commentary, see Juliet Mitchell, *Women's Estate* (Baltimore: Penguin, 1971).

machines they tended. Thus both Marx and Engels saw capitalism as destroying the humanity of the workers and the bourgeoisie, because wage slavery was degrading to both buyer and seller. Marx and Engels set out to understand capitalism, to destroy it, and to found a new, better world in its place.

Materialism

For Marx, general theoretical positions must always be related to the concrete, material world and vice versa. Questions of theory are never separated from practice; they are always closely related.

The basis of Marx's philosophy is found in the influence of the conditions of life on people. Although Marx did not develop the basis of this notion thoroughly himself, he once spelled out in capsule form the fundamental thesis, saying it "served as the guiding thread in my studies." Although the jargon is a bit difficult to follow, it is best to have this statement in Marx's own words; it summarizes thoroughly his basic ideas. The meaning will become clearer later.

> In the social production of their means of existence men enter into definite, necessary relations which are independent of their will, productive relationships which correspond to a definite state of development of their material productive forces. The aggregate of these productive relationships constitutes the economic structure of society, the real basis on which a juridical and political superstructure arises, and to which definite forms of social consciousness correspond. The mode of production of the material means of existence conditions the whole process of social, political, and intellectual life. It is not the consciousness of men that determines their existence, but, on the contrary, it is their social condition that determines their consciousness. At a certain stage of their development the material productive forces of society come into contradiction with the existing productive relationships within which they had moved before. From forms of development of the productive forces these relationships are transformed into their fetters. Then an epoch of social revolution opens. With the change in the economic foundation the whole vast superstructure is more or less rapidly transformed.[5]

The fundamental point, which is a truism today, is that the way people think is greatly affected by the way they live. As was noted in the introduction, the whole process known as socialization is the means by which an individual takes on the values of his or her particular society. The point made there was that an individual, by her or his position in life economically, socially, and so forth, and by family and religious background, educational experiences, and such daily influences as the mass media, is presented with a picture or a group of pictures of the world that helps form his or her basic value system. In other words, the way an individual lives does quite clearly affect the way she or he thinks.

5. Karl Marx, "Preface," in *A Contribution to the Critique of Political Economy,* trans. N. T. Stone (Chicago: Charles H. Kerr, 1913), 11–12.

But the point generally accepted today is not quite the same as the point Marx was making. Marx argued that the forms taken by the law, religion, politics, aesthetics, philosophy, and so forth, which he called the *superstructure,* are largely determined by the economic structure and processes of society.

Marx is often, with considerable truth, called an economic determinist, and taken at face value, that is the meaning of the phrase "their social condition . . . determines their consciousness." But earlier in the same passage Marx uses the word *conditions* instead of *determines.* In the simplest formulation, Marx can be read as saying there is a cause-and-effect relationship between the economic structure of society and the superstructure. However, Marx thinks in terms of interactions, not simple cause-and-effect relationships. In this case there is a continuing interaction between economic structure and superstructure, where changes in one produce changes in the other back and forth constantly. Marx's analysis is of a continuing process of change, with all aspects of both the economic structure and the superstructure constantly interacting. The economic structure is the driving force of social and intellectual change, but it is not a simple cause-and-effect relationship, even though Marx can be, has been, and still is read as a simple economic determinist.

The distinction here is a subtle but important one. For Marx, economic relationships are the most important factor determining the social forms produced at any time and place; but these economic relationships interact with aspects of the superstructure, opening up possibilities for changes in economic relationships that will then produce further changes in the superstructure, and so on. Thus Marx is almost a simple determinist, but not quite. Today, based in large part on the original insights of Marx, we tend to say that economic relationships are among the most important factors influencing the social and intellectual forms produced, but they are not always the most important factors.

In developing his materialistic approach, Marx was attacking a school of German philosophy known as idealism. Its major exponent had been Georg Wilhelm Friedrich Hegel (1770–1831), and it was particularly against Hegel that Marx directed his attack. Hegel's ideas and the diverse influence they had on Marx are a complex subject and cannot be explored thoroughly here. But some attempt at explanation must be made because Hegel's influence on Marx, both in what Marx accepted and what he rejected, was so great. Hegel's basic proposition, from Marx's viewpoint, was the existence of an Absolute Spirit—sometimes Hegel called it God—that gradually revealed more and more of itself in the form of higher and higher stages of human freedom. In Hegel's philosophy the ideal and the material, or concrete as he called it, were intimately connected, but not as cause and effect. The two were closely bound together, each influencing the other, even though ultimately the ideal was more important than the material.

Marx directed his main attack against Hegel's idealism. As Marx put it, he set Hegel on his feet by emphasizing the material rather than the ideal. Marx, of course, stressed economic relationships in his definition of the material, rather than physical nature or the like. By stressing the material, Marx was able to argue that his position was scientific (Marx's approach is often called *scientific socialism*)[6] because matter, the material, is subject to objective scientific analysis and laws; it behaves in a predictable manner. Marx was one of the first to argue that economics could be treated scientifically, that it followed certain laws. He also contended history followed certain patterns and these patterns could be discovered and projected into the future. Marx did not claim he could predict the future with certainty; he simply argued that, if conditions continued as they were at the present, certain things would probably happen in the future. If conditions changed, which they did (Marx had argued that they probably would not), the future would be different. Since they did change even within his lifetime, some of Marx's positions changed. Finally, it must be noted that Marx believed history was moving not only to a different stage but also to a better one.

Dialectical Materialism   The pattern Marx found in history, which he thought was a basic tool of analysis, was the dialectic. Hegel, too, had argued that history was moving to different and better stages; he also used the dialectic as his basic tool of analysis.

Marx's position is sometimes referred to as dialectical materialism. The dialectic seems to have originated in ancient Greece as a means of attaining truth through a process of questions and answers. In answer to an original question, such as the meaning of courage, beauty, justice, or the like, a position is stated. The questioner then criticizes this position through the question-and-answer process until an opposite or significantly different position is taken. Then, by a continuation of the process, an attempt is made to arrive at the truth contained in both positions. The process is then continued until all are satisfied that the correct answer has been reached. The most famous illustrations of this process can be found in the dialogues of Plato (427?–347 B.C.), such as the *Republic*.

Marx took the dialectic from Hegel, who argued that all ideas develop through this dialectical process of thesis (first position), antithesis (second position), and synthesis (truth of the opposites), which becomes a new thesis, and, thus continues the process. An illustration shows us something of what both Hegel and Marx are saying. Starting at the bottom with the original thesis (first position), we see its "opposite" antithesis (second position). This opposition is not one of complete difference; it is produced from the thesis in one of two ways, which are spelled out in the first two laws of the dialectic.

1. *The transformation of quantity into quality.* Changes in degree gradually produce a change in quality or kind. The usual example is the change in water from a solid (ice), to a liquid, to a gas. The changes Hegel had in mind were more basic, say H_2O to H_2O_2. In this process the combination of oxygen and hydrogen first produces H_2O, which is totally different from either hydrogen or oxygen. The continued addition of oxygen produces H_2O_2, which is again different.

---

6. The best statement of his argument is still Friedrich Engels, *Socialism: Utopian and Scientific* (1880). Many editions are available.

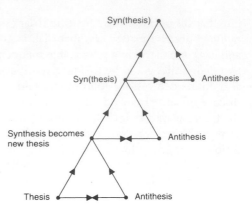

FIGURE 7.1 The Dialectic

2. *Unity or identity of opposites.* Contradictions in the thesis become the antithesis. Thus the opposites are actually similar because they are composed of similar elements. In addition, the thesis and antithesis become unified, differently, in the synthesis. This unification of the thesis and the antithesis is produced through the third law of the dialectic.

3. *Negation of the negation.* Contradictions continue to accumulate until another qualitative change occurs and the synthesis is reached. The synthesis, or the unity of the opposites, is a qualitative change, as was the original step from the thesis to the antithesis. In other words, a new position is reached that is not simply the combination of the thesis and antithesis. In a similar way, chemists sometimes speak of synthesizing a new product from two or more products. Thus water (H_2O) is a synthesis of two parts hydrogen with one part oxygen to produce a product that is significantly different from the original components. The synthesis is then treated as a new product, and the process continues in the same manner.

These three laws are often neglected or slighted by students of Marx, but, as will be seen later, they help to provide an understanding of the pattern taken by his analysis of history. Marx did not attempt to apply the dialectic systematically to the material world. Some of his followers, such as Engels and Lenin, tried to view nature as changing dialectically and spoke vaguely of scientific laws operating dialectically, but their attempts were not very successful.[7]

The general form of the dialectic is the interaction and intermingling of ideas, beliefs, and positions, not the specific form used here as an example of the dialectic. The dialectic is a way of understanding the constant interaction that characterizes the world. For a particularly relevant example, none of the ideologies presented here is, by itself, an accurate reflection of the world, but, on the other hand, each of them has something valuable to contribute to the under-

---

7. For a modern consideration, see Richard Levins and Richard Lewontin, *The Dialectical Biologist* (Cambridge: Harvard University Press, 1985).

Vladimir Ilyich Lenin (1870–1924, born Vladimir Ilyich Ulyanov) was a follower of Karl Marx. He is remembered primarily as the leader of the successful Bolshevik section of the Communist Party of the Soviet Union and as the first leader of the USSR, which he headed from the time of the Russian revolution in 1917 to his death. He was a major theorist of revolution as well as one of its successful practitioners. His books *What Is to Be Done?* (1902) and *One Step Forward, Two Steps Back* (1904) presented the case for a highly disciplined body of revolutionists as the only approach to a successful revolution. His *Imperialism: The Highest Stage of Capitalism* (1916) and *State and Revolution* (1918) were his major contributions to Marxist theory.

standing of how people behave. Ideological positions constantly interact in the world and are changed by that interaction. This very complex constant interaction and change is a more accurate description of the dialectic.

Historical Materialism Marx applied the dialectic to his interpretation of history. Since any change in the economic system is reflected in changes in the entire superstructure, Marx argued that it would be possible to interpret all history from this perspective. He also contended it might be possible to make some general statements about the future on the same basis. Marx did not say he could predict the future. He said there were patterns in history that would in all probability continue into the future. Thus an understanding of history should make it possible to argue that if conditions remain the same, certain things are likely to take place in the future.

Although Marx contended economics is an exact science and is basic to an understanding of his scientific socialism, he nowhere clearly and unambiguously defined the most important element in his economics, the *modes of production*. Most of the time they consist of (1) available natural resources and (2) productive techniques. At times Marx includes the organization of production as a third element, but this is more properly part of the superstructure.

Natural resources become available as we learn how to use them. Human knowledge is basic to both of the modes of production; this illustrates the interactive nature of Marx's materialism. Tools and knowledge grow together, each improvement in tools adding to knowledge and each improvement in knowledge making it possible to improve tools. Through this process more natural resources become available for use, and techniques of production change.

As humans gain knowledge of the uses of natural resources, their modes of production change, and they begin to develop more tools and manufacturing processes. They begin to produce pottery or weave baskets; they learn to form metals into tools and weapons. These changes in turn lead to further changes in both the modes of production and the superstructure.

Changes in productive techniques are brought about because previous changes were made. In other words, each development sets the stage for a further development. Also, major changes in productive techniques, such as the shift from herding to agriculture, produce major changes in the organization of the society and in the belief system of that society. In the case cited, Marx is right. If we look at any civilization where we know the pattern, we can see that the change from herding to agriculture was accompanied by changes in the political, religious, and social systems, as different activities became important. Although the change from herding to agriculture is an obvious case where major changes in productive techniques do change the organization of society, and specifically the political system of that society, Marx is probably correct in assuming that any such change produces a significant change in society. It is again obviously true that the change from a predominantly agricultural society to a predominantly industrial society has produced many far-reaching changes in contemporary society, and many argue that similar far-reaching changes will occur as production becomes more and more highly automated.

Part of the superstructure is a set of relations of production, or property relations. These constitute the second key to Marx's theory of history. Property relations in Marx's terminology refer to the ownership of the means of production: land, factories, and so on. These property relations change more slowly than do the modes of production, and thereby a conflict is formed that can be solved only by a change in the property relations. This point is important for an understanding of Marx's analysis of the changes in history and his criticism of contemporary society. Marx argued that property relations evolve more slowly than modes of production, and property relations will not change to meet changing needs. Since his analysis states that property relations are a product of the modes of production, it is clear that it is the property relations that must change to meet the new modes of production rather than the reverse. But, in the meantime, there is a tension between the modes of production and the property relations that is unresolved and cannot be resolved until the more slowly changing property relations have changed.

This tension produces conflict within society and is one of the major reasons for Marx's prediction of a revolution and his certainty that the proletariat will win the revolution. According to Marx, the owners of property will not be willing to give up their ownership, even though that is dictated by a change in the modes of production. At the same time, they ultimately must give up such ownership because of the change in the modes of production. Thus one can see in operation the three laws of the dialectic mentioned earlier. There is the transformation of quantity into quality in the changes in the modes of production. There is the unity of opposites in the growing contradiction between the economic foundation and the superstructure. And, finally, there is the negation of the negation in arriving at the new synthesis of modes of production and superstructure.

In addition, Marx uses the dialectic in his concept of progress to higher and higher, or better and better, stages of society. This is an aspect of the idea of progress or the notion that the human race and society are inevitably moving to better things. An extremely popular idea in Marx's time, the idea of progress, has fallen into disrepute today. Still, Marx's use of the idea of progress is worthy of some further consideration.

The idea of progress was not simply the notion of the world getting better and better every day in every way. Some believers in progress did think the world was constantly getting better and the human race had nothing to do with it. They argued that the world was moving in a straight line from some primitive state to some ultimate, perfect society in which everything would be good and beautiful; all people had to do was wait and things would get better. But most believers in progress did not accept this simple formulation. They believed that the world, although improving, constantly fell away from the line of progress into some sort of corruption, and then only by great effort, perhaps a revolution, could the world be brought back onto the correct path.

People could affect the path taken by the world in its gradual betterment both for good and evil. Marx seems to have assumed the world would gradually get better in spite of whatever humans did, but he contended that through concerted action people make a tremendous difference in the speed of improvement. Thus humanity's position would improve, but knowledgeable people such as Marx were in a position to recognize the direction that must be taken in order to achieve this.

The Class Struggle

A central part of Marxism is the class struggle, a hypothesis Marx used to explain change. The class struggle is based on the contradiction between the modes of production and the relations of production; this contradiction produces the class struggle. Marx said that in the mid-nineteenth century the means of production were controlled by a class he called the *bourgeoisie*. This class did little if any work but reaped immense profits from its control of the means of production. The actual labor was done by a class Marx called the *proletariat*. The modes of production required the proletariat, but did not, according to Marx, require the bourgeoisie; therefore, a struggle between these two classes resulted. For Marx there was no question concerning the result—the proletariat was necessary, the bourgeoisie was not. Although both he and later Marxists applied the theory of the class struggle to all history, Marx argued that the best example of class struggle existed in the mid-nineteenth century, in which society was clearly split into these two classes, the bourgeoisie (capitalists) and the proletariat (workers).

It is important at the outset to be clear regarding the nature of classes and of these two classes in particular. Classes are economic in nature and are groups ordered according to their relationship to the nonhuman powers of production and to each other. The proletariat is the class that makes its living from the sale of its labor power. The bourgeoisie consists of the owners of the productive resources on which the proletariat works. The bourgeoisie makes its living primarily from profit, interest, and rent, although it may earn some of its income from wages paid for managerial work and for the coordination of risk-taking ventures.

Many other smaller classes existed, but they were generally irrelevant to the unfolding conflict. In addition, Marx had a few problems with the manner in which he included certain groups within the class system. For example, he was always unclear as to exactly where the peasantry fit within his system. He often included the peasantry in a group loosely known as the *petite bourgeoisie* because they were landowners. At other times he split his definition of the peasantry into a variety of groups ranging from the bourgeoisie to the proletariat, but he was never clear exactly where to place the group of peasantry who owned their land and worked it themselves. This problem of classification has plagued Marxist theorists ever since. No one is ever quite certain where to place the peasant. In addition to the peasantry, Marx also added at the bottom of his classification scheme another class called the *lumpenproletariat,* which was composed of the dregs of society who made no contribution to production. Marx never clarified whether it would be possible to include this group within the proletariat itself, but one would assume from his writings that he thought that at some point after the revolution it would be possible to incorporate the lumpenproletariat into the proletariat in the same way the bourgeoisie was to be incorporated. For Marx in the nineteenth century, however, the most important classes were the proletariat and the bourgeoisie.

Revolution

The class struggle will, according to Marx, ultimately produce a revolution, and Marx worked for that revolution, arguing that we must move beyond simply understanding society to changing it. Marx was a revolutionary because he believed a revolution was both necessary and inevitable. The revolution was to develop as a result of a series of crises capitalism was to experience. These failed to appear as regularly or as seriously as Marx had expected, and thus the revolution did not develop, although some contemporary Marxists prefer to say it has not yet developed as anticipated.

In a small book entitled *Imperialism: The Highest Stage of Capitalism* (1916), Lenin attempted to show why these crises failed to occur as predicted. He argued that by colonizing and exploiting underdeveloped countries, the capitalists were temporarily able to stave off the crises. Colonial exploitation made it possible to pay workers slightly better by providing capitalists with (1) cheap raw materials, (2) cheap labor, and (3) markets for manufactured goods and excess capital. Lenin believed imperialism merely postponed the revolution; it did not put it off permanently, but it lulled the proletariat into believing revolution will not be necessary.

This position is of particular relevance today, and some Marxists argue that Lenin's analysis was correct, with the results only now developing. Cheap raw materials were provided for Western factories and higher wages were paid in the West by exporting exploitation to the colonies where very low wages were paid.

Today, Third World countries are beginning to control their own resources and are insisting on high prices, in part because of past exploitation. Some contemporary Marxists argue that capitalism will now experience the crises that Marx had predicted and that Lenin argued had been put off temporarily through imperialism. According to this argument the capitalist system will collapse and the revolution will come. So far this has not happened, and the price of raw materials has fluctuated dramatically. Marxists argue that this is only temporary and caused by the capitalists, who still control the markets for the raw materials.

In discussing the Marxian approach to revolution, it is instructive to distinguish between two different types of revolution—the political and the social. The political revolution takes place when political power is seized by the proletariat. The social revolution takes place later, first through changes made in the property relations of society and second as the superstructure adjusts to these changes.

Marx thought the political revolution would be violent, although he did allow for the possibility of peaceful change. The revolution would probably be violent for two reasons. First, Marx argued that achieving the synthesis would always be sudden; thus the gradualness implicit in peaceful change was ruled out by the dialectic. Second, the bourgeoisie would never agree to its disappearance as a class and would force the proletariat into a violent revolution.

Lenin Marx was a revolutionary. He believed revolution was necessary and good, and throughout his life he was involved in groups that tried to bring about revolutions in various countries. He was expelled from a number of countries for his activities. But it was his followers, particularly Lenin and Mao Zedong, who developed the tactics for and led successful communist revolutions.

Lenin's contribution was the development of the revolutionary party, which was an organizational weapon in the struggle to overthrow capitalism. Lenin argued that such a party was necessary because the proletariat was incapable of recognizing its role as the revolutionary class, whereas the party provided this necessary consciousness. As one scholar stated, "The party is conceived as the organization, incarnation, or institutionalization of class consciousness."[8] The party would be made up of those who had achieved this consciousness and had also become professional revolutionists. In the popular phrase, the party was to be the "vanguard of the proletariat"; it would point the way and lead the proletariat to its goal. The party would bring together the divided masses of workers and would express what they were truly feeling but were unable to express. It would mold them and unify them into a force for change.

Proletarians as individual members of a class would be unlikely to recognize their historic role. In the first place, they would be much too busy attempting to stay alive to be concerned with class questions. Second, very few would ever identify themselves as class members. Thus it would be left up to the few who became aware, the party members, to prepare for the great role the proletariat would play.

---

8. Alfred G. Meyer, *Leninism* (New York: Praeger, 1962), 31–33.

The importance of Lenin's party is found in the idea of the professional revolutionary and in the organizational principle of *democratic centralism*. The party would be composed of a small conspiratorial group of professional revolutionists. But, because no revolution could be successful without the support of, or at least little direct opposition from, the largest part of the population of a country, Lenin believed it should develop contacts throughout the society as a whole. This meant that party members would have to have a variety of organizational skills. They would have to be experts at agitation and propaganda. Since they had to be able to establish and maintain a vast network of "front" organizations, they would have to be expert administrators. Ideally, prior to the revolution, the majority of the population should be organized into a variety of these groups that would also provide the basis for organization once the revolution succeeded. In addition, the party members would have to prepare constantly for the revolution, because it would come only when the masses suddenly revolted against their oppressors.

The party might light the spark that set the masses afire, but the spark could come from anywhere, anytime, and the party had to be ready to ride the revolution into power. The theory of the spark was important to Lenin. One of his newspapers was called *The Spark (Iskra),* and he often referred to the necessity of some incident igniting the masses. Lenin believed it was possible for the party to produce the necessary conditions for a revolution, but he believed it was impossible to be absolutely sure when the revolution would come. Hence the party always had to be prepared for the revolution to come at an unexpected time, perhaps even at a time that was not favorable to the party.

The principle of organization making all this possible is *democratic centralism*. This principle combines freedom of discussion with centralized control and responsibility. Before any decision is made by the party, there should be complete freedom to dissent; after the decision is made, it must be accepted unanimously. Lenin believed this principle could work because all party members started from a position of agreement regarding goals. In practice, freedom of discussion was often forgotten. Democratic centralism would also serve as the principle of organization in the period immediately following the revolution, which will be discussed more completely later.

As a technique of revolutionary organization, democratic centralism has important characteristics. In planning a revolution, care must be taken to organize in order to act at a moment's notice. Everyone must also be able to act in a completely concerted manner without disagreements or squabbles over what is to be done now and what is to be done later, or arguments about the correct techniques of taking over the government or who is to do this or that at a particular moment. It is essential there be complete agreement among the revolutionists over the techniques of the revolution and the organization of society immediately after the successful revolution. Democratic centralism provides this by giving the leaders complete control over the actions of the revolutionists and at the same time allowing all members of the party to participate freely and openly in the process of reaching the appropriate decisions. Again, democratic centralism has usually been used in ways that stressed centralism.

Mao Zedong   Other Marxist theorists have also contributed to the tactics of revolution. For example, Mao Zedong's (1893–1976) theory of guerrilla warfare is also an organizational weapon. Mao's theory can be divided into two parts: the strictly military principles and some political principles derived from one of the military principles. Militarily, Mao developed what are now the commonly recognized principles of guerrilla warfare. These stress a hit-and-run approach, fighting only when fairly certain of victory, and keeping constant pressure on the enemy.[9]

According to Mao, this style of fighting requires a territorial base where the guerrillas will be virtually free from attack so they will be able to rest, train, and so on. In order to achieve this, they must have the positive support of the people in that area. This support is gained by (1) establishing a peasant government, (2) allowing the peasants to redistribute the land, and (3) helping the peasants in whatever rebuilding activities they undertake. The territorial base will provide food, manpower, and, perhaps most important, experience in organization. The network of tunnels used by the Vietcong during the Vietnam War provided a similar resting place. Thus Mao's theory of guerrilla warfare fulfills the same function as Lenin's theory of the revolutionary party. Mao's tactics are designed with the same purposes in mind as Lenin's strategies.

Marx had argued that revolution required an *industrial* proletariat. But the revolutions brought about by both Lenin and Mao took place in countries that were primarily agricultural; this was particularly the case in China. Lenin still argued that he was bringing about a proletarian revolution and worked to develop a base of industrial workers. Mao, while believing that China needed to industrialize quickly, knew that he had no industrial proletariat and changed his analysis to include the peasantry.

Dictatorship of the Proletariat

Marx envisioned a brief transitional period after the revolution, known as the *dictatorship of the proletariat*. This stage was to be characterized by the consolidation of the power of the proletariat through the gradual disappearance of the bourgeoisie and the minor classes, as they became part of the proletariat.

The bourgeoisie and the members of the other classes would be given jobs that would, over time, change their outlook and make them good members of the proletariat. The dictatorship of the proletariat would be the period in which the superstructure would change to adjust to the socialist mode of production. Loosely, the dictatorship of the proletariat should have the following characteristics:

1. distribution of income according to labor performed
2. gradual disappearance of classes
3. the state in the hands of the proletariat
4. increasing productivity

---

9. Mao Zedong, *Selected Works* (Bejing: Foreign Language Press, 1961), 4:161–62.

5. increasing socialist consciousness—people work with few incentives
6. increasing equality
7. a command economy
8. the economy managed by the state

All of these characteristics were expected to change fairly rapidly, and the dictatorship of the proletariat was to be brief. In practice, no country that has followed Marx's ideas has moved beyond the dictatorship of the proletariat. Contrary to Marx's vision, this "transitional" period does not seem to focus on the economic system; as practiced it is based on the political system, with all else as superstructure.

Marx refused to make specific predictions about the future. He argued that people who had themselves been shaped by new experiences would create the new social forms of the future. Except in the most general sense, those socialized in the old, bad society could have no notion of what the new, better society would look like; therefore, Marx never described the dictatorship of the proletariat in any detail. In addition, the dictatorship of the proletariat was to be a short period of transition and would be characterized more by change than by stable institutions. Still, it is possible to say something about the society of the dictatorship of the proletariat because Marx gave enough suggestions to allow some elaboration on the eight points listed previously.

During the dictatorship of the proletariat, the state, as always, will be the tool of the dominant class (in this case the proletariat). The state will be used to achieve a number of related goals. First, the economic system will be reorganized; the means of production must be taken from the capitalists and become the property of the state. The state must also establish a new way of administering the means of production so that the economy is kept running and goods produced, distributed, and consumed. As part of this process, the workers will all become employees of the state (public employees) and will be paid by the state on the basis of the quantity and quality of the work they perform, just as they had been by the previous owners. These previous owners and all other members of the bourgeoisie and the other classes will gradually be absorbed into the proletariat. They will be given jobs, and working for a living will resocialize them into the proletariat's way of thought and belief.

Together these show the operation of a command economy managed by a state in the hands of the proletariat, distribution of income on the basis of work performed, and the gradual disappearance of classes. With the gradual disappearance of classes, there should be greater productivity because there will be more workers available, no unproductive bourgeoisie, and no profit. As a result, equality will increase, and people will become more aware of their roles in society and will require fewer incentives to work.

The dictatorship of the proletariat, it can be seen, represents a unified view of a society in a period of transition. All these factors must be thought of as in a state of change. Some things will change quickly; others will change much more slowly. In practice, of course, a command economy was established that was managed by the state, but in no communist country has the state ever been in the hands of the proletariat, and none of the other changes have occurred. No communist country has even come close to the goals of the dictatorship of the proletariat, let alone the next, and final stage—Full Communism.

Full Communism

The changes in contemporary communism brought about by the fusion of nationalism, the early writings of Marx, and existentialism have given rise to a resurgence of utopian thinking by Marxists. But they have not significantly changed the characteristics of Marx's ideal system, Full or Pure Communism. Full Communism has the following characteristics:

1. Distribution of income according to need, no longer according to labor performed.
2. No classes.
3. The state withers away.
4. Very high productivity, so that there is plenty for all.
5. High socialist consciousness—people work without incentives.
6. More equality but not absolute equality.
7. No money.
8. A command economy.
9. The economy managed by a free and equal association of producers.
10. The differences between occupations disappear, so that there is no social distinction between town and country.
11. Each person does about as much physical as intellectual labor.
12. The system, as Stalin was the first to show, is worldwide.[10]

Full Communism is the goal of the entire system, the utopia or better society toward which all else is aimed. Its general characteristics are not much different from the utopias created by a variety of other socialists throughout the centuries, but some of these characteristics are worth further mention.

The economic aspects of Full Communism are outlined above; the major similarities and differences between it and the dictatorship of the proletariat can be seen by comparing this list with the list in the previous section. The command economy still exists, but it is no longer controlled by the state. Marx was primarily concerned with abolishing exploitation, and in Full Communism there are no exploiters, only workers. With the exploiters gone and the people working without incentives, there should be plenty so that all can be rewarded according to need.

The most direct effect of a change to Full Communism would be on the social stratification and mobility systems. Since classes would no longer exist and since no distinction would be made among types of labor, there would be

---

10. Adapted slightly and reprinted by permission of the author and the publishers from P. J. D. Wiles, *The Political Economy of Communism* (Cambridge: Harvard University Press, © 1962, by Basic Blackwell & Mott Ltd.), 332–33.

little social stratification. In the classless or single-class society, there would be no basis for any significant distinctions among people. *Significant* for Marx meant economic; he did not foresee a complete leveling. Individual differences would remain, but they no longer would be detrimental to the individual or the society as they had been under capitalism and all the other socioeconomic systems preceding it. Occupational mobility would be increased greatly, because an individual would be able to move freely among positions.

Marx envisioned other significant changes in the social system. There would, of course, be no religion. There would be education for all. All crime would disappear because there would be no reason for it. With the coming of Full Communism, prostitution and adultery would disappear, and the monogamous family would become a reality. The new family would be based on a love-sex relationship that Marx believed could have only one focus. At the same time, he wanted to free women from housework. A Marxist scholar has suggested that under Full Communism there will be a change from personal housekeeping functions, such as cooking and cleaning, to public or communal services, thus freeing women to choose among occupations in the same way men can.[11]

With the coming of the classless society, the state would no longer be necessary and would disappear. It would be replaced by "the administration of things," which means the economic system would have to be organized and somebody would have to administer it. It would be administered by "a free and equal association of producers" that would have the authority to direct, according to the needs of the people, what should be produced and in what amounts, and how it should be distributed. This "free and equal association of producers" could conceivably take a wide variety of forms, depending on the size of the territory and the complexity of the industries within the territory. Most such associations would undoubtedly take some such pattern as follows. A committee would be selected, probably by election, that would collect data on the productive capacity of the region and the needs of the people. It would then establish priorities and goals for the various manufacturing plants, farms, and craft industries. This assumes an economy based on abundance and, thus, would be more concerned with collecting accurate data on needs than with establishing priorities. The process would be continuous, and certainly the composition of the committee would change periodically. The committee would hold no coercive power, still assuming abundance, and would merely administer the economy.

This is the goal of Marxism. Many communists today believe Full Communism will never come. Others believe it is still possible. But, whichever position one takes, it illustrates some of the appeal communism has had and will continue to have in the future.

---

11. E. G. Balagushkin, "The Building of Communism and the Evolution of Family and Marital Relations," *Soviet Sociology* 1 (winter 1962–63): 43. Originally published in 1962 in *Voprosy Filosofii*. For some similar early U.S. plans, see Dolores Hayden, *The Grand Domestic Revolution: A History of Feminist Designs for American Homes, Neighborhoods, and Cities* (Cambridge: MIT Press, 1981).

Alternative Marxist Traditions

As mentioned earlier, an alternative tradition within Marxism emphasizes de-centralist and humanitarian aspects of Marx's thought. These alternative traditions provided the basis for the continuation of Marxism as a creative and useful social theory. The line of authoritarianism that Lenin developed was only successful after an intellectual and political struggle, and even Lenin regularly expressed reservations about the direction he took. But the centralization of authority that took place under Joseph Stalin (original name Iosif Vissariono-vich Dzhugashvili, 1879–1953) became the model for all communist countries and could be justified within the writings of Marx and Lenin. Lenin had rejected Stalin as his successor, but Stalin won the struggle for power after Lenin's death.

Those who lost the early struggle with Lenin, however, remained influential in Western Europe. The first stage of development of an alternative Marxism can be seen in the debate between Eduard Bernstein (1850–1932) and Rosa Luxemburg (1870–1919).

Eduard Bernstein Bernstein argued, in a work variously translated as *Evolutionary Socialism* and *The Preconditions of Socialism* (1899), that capitalism was more adaptable than Marx had thought, and, as result, evolution from capitalism to socialism was possible. This position, called Revisionism, led to the development of democratic socialism (see Chapter 4) and poses one of the central dilemmas for revolutionaries: whether to encourage or discourage reform. If reform is successful, the revolution is delayed, but opposing reform is likely to lose support from those who care more for immediate improvement than for a possible revolution. Bernstein's analysis gave strong support for those advocating reform.

Rosa Luxemburg Luxemburg was one of Bernstein's strongest opponents. In her *Social Reform and Revolution* (1899) she argued that revolution was essential. She advocated mass strikes as the best route to the revolution, but she explicitly rejected Lenin's notion of a centralized revolutionary party, believing that such a party would undermine the creativity of the mass of the workers.

Other opponents of the emphasis on centralism emerged in various countries. Three of the most important were Antonio Gramsci (1891–1937) of Italy, and Georg Lukács (1885–1971) of Hungary, and Anton Pannekoek (1873–1960) of the Netherlands.

Antonio Gramsci Gramsci was an advocate of democracy within factories. For example, he proposed that each factory be organized into workshops and each workshop into work crews based on similar skills. Each work crew would elect one of their number as a delegate. These delegates would meet and elect an executive committee, and, in a federal structure above the individual factories, elected representatives from the various factories in the area would meet in a variety of groupings. This system is democratic centralism with the emphasis on democracy.

Also, like Lukács, Gramsci rejected what he saw as Marx's overemphasis on materialism, particularly rejecting dialectical materialism. (See also the discussion of Gramsci's concept of *hegemony* in Chapter 1.)

Georg Lukács In his book *History and Class Consciousness* (1923), which was rejected by the orthodox Marxists of the time, Lukács stressed the need to recognize the role of human creativity in bringing about social change and argued, against what came to be called "vulgar Marxism," that human beings have the ability to think and act freely independent of their material and class positions. Lukács is often given credit for the rebirth of Marxist philosophy in the late twentieth century and is seen as a forerunner of post-Marxism.

Anton Pannekoek and Council Communism Anton Pannekoek went considerably further than Gramsci. He suggested that Full Communism be taken seriously and that there be no governing authority. The councils that he proposed would not be able to require obedience from the people. In this Pannekoek was very close to the type of federal communist anarchism described by Pyotr Kropotkin and discussed in the next chapter.

Marxists like Gramsci and Pannekoek provided the basis for the continuation of an alternative Marxist tradition among Western European and American Marxist theoreticians, and, until recently, among Eastern European Marxists.

The Frankfurt School The Frankfurt Institute for Social Research was founded in 1923, and, under the leadership of Max Horkheimer (1895–1973) and Theodor Adorno (1903–69), it became the foremost center in the West for Marxist research. The school is most noted for the development of *critical theory,* a general theory that views society from the point of view of the need to change it. Marx saw himself as always being both a social theorist and a revolutionary or someone who believed in the need to transform society. In his famous "Eleventh Thesis on Feuerbach," he even emphasized that change was more important than theory: "The philosophers have only *interpreted* the world in various ways; the point is to *change* it." [12]

Although there was great variety among the members, the Frankfurt School's most influential members have been Herbert Marcuse (1898–1979) and Jürgen Habermas (b. 1929). Marcuse combined the insights of Marx with those of Sigmund Freud to develop a vision of a nonrepressive society in his *Eros and Civilization* (1955) and *One-Dimensional Man* (1964). He greatly influenced the New Left. Habermas has focused on the concept of rationality as the basis of his theory. He has worked to develop a broad-based concept of rationality as a means of criticizing contemporary culture and as the foundation for

---

12. Karl Marx, "Theses on Feuerbach," in Karl Marx and Friedrich Engels, *Collected Works* (New York: International Publishers, 1976), 5:5. Emphasis in the original.

positive social change. In doing so he developed a theory of communicative action that he used to critique the concept of modernity while keeping those parts of modernity that he considered most valuable, universal rationality and morality. In his most recent work he explores the tension between law as a means of achieving stability and its normative role in each society. He argues that discursive or deliberative democracy in which there is a continuing process of discussion involving substantial parts of the population will overcome this tension.

Ernst Bloch Bloch (1885–1977) was a German Marxist philosopher who emphasized the utopian aspects of Marxism. In his magnum opus, *Das Prinzip Hoffnung* (*The Principle of Hope*) (1959), and other works, Bloch explored the various manifestations of hope in human history. He argued that the desire for betterment must be brought back to the center of Marxist thought as the real engine of social change. With the recent translation of his works into English, Bloch's writings are beginning to influence contemporary Marxist thought. Earlier Bloch had influenced the development of Liberation Theology.

CURRENT TRENDS

Communism has disappeared as the official ruling force in Eastern Europe and the former Soviet Union. It still exists in China, Cuba, and Vietnam and among numerous parties and groups throughout the world, including dominant parties with new names but the same leaders in parts of Eastern Europe. But, in general, communism as we have known it is coming to an end. It seems appropriate to ask, what happened?

The central problem is that the supposedly short-lived dictatorship of the proletariat, during which the various classes of capitalism were to become one class, became permanent and became a dictatorship in the name of the proletariat but not actually of the proletariat. As Milovan Djilas (1911–95) pointed out in *The New Class* (1955), communism simply replaced capitalist bosses with bureaucratic bosses who ruled in their own interest rather than in the interest of the proletariat. Some have actually called communism *state capitalism*.

Other problems include the fact that it is almost literally impossible to manage all the details of an economy from the center. As a result, many inefficiencies were built into the Soviet economy, gradually developing into the total breakdown we now see. On the other hand, central planning and control worked in the rebuilding of the Soviet Union after World War II and in their space program. We should not forget that it was the Soviet Union that put the first person into space.

In the past few years a small body of work has developed exploring the current situation of Marxism, particularly as a tool of social analysis. Most commentators argue that the greatest relevance of contemporary Marxism is found in the application of Marx's insight into capitalist exploitation to contemporary economic relationships in capitalism. For some, this analysis is particularly relevant to the Third World and neocolonialism. For others, it is most important for understanding developed capitalist societies like the United States, which most people are convinced have demonstrated the success of capitalism and the failure of Marxism. Marxists, to the contrary, argue that capitalism has only been successful in convincing people of its success, rather than being successful in overcoming exploitation. They point to the problems of contemporary American society, where many people find it necessary to work two jobs to earn enough to maintain the standard of living they believe they need. As a result, many people work as many long hours today as they did in Marx's time. And, although in many marriages both spouses choose to work outside the home, many couples feel that both spouses must work, even though they would prefer for one of them to be able to stay at home with the children. In these ways and others, contemporary Marxist theorists contend that Marxism is still relevant as a tool of analysis.[13]

The Relevance of Marxism Today

There are three schools of thought regarding Marxism today, which are often labeled post-Marxism, analytical Marxism, and ecological Marxism.

Post-Marxism   There are two forms of post-Marxism, which are generally called *post*-Marxism and post-*Marxism,* although it is reasonable to see the end results as not that different. *Post*-Marxism simply rejects Marxism as a way of thinking and uses whatever insights Marxists may have had without adopting a "Marxist" way of thinking. Jean-François Lyotard (1924–98) was an early *post*-Marxist who is best known for his exposition of postmodernism.[14]

The major theorists of post-*Marxism* are Ernesto Laclau and Chantal Mouffe, whose book *Hegemony and Socialist Strategy: Towards a Radical Democratic Politics* (1985) was an early challenge to Marxism as usual. Post-*Marxism* grafts developments in poststructuralism, deconstruction, postmodernism, and feminism onto Marxism.

Analytical Marxism   Analytical Marxism is particularly associated with John Elster and John Roemer. They apply the methodology of analytical philosophy and contemporary economic theory to Marxism. This admixture produces a complex, economically sophisticated form of market socialism.

Ecological Marxism   Ecological Marxism tends to focus on a critique of the capitalist mode of production's negative impact on the environment. In this way, it might be thought to be little different from such critiques advanced from within capitalism by environmentalists. But ecological Marxism, or ecosocialism as some prefer to call it, has had a political impact, particularly in Europe,

---

13. For discussions of the applicability of Marxism to a wide range of topics, see Andrew Gamble, David Marsh, and Tony Tant, eds., *Marxism and Social Science* (Urbana: University of Illinois Press, 1999).

14. On Marxism and postmodernism, see Terrell Carver, *The Postmodern Marx* (University Park: Pennsylvania State University Press, 1998).

where so-called Red-Green alliances have been and, in Germany, have been able to form a national government.

SUGGESTED READINGS

Classic Works

Bernstein, Eduard. *Evolutionary Socialism: A Criticism and Affirmation.* Translated by Edith C. Harvey. New York: Schocken Books, 1961. As *The Preconditions of Socialism.* Edited and translated by Henry Tudor. Cambridge: Cambridge University Press, 1993. Both are translations of *Die Voraussetzungen des Sozialismus und die Aufgaben der Sozialdemokratie.* Stuttgart: J H W Dietz, 1899.

Bloch, Ernst. *The Principle of Hope.* Translated by Neville Plaice, Stephen Plaice, and Paul Knight. 3 vols. Oxford: Basil Blackwell, 1986. Originally published as *Das Prinzip Hoffnung.* 3 vols. (Berlin: Aufbau-Verlag, 1955–59).

Debray, Régis. *Revolution in the Revolution? Armed Struggle and Political Struggle in Latin America.* Translated by Bobbye Ortiz. New York: Monthly Review Press, 1967.

Djilas, Milovan. *The New Class: An Analysis of the Communist System.* New York: Harcourt Brace Jovanovich, 1955.

Engels, Friedrich. *The Origin of the Family, Private Property, and the State* (1884).

———. *Socialism: Utopian and Scientific* (1880).

Gramsci, Antonio. *The Modern Prince and Other Writings.* New York: International Publishers, 1957.

Lenin, V. I. *Imperialism: The Highest State of Capitalism* (1916).

———. *State and Revolution* (1918).

———. *What Is to Be Done?* (1902).

Lukács, Georg. *History and Class Consciousness: Studies in Marxist Dialectics.* Translated by Rodney Livingstone. Cambridge: MIT Press, 1971.

Marx, Karl. *Capital* (1867).

———. *Economic and Philosophic Manuscripts of 1844* (first published in 1932).

Marx, Karl, and Friedrich Engels. *The Communist Manifesto* (1848).

Pannekoek, Anton. *Workers' Councils.* Melbourne, Australia: Southern Advocate for Workers' Councils, 1948.

Books and Articles

Albright, David E., ed. *Communism in Africa.* Bloomington: Indiana University Press, 1980.

Althusser, Louis. "Ideology and Ideological State Apparatuses (Notes towards an Investigation)." In his *Lenin and Philosophy and Other Essays,* 121–73. Translated by Ben Brewster. London: NLB, 1971.

———. "Marxism and Humanism." In Althusser, *For Marx,* translated by Ben Brewster, 219–47. New York: Pantheon, 1969.

Anderson, Kevin. *Lenin, Hegel, and Western Marxism.* Urbana: University of Illinois Press, 1995.

Aronson, Ronald. *After Marxism.* New York: Guilford Press, 1995.

Arthur, Christopher. *Engels Today. A Centenary Appreciation.* New York: St. Martin's Press, 1996.

Berman, Marshall. *Adventures in Marxism.* London: Verso, 1999.

Buhle, Paul. *Marxism in the United States: Remapping the History of the American Left.* Rev. ed. London: Verso, 1991.

Burkitt, Paul. *Marx and Nature: A Red and Green Perspective.* New York: St. Martin's Press, 1999.

Carver, Terrell. *The Postmodern Marx.* University Park: Pennsylvania State University Press, 1998.

Carver, Terrell, and Paul Thomas, eds. *Rational Choice Marxism.* University Park: Pennsylvania State University Press, 1995.

Cohen, G. A. *If You're an Egalitarian, How Come You're So Rich?* Cambridge: Harvard University Press, 2000.

Cowling, Mark, ed. *The Communist Manifesto: New Interpretations.* New York: New York University Press, 1998.

Cowling, Mark, and Paul Reynolds, eds. *Marxism, the Millennium and Beyond.* Basingstoke, England: Palgrave, 2000.

Djilas, Milovan. *Fall of the New Class: A History of Communism's Self-Destruction.* Edited Vasilije Kalezic. New York: Knopf, 1998.

Elster, Jon. *Making Sense of Marx.* Cambridge: Cambridge University Press; Paris: Éditions de la Maison des Sciences de l'Homme, 1985.

Elster, Jon, Claus Offe, and Ulrich K. Preuss, with Frank Boenker, Ulrike Goetting, and Friedbert W. Rueb. *Institutional Design in Post-communist Societies: Rebuilding the Ship at Sea.* Cambridge: Cambridge University Press, 1998.

Foster, John Bellamy. *Marx's Ecology: Materialism and Nature.* New York: Monthly Review Press, 2000.

Gamble, Andrew, David Marsh, and Toby Tant, eds. *Marxism and Social Science.* Urbana: University of Illinois Press, 1999.

Gramsci, Antonio. *Letters from Prison.* Translated and edited Lynne Lawner. New York: Harper & Row, 1973.

———. *Pre-Prison Writings.* Edited by Richard Bellamy. Cambridge: Cambridge University Press, 1994.

———. *Selections from Political Writings (1910–1920).* Edited by Quinton Hoare. Translated by John Mathews. London: Lawrence & Wishart, 1977.

———. *Selections from Political Writings (1921–1926).* Edited by Quinton Hoare. Minneapolis: University of Minnesota Press, 1978.

Habermas, Jürgen. *Communication and the Evolution of Society.* Translated by Thomas McCarthy. Boston: Beacon Press, 1979.

Howorth, David. "Post-Marxism." In *New Political Thought: An Introduction,* edited by Adam Lent, 126–42. London: Lawrence & Wishart, 1998.

Kagarlitsky, Boris. *New Realism, New Barbarism: Socialist Theory in the Era of Globalization.* Translated by Renfrey Clarke. London: Pluto Press, 1999.

Keller, Edmond J., and Donald Rothchild. *Afro-Marxist Regimes: Ideology and Public Policy.* Boulder, Colo.: Lynne Rienner, 1987.

Kolakowski, Leszek. *Main Currents of Marxism.* Translated by P. S. Falla. 3 vols. Oxford: Clarendon Press, 1978.

Laclau, Ernesto, and Chantal Mouffe. *Hegemony and Socialist Strategy: Towards a Radical Democratic Politics.* Translated by Winston Moore and Paul Cammack. London: Verso, 1985.

Lipset, Seymour Martin, and Gary Marks. *It Didn't Happen Here: Why Socialism Failed in the United States.* New York: Norton, 2000.

Lukács, Georg. *A Defence of "History and Class Consciousness": Tailism and the Dialectic.* Translated by Esther Leslie. London: Verso, 2000.

Luxemburg, Rosa. *The Accumulation of Capital.* Translated by Agnes Schwarzschild. New York: Monthly Review Press, 1964.

Lyotard, Jean-François. *Libidinal Economy.* Translated by Iain Hamilton Grant. London: Athlone Press; Bloomington: Indiana University Press, 1993. Originally published as *Economie libidinale* (Paris: Les Éditions de Minuit, 1974).

Marcuse, Herbert. *An Essay on Liberation.* Boston: Beacon Press, 1969.

Marx, Karl, and Friedrich Engels. *Collected Works.* 50 vols. New York: International Publishers, 1975–2002.

Munck, Ronaldo. *Marx @ 2000: Late Marxist Perspectives.* London: Macmillan; New York: St. Martin's Press, 2000.

O'Connor, James. "What Is Ecological Socialism?" In O'Connor, *Natural Causes: Essays in Ecological Marxism,* 324–39. New York: Guilford Press, 1998.

Robinson, Cedric J. *Black Marxism: The Making of the Black Radical Tradition.* London: Zed Books, 1983.

Roemer, John. *Analytic Foundations of Marxian Economic Theory.* New York: Cambridge University Press, 1981.

————. *A General Theory of Exploitation and Class.* Cambridge: Harvard University Press, 1982.

Sakwa, Richard. *Postcommunism.* Buckingham, England: Open University Press, 1999.

Service, Robert. *Lenin: A Biography.* Cambridge: Harvard University Press, 2000.

Sim, Stuart. *Post-Marxism: An Intellectual History.* London: Routledge, 2000.

————, ed. *Post-Marxism: A Reader.* Edinburgh: Edinburgh University Press, 1998.

Web Sites

http://www.anu.edu.au/polsci/marx/marx.html Marxism with links to texts

http://www.communist-party.ca/ Communist Party of Canada (Marxist-Leninist)

http://www.cpusa.org/ Communist Party of America

http://www.marxmail.org/ The Marxism Mailing List

http://www.shebeen.com/marx.htm Marxist Sites on the WWW

http://www.marxists.org/archive/Marxist Writers

8

Anarchism
and Libertarianism

Although its roots reach back to classical Greece, anarchism emerged as a major modern ideology at about the same time as Marxism. The word *anarchy* means without a chief or ruler, or rule by no one, but today it is suggestive of disorder or chaos and people connect it to violent protests. As a result, the words *anarchy* and *anarchist* are used indiscriminately to condemn protesters, whether or not any among the protesters are anarchists. This dual perception of anarchism originated in the nineteenth century along with the first statements by anarchist theorists.

Today forms of anarchism exist on the far left and far right of the political spectrum. While anarchism is traditionally identified with the left, a variant that is rooted in mid-nineteenth-century America, *anarcho-capitalism,* is generally identified with the right. And an offshoot of anarchism that developed mostly in the second half of the twentieth century, *libertarianism,* or *minimalism,* is also generally identified with the right.

This chapter examines the principles of both anarchism and libertarianism and shows how anarchism, in particular, has changed in the recent past. Libertarianism, because its followers have been willing to be involved in the political process, rests on the border between anarchism and some form of democracy, but its roots, particularly in the United States, are clearly in the anarchist tradition, and therefore it is discussed here rather than as another subtype of democracy.

PRINCIPLES OF ANARCHISM

The ideology we call anarchism has a variety of forms and includes a number of different ideas. Most studies of anarchism have focused on a select group of men: Prince Pyotr Kropotkin (1842–1921), Pierre-Joseph Proudhon (1809–65), Mikhail Bakunin (1814–76), Count Leo Tolstoi (1828–1910), Max Stirner (1806–56), William Godwin (1756–1836), and William Morris (1834–96), who rejected the label, with sometimes a bow in the direction of a few lesser-known figures such as Errico Malatesta (1853–1932), Élisée Réclus (1830–1905), Benjamin Tucker (1854–1939), and Josiah Warren (1798?-1874). Today anarchists and scholars of anarchism recognize the significant contribution made to the anarchist movement and anarchist theory by women. Emma Goldman (1869–1940) is generally recognized as the most important, but women have always been involved in all aspects of anarchism.

This approach, focused on individual anarchists, may produce a valid presentation and analysis of the clusters of ideas that make up anarchism, but it is just as likely to result in a misunderstanding of the important similarities and the equally important differences among anarchists. The best approach, therefore, seems to be to select those parts of the anarchist tradition that are most important today while striving to maintain a balanced presentation.

Kropotkin once defined *anarchism* as the name

> given to a principle or theory of life and conduct under which society is conceived without government—harmony in such a society being obtained, not by submission to law or by obedience to any authority, but by free agreements concluded between the various groups, territorial and professional, freely constituted for the sake of production and consumption, as also for the satisfaction of the infinite variety of needs and aspirations of a civilized being.[1]

Anarchism is, then, a political philosophy that holds that no group in society should be able to coerce anyone, and society should contain a wide variety of groups arranged to coordinate social functions. Anarchists differ somewhat on the interrelationships among these groups and on the importance of particular groups in the social system, but most would agree with this definition. As another anarchist, Alexander Berkman (1870–1936), stated, "Anarchism teaches that we can live in a society where there is no compulsion of any kind. A life without compulsion naturally means liberty; it means freedom from being forced or coerced, a chance to lead the life that suits you best."[2] Anarchists envision a peaceful, free life without rules and regulations. But many believe anarchism would result in chaos rather than the peaceful, noncoercive society of the vision.

---

1. Peter Kropotkin, "Anarchism," *Encyclopaedia Britannica,* 11th ed., 1:914.

2. Alexander Berkman, *ABC of Anarchism,* 3d ed. (London: Freedom Press, 1964), 10.

Pyotr (Peter) Kropotkin (1842–1921) was born into the Russian aristocracy but became the most important anarchist thinker of all time. Kropotkin's ideas originated during a long trip in Siberia as a geographer and naturalist. Intending to demonstrate that there was a "struggle for survival" and "survival of the fittest," he found instead cooperation and what he came to call "mutual aid." He published his findings in a series of essays between 1890 and 1896 and then collected them as *Mutual Aid* (1902). His argument that cooperation rather than competition is the basis of evolution became the foundation for all his thought. From this position he contended that anarchism, not Marxism, was scientific. After escaping from a Russian prison, he spent most of his life in western Europe, primarily in En-

The Bettmann Archive

gland, where he published his most famous books, *The Conquest of Bread* (1892), *Memoirs of a Revolutionist* (1898–99), and *Fields, Factories, and Workshops* (1899). He returned to Russia after the revolution in 1917 but quickly came into conflict with Lenin, whom he criticized for centralizing power.

The basic assumption of anarchism is that power exercised by one person or group over another is the cause of most of our contemporary problems. As one anarchist says, "Many people say that government is necessary because some men cannot be trusted to look after themselves, but anarchists say that government is harmful because no man can be trusted to look after anyone else."[3] All anarchists would agree with this statement. They all focus on the corrupting nature of power, and they believe that human beings are capable of organizing their affairs without anyone exercising authority over others. This does not mean there will be no order in society, except temporarily; it means people can cooperatively produce a better system than can be produced by any authority. "Given a common need, a collection of people will, by trial and error, by improvisation and experiment, evolve order out of chaos—this order being more durable than any kind of externally imposed order."[4] This order—this organization —will be better designed for human needs than any imposed system could be because it will be "(1) voluntary, (2) functional, (3) temporary, and (4) small."[5]

---

3. Nicolas Walter, *About Anarchism* (London: Freedom Press, 1969), 6. Originally published as *Anarchy* 100, vol. 9 (June 1969).

4. Colin Ward, "Anarchism as a Theory of Organization," *Anarchy* 62, vol. 6 (April 1966): 103.

5. Ward, "Anarchism," 101. See also Terry Phillips, "Organization—The Way Forward," *Freedom* 31 (August 22, 1970): 3.

Each of these last points is important for an understanding of anarchism. First, basic to all anarchism is the voluntary nature of any association. Second, an association will develop only to fill a fairly specific need and thus will be designed to fill that need alone. Therefore, third, it will disappear after the need is met. Finally, it must be small enough so people can control it rather than be controlled by it. There are many examples of such organizations functioning within contemporary society, such as many of the cooperatives discussed in Chapter 4.

The belief that it is possible to replace a coercive society with voluntary cooperation is about the only thing anarchists agree on. But "the essence of anarchism, the one thing without which it is not anarchism, is the negation of authority over anyone by anyone."[6]

Or, as another theorist put it, "Nobody is fit to rule anybody else. It is not alleged that people are perfect, or that merely through his/her natural goodness (or lack of same) he/she should (or should not) be permitted to rule. Rule as such causes abuse."[7]

Beyond this, anarchism divides loosely into two categories: (1) collectivist, with emphasis on the individual within a voluntary association of individuals; and (2) individualist, with emphasis on the individual separate from any association. The former is sometimes divided into communist anarchism and anarcho-syndicalism; the latter is usually divided into individualist anarchism and anarcho-capitalism. In each case, though, the similarities are more important than the differences.

Collectivist Anarchism

Communist anarchism, traditionally associated with Kropotkin, is the most developed and comprehensive anarchist theory. It starts, as does all anarchism, with the assumption that coercion in any form is bad. As the solution to the problem of order in a society without a government, it suggests the establishment of a series of small, voluntary communes or collectives. These communes would join together into a federation to deal with any common problems. As George Woodcock (1912–95) wrote, "The village would appoint delegates to the regional federations, which in their turn would appoint delegates to the national federations. No delegate would have the power to speak for anything but the decisions of the workers who elected him and would be subject to recall at any time."[8] He goes on to say that the delegates would be elected for a short period of time, and although expenses might be paid, the delegate would receive exactly the same salary as if still working at his or her regular job. In this way, the anarchist delegate is a very restricted representative.

---

6. Walter, *About Anarchism*, 8.

7. Albert Meltzer, *Anarchism, Arguments For and Against* (Edinburgh: AK Press, 1996), 19.

8. George Woodcock, *New Life to the Land* (London: Freedom Press, 1942), 26.

Anarcho-syndicalists take essentially the same approach, except that they refer specifically to the work situation, particularly industrial work. The basic principles are as follows:

1. Each industry is organized into a federation of independent syndicates.
2. The workers in that industry control each industry.
3. Policy questions and questions of relations among syndicates are handled by a coordinating council.

Rudolf Rocker (1873–1958), one of the theorists of anarcho-syndicalism, described the system as follows:

> The workers in each locality join the unions of their respective trades, and these are subject to the veto of no Central but enjoy the entire right of self-determination. The trade unions of a city or a rural district combine in a so-called labour cartel. The labour cartels are grouped according to districts and regions to form the National Federation of Labour Cartels, which maintain the permanent connection between the local bodies, arranges for free adjustment of the productive labour of the members of the different organizations on co-operative lines, provide for the necessary co-ordination in the work of education, in which the stronger cartels will need to come to the aid of the weaker ones, and in general support the local groups with counsel and guidance.[9]

The key to understanding anarcho-syndicalism is its industrial base. The central element of anarcho-syndicalism is workers' control,[10] in which the workers in that industry organize society on the basis of the control of each industry. The word *industry* is normally defined broadly to include such activities as the building industry, which then would be controlled by all the different workers who participate in building any structure. These individuals meet to resolve the particular problems of that industry; then representatives of each industry assemble to administer the economic life of the entire country. The key word here is *administer*.

This is the same as Engels's statement that in the final stage of communism, the government of people will become the administration of things. People will no longer be governed. They will be free from government, but they will participate in administering the economic life of the country. The contention is that there need be no such thing as a political decision. The administration of things should be, according to anarcho-syndicalism, a fairly simple and mechanical operation not giving rise to many conflicts. When conflicts do arise because of, for example, problems of allocating scarce goods, the workers will be in the best position to know what is most important, what can be produced least expensively, and how to improve production. Therefore, these workers

---

9. Rudolf Rocker, *Anarcho-Syndicalism* (1938; London: Pluto Press, 1989), 93.

10. There is a vast literature on workers' control. For a sampling, see *Workers' Control,* ed. Ken Coates and Tony Topham (London: Panther Books, 1970), and *Anarchy* 2, vol. 1 (April 1961).

rather than managers who are not in contact with the actual work should be making such decisions. The anarcho-syndicalist also argues that putting the workers in control will enable them to produce more, thus lessening the problem of the allocation of scarce goods. The anarcho-syndicalist argues that workers' control acts as a work incentive.

Some anarcho-syndicalists have argued that the basis for the new society is to be found in the organization of the present trade unions, but most anarcho-syndicalists view trade unions as conservative. Although the idea of syndicalism originated as part of the trade union movement in France, anarcho-syndicalism has moved away from the union movement. Modern anarcho-syndicalists oppose the existing union movement and argue that it fails to support workers against management and government.

The differences between communist anarchism and anarcho-syndicalism are not great. Anarcho-syndicalism is more directly concerned with the organization of industry than is communist anarchism, but both arrive at fundamentally the same conclusions. Both accept the notion that the people in a given area should administer that area for the benefit of the society as a whole. It is assumed in both cases that the entire population will be workers in that everyone will participate to some degree in the economic life of the society. Both believe that by removing coercion a viable society can develop. The primary difference is found in the emphasis in anarcho-syndicalism on the operation of the industrial system.

Anarcho-syndicalism and communist anarchism developed a secondary level of organization that is important for understanding the course of anarchist thought. Both stress the need for some way of developing cooperation among communes or industries as well as within the commune or industry. Although the focus of most studies of anarchist thought has been on individual freedom, anarchists have always argued that it is not possible to stop there. The primary focus of collectivist anarchism is not the isolated individual, but on an individual within a noncoercive society, one that will allow individual freedom. Most anarchists recognize that the small commune or industry is not sufficient for individuals in contemporary society. Some cooperation among communes and industries is necessary to produce enough goods in sufficient diversity for each individual.

This idea is most clearly recognized in anarcho-syndicalism because its basic form of organization—the industry—is specialized. Therefore, in order to give each individual the goods necessary for life, there must be a high degree of cooperation among industries to provide an efficient distribution system for the goods produced by the individual industries. The only way to handle this is through cooperation by the workers within the various industries. To some extent, what is looked for here is simply a form of enlightened self-interest, because each worker in a particular industry needs the products of a wide variety of industries. Therefore, all workers will cooperate because they all need the products of each and every industry. Anarcho-syndicalists believe this cooperation can be developed readily once coercion disappears. To achieve this, government and, for the collective anarchist, capitalism must go.

Getting rid of them raises the question of means, and this raises the question of violence. Anarchists believe no established authority will simply give up without a fight; therefore, revolution is likely to be the means of change.[11] The abolition of capitalism is a central concern for most anarchists because they believe workers are exploited by the capitalist in about the same ways Marx believed. Collectivist anarchists argue for common ownership of the means of production and the distribution of goods according to need. Anarcho-capitalists, discussed shortly, believe that this system would exploit the best workers. Collectivist anarchists respond that capitalism exploits all workers. It may be that this disagreement is incapable of being solved, but to put it in perspective, let us look at the individualist position.

Individualist Anarchism

The individualist anarchist recognizes nothing above his ego and rebels against all discipline and all authority, divine or human. He accepts no morality and when he gives himself to the feelings of love, friendship, or sociability, he does so because it is a personal need, an egoistic satisfaction —because it pleases him to do it.[12]

Individualist anarchism is traditionally associated with Max Stirner. Essentially the position is as stated above; individuals determine for themselves, out of their own needs and desires, what is right for them. Stirner even applies this to murder.[13]

Individualist anarchists do not completely reject cooperation. They argue that cooperation is essential for the fulfillment of some needs. But they contend that only the individualist of their own definition is capable of genuinely forming a voluntary association with others. In addition, they never see this association as an end in itself but merely as useful for a temporary purpose. It must serve the members, not dominate the members.

Individualist anarchists argue against the collective ownership of goods, but not all are convinced the capitalist system is any better. Here, one finds a major split in the ranks of individualist anarchists. On one hand, there are those that reject both capitalism and socialism and argue that they are not convinced that either system is valid. On the other hand, there are anarcho-capitalists.

Anarcho-Capitalism

Anarcho-capitalists contend that the only form of economic life compatible with individualism is capitalism. Usually their approach is connected with a view of life similar to that of the social Darwinist. They see life as a struggle for survival and hold that a socialist economic system supports those who do not

11. For a discussion, see Vernon Richards, ed., *Violence & Anarchism: A Polemic* (London: Freedom Press, 1993).

12. Enzo Martucci, "Individualist Amoralism," *Minus One,* no. 16 (November–December 1966): 5, trans. J.-P.S. from *L'Unique,* no. 37.

13. See Max Stirner [Johan Kasper Schmidt], *The Ego and His Own,* ed. David Leopold, trans. Steven T. Byington, 167–68 (Cambridge: Cambridge University Press, 1995).

deserve to survive. Anarcho-capitalists take the position that all essential social services can be better operated privately for profit than by any government or commune; this includes the police, education, the military, and so forth.

Anarcho-capitalists trace their origins to Max Stirner and the individualist anarchist tradition; in the United States one of the earliest anarcho-capitalists was Lysander Spooner (1808–87), who argued for the abolition of slavery on anarchist grounds and, after the Civil War, wrote tracts opposing all government. In the twentieth century, much U.S. anarcho-capitalism stems from Ayn Rand (1905–82), but its most sophisticated advocate was Murray Rothbard (1926–95).

Libertarianism

Closely related to anarcho-capitalism is libertarianism, sometimes called *minimalism* because some theorists include a role for government. Probably the best-known libertarian/minimalist text is *Anarchy, State, and Utopia* (1974) [14] by Robert Nozick (1938–2002), in which Nozick argues for a minimal government, saying "Our main conclusions about the state are that a minimal state, limited to the narrow functions of protection against force, theft, fraud, enforcement of contracts, and so on is justified; that any more extensive state will violate persons' rights not to be forced to do certain things, and is unjustified; and the minimal state is inspiring as well as right." [15] His ideal system consists of a number of small communities where the members have agreed on a particular way of life, and there would be many different communities so that a wide variety of ways of living would be possible. But in 1989 Nozick at least partially backed away from his libertarian position, saying "The libertarian position I once propounded now seems to me seriously inadequate, in part because it did not fully knit the humane considerations and joint cooperative activities it left room for more closely into its fabric." [16] As a result, its author has undermined the most sophisticated and well worked out defense of libertarianism.

In the United States, one of the forms taken by libertarianism is the Libertarian Party, a political party supporting candidates for office who are pledged to severely reduce government.

The "Preamble" to the Libertarian Party platform for the 2000 election says, "As Libertarians, we seek a world of liberty; a world in which all individuals are sovereign over their own lives, and no one is forced to sacrifice his or her values for the benefit of others." [17] In language repeated from previous platforms, the 2000 platform says,

14. For discussions of this book, see Jeffrey Paul, ed., *Reading Nozick: Essays on Anarchy, State, and Utopia* (Totowa, N.J.: Rowman & Littlefield, 1981); J. Angelo Corlett, ed., *Equality and Liberty: Analyzing Rawls and Nozick. Property, Justice, and the Minimal State* (Stanford, Calif.: Stanford University Press, 1991).

15. Robert Nozick, *Anarchy, State, and Utopia* (New York: Basic Books, 1974), ix.

16. Robert Nozick, "The Zigzag of Politics," in Nozick, *The Examined Life: Philosophical Meditations* (New York: Simon & Schuster, 1989), 186–87.

17. 2000 Libertarian Party Platform. http://www/lp/org/issues/platform/

> We, the members of the Libertarian Party, challenge the cult of the om-
> nipotent state and defend the rights of the individual. We hold that all
> individuals have the right to exercise sole dominion over their own lives,
> and have the right to live in whatever manner they choose, so long as
> they do not forcibly interfere with the equal right of others to live in
> whatever manner they choose.[18]

And the platform stresses that to achieve these goals, government power must
be strictly limited:

> where governments exist, they must not violate the rights of any individ-
> ual: namely, (1) the right to life—accordingly we support the prohibition
> of physical force against others; (2) the right to liberty of speech and action
> —accordingly we oppose all attempts by government to abridge the free-
> dom of speech and press, as well as government censorship in any form;
> and (3) the right to property—accordingly we oppose all government in-
> terference with private property, such as confiscation, nationalization, and
> eminent domain, and support the prohibition of robbery, trespass, fraud,
> and misrepresentation.[19]

The platform specifies many areas in which government should not be involved, such as the use of drugs, alcohol, consensual sexual relations (both heterosexual and homosexual), pornography, and gambling, all of which are called
"victimless crimes," but much of the platform is concerned with property. Regarding property, in language again repeated from earlier platforms, the 2000
platform says, "There is no conflict between property rights and human rights.
Indeed, property rights are the rights of humans with respect to property and,
as such, are entitled to the same respect and protection as all other human
rights."[20] All human rights are property rights based on self-ownership. "Our
bodies are our property every bit as much as is justly acquired land or material
objects. We further hold that the owners of property have the full rights to control, use, dispose of, or in any manner enjoy their property without interference, until and unless the exercise of their control infringes the valid rights of
others."[21]

ANARCHIST SOCIAL THOUGHT

All of anarchism, whether communist, anarcho-syndicalist, or individualist, is
concerned with the freedom of the individual. Anarchism rejects control by
any group, but particularly by the organized group we call the state or government. Anarchists argue that people are capable of both freedom and coopera-

---

18. Ibid.
19. Ibid.
20. Ibid.
21. Ibid.

tion. They believe human beings are willing and able to help each other. They believe the human being's best instincts are destroyed by the present organization of society. They believe, as did Marx, that true love between individuals is impossible, or virtually impossible, under contemporary conditions. They believe a morality system that rejects physical relationships without the sanction of church and state destroys the possibility of developing what Marx called the love-sex relationship. The anarchist does not insist on or reject the simple monogamous marriage relationship. Individuals, they contend, must decide about what kind of relationship they want. It is their life; they must be free to live it as they choose.

The anarchist also contends that parents have a real responsibility to ensure freedom for their children. Anarchists believe the contemporary educational system is destructive of freedom, creativity, and learning. They believe there must be an educational system directed to the individual child, whatever her or his needs. Education directed to the individual child cannot be found, they contend, in the highly organized, overly complex system we have today. It can be found in the small group concerned with educating for freedom. Anarchists believe a child, given the freedom to choose and the encouragement to follow his or her own bent, will gradually find distinct interests and, getting interested, will apply to those interests the tremendous energies children can develop. Children will learn more this way than by traditional methods.

Much of what we are taught in our schools, the anarchist believes, is irrelevant to our lives; we waste many years in attempting to learn things that will never interest us or be of any use to us. A child should be encouraged to look at the world and interpret it on her or his own rather than being given answers. This approach to education puts a tremendous burden on parents and teachers. Teachers must develop a close relationship with the child in order to be able to understand the child's changing interests and to suggest ways in which the child might best fulfill them. This must be done without too much direction. Parents must be capable of giving the child freedom. Parents must not control children too much. Anarchist theories of child rearing and education have been some of the most innovative, instructive, and successful of any of the anarchist approaches to contemporary life.[22] Related to these theories is the *homeschooling* movement in which parents choose to educate their children at home rather than expose them to public education. For some parents the motivation is religious; for some it is concern over the quality of education; and for others it centers on educating their children for freedom.[23]

There is no anarchist proscription or support of religion. Within anarchist circles, considerable debate takes place over the question of religious affiliation.

---

22. See, for example, Herbert Read, *The Education of Free Men* (London: Freedom Press, 1944); A. S. Neill, *Summerhill: A Radical Approach to Child Rearing* (New York: Hart Publication, 1960); Neill, *A Dominie's Log* (1915; London: Hogarth Press, 1986); Ivan D. Illich, *Deschooling Society* (London: Calder; New York: Harper & Row, 1971); and *Education without Schools,* ed. Peter Buckman (London: Souvenir Press, 1973).

23. http://www.homeschooltoday.com/home/htm; http://www.home-ed-magazine .com/wlcm_HEM.html; http://www.home-school.com/; http://www.montessori .edu/homeschooling.html

Many argue that such affiliation is incompatible with anarchism, while others argue that it depends on the type of organization or church. Still others, including Catholic anarchists such as Dorothy Day (1897–1980) and Ammon Hennacy (1893–1970) (who left the church shortly before he died), argued that faith in the doctrines of the church did not affect them as anarchists. They held that the church speaks only on matters of faith and morals. Outside of these areas, Catholic anarchists consider themselves free of the church. The Catholic anarchist is merely a special case of contemporary anarchism. Individuals such as Day and Hennacy, who accepted an authoritarian religion and at the same time considered themselves anarchists, were merely taking one part of their lives, that part dealing with questions of religious faith, and there accepting the dictates of the church. As long as this acceptance is restricted to religious and, perhaps, moral questions, it does not necessarily affect the social and political positions of the anarchist. Today Dorothy Day's Catholic Worker Movement continues in cities and country communities devoted to assisting those at the very bottom of the social ladder. Recently, church authorities, who opposed Day during her lifetime, have suggested that she be considered for sainthood.

Anarchist theory has developed mostly as a series of commentaries on specific areas of life that are believed to be coercive and that could be improved by providing a free atmosphere. The ultimate goal is a truly free life in a commune that weaves together the various ways of being free.

Anarchism will probably always remain a minor ideology. While unlikely to ever succeed in this world, anarchism is the ideology that has the most faith in people. It believes, more than any other ideology does, that people are capable of freedom and cooperation.

As Colin Ward wrote, "Anarchism in all its guises is an assertion of human dignity and responsibility."[24]

CURRENT TRENDS

In the last quarter of the twentieth century a number of creative anarchist thinkers have published innovative applications of anarchist theory to current issues of public policy. The most important of these writers is Colin Ward (b. 1924), a freelance writer who has been particularly concerned with transportation policy, housing and town planning, and environmental policy. Ward's most recent work has focused on architecture. Alex Comfort (1920–2000) is best known for his writings arguing for a freed sexuality, but he has contributed substantially to anarchist theory in the area of aging.

Recently Murray Bookchin (b. 1921), in *Social Anarchism or Lifestyle Anarchism* (1995) has argued that anarchism is in serious danger of losing its value because many anarchists are what he calls "lifestyle anarchists" rather than being seriously involved in trying to change social policy. "Lifestyle anarchists" are, according to Bookchin, committed to individual autonomy rather than to a

---

24. Colin Ward, *Anarchism in Action,* 2d ed. (London: Freedom Press, 1982), 143.

Library of Congress

Emma Goldman (1869–1940), also known as "Red Emma," was a leading anarchist, lecturer, popularizer of the arts, and agitator for birth control, women's rights, and free speech. Born in Russia, she emigrated to the United States in 1885. In 1889 she moved from Rochester, New York to New York City, where she met Johann Most (1846–1906) and Alexander Berkman (1870–1936) and became active with them in anarchist circles. In 1892 she and Berkman attempted to assassinate the industrial leader Henry Clay Frick. She edited the journal *Mother Earth* (1906–17) and wrote a number of books, including *Anarchism and Other Essays* (1911), *The Social Significance of Modern Drama* (1914), and *Living My Life* (1931). She was involved in most radical activities in the United States until she was deported as an undesirable alien in 1919. After she was deported she traveled in the Soviet Union and wrote *My Disillusionment with Russia* (1923) and *My Further Disillusionment with Russia* (1924), both of which discussed the authoritarian nature of the Soviet government. After leaving Russia she continued her career as a radical agitator through involvement in the Spanish civil war.

collective vision of social freedom for all. The issue Bookchin raises is important; many people who believe in anarchism do not think that a fully anarchist society is possible. As a result, they choose to try to live their own lives as freely as possible, but with little or no concern for others. But unless anarchism remains a major critic of contemporary social and political policy, it will lose all claim to be taken seriously as a living ideology.

Bookchin, who will also be discussed in Chapter 12, is a critic of contemporary technology and an advocate of what he calls social ecology. Bookchin writes that "social ecology 'radicalizes' nature, or more precisely, our understanding of natural phenomena, by questioning the prevailing marketplace image of nature from an ecological standpoint: nature as a constellation of communities that are . . . freed of all anthropocentric moral trappings, a *participatory* realm of interactive life-forms whose most outstanding attributes are fecundity, creativity, and directiveness, marked by complementarity that renders the natural world the *grounding* for an ethics of freedom rather than domination." [25]

Anarchism and Globalism

Anarchism has been making headlines in the past few years. Those producing the violence at the WTO (World Trade Organization) meeting in Seattle, the G-8 (Group of 8) meeting in Genoa, Italy, and at other economic and political meetings designed to foster globalism have identified themselves as anarchists and, in a few cases, have worn black clothes and carried the black flag symbolic of anarchism. Most of the protesters have tried to distance themselves from these anarchists, but officials, particularly in Genoa, used the anarchists as an excuse for a violent attack on all the protesters.

Anarchists have long had an ambivalent attitude toward the use of violence. Many anarchists have argued that violence is most often ineffective and commonly counterproductive. It may give the violent demonstrators the feeling that they are personally doing something about the evil they oppose, and it certainly gets the attention of the media (these days the main reason for its use), but it rarely changes policy and frequently produces a backlash against the position being advocated.

The supporters of violence as a tool/weapon contend that it is the only way to get the attention of the media, who without it would ignore the opposition at such meetings. Indeed, violence staged for the cameras, sometimes with the collusion of the media, is a regular feature of demonstrations. Violence is also used by the ignored powerless simply as an expression of frustration. Those whose beliefs fall outside the dominant ideologies/paradigms of the countries in which they live rarely have ways to be heard. They may come to believe that the only way to get heard is to throw a stone through the window of a shop, attack the police, or trash a city center.

And there is some merit to the argument. When a protester in Genoa was killed by a police officer, the G-8 leaders all said that they were responsive to the concerns expressed by the protesters, that they were actually trying to solve the problems the protesters raised. The protesters' response was that they wanted action, not talk, and that the leaders would not even have *said* they were aware of the issues without the protests. Therefore, both peaceful and violent protesters will be at future meetings. In hopes of being able to control protesters' access, the next G-8 meeting was scheduled for a very small resort in the Canadian Rockies.

TAZ, or Temporary Autonomous Zones

One of the most interesting developments within anarchism is what Hakim Bey (Peter Lamborn Wilson) calls TAZ, or Temporary Autonomous Zones, and George McKay (b. 1950) called DiY (Do-it-Yourself) culture. Both labels

---

25. Murray Bookchin, *The Modern Crisis,* 2d rev. ed. (Montreal: Black Rose Books, 1987), 55.

suggest a free space in which people can temporarily create the life they want, where one can, briefly, be free.

The collection *DiY Culture* (1998) uses, among other examples, the long-term protests against military bases and construction projects in the United Kingdom as instances in which free communities were established. Other examples include New Age Travelers and the Rainbow Gatherings.[26] A much more temporary version are the "raves," or music and dance festivals, that occur apparently spontaneously but actually mostly by word of mouth in urban and rural settings and last, most often, for one night. In Britain, there has been a collective creating them; in the United States they are often quasi-commercial enterprises.

TAZ opens up a space in which it is possible for believers to live their beliefs for a while. Julia "Butterfly" Hill lived in her tree for two years; a few of the women protesting the siting of nuclear missiles at Greenham Common Air Base stayed for years, but most were there for short periods. Woodstock and other music festivals are short-lived but still provide a different space for that length of time. There is a lesbian music camp and some lesbian communes that are re-created each summer (other lesbian communes are permanent) in which the women say that they are able to truly be themselves, as they cannot be the rest of the year.

For some, the temporary can become permanent. New Age Travelers are noticed only when they gather in groups for one of their periodic festivals. While for some the Rainbow Gatherings are a once-a-year festival, others travel from gathering to gathering, which now occur in Europe as well as in North America.

These are people who used to be called "dropouts," although most of them prefer to say that they "dropped in" to a better life. But the most common way anarchism is practiced is through individual life choices—for example, to teach in a school in which pupils are given freedom as opposed to teaching in a traditional, hierarchical public or private school.[27]

LETS, or Local Exchange and Trading Systems

An example of TAZ is LETS, or local exchange and trading systems in which, "a number of people get together to form an association. They create a unit of exchange, choose a name for it, and offer each other goods and services priced in these units. These offers and wants are listed in a directory, which is circulated periodically to members. Members decide who to trade with and how much trading they want to do."[28] There are many LETS groups, ranging from

---

26. Richard Lowe and William Shaw, *Travellers: Voices of the New Age Nomads* (London: Fourth Estate, 1993); Michael I. Niman, *People of the Rainbow: A Nomadic Utopia* (Knoxville: University of Tennessee Press, 1997).

27. Colin Ward describes DiY culture (although he does not call it that) at work in a community in "Anarchy in Milton Keynes," *The Raven*, no. 18 (5.2) (April-June 1992): 116–31.

28. Harold Sculthorpe, "LETS: Local Exchange and Trading Schemes," *The Raven*, no. 31 (8.3) (autumn 1995): 237.

child–care groups in which parents in a neighborhood exchange taking care of children so that they can sometimes have a night out, to Womanshare in New York City, which has created a "Skill Bank" in which each woman gains credit for the work she contributes,[29] to Tucson Traders, a bartering and trading network,[30] to local currency schemes like Ithaca HOURS, BloomingHours, the Maine Time Dollar Network, and Bread Hours in the San Francisco Bay area.[31] There are hundreds of such groups in existence today.

SUGGESTED READINGS

Some Classic Works

Bakunin, Mikhail. *God and the State*. New York: Mother Earth Press, 1916.

Berkman, Alexander. *ABC of Anarchism*. 3d ed. London: Freedom Press, 1964.

Bookchin, Murray. *Post-Scarcity Anarchism*. Berkeley, Calif.: Ramparts Press, 1971.

Freire, Paulo. *Pedagogy of the Oppressed*. Translated by Myra Bergman Ramos. New York: Seabury Press, 1970.

Godwin, William. *Enquiry Concerning Political Justice and Its Influence on Morals and Happiness*. Edited by R. E. L. Priestley. 3 vols. Toronto: University of Toronto Press, 1946. Originally published 2 vols., London: Printed for G. G. J. and J. Robinson, 1793.

Goldman, Emma. *Anarchism and Other Essays*. New York: Mother Earth Press, 1910.

————. *Living My Life*. 2 vols. New York: Dover, 1970.

Kropotkin, Peter. *The Conquest of Bread*. New York: Putnam's, 1907.

————. *Fields, Factories, and Workshops*. New York: Benjamin Blom, 1968.

————. *Fields, Factories, and Workshops Tomorrow*. Edited by Colin Ward. London: George Allen & Unwin, 1974.

————. *Kropotkin's Revolutionary Pamphlets*. Edited by Roger N. Baldwin. New York: Dover, 1970.

————. *Memoirs of a Revolutionist*. Edited by James Allen Rogers. Garden City, N.Y.: Doubleday, 1962.

————. *Mutual Aid: A Factor of Evolution*. Boston: Extending Horizons Books, 1955.

Malatesta, Errico. *Anarchy*. 8th ed. London: Freedom Press, 1949.

Nozick, Robert. *Anarchy, State, and Utopia*. New York: Basic Books, 1974.

Proudhon, Pierre-Joseph. *What Is Property? An Inquiry into the Principle of Right and of Government*. Edited and translated by Donald R. Kelley and Bonnie G. Smith. 1840. Cambridge: Cambridge University Press, 1994.

Stirner, Max [Johan Kasper Schmidt]. *The Ego and His Own*. Edited by David Leopold. Translated by Steven T. Byington. Cambridge: Cambridge University Press, 1995.

Tolstoy, Leo. *The Law of Love and the Law of Violence*. Translated by Mary Koutouzow Tolstoy. London: Anthony Blond, 1970.

Tucker, Benjamin R. *Individual Liberty: Selections from the Writings of Benjamin R.*

---

29. http://www.angelfire.com/ar2/womanshare/

30. http://www.tucsontraders.org/

31. http://www.ithacahours.org/; http://www.bloomington.in.us~blmghour/; http://www.mtdn.org/; and http://www.breadhours.org/.
    For a listing of such currency schemes in North America, see http://www.schumachersociety.org/cur_grps.html/.

Tucker. Edited by C. L. S. New York: Vanguard Press, 1926.

Ward, Colin. *Anarchy in Action.* 2d ed. London: Freedom Press, 1982.

Books and Articles

Avrich, Paul. *Anarchist Portraits.* Princeton, N.J.: Princeton University Press, 1988.

———. *Bakunin & Nechaev.* London: Freedom Press, 1974.

———. *The Modern School Movement: Anarchism and Education in the United States.* Princeton, N.J.: Princeton University Press, 1980.

Bendall, Lisa. "Anarchism and Feminism." *The Raven,* no. 21 (6.1) (January–February 1993): 34–42.

Berneri, Camillo. *Peter Kropotkin: His Federalist Ideas.* London: Freedom Press, 1942.

Bey, Hakim [Peter Lamborn Wilson]. *Immediatism.* Edinburgh: AK Press, 1994. Originally published as *Radio Sermonettes* (New York: Libertarian Book Club, 1992).

———. *Millennium.* Brooklyn, N.Y.: Autonomedia; Dublin: Garden of Delight, 1996.

———. *T. A. Z. The Temporary Autonomous Zone, Ontological Anarchy, Poetic Terrorism.* Brooklyn, N.Y.: Autonomedia, 1991.

Boaz, David. *Libertarianism: A Primer.* New York: Free Press, 1997.

Bookchin, Murray. *Anarchism, Marxism, and the Future of the Left.* Edinburgh: AK Press, 1999.

———. *The Modern Crisis.* 2d rev. ed. Montreal: Black Rose Books, 1987.

———. *Social Anarchism or Lifestyle Anarchism: An Unbridgeable Chasm.* San Francisco: AK Press, 1994.

Brooks, Frank H., ed. *The Individualist Anarchists: An Anthology of "Liberty" (1881–1908).* New Brunswick, N.J.: Transaction, 1994.

Carter, April. *The Political Theory of Anarchism.* London: Routledge & Kegan Paul, 1971.

Christie, Stuart, and Albert Meltzer. *The Floodgates of Anarchy.* London: Kahn & Averill, 1970.

Debord, Guy. *The Society of the Spectacle.* Translated by Donald Nicholson-Smith. New York: Zone Books, 1994.

De Cleyre, Voltairine. *Selected Works of Voltairine de Cleyre.* Edited by Alexander Berkman. New York: Mother Earth Press, 1914.

DeLeon, David. *The American as Anarchist: Reflections on Indigenous Radicalism.* Baltimore: Johns Hopkins University Press, 1978.

DuBrul, Sascha Altman. *Carnival of Chaos: On the Road with the Nomadic Festival.* Philadelphia: Bloodlink Press, 1997.

Freire, Paulo. *Pedagogy of Freedom: Ethics, Democracy, and Civic Courage.* Translated by Patrick Clarke. Lanham, Md.: Rowman & Littlefield, 1998.

———. *Pedagogy of Hope: Reliving Pedagogy of the Oppressed. With Notes by Ana Maria Araújo Freire.* Translated by Robert R. Barr. New York: Continuum, 1999.

———. *Pedagogy of the City.* Translated by Donaldo Macedo. New York: Continuum, 1993. Interviews that Freire gave while head of the school system in São Paulo, Brazil.

Gladstein, Mimi Reisel. *The Ayn Rand Companion.* Westport, Conn.: Greenwood Press, 1984.

Goodway, David. "The Politics of Herbert Read." In *Herbert Read Reassessed,* edited by David Goodway, 177–95. Liverpool: Liverpool University Press, 1998.

Guérin, Daniel. *Anarchism from Theory to Practice.* Translated by Mary Klopper. New York: Monthly Review Press, 1970.

———, ed. *No Gods No Masters.* Translated by Paul Sharkey. 2 vols. Edinburgh: AK Press, 1998.

Hennacy, Ammon. *The Book of Ammon.* The author, 1965.

———. *The One-Man Revolution in America.* Salt Lake City: Ammon Hennacy Publications, 1965.

Hirsh, Jesse. "The Mythology of Technology: The Internet as Utopia." *The Raven,* no. 34 (9.2) (spring 1997): 155–60.

Holterman, Thom, and Henc van Maarseveen, eds. *Law in Anarchism.* Rotterdam: Erasmus University, 1980.

Hospers, John. *Libertarianism: A Political Philosophy for Tomorrow.* Santa Barbara, Calif.: Reason Press, 1971.

Illich, Ivan. *Celebrating Awareness: A Call for Institutional Revolution.* London: Calder & Boyars, 1971.

———. *Deschooling Society.* New York: Harper & Row, 1971.

———. *The Right to Useful Unemployment and Its Professional Enemies.* London: Marion Boyars, 1978.

———. *Tools for Conviviality.* London: Calder & Boyars, 1973.

Jackson, Corrine. *The Black Flag of Anarchy: Antistatism in the United States.* New York: Scribner, 1968.

Joll, James. *The Anarchists.* 2d ed. London: Methuen, 1979.

Kornbluth, Joyce L. *Rebel Voices: An I.W.W. Anthology.* Ann Arbor: University of Michigan Press, 1968.

Marshall, Peter. *Demanding the Impossible: A History of Anarchism.* London: HarperCollins, 1992.

Martin, Brian. *Information Liberation: Challenging the Corruptions of Information Power.* London: Freedom Press, 1998.

Martin, James J. *Men against the State: The Expositors of Individualist Anarchism in America, 1827–1908.* Colorado Springs, Colo.: Ralph Myles, 1970.

Mbah, Sam, and I. E. Igariwey. *African Anarchism: The History of a Movement.* Tucson, Ariz.: See Sharp Press, 1997.

McKay, George, ed. *DiY Culture: Party & Protest in Nineties Britain.* London: Verso, 1998.

———. *Senseless Acts of Beauty: Cultures of Resistance since the Sixties.* London: Verso, 1996.

Meltzer, Albert. *Anarchism Arguments, For and Against.* Edinburgh: AK Press, 1996.

Morland, David. *Demanding the Impossible? Human Nature and Politics in Nineteenth-Century Social Anarchism.* London: Cassell, 1997.

Narveson, Jan. *The Libertarian Idea.* Philadelphia: Temple University Press, 1988.

Piehl, Mel. *Breaking Bread: The Catholic Worker and the Origin of Catholic Radicalism in America.* Philadelphia: Temple University Press, 1982.

Purchase, Graham. *Anarchism & Environmental Survival.* Tucson, Ariz.: See Sharp Press, 1994.

Purkis, Jon, and James Bowen, eds. *Twenty-first Century Anarchism: Unorthodox Ideas for a New Millennium.* London: Cassell, 1997.

Raimondo, Justin. *An Enemy of the State: The Life of Murray Rothbard.* Amherst, N.Y.: Prometheus Books, 2000.

Rand, Ayn. *Anthem.* Exp. 50th anniv. ed. New York: Dutton, 1995.

———. *Atlas Shrugged.* New York: Random House, 1957.

———. *Capitalism, the Unknown Ideal.* With additional articles by Nathaniel Branden, Alan Greenspan, and Robert Hessen. New York: New American Library, 1966.

———. *For the New Intellectual: The Philosophy of Ayn Rand.* New York: Random House, 1961.

———. *The Fountainhead.* Indianapolis: Bobbs-Merrill, 1943.

———. *The Virtue of Selfishness: A New Concept of Egoism.* With additional articles by Nathaniel Branden. New York: New American Library, 1964.

———. *We the Living.* New York: Macmillan, 1936.

Read, Herbert. *Anarchy and Order: Essays in Politics.* London: Faber & Faber, 1954.

———. *The Philosophy of Anarchism.* London: Freedom Press, 1940.

———. *Poetry and Anarchism.* 2d ed. London: Freedom Press, 1947.

Reichert, William O. *Partisans of Freedom: A Study in American Anarchism.* Bowling Green, Ohio: Bowling Green State University Popular Press, 1976.

Richards, Vernon, ed. *Violence & Anarchism*. London: Freedom Press, 1993.

Roberts, Nancy J. *Dorothy Day and the "Catholic Worker."* Albany: State University of New York Press, 1984.

Rocker, Rudolf. *Anarcho-Syndicalism*. 1938. London: Pluto Press, 1989.

————. *Nationalism and Culture*. Translated by Ray E. Chase. Los Angeles, Calif.: Rocker Publications Foundation, 1937.

Rothbard, Murray. *The Ethics of Liberty*. Atlantic Highlands, N.J.: Humanities Press, 1982.

————. *For a New Liberty*. New York: Macmillan, 1973.

Roussopoulos, Dimitrios I., ed. *The Anarchist Papers*. 3 vols. Montreal: Black Rose Books, 1986–90.

Schuster, Eunice Minette. *Native American Anarchism: A Study of Left-Wing American Individuals*. 1932. New York: AMS Press, 1970.

Taylor, Michael. *Anarchy and Cooperation*. New York: Wiley, 1976.

————. *Community, Anarchy, and Liberty*. Cambridge: Cambridge University Press, 1982.

Tullock, Gordon, ed. *Explorations in the Theory of Anarchy*. Blacksburg, Va.: Center for the Study of Public Choice, Virginia Polytechnic Institute and State University, 1972.

————, ed. *Further Explorations in the Theory of Anarchy*. Blacksburg, Va.: University Publications, 1974.

Vallentyne, Peter, and Hillel Steiner, eds. *Left Libertarianism and Its Critics: The Contemporary Debate*. London: Palgrave, 2000.

————. *The Origins of Left Libertarianism: An Anthology of Historical Writings*. London: Palgrave, 2000.

Ward, Colin. *Housing: An Anarchist Approach*. London: Freedom Press, 1982.

————. *Reflected in the Water: A Crisis in Social Responsibility*. London: Cassell, 1997.

————. *Social Policy: An Anarchist Response*. Rev. ed. London: Freedom Press, 2000.

Wilson, Charlotte. *Anarchist Essays*. Edited by Nicolas Walter. London: Freedom Press, 2000.

Woolf, Robert Paul. *In Defense of Anarchism*. New York: Harper & Row, 1970.

Worple, Ken, ed. *Richer Futures: Fashioning a New Politics*. London: Earthscan, 1999.

Web Sites

http://burn.ucsd.edu/~anow/world/na/ Anarchism in North America

http://website.lineone.net/~grandlaf/Sotiga.htm Green Anarchist (UK)

http://www.anarchism.net/ Anarchism Net (Anarcho-capitalism)

http://www.anarchistcommunitarian.net/ Anarchist Communitarian Network

http://www.saccovanzettiproject.org/ The Sacco-Vanzetti Project

http://www.social-ecology.org/ Institute for Social Ecology

9

Fascism and National Socialism

For the generation that lived through World War II, the words *fascism, National Socialism,* and *Nazism* raise indescribably horrible pictures of brutality and inhumanity. For those who have grown up since the end of the war, the horror associated with the concentration camps has faded. For many years now the words *fascist* and *Nazi* have been used loosely to refer to various authoritarian countries and individuals, but using the words loosely tends to hide the fact that fascism and National Socialism have recently revived as small but active movements in many countries, including the United States.

Fascism and National Socialism are similar enough to be called one ideology. There are differences, but National Socialism is more accurately seen as one of a number of varieties of fascism rather than different in kind. We identify National Socialism with Adolf Hitler (1889–1945), which tends to isolate it in time and space; but National Socialism continues without Hitler, even though he is one of its heroes. Fascism as an ideology developed early in this century in France and Italy, and the first successful fascist movement was in Italy in the 1920s. The discussion here focuses on the major movements in Germany and Italy prior to World War II because they provide the ideological basis for the contemporary movements. But it is essential to keep in mind that both fascist and National Socialist groups, often labeled neofascist and neo-Nazi, are currently flourishing throughout North America and Europe.

THE THEORETICAL BASE

Any discussion of fascism and National Socialism must stress seven basic ideas listed below. Although the emphasis varies, these ideas are almost always found in fascist and national socialist writing.

1. irrationalism
2. social Darwinism
3. nationalism
4. glorification of the state
5. the leadership principle
6. racism (more important in National Socialism than in fascism)
7. anticommunism

The first two are basic themes that are rarely explicitly stated. All seven concepts are interrelated but can be separated for analysis.

Irrationalism

Irrationalism permeates the approach of fascism and National Socialism but by its very nature is difficult to analyze. Irrationalism rejects the idea that reason or science can solve social problems. In the nineteenth and early twentieth centuries, reason and science were the central tenets of liberal and Marxist approaches to social change, and irrationalism specifically rejects those approaches. Fascism and National Socialism reject the application of reason and science to social problems and use myth, emotion, and hate as tools of manipulation. National Socialism in particular had an affinity for astrology, the occult, and various pseudosciences, and that affinity continues into contemporary neo-Nazi movements.[1]

The basic assumption is that humans are not rational beings. They need not and cannot be reasoned with; they can only be led and manipulated. Other ideologies take note of the irrational aspects of human psychology and behavior, and some stress the positive aspects of human psychology and behavior. But only fascism and National Socialism emphasize the irrational and treat it as a central part of the ideology.

The emphasis in National Socialism is on myths of blood (racism) and soil (nationalism) and on violence as a constant part of life. Violence is not only directed at the national and racial enemies but is a normal aspect of political life.

---

1. See Nicholas Goodrick-Clarke, *The Occult Roots of Nazism: Secret Aryan Cults and Their Influence on Nazi Ideology. The Ariosophists of Austria and Germany, 1890–1935* (New York: New York University Press, 1992); Goodrick-Clarke, *Hitler's Priestess: Savitra Devi, the Hindu-Aryan Myth, and Neo-Nazism* (New York: Oxford University Press, 2000); and Goodrick-Clarke, *Black Sun: Aryan Cults, Esoteric Nazism, and the Politics of Identity* (New York: New York University Press, 2001).

Germans who did not fit Hitler's image of racial purity were executed along with Jews, homosexuals, and the physically and mentally disabled.

Paradoxically, racial hatred and intense nationalism are part of the appeal of fascism and National Socialism. If you are insecure—financially, socially, or emotionally—an appeal based on racial hatred and intense nationalism, which promotes a feeling of worth in you as a member of a superior race or nation and which identifies people who are said to be inferior, can be very effective. Fascism and National Socialism give a sense of belonging, superiority, and security to those who feel cut off, inferior, or insecure. It does this in such a way that the feeling need not be questioned. This is very clear in contemporary racist fascism in the United States.

Social Darwinism

Social Darwinism is the name generally given to social theories viewing life as a struggle for survival within each species as well as between species. While Charles Darwin (1809–82) was not the first one to use the phrase, in *On the Origin of Species by Means of Natural Selection* (1859), Darwin stated that life evolved through a struggle for survival *between* species. Herbert Spencer (1820–1903), the real father of social Darwinism, first coined that phrase. The social Darwinists took this idea and applied it to each species. In other words, rather than seeing a struggle for survival *between* species, they saw a struggle for survival *within* each species.

Pyotr Kropotkin (1842–1921) argued in his book *Mutual Aid* (1902) that there is considerable evidence for cooperation within a species. In contrast, Fascists and National Socialists applied social Darwinism to their theories of nationalism and racism, and we will return to it in that context.[2] Not all social Darwinists are racists. Social Darwinism is a general theory that the Fascists and National Socialists applied to their theories.

Nationalism

By far the most important theme, as illustrated in the phrase *National Socialism,* is nationalism. In Chapter 2 we looked at the basic characteristics of nationalism. Here we will see what they mean to the Fascist. In fascism and National Socialism, nationalism takes on a different meaning, to the extent that some scholars call it by a modified name, such as "integral" nationalism.[3]

The nation is the key unit to which the Fascist relates. For the National Socialist, the key factor is race, with the nation as a secondary concern. For the Fascist, individuals are first and foremost members of the nation to which they give all of their loyalty, dedication, and love. The individual does not exist apart

---

2. For further analysis of the role of social Darwinism in National Socialism, see Hajo Holborn, "Origins and Political Character of Nazi Ideology," *Political Science Quarterly* 74 (December 1964): 542–54.

3. See, for example, Carlton J. H. Hayes, *The Historical Evolution of Modern Nationalism* (New York: Macmillan, 1931), 164–231.

from his or her existence in the nation. There is almost no such thing as an individual within fascist ideology. An individual is one small part of the nation. The individual and the nation are inseparable. Individuals should not be able to conceive of themselves as distinct entities, separate from existence in the nation. People should be completely wrapped up in the nation. Only some of the citizens of fascist countries felt this strongly, but this was the fascist ideal.

For the National Socialist, nationalism was usually so closely connected with racism that it formed one concept rather than two. For example, among the basic principles on which the National Socialists intend to reform the legal system, race is considered the most important:

> The legal protection of the race, which has created a new concept of nationality [*Volkszugehörigkeit*], is consciously put in first place, for the most significant historical principle which has been established by the victory of National Socialism is that of the necessity for keeping race and blood pure. All human mistakes and errors can be corrected except one: "the error regarding the importance of maintaining the basic values of a nation."
>
> The purpose of this legal protection of the basic value of *race* must be the prevention for all time of a further mixture of German Blood with foreign blood, as well as the prevention of continued procreation of racially unworthy and undesirable members of the people.[4]

For most Fascists, racism is not closely connected to nationalism. In fact, racism, although part of their fascist outlook, played a fairly minor role in both ideology and practice in a number of countries, such as Italy. In other countries with fascist groups today, racism is an important part of small groups that are either National Socialist or fascist and racist.

Nonracist fascism holds a strongly nationalist position usually presented in connection with the concept of the state. The following statement by Benito Mussolini (1883–1945) is a good example: "The keystone of the Fascist doctrine is the conception of the State, of its essence, of its functions, its aims. For Fascism the State is absolute, individuals and groups relative."[5] Mussolini continued in the same vein, contending that the state is the carrier of the culture and spirit of the people or nation; that it is the past, present, and future; that it represents the "immanent conscience of the nation"; and that it educates the citizens in all the virtues.[6] Here is the connection between the state and nationalism in fascist ideology. The state is seen as the physical embodiment of the spirit of the nation. The state brings together the ideas and ideals that form

---

4. Otto Gauweiler, *Rechtseinrichtungen and Rechtsaufgaben der Bewegung* (Munich: Zentral verlag der NSDAP, Franz Eher, Nachfolger, 1939); trans. in *National Socialism: Basic Principles. Their Application by the Nazi Party's Foreign Organization, and the Use of Germans Abroad for Nazi Aims*, prepared in the Special Unit of the Division of European Affairs by Raymond E. Murphy, Francis B. Stevens, Howard Trivers, and Joseph M. Roland (Washington, D.C.: GPO, 1943), 208–9.

5. Benito Mussolini, "The Doctrine of Fascism," in Mussolini, *Fascism: Doctrine and Institutions* (New York: Howard Fertig, 1968), 27.

6. Ibid., 27–28.

the basis of nationalism. Nationalism and the state cannot be easily separated for the Fascist. The state, as Mussolini said, is the carrier of the culture and spirit of the people, the driving force that welds the people together. The state is capable of focusing the spirit of the people and the nationalism of the country. The state, therefore, must be strong; it must have the power necessary to achieve these goals.

Glorification of the State

The state is the vehicle through which the attributes of the nation, the nationality, or the race are expressed, but the state, at least as seen by Hitler, is a "rigid formal organization," and the nation or the people is a "living organism" that must replace the state.[7] In other words, the people or the nation is the locus of emotion and the state is the structure through which that emotion is expressed. The theory of the state as actually presented by Fascists and National Socialists combines these two notions into the idea of an organic or corporate state.

The word *totalitarian* emerged in the 1920s and 1930s as a way of characterizing governments in Italy under fascism and then Germany under National Socialism. It was later extended to the Soviet Union under Communism, particularly the regime of Joseph Stalin. It refers to a government that controls or attempts to control the totality of human life and completely subordinates the individual to the state.[8]

This conception of the state stresses the continuity of the entire society over generations. In this context, the word *organic* means "social groups as fractions of the species receive thereby a life and scope which transcends the scope and life of the individuals identifying themselves with the history and finalities of the uninterrupted series of generations."[9] Put somewhat differently, this means society, represented by the state, is a separate entity having a life or existence at once different from, and greater than, the life of any individual within that society. This also means the life of the individual is less important than the life of the society.

This point is best illustrated by the idea of the folkish state that we find expressed by Hitler in *Mein Kampf:* "Thus, the highest purpose of a *folkish* state is concern for the preservation of those original racial elements which bestow culture and create the beauty and dignity of a higher humanity."[10] The folkish state is the best symbol for the full idea of the identification of the individual with the mass. Here, the ideas of blood and soil are intermingled in a way that

---

7. Adolf Hitler, *The Speeches of Adolf Hitler, April 1922–August 1939,* ed. Norman H. Baynes (London: Oxford University Press, 1942), 1:178, speech of September 1930.

8. For different perspectives on the concept of totalitarianism, see Carl J. Friedrich, Michael Curtis, and Benjamin R. Barber, *Totalitarianism in Perspective: Three Views* (New York: Praeger, 1969).

9. Some Fascists reject the idea that they are presenting the "organic theory of the state." See, for example, Alfredo Rocco, "The Political Doctrine of Fascism," trans. D. Bigongiari, *International Conciliation,* no. 223 (October 1926): 402.

10. Adolf Hitler, *Mein Kampf,* trans. Ralph Manheim (Boston: Houghton Mifflin, 1943), 394. Emphasis in the original.

Culver Pictures, Inc.

Adolf Hitler (1889–1945) was founder and leader of the National Socialist German Workers' Party, chancellor (1933–45), and head of state (1934–45) of Germany. He was the leading figure of the Nazi movement and is still venerated as such by Nazis everywhere. He was violently nationalist and anti-Semitic. He was the author of one of the classic texts of National Socialism, *Mein Kampf* (1925–27). The swastika on his uniform is the symbol of National Socialism. Standing next to him is Benito Mussolini (1883–1945). In this picture he is giving the Nazi salute. Mussolini, known as *Il Duce* (the Leader), ruled Italy from 1922 until shortly before his death.

illustrates why they are so important to National Socialism. The folkish state is a racial state. It is a state in which only the members of the true Aryan race may participate, but they participate only in the sense of giving of themselves to the state. They do not govern. The folkish state, then, is a state based on racial purity, and it is a state based on ideas of soil—myths of racial content connected with the particular history of the German nation. Here race and nationalism, blood and soil, combine in the folkish state. An understanding of National Socialism as it developed in Germany cannot be separated from an understanding of race and nationalism and the combination of the two in a folkish state.

Mussolini said the state is the source of the life of the people of all generations that compose it.[11] The state is owed supreme loyalty by the individuals who live in it, but the state is also something more than what these somewhat mechanical notions imply. It is also a "spiritual" unit, but this "spiritual" side is closely related to the authority controlling the state. The state "enforces discipline and uses authority, entering into the soul and ruling with undisputed sway."[12] It does this through the leadership principle.

The Leadership Principle

The state is the mechanism for enforcing fascist beliefs, and the state is run on the *leadership* or *Führer principle,* under which each subordinate owes absolute obedience to his or her immediate superior, with everyone ultimately subordinate to the absolute leader, the *Führer,* which was Hitler's title. Mussolini's title was *Il Duce,* which also means "the leader." This hierarchy of leaders with a single, absolute leader at the top is an important characteristic of fascism and National Socialism. The only limit on the leader's power is that the *Führer* must

---

11. Mussolini, "Doctrine of Fascism," 11–12.

12. Ibid., 14.

reflect the collective will of the people. In practice, this does not limit power because the leader's will is, by definition, the same as the collective will. "His will is not the subjective individual will of a single man, but the collective national will."[13] The leader's authority is absolute. Hitler and Mussolini were each charismatic leaders, able to attract people by sheer force of personality. Therefore, few fascist movements have survived the death of the leader.

The *Führer* principle on which Hitler based his power and organization seems, on the surface, to be complicated. But it is similar to the notion of a representative as embodying the will of the constituency. Hitler, as leader, was the representative of the German nation and the Aryan race in that he embodied within himself all the aspirations of the people. This does not mean that Hitler followed the will of the people, but that he, by embodying their will, was capable of *rightly* interpreting it. This is the key to the whole *Führer* principle — the *Führer* is the only one capable of rightly interpreting the will of the people. When the *Führer* speaks, he represents what the people truly want. In this sense he is virtually infallible, and this is clearly how Hitler viewed himself. Hitler as *Führer* could do no wrong.

But no one person, even a *Führer,* can rule an entire country; even an absolute ruler needs some apparatus to enforce rules. This apparatus is the party. Party members are separate from and above the rest of the population. Some clearly recognizable sign, such as a uniform, usually identifies them. Finally, there is a corps within this elite to check on the rest of the party. The two groups that served this function within the National Socialist German Workers' Party (the official name of Hitler's party) were the SA (*Sturmabteilung*) and the SS (*Schutzstaffel*). Hitler defined the task of the SA as follows: "The SA on behalf of our German people must educate the young German in mind and body so that he becomes a man hard as steel and ready to fight. Out of hundreds of thousands of individuals it must forge one united, disciplined, mighty organization."[14] The party was the effective ruling mechanism. But as Hitler said, "Every member of the Party has to do what the leader orders."[15]

In fascism and National Socialism the party plays a role similar to that of the Communist Party in Lenin's thought. The party is the vanguard of the nation or the race rather than of the proletariat, but the general notion is the same. The party is the forerunner of the new order to come. The National Socialist believes the new order is based on race.

Racism

Probably the single, best-known part of National Socialism is its racism. The words *racism* and *racist* were first used in the 1930s to refer to the beliefs of the National Socialists, and they reflect the belief that the human species can be sub-

---

13. Ernst Rudolf Huber, *Verfassungsrecht des grossdeutschen Reiches* (Hamburg, 1939), 195;
    trans. and quoted in *Readings on Fascism and National Socialism* (Denver, Colo.: Alan
    Swallow, n.d.), 75.

14. Adolf Hitler, "Introduction to the Service-Order of the SA," quoted in Hitler,
    Speeches, 1:169.

15. Ibid., 1:459, speech of May 21, 1930.

divided into races, or subgroups with similar cultural and/or physical character-istics, and that one of these races is superior to the others. Modern science does not provide support for these beliefs.[16]

Hitler based racism originally on the right of the stronger, and he believed that from the very beginning the Aryan, or Nordic, or white, or sometimes German, race dominated all others. He contended this domination was good for all because it was natural and founded on reason, and it would also ultimately be accepted by the dominated races.

Here is the thesis of the struggle for survival among races. Hitler believed the dominated races would gladly accept racial domination by the Aryans, but the social Darwinian struggle for survival as interpreted by the National Socialists does not include the survival of the dominated races. The logic of the position is that the inferior races will be eliminated, not merely dominated.

For National Socialism, racism (1) represents the underlying current of social Darwinism and (2) is a mechanism of social control, negatively by destroying the Jews and others identified by the regime—primarily Gypsies and homosexuals—and thus instilling fear in the Germans, and positively by instilling a pride in the Germans in their so-called racial heritage. Nazi policy stressed what was known as both negative and positive eugenics. Negative eugenics was aimed at keeping those perceived to be unfit from having children. Positive eugenics was aimed at encouraging the fit to have children.

The racial policies of Hitler were not limited to extermination and breeding. They included the belief that all that is good in culture stems from the Aryan race and that, therefore, the Germans as the representative of the Aryans had the best cultural heritage of the Western world and would have an even better culture in the future. In the chapter on nationalism it was noted that one of Hitler's great loves was Wagner. This is because Wagner's operas were in some ways operas of the folkish state. They represented the myths of blood and soil that were so important to Hitler. In particular, they represented what he saw as a high point in German culture—an illustration that the Germans did have a great culture and particularly that Wagner, as a representative of German culture, seemed to agree with some of the ideas put forth by Hitler. Therefore, Hitler was able to present National Socialism as a logical outgrowth of German culture and the German nation.

The relationship of the state to racism is seen in *Mein Kampf,* where Hitler wrote, "The state is a means to an end. Its end lies in the preservation and advancement of a community of physically and psychically homogenous creatures." [17]

The effect of racism on other aspects of the society is fairly obvious. For example, social stratification would be based on racial purity and party membership. Also taken into account would be positive support for the regime and contributions to the country. In addition, the racist ideology would indicate the control of marriage, and the desire to control the minds of the children would

---

16. For contemporary perspectives, see Bernard Boxill, ed., *Race and Racism* (Oxford: Oxford University Press, 2001).

17. Hitler, *Mein Kampf,* 393.

dictate control of the family system. Along these lines, German women were encouraged to have many children—that is, if they were of the correct racial type. As Goebbels put it, "The mission of woman is to be beautiful and to bring children into the world."[18] She was also supposed to be athletic and to refrain from wearing makeup or from such things as smoking in public. But, above all, she was to have children. We have seen the way in which the educational system was used to develop the correct values in children. The family and religion were used in the same way. Parents were to teach their children the true National Socialist ideas from birth. National Socialism also contended God supported it; thus, religion was used for the same purpose.

Anticommunism

One of the aspects of the ideologies of fascism and National Socialism that made them acceptable to many was their anticommunist stance. As one scholar of fascism put it, "Before all else, it was anticommunist. It lived and throve on anticommunism."[19] This was an aspect of fascism's antirationalist approach, and its general rejection of the modern world, but it became a significant element in the appeal of fascism.[20]

Fascism and National Socialism were not only anticommunist, but also antiintellectual, antirational, and antimodern because they glorified the past with myths of blood and soil. The ideologies of fascism and National Socialism developed first as practice and were never tightly tied together by theory, but the very lack of rational coherence is an integral part of the ideologies and part of the rejection of what was seen as the overly intellectual, overly rational approach of communism.

THE ECONOMIC SYSTEM

The economic theory of fascism and National Socialism was never developed very systematically, and there were marked differences in the countries involved. Even though socialism is part of the name National Socialism and Mussolini was originally a socialist, neither fascism nor National Socialism was actually socialist. National Socialism began from that position, but it quickly

---

18. Joseph Goebbels, quoted in Mosse, *Nazi Culture: Intellectual, Cultural, and Social Life in the Third Reich* (New York: Grosset & Dunlap, 1966), 41. A good introduction to the socialization process is [Fritz Brennecke], *The Nazi Primer: Official Handbook for Schooling the Hitler Youth,* trans. Harwood L. Childs (New York: Harper & Brothers, 1938; New York: AMS Press, 1972).

19. H. R. Trevor-Roper, "The Phenomenon of Fascism," in S. J. Woolf, ed., *European Fascism* (New York: Vintage Books, 1969), 24.

20. See, for example, Alastair Hamilton, *The Appeal of Fascism: A Study of Intellectuals and Fascism 1919–1945* (New York: Macmillan, 1971).

changed as it gained the support of capitalists.[21] Probably the best statement of the general economic theory of National Socialism is, "All property is common property. The owner is bound by the people and the Reich [government] to the responsible management of his goods. His legal position is only justified when he satisfies this responsibility to the community."[22] Thus property under National Socialism was held in private hands, but it had to be used as the government dictated or it would be confiscated. Here again is the idea of the people as a whole acting for the best interests of the state.

A major concern in the economic theory is to establish economic self-sufficiency. For fascism and National Socialism to achieve their goals, the countries involved must be self sufficient; they must not depend on other countries for supplies.[23] All the stress on the nation, the state, the race, and the people would lose considerable force if these entities were dependent on other nations, states, races, and peoples.

The economic system of National Socialism clearly states that, even though an individual may have temporary control of some economic good, be it land, capital, or whatever, this control must serve the interests of the collectivity as interpreted by the *Führer,* or the control must be terminated.

The economic system of fascism includes the idea of state-controlled syndicates. The state creates all economic organizations, as the Labour Charter of April 21, 1927, says: "Work in all its forms—intellectual, technical and manual—both organizing or executive, is a social duty. On this score and only on this score, it is protected by the State. From the national standpoint the mass of production represents a single unit; it has a single object, namely, the well-being of individuals and the development of national power."[24] All economic organization under fascism is ultimately controlled by the state. All economic organizations under fascism are designed to include both workers and employers in the same organization so that all of the economy can be directly controlled from above; this is called *corporatism* or the *corporate economy.* In this way, the state is made superior to every part of the economy. The syndicates are designed to ensure that production continues as long as the state requires it. The right to strike is taken away from the workers, but at the same time the syndicate, operating as an arm of the state, usually has the power to set wages; thus the syndicate acts as a policymaking arm of the state in economic affairs. It should be clear that, as in Germany, the Fascist Party in Italy with Mussolini at the head had ultimate power. In many ways, the syndicates were merely administrative arms of the Fascist Party and of Mussolini rather than having any real power to make decisions. The leadership principle was not abrogated in Italy. It was

---

21. On this point, see Martin Broszat, *German National Socialism 1919–1945,* trans. Kurt Rosenbaum and Inge Pauli Boehm (Santa Barbara, Calif.: CLIO Press, 1966), 22–24.

22. Huber, *Verfassungsrecht,* 372–73, quoted in *Readings on Fascism,* 91.

23. See the discussion in Paul M. Hayes, *Fascism* (London: George Allen & Unwin, 1973), 89–105.

24. "The Labour Charter," in Benito Mussolini, *Four Speeches on the Corporate State* (Rome: "Laboremus," 1935), 53.

maintained, and the syndicates acted as lower-level leaders following the dictates of the leader.

CURRENT TRENDS

Neofascism

In the past few years fascism and National Socialism have been revived in a number of countries, including Germany, Italy, and the United States. In Italy parties associated with fascism have made substantial electoral gains. In Germany direct reference to National Socialism is rare, but opposition to immigration has produced groups that are quite similar to early National Socialism. This is particularly true in the former East Germany where the unification of Germany has produced substantial unemployment and poverty in contrast to the obvious wealth of the former West Germany. In the United States quite a number of groups, most fairly small, either identify with National Socialism through the use of its traditional symbols (mostly the swastika) or support social and political traditions closely associated with National Socialism.

Although these small groups clearly exist, most of the extreme right political movements are not necessarily fascist, and were discussed under the heading "The Extreme Right" in Chapter 5. If we take the seven points with which the chapter began, most of the movements are anticommunist, racist, and nationalist, but they generally do not stress the other four. Anticommunism, racism, and nationalism are the most important of the seven, so there is certainly a close affinity between the contemporary extremist groups and fascism, and perhaps that is enough for us to use the word *neofascism* to describe them. Such groups are particularly strong in France, where the National Front led by Jean-Marie Le Pen (b. 1928) has gained considerable electoral success, and in the United States, where the various militia groups are clearly growing rapidly.

There are, though, groups in the United States that are clearly fascist and others that explicitly align themselves with National Socialism. For example, the World Church of the Creator, currently led by Matt Hale (b. 1971), who identifies himself as the Pontifex Maximus of the church, preaches what it calls RAHOWA or RAcial HOly WAr, uses the Nazi salute, and is virulently anti-Semitic. One of its members, Benjamin Nathaniel Smith, killed two people, wounded seven, and shot at many more in Illinois and Indiana on July 4, 1999 before committing suicide. All of his targets and victims were black, Jewish, or ethnic minorities. He was lauded by Matt Hale as a "martyr for free speech."[25] The leader of the National Alliance, William J. Pierce (b. 1933), was once an associate of George Lincoln Rockwell (1918–67), the longtime leader of the American Nazi Party, which still exists, together with other U.S. groups that explicitly align themselves with National Socialism.

---

25. Duncan Campbell, "Hate Spawned on the Fourth of July," *Guardian* (London), 6 July 1999, p. 3.

A recent study argues that fascism is currently emerging in Russia, the states of the former Soviet Union, and China.[26] In Austria, Jörg Haider (b. 1950), chairman of the Freedom Party (FPÖ), was briefly a member of a coalition government in 2000 but resigned in part as a result of controversy that arose from his oft-stated sympathies with National Socialism.

In Europe the issue that seems to most attract people to the neofascist ranks is immigration. Immigration is an increasingly volatile issue in the United States, but the focus of the neofascist right in the United States is race followed by internationalism, the power of the Federal Reserve and the Internal Revenue Service, and the perceived desire of the central government to restrict the freedoms of dissenters on the right.

SUGGESTED READINGS

Some Classic Works

Hitler, Adolf. *Mein Kampf.* Translated by Ralph Manheim. Boston: Houghton Mifflin, 1943.

Mussolini, Benito. *Four Speeches on the Corporate State.* Rome: "Laboremus," 1935.

———. *My Autobiography.* New York: Scribner, 1928.

Books and Articles

Barkun, Michael. *Religion and the Racial Right: The Origins of the Christian Identity Movement.* Chapel Hill: University of North Carolina Press, 1994.

Boxill, Bernard, ed. *Race and Racism.* Oxford: Oxford University Press, 2001.

[Brennecke, Fritz]. *The Nazi Primer: Official Handbook for Schooling the Hitler Youth.* Translated by Harwood L. Childs. New York: Harper & Brothers, 1938; New York: AMS Press, 1972.

Campbell, Duncan. "Hate Spawned on the Fourth of July." *Guardian* (London), 6 July 1999, p. 3.

De Grand, Alexander. *Italian Fascism: Its Origin & Development.* 3d ed. Lincoln: University of Nebraska Press, 2000.

Durham, Martin. *Women and Fascism.* London: Routledge, 1998.

Eatwell, Roger. *Fascism: A History.* London: Chatto & Windus, 1995.

Eley, Geoff, ed. *The "Goldhagen Effect": History, Memory, Nazism—Facing the German Past.* Ann Arbor: University of Michigan Press, 2000.

Fraser, Nicholas. *The Voice of Modern Hatred: Tracing the Rise of Neo-Fascism in Europe.* Woodstock, N.Y.: Overlook Press, 2000.

Goldhagen, Daniel Jonah. *Hitler's Willing Executioners: Ordinary Germans and the Holocaust.* New York: Knopf, 1996.

Golsan, Richard J. *Fascism's Return: Scandal, Revision, and Ideology since 1980.* Lincoln: University of Nebraska Press, 1998.

Gonen, Jay Y. *The Roots of Nazi Psychology: Hitler's Utopian Barbarism.* Lexington: University Press of Kentucky, 2000.

Goodrick-Clarke, Nicholas. *Black Sun: Aryan Cults, Esoteric Nazism, and the Politics of Identity.* New York: New York University Press, 2001.

———. *Hitler's Priestess: Savitra Devi, the Hindu-Aryan Myth, and Neo-Nazism.* New York: Oxford University Press, 2000.

———. *The Occult Roots of Nazism: Secret Aryan Cults and Their Influence on Nazi*

---

26. A. James Gregor, *Phoenix: Fascism in Our Time* (New Brunswick, N.J.: Transaction, 1999).

Ideology. The Ariosophists of Austria and Germany, 1890–1935. New York: New York University Press, 1992.

Gregor, A. James. *Giovanni Gentile: Philosopher of Fascism*. New Brunswick, N.J.: Transaction, 2001.

———. *Interpretations of Fascism*. New Brunswick, N.J.: Transaction, 1997.

———. *Phoenix: Fascism in Our Time*. New Brunswick, N.J.: Transaction, 1999.

Griffin, Roger. *The Nature of Fascism*. New York: St. Martin's Press, 1991.

———, ed. *Fascism*. Oxford: Oxford University Press, 1995.

———, ed. *International Fascism: Theories, Causes, and the New Consensus*. London: Arnold, 1998.

Guernsey, Lisa. "Mainstream Sites Serve as Portals to Hate." *New York Times,* 30 November 2000, pp. D1, D12.

Hamm, Mark S. *Apocalypse in Oklahoma: Waco and Ruby Ridge Revenged*. Boston: Northeastern University Press, 1997.

Hilliard, Robert L., and Michael C. Keith. *Waves of Rancor: Tuning in the Radical Right*. Armonk, N.Y.: M. E. Sharpe, 1999.

Hitler, Adolf. *The Speeches of Adolf Hitler, April 1922–August 1939*. Edited by Norman H. Baynes. 2 vols. London: Oxford University Press, 1942.

Kallis, Aristotle A. *Fascist Ideology: Territory and Expansionism in Italy and Germany, 1922–1945*. London: Routledge, 2000.

Kaplan, Jeffrey, ed. *Encyclopedia of White Power: A Sourcebook on the Radical Racist Right*. Walnut Creek, Calif.: AltaMira Press, 2000.

Kershaw, Ian. *Hitler*. 2 vols. New York: Norton, 1999–2000.

Kettle, Martin. "Church of Hates Hand Seen in Killing of Gays." *Guardian* (London), 12 July 1999, p. 13.

Kühl, Stefan. *The Nazi Connection: Eugenics, American Racism, and German National Socialism*. New York: Oxford University Press, 1994.

Lee, Martin A. *The Beast Reawakens*. Boston: Little, Brown, 1997.

Littell, Franklin H., ed. *Hyping the Holocaust: Scholars Answer Goldhagen*. Merion Station, Pa.: Merion Westfield Press International, 1997.

Mariani, Mack. "The Michigan Militia: Political Engagement or Political Alienation?" *Terrorism and Political Violence* 10, no. 4 (winter 1998): 122–48.

Mosse, George L. *The Crisis of German Ideology: Intellectual Origins of the Third Reich*. New York: Grosset & Dunlap, 1964.

———. *The Fascist Revolution: Toward a General Theory of Fascism*. New York: Howard Fertig, 1999.

Mussolini, Benito. *Fascism: Doctrine and Institutions*. New York: Howard Fertig, 1968.

———. *My Rise and Fall*. New York: Da Capo Press, 1998.

Neocleous, Mark. *Fascism*. Minneapolis: University of Minnesota Press, 1997.

Nolte, Ernst. *Three Faces of Fascism: Action Française, Italian Fascism, National Socialism*. Translated by Leila Vennewitz. New York: Holt, Rinehart & Winston, 1965.

Perlmutter, Philip. *Legacy of Hate: A Short History of Ethnic, Religious, and Racial Prejudice in America*. Armonk, N.Y.: M.E. Sharpe, 1999. Rev. ed. of *Divided We Fall: A History of Ethnic, Religious, and Racial Prejudice in America*. Ames: Iowa State University Press, 1992.

Pine, Lisa. *Nazi Family Policy, 1933–1945*. Oxford, England: Berg, 1997.

Renton, Dave. *Fascism: Theory and Practice*. London: Pluto Press, 1999.

Rocco, Alfredo. "The Political Doctrine of Fascism." Translated by D. Bigongiari. *International Conciliation,* no. 223 (October 1926): 393–415.

Sargent, Lyman Tower, ed. *Extremism: A Reader*. New York: New York University Press, 1995.

Schnapp, Jeffrey T. ed. *A Primer of Italian Fascism*. Translated by Jeffrey T. Schnapp, Olivia E. Sears, and Maria

G. Stampino. Lincoln: University of Nebraska Press, 2000.

Shandley, Robert R. *Unwilling Germans: The Goldhagen Debate*. Minneapolis: University of Minnesota Press, 1998.

Shenfield, Stephen D. *Russian Fascism: Traditions, Tendencies, Movements*. Armonk, N.Y.: M.E. Sharpe, 2001.

Simonelli, Frederick J. *American Fuehrer: George Lincoln Rockwell and the American Nazi Party*. Urbana: University of Illinois Press, 1999.

Viereck, Peter. *Metapolitics: The Roots of the Nazi Mind*. Rev. ed. New York: Capricorn Books, 1961.

Web Sites

http://www.americannaziparty.com/ American Nazi Party

http://www.creator.org/ World Church of the Creator

http://www.naawp.com/ National Association for the Advancement of White People

http://www.natvan.com/ National Alliance

http://www.nazi.org/ Libertarian National Socialist Green Party

http://www.nordland.net/vinland/ Vinland Records

http://www.nsm88.com/ National Socialist Movement

http://www.panzerfaust.com/ Panzerfaust Records

http://www.resistance.com/ Resistance Records

http://www.national-socialist.org/ National Socialist Christianity

10

○

Political Islam

Islam is a religion that has become a major political force in the contemporary world.[1] *Islam* is an Arabic word meaning submission, specifically submission to the will of God or Allah (the Arabic word meaning God); *Muslim* means one who submits. Islam is the second largest world religion, after Christianity, with about a billion adherents. They live mostly in a wide belt from Senegal on the west coast of Africa, east to Indonesia on the western edge of the Pacific Ocean, and reaching south into sub-Saharan Africa and north into the southern part of the former Soviet Union. This area contains forty-four countries that are

---

1. Islamic political thought has not yet been studied very much in the West. The following sources in English include works both for the beginner and for someone wanting some depth. Good places for the neophyte to start are Aziz Al-Azmeh, "Islamic Political Thought," in *Blackwell Encyclopedia of Political Thought,* ed. David Miller (Oxford, England: Blackwell Reference, 1987), 249–53; and Phil Marfleet, "Islamist Political Thought," in *New Political Thought: An Introduction,* ed. Adam Lent (London: Lawrence & Wishart, 1998), 89–111. Other works to consult include Hamid Enayat, *Modern Islamic Political Thought: The Response of the Shi'i and Sunni Muslims to the Twentieth Century* (London: Macmillan, 1982); Abdulrahman Abdulkadir Kurdi, *The Islamic State: A Study Based on the Islamic Holy Constitution* (London: Mansell, 1984); Bernard Lewis, *The Political Language of Islam* (Chicago: University of Chicago Press, 1988); E. I. J. Rosenthal, *Political Thought in Medieval Islam: An Introductory Outline* (Cambridge: Cambridge University Press, 1962); and W. Montgomery Watt, *Islamic Political Thought: The Basic Concepts* (Edinburgh: Edinburgh University Press, 1968). Some texts can be found in "Political Philosophy in Islam," ed. Muhsin Mahdi, in *Medieval Political Philosophy: A Sourcebook,* ed. Ralph Lerner and Muhsin Mahdi (New York: Free Press, 1963), 22–186; and Kemal H. Karpat, ed., *Political and Social Thought in the Contemporary Middle East,* rev. and enl. ed. (New York: Praeger, 1982).

predominantly Islamic; in addition, there are growing Muslim communities throughout the rest of the world, including America and Europe.

There are similarities of belief among Muslims that allow us to identify a community of believers, just as there are similarities of belief among the widely divergent sects of Christianity. But Islam is not a single, unified religion. There is one major division between two sects, the Sunni with about 85 percent of all Muslims and the Shiite with the other 15 percent, which will be discussed in this chapter, and there are a number of smaller sects. Equally important, there are significant differences in Islamic practice from country to country as well as from individual to individual.

For most of the twentieth century Islam was not a significant political force in world affairs. Most Islamic countries were attempting to modernize and join the developed world. Four things changed this. First, the establishment of the state of Israel in 1948 on land then occupied by Palestinians united Islamic countries that had been previously divided. Second, the rapid rise in the price of oil meant that some poor countries were suddenly rich. Third, the Iranian revolution, combined with Iranian attempts to foment revolution in other Islamic countries, led to a much greater focus on Islamic thought both in the Middle East and elsewhere. Fourth, the process of decolonization and the connected revitalization of national cultures led to a revival of divisions in Islam that had lain dormant during the colonial period.

Many Muslims reject modernization and Westernization, seeing it as corrupting basic Islamic values. This rejection is most frequently labeled *Islamic fundamentalism,* even by many Islamic scholars. While *Islamic revivalism* or *re-Islamization* are better labels because they avoid the too easy identification with Christian fundamentalism, these terms are currently used interchangeably with *Islamic fundamentalism.*

BELIEFS

Although it is neither possible nor relevant to discuss Islamic theology here, a few points of religious belief are necessary as background to help understand Islam. Islam is unified by its faith in Allah, the holy book the Qur'an, and the teachings of its prophet, Muhammad. Islam sprang from the same roots and the same geographic area as Judaism and Christianity, and Islam accepts the Jewish prophets and Jesus as great religious teachers who were forerunners to Muhammad. Islam, like both Judaism and Christianity, is monotheistic. Jews, Christians, and Muslims are all thought of as "People of the Book."

There are five "pillars" of Islam that every pious Muslim must perform:

1. In a lifetime the believer must at least once say, "There is no god but God and Muhammad is the messenger of God," in full understanding and acceptance.
2. The believer must pray five times a day (at dawn, noon, midafternoon, dusk, and after dark).

3. The believer must give alms generously.

4. The believer must keep the fast of Ramadan (the ninth month of the Muslim year).

5. The believer must once make the pilgrimage (*hajj*) to Mecca, (generally spelled Makkah in the Middle East).

A sixth pillar is sometimes included, the *jihad,* usually thought of in the West as denoting "holy war" but actually meaning "to struggle" and signifying that believers must struggle with themselves and their communities to be good Muslims and to proselytize to enlarge the Muslim community.[2] Today, of course, *jihad* is being used by radical Islamic sects to describe a holy war against the West.

Beyond these basic beliefs and duties, the believer refers for guidance to the *Shari'a* (path or way), the religious law.[3] Islamic law gives both legal and moral guidance and has provided an additional point of reference for the widely divergent cultures represented by the many Islamic countries. For radical Muslims, one central goal is the adoption of the *Shari'a* as the law of the land. Of course, any law requires interpreters, and who is to interpret the law is the basis for certain disagreements within Islam.

Islamic law is derived from the Qur'an, the *Sunna* of the Prophet (the life of Muhammad), legal reasoning, and the consensus of the community.[4] It is more like a set of moral and ethical principles than what Westerners today think of as law, and it was, and in many Muslim countries is, interpreted and applied by a variety of courts and officials. In addition, in most countries the *Shari'a* was gradually supplemented and, in the eyes of some, supplanted by laws designed to deal with changing economic and political conditions.

Islamic countries have traditionally been theocratic (*theo* = God, *kratos* = rule), or societies where there is no separation of church and state and politics is subordinate to religion. Part of Islamic liberalism is the result of the political leaders in some countries changing or trying to change that relationship.

HISTORY

It is impossible to understand contemporary Islam without a little history. Muhammad lived from about 570 to 632, and the major division in Islam relates to his succession. Most Islamic groups accept that the first four *Caliphs* (successors) were correctly chosen. The dispute involves the line of succession after the fourth Caliph. The main Shiite sect, the Twelvers (believers in the Twelfth Imam), believe that the correct succession was through the fourth Caliph's descendants by his wife Fatima, Muhammad's daughter, through a line of infallible Imams, beginning with Ali ben Abi Talib, the fourth Caliph, and his two sons to the Twelfth Imam, who disappeared while still a boy. The Twelvers be-

---

2. John L. Esposito, *Islam: The Straight Path,* exp. ed. (New York: Oxford University Press, 1991), 93.

3. Ibid., 75–76.

4. Ibid., 79–85.

The Great Mosque, or *Haran,* at Mecca, Saudi Arabia is the spiritual center of Islam. At the center of the mosque is the Kaaba, or Caaba, the most sacred sanctuary in Islam. Mecca and the mosque are the destination of the hajj, or the pilgrimage that every Muslim is required to make in their lifetime. The towers are minarets, and from them a muezzin calls the faithful to prayer five times a day.

lieve that the Twelfth Imam is waiting for the right time to return, at which time he will bring justice to the earth and overthrow oppression. The Sunni, on the other hand, believe that the Caliphs that followed Ali were correctly chosen. They also accept a different basis for the choice—consensus—whereas the Shiites believe in divine appointment.

Although the division between the Sunni and the Shiite is the most important division within Islam, there are many other subgroups. For example, Saudi Arabia is ruled by followers of Wahabism, which was named after Muhammad bin Abd al-Wahab, an eighteenth-century clan leader. His descendants unified the country in 1932 and still rule; they consider Wahabism a purified form of Islam. Another important group within Islam is the Sufi, a mystical sect that exists throughout Islam, and there are numerous other distinct sects within Islam.

The next great division within Islam that is relevant to the contemporary political situation was brought about by the impact of the West. As with most other colonized areas, Islamic countries went through a process of combined acceptance and rejection of Western values and practices. While it was clear that Western technology, which allowed colonization to take place, was useful, perhaps even necessary, there was a deep division over the acceptance of Western values, particularly those related to individual freedom and equality.

Islamic thought has no concept of individual freedom or rights.[5] The emphasis is on the community of believers rather than the individual. An Islamic

5. Watt, *Islamic Political Thought,* 96.

government is expected to provide the internal and external security that will allow the believer to worship and to earn a living. But these are not rights that an individual can claim against a government. The process of government is dependent on the *Shari'a,* which means that religious teachers and interpreters are very powerful, as was the Imam Khomeini (1900–1989) in Iran during his lifetime.

The ideas of freedom, rights, and equality proved appealing to some believers, however, and groups of Westernizers, Islamic liberals, Islamic socialists, and advocates of women's rights began to appear in the nineteenth and early twentieth centuries. Thus, in practice the ideals of Islam have been challenged and compromised, particularly through contact with the West and its emphasis on individual liberty, the rights of the individual against the state, and the equality of women and men.

ISLAM TODAY

Politically, Islam is deeply divided between those who accept modernization and those who reject it. In the West today we mostly hear about the latter. The primary issue is not technology but the attitudes and beliefs of the West, and the modernizers are under great pressure to reject Western beliefs and attitudes even while encouraging the use of modern technologies.

Islamic Liberalism or Modernism

In the nineteenth and early twentieth centuries Islam went through a lengthy period during which Islamic thought experienced a transformation similar to the changes Christianity experienced in the seventeenth through nineteenth centuries. Specifically, Islamic liberal thinkers accepted the notion of historical change and, in particular, the idea that Islamic texts could be reinterpreted to meet changing conditions. These thinkers also argued for the reconciliation of reason and faith, the need for educational reform to take advantage of Western science and technology, and the desirability of greater equality for women.[6] For quite some time and in many countries, Islamic liberalism was dominant, but in the second quarter of the twentieth century a shift began to take place, based on the experience of colonialism, that rejected Islamic liberalism as too Western. The identification of Islamic liberalism with the West and colonialism provided the ideological basis for the emergence of Islamic revivalism.

Islamic liberalism or modernism survives as a strong intellectual force throughout Islam and in movements that stem from the earlier liberal period but has made compromises with Islamic revivalism.[7]

---

6. See Nader Saiedi, "What Is Islamic Fundamentalism?" in *Prophetic Religions and Politics: Religion and the Political Order,* ed. Anson Shupe and Jeffrey K. Hadden (New York: Paragon House, 1986), 179–82.

7. See, for example, Charles Kurzman, ed., *Liberal Islam: A Sourcebook* (New York: Oxford University Press, 1998).

In Egypt the movement started by Gamal Abdel Nasser (1918–70) still exists but is of much less importance than it once was, even though the current leaders of Egypt see themselves as the heirs of Nasser. Nasserism was essentially secular but used Islamic symbols. In Libya, Colonel Mu'ammar Gadhafi (Qadahafi) (b. 1942) established a highly idiosyncratic version of Islam that hides a dictatorship behind most of the policies of Islamic liberalism. In Syria the Baath Party, which was founded in 1940 by Michel Aflaq (1910–89), a Christian, and Salah al-Din Baytar (1911–80), a Muslim, is essentially secular while using Islamic symbols. It rejects both capitalism and communism because both are based on materialism; economically the Baath Party is socialist. Its greatest emphasis, though, is on Arab nationalism and the desirability of a single Arab nation; the party finds Islamic origins for this position.

Intellectually, Islamic liberalism or modernism centers on democratization and what Western intellectuals and a growing number of Islamic scholars see as related issues, freedom and equality, the latter particularly as it relates to the status of women. Although they approach the question from a number of different angles, many Islamic scholars argue that democracy, with its attendant elections and the loss and gain of power, is completely acceptable within Islam as a way of fulfilling the traditional obligation that rulers have to consult widely.[8]

Islamic Revivalism or Fundamentalism

In the West revivalism is usually associated with the Shiites, but revivalism is also strong among the Sunni. Although there are significant differences between Sunni and Shiite revivalists, there are also major agreements. In particular, all revivalists want the reestablishment of the *Shari'a,* which they believe will result in an Islamic theocracy and the full realization of the ideal Islamic community.

The intellectual grounding of Islamic revivalism is usually traced to Ayatollah Ruhollah Khomeini (1900–1989), Abu al-A'la al-Mawdudi (1903–79), and Sayyid Qutb (1906–66). Qutb is best known for the concept *jahiliyya,* which originally referred to the period of "ignorance" or "barbarism" that existed before Muhammad preached in Arabia. Qutb used *jahiliyya* to refer to the present day, explicitly to the influence of the West. While these revivalists had serious differences, they all wanted to create theocracies in which Allah delegated political power to the current rulers. In other words, all temporal power was to be held in the name of Allah, and the leader was to be responsible to Allah for his (none of them could conceive of a woman as a ruler) use of that power.

The Muslim Brotherhood   The fact that revivalism can combine modernization with a rejection of Westernization is demonstrated best by the Muslim Brotherhood (al-Ikhwan al-Muslimun), the first major revivalist movement, founded in 1928 in Egypt by Hasan al-Banna (1906–49). The Muslim Brotherhood, which became one of the most powerful movements ever to exist within

---

8. See, for example, Azzam Tamimi, ed., *Power-Sharing Islam?* (London: Liberty for Muslim World Publications, 1993), particularly the essays by Rachid Ghannouchi, Muhammad Salim Al-Awa, and Hassan Al-Alkim.

Islam and still exists today, emphasizes both a return to Islamic traditions and scientific and technical education. The Muslim Brotherhood also argues for major social and economic reforms within the framework of Islam. In addition, the Brotherhood seeks the unification of all Muslims.

Politics For Muslims, Allah is the only legislator; any earthly ruler is only to ensure that God's laws are practiced. Therefore, any such ruler is an administrator, not a lawgiver. Sunni and Shiite revivalists disagree on who should rule. The most extreme Sunni believe that a Caliph (successor) should administer the Divine Law. Shiite Islam requires the presence of the Mahdi, or Twelfth or Hidden Imam, for the correct government to be established. In his absence a monarch or sultan who rules with the consent of the *ulama*—religious teachers or those who are learned in the divine law—is the best possible solution.

As was seen in Iran under Ayatollah Khomeini, a legislature composed of the *ulama* operating with the advice of an imam (leader) can replace the monarch or sultan, but that legislature is still subordinate to the *Shari'a*. Khomeini believed that the clergy were the appropriate rulers. He also argued that the most preeminent among the clergy—that is, the most learned, just, and pious —should hold the highest office, that of deputy to the Hidden or Twelfth Imam. Khomeini saw himself in that role and was accepted as such.

Social Organization The traditional, patriarchal family with the man as its head is at the center of the Islamic community. A Muslim man may have up to four wives as long as he can support them. Under the law the testimony of two women is equal to that of one man. However, the Qur'an gives women specific rights. Most important, women can hold and inherit property, although these rights have been frequently violated and some revivalists would like them limited. But women are to function only in the private sphere; only men are to act publicly.

In traditional Islam, which the revivalists want to see reestablished, equality between women and men is impossible—the concept is meaningless. According to one scholar's interpretation, the functions of men and women could be divided into privileges and duties. Men have the privileges of social authority and mobility and the duty of economic responsibility.[9] Women have three privileges:

1. "A woman in traditional Islamic society does not have to worry about earning a living."

2. "A women does not have to find a husband for herself."

3. A woman "is spared direct military and political responsibility." Her primary duty "is to provide a home for her family and to bring up her children properly."[10]

---

9. Seyyad Hossein Nasr, *Ideals and Realities of Islam,* 2d ed. (London: George Allen & Unwin, 1975), 112.

10. Ibid., 112–13.

The Taliban In September 2001 Americans suddenly became aware of the Taliban, an obscure sect of Islam then ruling most of Afghanistan.[11] The word *taliban* means "student" and the movement is sometimes called the "Religious Students' Movement." The goal of the Taliban has been to create a pure Islamic state in Afghanistan under its founder and leader Mullah Mohammad Omar Akhund (b. 1961).

Although mostly representing one of the many ethnic groups in the country (the Pashtuns, the largest ethnic group in Afghanistan), the Taliban were initially very popular because they brought relative peace to a country that had been at war with its neighbors and within itself since 1978. The Soviet Union invaded Afghanistan in 1979 and was finally forced to withdraw in 1988, at which time a struggle for power among various factions within Afghanistan began. The Taliban captured the capital, Kabul, in 1996 and began to enforce their very narrow interpretation of the Islamic rule of law, one in which women must wear the *burqa,* a dress that covers them completely from head to toe, and men must grow their beards. Women, in particular, were severely restricted in that few were allowed to work or be educated, and, with almost no women doctors, their access to health care was almost nonexistent.[12]

Since September 2001, the Taliban have become best known for protecting Osama bin Laden (b. 1957), head of Al Qaeda, an organization designed to overthrow both Western and Muslim governments, all of which are seen as corrupted by Western influences. The ultimate goal appears to be to abolish all contemporary political boundaries and reestablish the rule of the Caliphs.

ISLAM IN THE UNITED STATES

Islam has deep roots in the United States and is growing rapidly. Muslims were among the earliest explorers and settlers in North America, but significant numbers began to arrive in the late 1800s, with later waves of immigrants in the periods 1947 to 1960 and 1967 to the present. As a result, there are Islamic communities in the United States that are one hundred years old. In addition, many African Americans converted to Islam. This movement began early in the twentieth century but its greatest growth was in the 1950s and 1960s with the development of the Nation of Islam under the leadership of Elijah Muhammad (1897–1975) and Malcolm X (1925–65). It continues today in a variety

---

11. On the Taliban, see M. J. Gohari, *The Taliban: Ascent to Power* (Karachi, Pakistan: Oxford University Press, 2000); Peter Marsden, *The Taliban: War, Religion, and the New Order in Afghanistan* (Karachi, Pakistan: Oxford University Press; London: Zed Books, 1998); Kamal Matinuddin, *The Taliban Phenomenon: Afghanistan 1994–1997* (Karachi, Pakistan: Oxford University Press, 1999); Ahmed Rashid, *Taliban: Militant Islam, Oil, and Fundamentalism in Central Asia* (New Haven, Conn.: Yale University Press, 2000); and *The Taliban's War on Women: A Health and Human Rights Crisis in Afghanistan. A Report by Physicians for Human Rights* (Boston: Physicians for Human Rights, 1998).

12. For some of the actual rules, see "A Sample of Taliban Decrees Relating to Women and Other Cultural Issues, after the Capture of Kabul, 1996," in Rashid, *Taliban,* 217–19.

of groups that emerged from the Nation of Islam. About 30 percent of the Muslims in America today are African American.

Immigrant Islam Islam is among the fastest growing religions in both Europe and the United States. Although estimates of the number of Muslims in the United States vary widely and are considered unreliable, there are more Muslims in the United States than in a number of Islamic countries in the Middle East. In the United States Islam tends to center on local mosques, which generally operate quite independently, although there are the beginnings of a number of regional and countrywide federations of mosques, mostly based on the country of origin of the immigrant community attending the mosques.[13] At present, there are about 1,200 mosques in the United States, and about a third of the Muslims in America today come from South and East Asia and 25 percent from various Arab countries.

Since many Islamic students come to the United States to attend university, there are also a number of Muslim student groups, the Muslim Student Association being the largest. There are also a number of immigrant Islamic sectarian communities.[14] The largest and best established of these is the Sufi.

American Muslims have the full range of immigrant responses that have been experienced by immigrants of other faiths. Some return to the home country (sometimes with the idea of building an Islamic state); others work to establish Islamic communities in the United States so that it will be possible to live an Islamic life within the United States; and yet others assimilate. As with other immigrants, the second and third generations tend toward the third option but often, again as with other immigrants, with the desire to reconnect with their national and religious roots.[15] An indication of the adjustment to U.S. conditions is that women now head the boards running two mosques in the United States. It is, of course, entirely possible that the attacks on Muslims in the United States since September 11, 2001 will produce future terrorists of people who

---

13. On Islam in America, see Yvonne Yazbeck Haddad and Jane Idleman Smith, *Mission to America* (Gainesville: University Press of Florida, 1993), which discusses Islamic groups in America outside the mainstream; Haddad and Smith, eds., *Muslim Communities in North America* (Albany: State University of New York Press, 1994), a collection of essays on many specific Muslim communities in the United States and Canada; Haddad, ed., *The Muslims of America* (New York: Oxford University Press, 1991); Gilles Kepel, *Allah in the West: Islamic Movements in America and Europe,* trans. Susan Milner (Stanford: Stanford University Press, 1997); Michael A. Koszegi and J. Gordon Melton, eds., *Islam in North America: A Sourcebook* (New York: Garland, 1992); Jane I. Smith, *Islam in America* (New York: Columbia University Press, 1999); and Earle H. Waugh, Sharon McIrvin Abu-Laban, and Regula Burckhardt Qureshi, eds., *Muslim Families in North America* (Calgary: University of Alberta Press, 1991).

14. For a now somewhat dated list of Islamic organizations in North America, see "A Directory of Islamic Organizations and Centers in North America," in Koszegi and Melton, *Islam in North America,* 291–395. For a list of Internet sources (though be aware that many of these will have changed), see Smith, *Islam in America,* 225–26.

15. On the immigrant experience, see Yvonne Yazbeck Haddad and Adair T. Lummis, *Islamic Values in the United States: A Comparative Study* (New York: Oxford University Press, 1987); Haddad and John L. Esposito, eds., *Muslims: The New Generation* (New York: Continuum, 2000).

were good, loyal American citizens until they and their coreligionists were targeted by U.S. ethnic nationalists.

African American Islam African Americans have been affiliated with Islam from at least 1913, when the Moorish American Science Temple was founded in Newark, New Jersey, but African American Islam is most commonly identified with the Nation of Islam (better known as the Black Muslims), which was a direct response to the conditions of African Americans in the twentieth century in the United States. As taught by Elijah Muhammad, the Nation of Islam combined traditional Islamic teachings with an interpretation of the African American experience in the United States that saw whites as the devil.

After the death of Elijah Muhammad and the assassination of Malcolm X, who, after a pilgrimage to Mecca, rejected the racial message of the Nation of Islam, the Nation fragmented. One of Elijah Muhammad's sons, Warith Deen Muhammad (b. 1933), rejected the racial message of his father, decentralized the organization, changed its name to the American Muslim Mission, and encouraged African American Muslims to join mainstream Islam. The best known contemporary descendent of the Nation, Louis Farrakhan (b. 1933) kept both the name and centralized structure of the Nation of Islam, and, although not consistently, has kept at least some of the racial message.[16]

CURRENT TRENDS

There are a number of issues within Islam today.[17] One of the most widespread is the status of women. In the West, probably the best-known aspect of traditional Islam is the veiling of women. Veiling—which can range from a scarf covering the hair to the *burqa* required by the Taliban—is not found in the Qur'an but developed differently within the different Islamic countries. In fact, most of the rules that keep women in an inferior position in some Islamic countries are not found in either the Qur'an or the *Shari'a*. As a result, Islamic feminists argue that there are serious grounds for an Islamic version of female-male equality. It must be recognized, though, that many modern Islamic women accept the veil or scarf covering the head as a way of respecting their religion; for many it is definitely not a symbol of inferiority.[18] It is difficult to generalize about Islam. For example, in March of 2001 I flew from New Zealand to Europe and

---

16. On the Nation of Islam, see Essien Udosen Essien-Udom, *Black Nationalism: A Search for Identity in America* (Chicago: University of Chicago Press, 1962); Mattias Gardell, *In the Name of Elijah Muhammad: Louis Farrakhan and the Nation of Islam* (Durham, N.C.: Duke University Press, 1996); C. Eric Lincoln, *The Black Muslims in America* (Boston: Beacon Press, 1973); and Vibert L. White, Jr., *Inside the Nation of Islam: A Historical and Personal Account by a Black Muslim* (Gainesville: University Press of Florida, 2001).

17 For general coverage, see Mansoor Moaddel and Kamran Talattof, eds., *Contemporary Debates in Islam: An Anthology of Modernist and Fundamentalist Thought* (New York: St. Martin's Press, 2000).

18. On veiling specifically, see Fadwa El Guindi, *Veil: Modesty, Privacy, and Resistance* (Oxford, England: Berg, 1999); and Nancy J. Hirschmann, "Eastern Veiling, Western Freedom?" *Review of Politics* 59, no. 3 (summer 1997): 461–88.

back on Air Malaysia, and I spent a few hours in each direction waiting in the airport in Kuala Lumpur. Malaysia is an Islamic country, and one of the most striking things in the airport was that women, both those working in the airport and those traveling, wore clothes that ranged from blue jeans and short skirts to complete coverings, including face masks or the *burqa*.

A second issue that is currently significant is the development of an Islamic concept of civil society (see the discussion in Chapter 3). The supporters of an Islamic conception of civil society reject the Western identification of civil society with secularism, arguing that it is possible to develop a distinctively Islamic civil society centered on the mosque. This has clearly already happened in North America.[19]

A third issue that has come up from time to time but is currently most important in Nigeria, an African country with a large Muslim population, is the extent to which Islamic law or the *Shari'a* should replace the legal codes currently in place. Most of these codes are based on Western models, either left over from colonial times or put into place by the first postindependence governments, and putting the *Shari'a* in place serves the dual purpose of rejecting the West and enhancing the Islamic identity of the country. But non-Muslims are afraid that they will lose the rights they had under the previous codes and become an oppressed minority. In Nigeria, this dispute has led to sporadic violence.

But of course, the central issue in Islam today is that between radical Islamic sects and mainstream Islam and between those sects and the West.

SUGGESTED READINGS

Some Classic Works

Ahmad, Jalal Al-E. *Gharbzadegi* (*West-struckness*). Translated by John Green and Ahmad Alizadeh. Lexington, Ky.: Mazdâ Publishers, 1982.

Banisadr, Asbolhassan. *The Fundamental Principles and Precepts of Islamic Government.* Translated by Mohammad R. Ghanoonparvar. Lexington, Ky.: Mazdâ Publishers, 1981.

El Saadawi, Nawal. *The Hidden Face of Eve: Women in the Arab World.* Translated and edited by Sherif Hetata. London: Zed Books, 1980.

Khomeini, Ayatollah Sayyed Ruhollah Mousavi. *Islam and Revolution.* Translated by Hamid Algar. Berkeley, Calif.: Mizan Press, 1981.

———. *Islamic Government.* Translated by Joint Publications Research Service. New York: Manor Books, 1979.

The Koran. With Parallel Arabic Text. Translated by N. J. Dawood. London: Penguin Books, 1990.

Books and Articles

Abdo, Geneive. *No God but God: Egypt and the Triumph of Islam.* Oxford: Oxford University Press, 2000.

Abrahamian, Ervand. *Khomeinism: Essays on the Islamic Republic.* Berkeley: University of California Press, 1993.

Abu-Rabi', Ibrahim M. *Intellectual Origins of Islamic Resurgence in the Modern Arab World.* Albany: State University of New York Press, 1996.

Afshar, Haleh. *Islam and Feminisms: An Iranian Case-Study.* London: Macmillan; New York: St. Martin's Press, 1998.

———, ed. *Women and Politics in the Third World.* London: Routledge, 1996.

---

19. See Augustus Richard Norton, ed., *Civil Society in the Middle East,* 2 vols. (Leiden, The Netherlands: E. J. Brill, 1995–96).

Ahmed, Akbar S. *Islam Today: A Short Introduction to the Muslim World.* London: I. B. Tauris, 1999.

Blank, Jonah. *Mullahs on the Mainframe: Islam and Modernity among the Daudi Bohras.* Chicago: University of Chicago Press, 2001.

Brown, L. Carl. *Religion and State: The Muslim Approach to Politics.* New York: Columbia University Press, 2000.

Brumberg, Daniel. *Reinventing Khomeini: The Struggle for Reform in Iran.* Chicago: University of Chicago Press, 2001.

Butterworth, Charles E., and I. William Zartman, eds. *Between the State and Islam.* Washington, D.C.: Woodrow Wilson Center Press; Cambridge: Cambridge University Press, 2001.

Cook, Michael. *The Koran: A Very Short Introduction.* Oxford: Oxford University Press, 2000.

Davidson, Lawrence. *Islamic Fundamentalism.* Westport, Conn.: Greenwood Press, 1998.

El Guindi, Fadwa. *Veil: Modesty, Privacy, and Resistance.* Oxford, England: Berg, 1999.

Esposito, John L. *The Islamic Threat: Myth or Reality.* 3d ed. New York: Oxford University Press, 1999.

———. *The Oxford Encyclopedia of the Modern Islamic World.* 4 vols. New York: Oxford University Press, 1995.

———, ed. *The Oxford History of Islam.* New York: Oxford University Press, 1999.

Esposito, John L., and John O. Voll. *Makers of Contemporary Islam.* Oxford: Oxford University Press, 2001.

Essien-Udom, Essien Udosen. *Black Nationalism: A Search for Identity.* Chicago: University of Chicago Press, 1962.

Euben, Roxanne L. *Enemy in the Mirror: Islamic Fundamentalism and the Limits of Modern Rationalism. A Work of Comparative Political Theory.* Princeton, N.J.: Princeton University Press, 1999.

Fluehr-Lobban, Carolyn. *Against Islamic Extremism: The Writings of Muhammad Sa'id al-'Ashmawy.* Gainesville: University Press of Florida, 1998.

Foltz, Richard. "Is There an Islamic Environmentalism?" *Environmental Ethics* 22, no. 1 (spring 2000): 63–72.

Gardell, Mattias. *In the Name of Elijah Muhammad: Louis Farrakhan and the Nation of Islam.* Durham, N.C.: Duke University Press, 1996.

Gerges, Fawaz A. *America and Political Islam: Clash of Cultures or Clash of Interests?* Cambridge: Cambridge University Press, 1999.

Gohari, M. J. *The Taliban: Ascent to Power.* Karachi, Pakistan: Oxford University Press, 2000.

Goodson, Larry P. *Afghanistan's Endless War: State Failure, Regional Politics, and the Rise of the Taliban.* Seattle: University of Washington Press, 2001.

Haddad, Yvonne Yazbeck, ed. *The Muslims of America.* New York: Oxford University Press, 1991.

Haddad, Yvonne Yazbeck, and John L. Esposito, eds. *Islam, Gender, & Social Change.* New York: Oxford University Press, 1998.

———, eds. *Muslims on the Americanization Path?* Atlanta: Scholars Press, 1998.

Haddad, Yvonne Yazbeck, and John L. Esposito, with Elizabeth Hiel and Hibba Abugideiri. *The Islamic Revival since 1988: A Critical Survey and Bibliography.* Westport, Conn.: Greenwood Press, 1997.

Haddad, Yvonne Yazbeck, and Adair T. Lummis. *Islamic Values in the United States: A Comparative Study.* New York: Oxford University Press, 1987.

Haddad, Yvonne Yazbeck, and Jane Idleman Smith. *Mission to America: Five Islamic Sectarian Communities in North America.* Gainesville: University Press of Florida, 1993.

———, eds. *Muslim Communities in North America.* Albany: State University of New York Press, 1994.

Halliday, Fred. *Nation and Religion in the Middle East.* Boulder, Colo.: Lynne Rienner, 2000.

Hasan, Asma Gull. *American Muslims: The New Generation.* New York: Continuum, 2000.

Hekmat, Anwar. *Women and the Koran: The Status of Women in Islam.* Amherst, N.Y.: Prometheus Books, 1997.

Huband, Mark. *Warriors of the Prophet: The Struggle for Islam.* Boulder, Colo.: Westview Press, 1998.

Keane, John. *Civil Society.* London: Polity Press, 1998.

Kepel, Gilles. *Allah in the West: Islamic Movements in America and Europe.* Translated by Susan Milner. Stanford: Stanford University Press, 1997. Originally published as *A l'Ouest d'Allah* (Paris: Éditions du Seuil, 1994).

Khadduri, Majid. *The Islamic Conception of Justice.* Baltimore: Johns Hopkins University Press, 1984.

Khuri, Richard K. *Freedom, Modernity, and Islam: Toward a Creative Synthesis.* Syracuse, N.Y.: Syracuse University Press, 1998.

Koszegi, Michael A., and J. Gordon Melton, eds. *Islam in North America: A Sourcebook.* New York: Garland, 1992.

Kurzman, Charles, ed. *Liberal Islam: A Sourcebook.* New York: Oxford University Press, 1998.

Lawrence, Bruce B. *Shattering the Myth: Islam beyond Violence.* Princeton, N.J.: Princeton University Press, 1998.

Lee, Martha F. *The Nation of Islam: An American Millenarian Movement.* Lewiston, N.Y.: Edward Mellen Press, 1988. Reprint, Syracuse, N.Y.: Syracuse University Press, 1996.

Lincoln, C. Eric. *The Black Muslims of America.* Rev. ed. Boston: Beacon Press, 1973.

Malcolm X. *The Autobiography of Malcolm X.* New York: Grove Press, 1965.

Marfleet, Phil. "Islamist Political Thought." In *New Political Thought: An Introduction,* edited by Adam Lent, 89–111. London: Lawrence & Wishart, 1998.

Marlow, Louise. *Hierarchy and Egalitarianism in Islamic Thought.* Cambridge: Cambridge University Press, 1997.

Marsden, Peter. *The Taliban: War, Religion, and the New Order in Afghanistan.* Karachi, Pakistan: Oxford University Press; London: Zed Books, 1998.

Matinuddin, Kamal. *The Taliban Phenomenon: Afghanistan 1994–1997.* Karachi, Pakistan: Oxford University Press, 1999.

Mernissi, Fatima. *Beyond the Veil: Male-Female Dynamics in Modern Muslim Society.* Rev. ed. Bloomington: Indiana University Press, 1987.

Messaoudi, Khalida. *Unbowed: An Algerian Woman Confronts Islamic Fundamentalism.* Interviews with Elisabeth Schemla. Translated by Anne C. Vila. Philadelphia: University of Pennsylvania Press, 1998. Originally published as *Une Algérienne debout* (Paris: Flammarion, 1995).

Moaddel, Mansoor, and Kamran Talattof, eds. *Contemporary Debates in Islam: An Anthology of Modernist and Fundamentalist Thought.* New York: St. Martin's Press, 2000.

Moghissi, Haideh. *Feminism and Islamic Fundamentalism: The Limits of Postmodern Analysis.* London: Zed Books, 1999.

Moin, Baqer. *Khomeini: Life of the Ayatollah.* New York: Thomas Dunne Books, 1999.

Moses, Wilson Jeremiah, ed. *Classical Black Nationalism: From the American Revolution to Marcus Garvey.* New York: New York University Press, 1996.

Moussalli, Ahmad S. *Moderate and Radical Islamic Fundamentalism: The Quest for Modernity, Legitimacy, and the Islamic State.* Gainesville: University Press of Florida, 1999.

Norton, Augustus Richard, ed. *Civil Society in the Middle East.* 2 vols. Leiden, The Netherlands: E. J. Brill, 1995–96.

Rahnema, Ali. *An Islamic Utopian: A Political Biography of Ali Shari'ati.* London: I.B. Tauris, 1998.

———, ed. *Pioneers of Islamic Revival.* London: Zed Books, 1994.

Rashid, Ahmed. *Taliban: Militant Islam, Oil, and Fundamentalism in Central Asia.* New Haven, Conn.: Yale University Press, 2000.

Robinson, Dean E. *Black Nationalism in American Politics and Thought.* Cambridge: Cambridge University Press, 2001.

Rubin, Barry. *The Transformation of Palestinian Politics: From Revolution to State-Building.* Cambridge: Harvard University Press, 2000.

Ruthven, Malise. *Islam: A Very Short Introduction.* Oxford: Oxford University Press, 1997.

Sadri, Mahmoud, and Ahmad Sadri, eds. and trans. *Reason, Freedom, & Democracy in Islam: Essential Writings of 'Abdolkarim Soroush.* Oxford: Oxford University Press, 2000.

Sciolino, Elaine. *Persian Mirrors: The Elusive Face of Islam.* New York: Free Press, 2000.

Shadid, Anthony. *Legacy of the Prophet: Despots, Democrats, and the New Politics of Islam.* Boulder, Colo.: Westview, 2001.

Sidahmed, Abdel Salam, and Anoushiravan Ehteshami, eds. *Islamic Fundamentalism.* Boulder, Colo.: Westview Press, 1996.

Smith, Jane I. *Islam in America.* New York: Columbia University Press, 1999.

The Taliban's War on Women: A Health and Human Rights Crisis in Afghanistan. A Report by Physicians for Human Rights. Boston: Physicians for Human Rights, 1998.

Tamimi, Azzam, ed. *Power-Sharing Islam?* London: Liberty for Muslim World Publications, 1993.

Tamimi, Azzam, and John L. Esposito, eds. *Islam and Secularism in the Middle East.* New York: New York University Press, 2000.

Tibi, Bassam. *The Challenge of Fundamentalism: Political Islam and the New World Disorder.* Berkeley: University of California Press, 1998.

Van Deburg, William L., ed. *Modern Black Nationalism: From Marcus Garvey to Louis Farrakhan.* New York: New York University Press, 1997.

Viorst, Milton. *In the Shadow of the Prophet: The Struggle for the Soul of Islam.* New York: Anchor Books, 1998.

Wadud-Muhsin, Amina. *Qur'an and Woman.* Kuala Lumpur, Malaysia: Penerbit Fajar Bakti, 1992.

Waugh, Earle H., Baha Abu-Laban, and Regula B[urckhardt] Qureshi, eds. *The Muslim Community in North America.* Calgary: University of Alberta Press, 1983.

Waugh, Earle H., Sharon McIrvin Abu-Laban, and Regula Burckhardt Qureshi, eds. *Muslim Families in North America.* Calgary: University of Alberta Press, 1991.

Waugh, Earle H., and Frederick M. Denny, eds. *The Shaping of an American Islamic Discourse: A Memorial to Fazlur Rahman.* Atlanta: Scholars Press, 1998.

Webb, Gisela. "Expressions of Islam in America." In *America's Alternative Religions,* edited by Timothy Miller, 233–42. Albany: State University of New York Press, 1995.

———. "Sufism in America." In *America's Alternative Religions,* edited by Timothy Miller, 249–58. Albany: State University of New York Press, 1995.

White, Vibert L., Jr. *Inside the Nation of Islam: A Historical and Personal Account by a Black Muslim.* Gainesville: University Press of Florida, 2001.

Web Sites

http://global.globale.net/~mag/ Islam in America

http://www.daralislam.org/ Dar al Islam

http://www.iananet.org/ Islamic Assembly of North America

http://www.icna.org/ Islamic Circle of North America

http://www.icofa.com Islamic Center of North America

http://www.islamicedfoundation.com/ Islamic Foundation of North America

http://www.universalsufism.com/ International Sufi Movement, America

11

@

Liberation Theology

Liberation Theology began as a movement within the Roman Catholic Church in Latin America. As a movement it struggled to define itself against the opposition of most of the church hierarchy in Latin America and against the opposition of the papacy, particularly the opposition of Pope John Paul II (the current pope). From these roots Liberation Theology spread to Protestantism and to Africa, Asia, Ireland, and the United States. Because of the continuing opposition of the Roman Catholic Church, today Liberation Theology may be most dynamic in Protestantism, particularly in Black Theology in the United States, but it remains of great significance, although quietly, within Roman Catholicism, particularly in Latin America. Coordination among liberation theologies is provided by the Ecumenical Association of Third World Theologians (EATWOT).

Liberation Theology has a conflicted relationship with European theology, which clearly provided some of its ideas and early thinkers. Particularly outside Latin America, the European, or in the United States the white, nature of theology is seen as a problem to be overcome, overcome because European/white theology ignored or, to some degree, opposed the concerns of the poor, minorities, colonized peoples, and women. As one Asian theologian put it, "we find that many elements in the Christian teachings are not relevant to us."[1]

---

1. Tissa Balasuriya, "Towards the Liberation Theology of Asia," in *Asia's Struggle for Full Humanity: Towards a Relevant Theology. Papers from the Asian Theological Conference, January 7–20, 1979, Wennappuwa, Sri Lanka,* ed. Virginia Fabella (Maryknoll, N.Y.: Orbis Books, 1980), 19.

Liberation Theology is based on the message that Jesus was and is a liberator. It brings "the good news of liberation" from unjust social structures, the
power of fate, and personal sin and guilt through divine mercy and the action
of people to transform their own lives. It brings hope to and requires commitment from its adherents, hope that the Kingdom of God can be created on earth
and commitment to the effort to prepare the way.

Liberation Theology developed as a response to the poverty found in Latin
America together with the fact that the Roman Catholic Church, the dominant
church in the area, was identified with the rich and powerful. The Church was
having difficulty providing priests for rural areas where most of the poor lived.
As a result, those who were concerned with these problems began, first in Brazil
as early as the late 1950s, to encourage community-based organizations, later to
be called Base Christian Communities, to provide for their own religious needs.
This led, quite rapidly, to these same groups identifying social, economic, and
political needs and organizing themselves to try to meet those needs.

As the movement developed, intellectuals began to look for theological and
theoretical justification. They found the French worker-priest movement,[2] and
they found Western Marxism with its concern for the poor. The worker-priest
movement helped them encourage priests to work in communities as equals
with the people. Marxism, but particularly the so-called Marxist-Christian dialogue of the late 1960s, provided a theory that could be integrated with the theological movements that had produced the Ecumenical Council of 1962–65,
better known as Vatican II, with its emphasis on modernizing the Church and
making it more responsive to laypeople. Vatican II also stressed collective responsibility in the Church, which fit nicely with the community organizations
that Liberation Theology was developing.

THE MARXIST-CHRISTIAN DIALOGUE

Much of the Marxism found in Liberation Theology came through Ernst Bloch
(1885–1977), who was discussed in Chapter 7. Bloch, a Marxist who chose to
spend much of his life in what was then East Germany, argued that Christianity had a tremendous radical potential. And theologians within Liberation Theology found that Marx's emphasis on the poor resonated with their concerns
and the needs of their people.

In 1965 the French Marxist Roger Garaudy (b. 1913) published a book entitled *From Anathema to Dialogue: The Challenge of Marxist-Christian Cooperation.*
The publication of this book began a long-lasting debate on the degree to which
Marxists and Christians could learn from each other or even actively cooperate. The basis of the developing dialogue was the writings of the young Marx,
which focus on human alienation and the dehumanizing effects of capitalist
society. These writings attracted theologians with similar concerns, and some

---

2. The worker-priest movement was a movement in French Catholicism in which priests
   took factory jobs so that they would experience the lives of the people more completely.

Marxists have found in Christianity, particularly early Christianity, both a deep concern with the oppressed and a message of hope for the future in this life. As a result, both Marxists and Christians began to consider what they could say to each other without losing the essential characteristics of their beliefs.

For Liberation Theology the key is found in accepting that Marx made major contributions to our understanding of capitalism and helped illuminate the position of the poor in modern society but also in recognizing that he was limited by his rejection of God. Thus "Marx (like any other Marxist) can be a companion on the way . . . but he can never be the guide, because 'You have only one teacher, the Christ' (Matt. 23:10)."[3] In addition to Marx, one of the most important nontheological sources of Liberation Theology is the work of the Brazilian Paulo Freire (1921–97), particularly his *Pedagogy of the Oppressed* (1970). Freire advocated what he calls conscientization, or consciousness-raising, a process in which the oppressed become aware of their oppression through participation in group discussion with others in similar circumstances. Anarchists also claim Freire as an important theorist, and he is best known as an educational theorist who successfully headed the school system in São Paulo, Brazil.

THE PRINCIPLES OF LATIN AMERICAN LIBERATION THEOLOGY

Liberation Theology arose out of the above-mentioned dialogue. It has also been said that "Liberation theology was born when faith confronted the injustice done to the poor."[4] Although John Paul II condemned Liberation Theology in the past, he subsequently accepted some of its basic positions. Most conservatives within the Roman Catholic Church still reject most of Liberation Theology.

In broad outline the position of Liberation Theology is as follows:

1. The church should be concerned with poverty.

2. The church should be concerned with political repression.

3. The church should be concerned with economic repression.

4. Priests should become actively involved in trying to solve these problems.

5. Priests should move beyond general activity to

   a. direct political action, and, possibly,

   b. direct involvement in attempts to change political and economic systems, even by actual participation in revolutionary activity.

---

3. Leonardo Boff and Clodovis Boff, *Introducing Liberation Theology,* trans. Paul Burns (Maryknoll, N.Y.: Orbis Books, 1987), p. 28.

4. Boff and Boff, *Introducing Liberation Theology,* 3.

6. Base communities or communities that include both religious (priests and nuns) and laypeople should be established. These communities should be designed to overcome the division between religious and laypeople.

The Roman Catholic Church specifically rejects item five and is not sure about item three. Pope John Paul II once rejected item six but has accepted it in some circumstances. Camilo Torres (1929–66) was one of the priests who took the political messages to heart and became an active revolutionary.[5]

One of the early theorists of Liberation Theology was Gustavo Gutiérrez (b. 1928) of Chile. His *Theology of Liberation* (1971, English trans. 1973) was the first work to bring together the elements of Liberation Theology. Gutiérrez argued, based on Freire and Bloch, that the Church must recognize the positive function of the idea of utopia. Utopia includes the condemnation of the evils of the present and an affirmation of the possibilities of the future. As Gutiérrez put it,

> The theology of liberation attempts to reflect on the experience and meaning of the faith based on the commitment to abolish injustice and to build a new society; this theology must be verified by the practice of that commitment, by active, effective participation in the struggle which the exploited social classes have undertaken against their oppressors. Liberation from every form of exploitation, the possibility of a more human and more dignified life, the creation of a new man—all pass through this struggle.[6]

Today the best known theorist of Latin American Liberation Theology is Leonardo Boff (b. 1938). He argues that Liberation Theology developed as and where it did because Latin Americans are both poor and Christian. The Church was generally supportive of the rich and powerful, and many both inside and outside the Church found this fact morally repugnant. As Boff and Clodovis Boff (b. 1944) wrote, "we can be followers of Jesus and true Christians only by making common cause with the poor and working out the gospel of liberation."[7]

Liberation Theology, like other radical movements in the 1960s and 1970s, stressed consciousness-raising, the direct participation of the people, and socialism, but Liberation Theology differs from these radical movements in that it focuses on religion. Although it is beyond the scope of this book to explore the theology of Liberation Theology, it must always be remembered that it is a theology and bases its political and economic message on an understanding of the Bible and, particularly, the mission of Christ.

Like many radical theologians and spiritual leaders of the past, the leading thinkers of Liberation Theology see the Christian message as directed particu-

---

5. For his writings, see *Revolutionary Priest: The Complete Writings & Messages of Camilo Torres,* ed. John Gerassi (New York: Random House, 1971).

6. Gustavo Gutiérrez, *A Theology of Liberation: History, Politics, and Salvation,* 15th anniv. ed., trans. and ed. Sister Caridad Inda and John Eagleson (Maryknoll, N.Y.: Orbis Books, 1988), 174.

7. Boff and Boff, *Introducing Liberation Theology,* 7.

Leonardo Boff (b. 1938) is a Franciscan priest and professor of Systematic Theology at the Institute for Philosophy and Theology in Petrópolis, Brazil. He is one of the best-known theologians of Liberation Theology. He was "silenced" (meaning he could not publish) by the Vatican for one year in response to his writings on Liberation Theology.

Claus Meyer/Black Star

larly to the poor and oppressed. One of the earlier spiritual leaders to whom the Liberation Theologians look is St. Francis of Assisi (1182–1226), who, it should be remembered, insisted on the absolute poverty of his followers.[8] St. Francis was too radical for the church of his day, as is Liberation Theology today.

A central political-theological tenet of Liberation Theology is the idea of the poor, or, as they call it, "the preferential option for the poor." This means that all actions should be judged on whether or not they help the poor. The Boffs argue that the idea of the poor must be expanded to include all the oppressed —specifically, blacks, indigenous peoples, and women. The poor are, for the Boffs, "the Disfigured Son of God."[9]

Liberation Theology holds out hope for the transformation of the world in which we live today. "The holy city, the new Jerusalem that comes down from heaven (Rev. 21:2), can be established on earth only when men and women filled with faith and passion for the gospel, united with each other, and hungry and thirsty for justice, create the human dispositions and material conditions for it."[10] This desired transformation will be a gift from God, but people can prepare the way for it.

Base Communities

In a phrase reminiscent of Karl Marx's statement, "The philosophers have only *interpreted* the world in various ways; the point is to *change* it,"[11] Boff says,

---

8. Leonardo Boff, *Saint Francis: A Model for Human Liberation,* trans. John W. Diercksmeier (New York: Crossroad Press, 1982).

9. Boff and Boff, *Introducing Liberation Theology,* 31.

10. Ibid., 95.

11. See Chapter 7.

"More important than to see and to judge is to act." [12] A key to action in Latin American Liberation Theology has been the establishment of base communities, or base ecclesial communities. These communities both aid consciousness-raising and provide a setting in which people learn to take control of their own lives. "From its own identity in faith, the Church organizes the people in Christian communities, those in which the lowly meet, meditate on the Word of God, and, enlightened by that Word, discuss their problems and find ways of solution. These base communities have an immediate and direct religious value, but they also achieve social importance because they are places for the formation of social conscience, responsibility, and the desire for change." [13]

In 1979 Latin American bishops meeting at Puebla, Mexico recognized the base communities as an important new form of both evangelizing and liberating the poor and oppressed. "We have found that small communities, especially the CEBs [Base-level Ecclesial Communities], create more personal interrelations, acceptance of God's Word, re-examination of one's life, and reflection on the reality of the Gospel. They accentuate committed involvement in the family, one's work, the neighborhood, and the local community." [14]

In Liberation Theology, communitarianism rather than individualism is considered the way forward. Ever since Vatican II (1962–65) there has been a movement in the Roman Catholic Church to involve the laity more fully in the Church. The development of base communities is one of the responses to this movement. Boff describes a typical community as follows:

> The base ecclesial community is generally made up of fifteen to twenty families. They get together once or twice a week to hear the Word of God, to share their problems in common, and to solve those problems through the inspiration of the Gospel. They share their comments on the biblical passages, create their own prayers, and decide as a group what their tasks should be. After centuries of silence, the People of God are beginning to speak. They are no longer just parishioners in their parish; they have their own ecclesiological value; they are recreating the Church of God. [15]

The sense of participation that is encouraged is a radical departure for the Roman Catholic Church, which has traditionally been hierarchical and authoritarian. Many in the Church have difficulty accepting the empowerment of the laity and the degree of control over the forms of worship that are being demanded. For reasons that are not entirely clear, such communities have developed only in Latin America.

---

12. Boff, *Saint Francis*, 87.

13. Ibid.

14. *Puebla and Beyond: Documentation and Commentary,* ed. John Eagleson and Philip Scharper (Maryknoll, N.Y.: Orbis Books, 1979), 211.

15. Leonardo Boff, *Church: Charism and Power—Liberation Theology and the Institutional Church,* trans. John W. Diercksmeier (New York: Crossroad Press, 1985), 125–26. From *Church: Charism and Power—Liberation Theology and the Institutional Church* by Leonardo Boff, trans. John W. Diercksmeier. English translation © 1985 by T. C. P. C. Reprinted by permission of The Crossroad Publishing Company.

LIBERATION THEOLOGY IN ASIA

Minjung theology is a Korean Liberation Theology that emerged initially within the Korean Methodist Church in the 1970s in response to oppression by the Korean government. The central theologian of Minjung theology is Ahn Byung-mu (1922–96). Minjung is Korean derived from Chinese *min* = "people" and *jung* = "mass," but the word cannot be translated into English.[16] Minjung theology is millenarian, believing that the Kingdom of God will be established on earth in the near future.

Minjung refers to the common people oppressed by an elite. "Minjung are the people of God, and their experience of suffering owing to the injustice of the ruling group has to be eliminated from this world. Therefore, the act of liberation becomes the central focus of minjung theology. Moreover, the realization of the fruits of liberation produces the establishment of the Messianic Kingdom or the Reign of God on earth."[17] The key concepts are *Han* and *Dan*. "*Han* is the feeling of resentment, depression, repressed anger, helplessness, just indignation, etc., which is combined with a desire for a better future."[18] *Dan* is a more complex and more clearly political concept and refers to the ability to overcome *Han* with the help of God by breaking through the repression that creates *Han*. Thus, using different concepts, Minjung theology is quite similar to Latin American Liberation Theology. It focuses on the poor and repressed and fashions a theology that energizes people to help themselves overcome their situation. It is different from Latin American Liberation Theology in being millenarian, relying on local congregations rather than base ecclesial communities, and, of course, occurring within Protestantism rather than Roman Catholicism.

LIBERATION THEOLOGY IN AFRICA

Contemporary Christian theology in Africa can be divided into liberation, most obviously in South Africa, and inculturation, found throughout the rest of Christian Africa. Inculturation means that indigenous African religious practices have been grafted onto Christian theology. This has generally been easier within Protestantism, but is also found in Roman Catholicism. Liberation Theology took hold in South Africa because it provided a response to the oppres-

---

16. David Suh Kwang-sun, "A Biographical Sketch of an Asian Theological Consultation," in *Minjung Theology: People as the Subjects of History,* ed. Commission on Theological Concerns of the Christian Conference of Asia (CTC-CCA), rev. ed. (Maryknoll, N.Y.: Orbis Books; London: Zed Books, 1983), 16.

17. Jung Young Lee, "Minyung Theology: A Critical Introduction," in *An Emerging Theology in World Perspective: Commentary on Korean Minjung Theology,* ed. Jung Young Lee (Mystic, Conn.: Twenty-Third Publications, 1988), 11.

18. Michael Amaladoss, S.J., *Life in Freedom: Liberation Theologies from Asia* (Maryknoll, N.Y.: Orbis Books, 1997), 4.

sion of the black majority by the white majority.[19] The best known of the South African Liberation Theologians is Allan Boesak (b. 1946), who in *Farewell to Innocence* (1976, English trans. 1977) argued that African theology, Latin American Liberation Theology, Black Theology in the United States, and black theology in South Africa are all expressions of the same fundamental theology of liberation.

Liberation Theology in Africa is similar to and different from Latin American Liberation Theology in much the same ways as Minjung theology, with the added ingredient of race. The oppressed group was oppressed because it was black, which resonates with the development of Black Liberation Theology in the United States.

BLACK LIBERATION THEOLOGY
IN THE UNITED STATES

From the perspective of the United States, the most interesting development is the spread of Liberation Theology within African American Protestantism. James H. Cone (b. 1938), certainly one of the most important theologians of the twentieth century, was the first exponent of Black Theology, a distinct movement not initially connected to Liberation Theology, and is still its best-known advocate. Cone initially kept his distance from Latin American Liberation Theology because it was rooted in Roman Catholicism and because he saw its proponents as white. But Cone came quite quickly to recognize the commonalities between his position and theirs, and he also helped introduce Asian Liberation Theology to U.S. theologians and Black Theology to both Latin American and Asian theologians. Cone has been a key figure internationally in bringing the various strands of Liberation Theology together. He has recognized and corrected weaknesses in his own initial analysis, particularly regarding women and class.

Cone stresses that Black Theology derives from the lived experiences of African Americans in racist America and their experiences in the black church. He calls white theology *ideology* and means it negatively, saying, "Christ *really* enters into our world where the poor, the despised, and the black are, disclosing that he is with them, enduring their humiliation and pain and transforming oppressed slaves into liberated servants. Indeed, if Christ is not *truly* black, then the historical Jesus lied."[20] This strong language emphasizes Black Theology's alienation from the dominant theological culture in Europe and North America in which Christ is always depicted as white. It also stresses that for African Americans, Christ as liberator reflects their community.

---

19. For a discussion of both trends, see Emmanuel Martey, *African Theology: Inculturation and Liberation* (Maryknoll, N.Y.: Orbis Books, 1993).

20. James H. Cone, *God of the Oppressed* (New York: Seabury Press, 1975), 136. Emphasis in the original.

James H. Cone (b. 1938) is the Charles A. Briggs Distinguished Professor of Systematic Theology at Union Theological Seminary. His book *A Black Theology of Liberation* (1970) founded the school of thought now known as Black Theology. Over the years, he has enriched his thought by incorporating work by theologians from North America, Africa, Asia, and Latin America, including black women theologians, and later editions of *A Black Theology of Liberation* (1986 and 1990) illustrate the evolution of his thought. His books *Black Power and Black Theology* (1969, new ed. 1989) *The Spirituals and the Blues* (1972), *God of the Oppressed* (1975, rev. ed. 1997),

Sheila Turner, Atlanta, GA

For My People: Black Theology and the Black Church (1984), *Speaking the Truth: Ecumenism, Liberation, and Black Theology* (1986), *My Soul Looks Back* (1986), and *Martin & Malcolm & America: A Dream or a Nightmare?* (1991) reflect his growing stature as both a theologian and a cultural critic.

Womanist Theology

As indicated above, Cone was criticized for ignoring gender issues, and while he responded positively to the criticisms, African American women have developed a variant of Black Liberation Theology known as "Womanist Theology." Womanist comes from Alice Walker's (b. 1944) *In Search of Our Mothers' Gardens* (1983), in which she defines the term as follows:

> **Womanist** 1. From *womanish*. (Opp. of "girlish." i.e., frivolous, irresponsible, not serious.) A black feminist or feminist of color. From the black folk expression of mothers to female children, "You acting womanish," i.e., like a woman. Usually referring to outrageous, audacious, courageous or *willful* behavior. Wanting to know more and in greater depth than is considered "good" for one. Interested in grown-up doings. Acting grown up. Being grown up. Interchangeable with another black folk expression: "You trying to be grown." Responsible. In charge. Serious.
>
> • • •
>
> 2. *Also:* A woman who loves other women, sexually and/or nonsexually. Appreciates and prefers women's culture, women's emotional flexibility (values tears as natural counterbalance to laughter), and women's strength. Sometimes loves individual men, sexually and/or nonsexually. Committed to survival and wholeness of entire people, male *and* female. Not a separatist, except periodically, for health. Traditionally universalist, as in: "Mama, why are we brown, pink, and yellow, and our cousins are white, beige,

and black?" Ans.: "Well, you know the colored race is just like a flower garden, with every color flower represented." Traditionally capable, as in: "Mama, I'm walking to Canada and I'm taking you and a bunch of other slaves with me." Reply: "It wouldn't be the first time."

• • •

3. Loves music. Loves dance. Loves the moon. *Loves* the Spirit. Loves food and roundness. Loves struggle. *Loves* the Folk. Loves herself. *Regardless.*

• • •

4. Womanist is to feminist as purple to lavender.[21]

The phrase "A woman who loves other women, sexually and/or nonsexually" has divided Womanist theologians.

Womanist theologians argue, as did Cone, that "Christ is Black. That is to say, Christ has Black skin and features and is committed to the Black community's struggle for life and wholeness."[22] Womanist theologians are explicit that African American women must free themselves from their own acceptance "of sexist oppression, the black man's acceptance of patriarchal privilege, and the white woman's acceptance of white racist privilege."[23] Womanist theologians also argue, as do most feminists, that liberation must be for all peoples regardless of race, gender, and ethnicity.

LIBERATION THEOLOGY
IN EUROPE—IRELAND

Liberation Theology took hold in Ireland because Ireland was the first British colony. Ireland gained its independence from Britain only in 1922, and the existence of Northern Ireland as a part of the United Kingdom of Great Britain and Northern Ireland constantly reminds the Irish of this colonial past and, as many see it, the continuing colonial status of this part of their country. Until quite recently Ireland was one of the poorest countries in Europe, and therefore the stress on poverty in Liberation Theology appealed to some Irish theologians. At the same time, Ireland, like Latin America, had a church hierarchy opposed to Liberation Theology and the closeness of Rome and the Papacy appears to have led to an almost complete suppression of Liberation Theology in Ireland in the recent past.[24]

---

21. Alice Walker, "Womanist" from *In Search of Our Mothers' Gardens: Womanist Prose,* copyright © 1983 by Alice Walker, reprinted by permission of Harcourt, Inc. and The Women's Press.

22. Kelly Brown Douglas, *The Black Christ* (Maryknoll, N.Y.: Orbis Books, 1994), 106–7.

23. Marcia Y. Riggs, *Awake, Arise, and Act: A Womanist Call for Black Liberation* (Cleveland: Pilgrim Press, 1994, 2.

24. On Irish Liberation Theology, see, for example, Dermot Lane, ed., *Liberation Theology: An Irish Dialogue* (Dublin: Gill and Macmillan, 1977), reprinted as *Ireland, Liberation, and Theology* (Maryknoll, N.Y.: Orbis Books, 1978); and Joe McVeigh, *Renewing*

CURRENT TRENDS

Today Liberation Theology is still predominantly a Third World movement and the Ecumenical Association of Third World Theologians (EATWOT) provides a recurring venue for dialogue among theologians from Africa, Asia, the Caribbean, Latin America, the Pacific Islands, and North America. They are trying to deal with how Protestants and Roman Catholics, men and women, and peoples of all colors, ethnicities, and nationalities can forge a common understanding within Christianity of a common theology of liberation. Liberation Theology is perhaps more active today than at any time in the past.

Liberation Theology is now a worldwide movement, and for all their differences, these theologians agree on the central role of the poor and the oppressed and the need for committed action to achieve their liberation. Thus, Liberation Theology is explicitly and consciously a political movement that challenges economic and political oppression as well as the acceptance of such oppression by religious hierarchies.

SUGGESTED READINGS

Some Classic Works

Boff, Leonardo. *Jesus Christ Liberator: A Critical Christology for Our Times*. Translated by Patrick Hughes. Maryknoll, N.Y.: Orbis Books, 1981.

———. *Saint Francis: A Model for Human Liberation*. Translated by John W. Diercksmeier. Maryknoll, N.Y.: Orbis Books, 1982.

Bonino, José Míguez. *Doing Theology in a Revolutionary Age*. Philadelphia: Fortress Press, 1975. Published in the United Kingdom as *Revolutionary Theology Comes of Age* (London: SPCK, 1975).

Cone, James H. *A Black Theology of Revolution*. 20th anniv. ed. Maryknoll, N.Y.: Orbis Books, 1990.

Dussel, Enrique. *History and Theology of Liberation: A Latin American Perspective*. Translated by John Drury. Maryknoll, N.Y.: Orbis Books, 1975.

Gutiérrez, Gustavo. *The Power of the Poor in History*. Translated by Robert R.

Barr. Maryknoll, N.Y.: Orbis Books, 1983.

———. *A Theology of Liberation: History, Politics, and Salvation*. 15th anniv. ed. Maryknoll, N.Y.: Orbis Books, 1988.

Segundo, Juan Luis. *Liberation Theology*. Translated by John Drury. Maryknoll, N.Y.: Orbis Books, 1976.

Books and Articles

Amaladoss, Michael, S.J. *Life in Freedom: Liberation Theologies from Asia*. Maryknoll, N.Y.: Orbis Books, 1997.

Boesak, Allan [Aubrey], and Charles Villa-Vicencio. *A Call for an End to Unjust Rule*. Edinburgh: Saint Andrew Press, 1986.

———. *Farewell to Innocence: A Socio-Ethical Study on Black Theology and Black Power*. Maryknoll, N.Y.: Orbis Books, 1977.

Boff, Leonardo. *Church, Charism, and Power: Liberation Theology and the Institutional Church*. Translated by John W.

the Irish Church: Towards an Irish Liberation Theology (Dublin: Mercier Press, 1993). An interesting sidelight on Irish Liberation Theology is found in the recognition by a Protestant minister from Northern Ireland that Liberation Theology may also speak to their concerns. See Sidney John Garland, "Liberation Theology: An Irish Perspective" (master's thesis, Westminster Theological Seminary, Philadelphia, 1984).

Diercksmeier. New York: Crossroad Press, 1985.

————. *Ecclesiogenesis: The Base Communities Reinvent the Church*. Translated by Robert R. Barr. Maryknoll, N.Y.: Orbis Books, 1986.

————. *Liberating Grace*. Translated by John Drury. Maryknoll, N.Y.: Orbis Books, 1981.

————. *The Lord's Prayer: The Prayer of Integral Liberation*. Translated by Theodore Morrow. Maryknoll, N.Y.: Orbis Books, 1983.

————. *Trinity and Society*. Translated by Paul Burns. Maryknoll, N.Y.: Orbis Books, 1986.

————. *Way of the Cross—Way of Justice*. Translated by John Drury. Maryknoll, N.Y.: Orbis Books, 1982.

Boff, Leonardo, and Clodovis Boff. *Introducing Liberation Theology*. Translated by Paul Burns. Maryknoll, N.Y.: Orbis Books, 1987.

————. *Salvation and Liberation: In Search of a Balance between Faith and Politics*. Translated by Robert R. Barr. Maryknoll, N.Y.: Orbis Books; Melbourne, Australia: Dove Communications, 1984.

Boff, Leonardo, and Virgil Elizondo, eds. *Convergences and Differences* [Cover title: *Theologies of the Third World*]. Edinburgh: T. & T. Clark, 1988.

————, eds. *The People of God Amidst the Poor*. Edinburgh: T. & T. Clark, 1988.

Brown, Robert McAfee. *Liberation Theology: An Introductory Guide*. Louisville, Ky.: Westminster/John Knox Press, 1993.

Commission on Theological Concerns of the Christian Conference of Asia (CTC-CCA), ed. *Minjung Theology: People as the Subjects of History*. Rev. ed. Maryknoll, N.Y.: Orbis Books; London: Zed Books; Singapore: Christian Conference of Asia, 1983.

Cone, James H. *Black Theology and Black Power*. Maryknoll, N.Y.: Orbis Books, 1997.

————. *God of the Oppressed*. New York: Seabury Press, 1975.

————. *Martin & Malcolm & America: A Dream or a Nightmare*. Maryknoll, N.Y.: Orbis Books, 1991.

————. *Risks of Faith: The Emergence of a Black Theology of Liberation, 1968–1998*. Boston: Beacon Press, 1999.

————. *The Spirituals and the Blues: An Interpretation*. New York: Seabury Press, 1972.

Cone, James H., and Gayraud S. Wilmore, eds. *Black Theology: A Documentary History, 1966–1979*. 2d ed., rev. Maryknoll, N.Y.: Orbis Books, 1993.

————, eds. *Black Theology: A Documentary History, 1980–1902*. Maryknoll, N.Y.: Orbis Books, 1993.

Douglas, Kelly Brown. *The Black Christ*. Maryknoll, N.Y.: Orbis Books, 1994.

Dussel, Enrique. *Philosophy of Liberation*. Translated by Aquilina Martinez and Christine Morkowsky. Maryknoll, N.Y.: Orbis Books, 1985.

Elwood, Douglas J., ed. *Asian Christian Theology: Emerging Themes*. Rev. ed. of *What Asian Christians Are Thinking*. Philadelphia: Westminster Press, 1980.

Eze, Emmanuel Chukwudi, ed. *African Philosophy: An Anthology*. Oxford: Blackwell, 1998.

Fabella, Virginia, ed. *Asia's Struggle for Full Humanity: Towards a Relevant Theology. Papers from the Asian Theological Conference, January 7–20, 1979, Wennappuwa, Sri Lanka*. Maryknoll, N.Y.: Orbis Books, 1980.

Fabella, Virginia, and R. S. Sugirtharajah, eds. *Dictionary of Third World Theologies*. Maryknoll, N.Y.: Orbis Books, 2000.

Fabella, Virginia, and Sergio Torres, eds. *Irruption of the Third World: Challenge to Theology. Papers from the Fifth International Conference of the Ecumenical Association of Third World Theologians, August 17–29, 1981, New Delhi, India*. Maryknoll, N.Y.: Orbis Books, 1983.

Fagan, Seán, S.M. "Liberation Theology in Ireland." *Doctrine and Life* (Dublin), 27.2 (May 1977): 22–28.

Garland, Sidney John. "Liberation Theology: An Irish Perspective." Master of

Theology thesis, Westminster Theological Seminary, Philadelphia, 1984.

Gerassi, John, ed. *Revolutionary Priest: The Complete Writings & Messages of Camilo Torres*. New York: Random House, 1971.

Gilkes, Cheryl Townsend. *"If It Wasn't for the Women . . .": Black Women's Experience and Womanist Culture in Church and Community*. Maryknoll, N.Y.: Orbis Books, 2001.

Hayes, Diana L. *And Still We Rise: An Introduction to Black Liberation Theology*. New York: Paulist Press, 1996.

Hebblethwaite, Margaret. *Base Communities: An Introduction*. London: Geoffrey Chapman, 1993.

Hopkins, Dwight N. *Introducing Black Theology of Liberation*. Maryknoll, N.Y.: Orbis Books, 1999.

King, Ursula, ed. *Feminist Theology from the Third World: A Reader*. Maryknoll, N.Y.: Orbis Books, 1994.

Lane, Dermot, ed. *Liberation Theology: An Irish Dialogue*. Dublin: Gill & Macmillan, 1977. Reprinted as *Ireland, Liberation, and Theology* (Maryknoll, N.Y.: Orbis Books, 1978).

Lee, Jung Young, ed. *An Emerging Theology in World Perspective: Commentary on Korean Minjung Theology*. Mystic, Conn.: Twenty-Third Publications, 1988.

Martey, Emmanuel. *African Theology: Inculturation and Liberation*. Maryknoll, N.Y.: Orbis Books, 1993.

McVeigh, Joe. *Renewing the Irish Church: Towards an Irish Liberation Theology*. Dublin: Mercier Press, 1993.

O'Sullivan, Michael, S. J., ed. *The Liberation of Theology*. Dublin: Irish Student Christian Movement, 1977.

Park, Jong Chun. *Crawl with God, Dance in the Spirit: A Creative Formulation of Korean Theology of the Spirit*. Nashville, Tenn.: Abingdon Press, 1998.

Rieger, Joerg. *Remember the Poor: The Challenge to Theology in the Twenty-First Century*. Harrisburg: Trinity Press International, 1998.

Riggs, Marcia Y. *Awake, Arise, and Act: A Womanist Call for Black Liberation*. Cleveland: Pilgrim Press, 1994.

Rowland, Christopher, ed. *The Cambridge Companion to Liberation Theology*. Cambridge: Cambridge University Press, 1999.

Setiloane, Gabriel M. *African Theology: An Introduction*. Johannesburg: Skotaville Publishers, 1986.

Williams, Delores S. *Sisters in the Wilderness: The Challenge of Womanist God-Talk*. Maryknoll, N.Y.: Orbis Books, 1993.

Wilmore, Gayraud S. *Black Religion and Black Radicalism: An Interpretation of the Religious History of African Americans*. 3d ed., rev. and enl. Maryknoll, N.Y.: Orbis Books, 1998.

Web Sites

http://minjungtheology.org/english.htm Institute of Minjung Theology

http://www.kuleuven.ac.be/studeng/interrelations/developco/fisches/c_theo5.htm
    Centre for Liberation Theology (Belgium)

http://www.osjspm.org/cst/libtheo2.htm Vatican Statement on Liberation Theology

12

@

Environmentalism

Even though it does not yet have an agreed-on name, a new ideology has emerged. This chapter briefly examines the origins and development of what is variously called *ecologism, environmentalism, Green politics,* or *Green political thought.* Here it is simply called environmentalism because in the United States it is most often called that. In Europe, where the movement is more developed, the word *environmentalism* reflects a fairly conservative approach, rather like the word *conservationism* does in the United States. Thus European thinkers tend more toward words like *ecologism,* which have not caught on in the United States.

In Europe many countries have Green political parties that have elected members to various local and regional legislative bodies; a number have elected members to national legislative bodies and to the European Parliament of the European Union. Green political parties are uncommon in North America. This changed, at least temporarily, when Ralph Nader (b. 1934) ran for president in 2000 as the candidate of the Green Party. But Nader received only 2.7% of the votes cast, which does not qualify the Green Party for federal funding in the 2004 election.

The Green Movement is primarily a movement of the developed North (including Australia and New Zealand in the South but generally excluding Japan) but is beginning to be felt in the rest of the world. Many, but not all, thinkers in the Third World argue that although they would like to encourage environmentally sound policies, they can't afford to; they see the Green Movement as a luxury that only the developed world can afford. However, the Green Movement is beginning to convince some of them that environmentalism is good economic policy.

ORIGINS

In North America two major sources have coalesced in the development of environmentalism. One source is the conservationism that developed in the United States as a result of such works as *Silent Spring* (1962) by Rachel Carson (1907–1964) and out of concern about the effects of overpopulation stemming from works like *The Population Bomb* (1968) by Paul Ehrlich (b. 1932). The other main source is the environmental theorists and activists who give the movement its belief system. It is possible to follow the careers and writings of major figures of this second source back to the ferment of the 1960s.

In North America, protests against the Vietnam War, nuclear weapons, and nuclear power produced a broadening awareness of the way these issues interact with issues related to political power and social conflict. There was a strong concern with self-sufficiency and a "back-to-the-land" component to some of the movements of the 1960s and 1970s. In the United States, the immensely successful series *The Whole Earth Catalog* (1968–1981) and the related *CoEvolution Quarterly* (1974–84) are evidence of this. The fact that a new edition of the *Whole Earth Catalog* was published in 1994 and that the *CoEvolution Quarterly* continues as the *Whole Earth Review* suggests that these movements did not end with the end of the earlier social movements. Related activities exist in Europe, Canada, Australia, and New Zealand based on similar earlier activities.

In Europe, the development of the movement was similar, but the failed revolutions of 1968 were of central importance, followed by the campaign against nuclear weapons, a growing recognition of the cross-national effects of pollution, and an early awareness that political and economic systems were centrally involved in the existing environmental problems as well as in any possible solutions. The key difference is that in Europe political parties were formed as well as interest or pressure groups as in North America.

A slightly different path involving the same issues can be traced in the writings of major theorists of environmentalism such as André Gorz (b. 1924), Ivan Illich (b. 1926), and Murray Bookchin (b. 1921). These theorists usually started from a position of general radicalism and then focused more and more on ecological issues.

Environmentalism has more remote origins that are difficult to define precisely. In North America these origins can be found in the writings of early environmentalists like John Muir (1838–1914), who was a campaigner for forest reserves and is now a "patron saint" of radical environmentalists, and Henry David Thoreau (1817–62), a writer whose *A Week on the Concord and Merrimack Rivers* (1849) and, especially, *Walden, or Life in the Woods* (1854) are imbued with a sensuous love of nature and a political rebelliousness that are echoed in many contemporary works.

Ecotopia

In 1975 Ernest Callenbach (b. 1929) self-published a novel that was to become the classic ecological utopia, particularly after it was republished in 1977 in a mass-market edition.[1] *Ecotopia* also produced a small body of literature of related materials.[2]

Ecotopia is a country formed out of what used to be the Northwest of the United States (Washington, Oregon, and Northern California). The story of the revolution that led to this successful secession is told in Callenbach's *Ecotopia Emerging* (1981) and need not detain us here. In 1999, when *Ecotopia* is set, a reporter is visiting Ecotopia for the first time since the 1980 secession. Although Ecotopia has a decentralized economic system, it also has a strong political system. There is more political power at the local level than in the United States, but Ecotopia has a chief of state (a concept that would be anathema in most of the other ecological utopias).

The description of a train trip in *Ecotopia* is a good example of what the environmentalism hopes to achieve.

> Their sentimentality about nature has even led the Ecotopians to bring greenery into their trains, which are full of hanging ferns and small plants I could not identify. (My companions however reeled off their botanical names with assurance.) At the end of the car stood containers rather like trash bins, each with a large letter—M, G, and P. These, I was told, were "recycle bins." It may seem unlikely to Americans, but I observed that during our trip my fellow travelers did without exception dispose of all metal, glass, or paper and plastic refuse in the appropriate bin. That they did so without the embarrassment Americans would experience was my first introduction to the rigid practices of recycling and re-use upon which Ecotopians are said to pride themselves to fiercely.[3]

The principles behind Callenbach's description and the rest of the utopia he presents in *Ecotopia* include closeness to nature, with plants inside the train, knowledge of the natural world, as shown by the passengers' ability to name the plants, and recycling.

---

1. Ernest Callenbach, *Ecotopia: The Notebooks and Reports of William Weston* (Berkeley, Calif.: Banyan Tree Books, 1975; New York: Bantam Books, 1977).

2. See Ernest Callenbach, *Ecotopia Emerging* (Berkeley, Calif.: Banyan Tree Books, 1981); and Callenbach, *The Ecotopian Encyclopedia for the 80s: A Survival Guide for the Age of Inflation* (Berkeley, Calif.: And/Or, 1980). See also Judith Clancy, *The Ecotopian Sketchbook: A Book for Drawing, Writing, Collaging, Designing, Thinking About, and Creating a New World, Based on the Novel Ecotopia by Ernest Callenbach* (Berkeley, Calif.: Banyan Tree Books, 1981).

3. Callenbach, *Ecotopia*, 10. Reprinted by permission of the author.

NASA

Photographs of Earth taken from outer space make the point that all human beings are inhabitants of a single place. Such photographs have struck a chord in many people and encouraged them to become aware of themselves as part of an international community. In addition, seen from outer space Earth has a fragile beauty that has helped fuel the recognition that ecological and environmental concerns cross all national borders.

THE PRINCIPLES OF
ENVIRONMENTALISM

Other writers have explicitly spelled out what they see as the fundamental principles of environmentalism. Lester W. Milbrath (b. 1925) has argued that there is a "new environmental paradigm" that includes a "high valuation on nature"; compassion toward other peoples, generations, and species; planning to avoid technology that is not environmentally sensitive; limiting growth; and, most important for the development of a new ideology, a new social paradigm and a new politics. The latter will require, among other things, greater participation, simpler living, cooperation, public versus private solutions to many issues, and a greater emphasis on worker satisfaction.[4] These principles make a good starting point because Milbrath establishes a middle ground; others would generally differ only in degree.

Elsewhere Milbrath has expanded on these characteristics with proposals that are more radical while rejecting any sort of right/left political dichotomy. In a later work, he insists on the necessity of eliminating the whole concept of dominance over nature; but much more important is his argument that we must both reduce the population in the world and lower the standard of living in the West.[5] While many agree with this position, it is not frequently stated because there is a fear that it will frighten people away from the movement.

---

4. Lester W. Milbrath, "Environmental Beliefs and Values," in *Political Psychology* (San Francisco: Jossey-Bass, 1986), 100.

5. See his argument in *Envisioning a Sustainable Society: Learning Our Way Out* (Albany: State University of New York Press, 1989).

Another author who has outlined the basic principles is Robert C. Paehlke. His "central value assertions of environmentalism" include a recognition of human beings as part of a global ecosystem, political decentralization and participation, concern with the future, simplicity, nonmaterial values, and less concern with technical solutions.[6] A third list, deriving from a leaflet put out by the Denver Region Greens in 1989, has these elements: Ecological Wisdom, Grassroots Democracy, Personal and Social Responsibility, Nonviolence, Decentralization, Community-based Economics, Postpatriarchal Values, Respect for Diversity, Global Responsibility, and a Future Focus.[7]

These three lists show the similarities and differences among those trying to define a Green ideology. The fact that the lists have such basic similarities begins to make the case for the existence of a coherent Green ideology. At the same time, some differing positions within the Green Movement are reflected in some of the differences found in these lists. Here we will look briefly at three of these different positions—ecosocialism, ecofeminism, and Deep Ecology.

ECOSOCIALISM

André Gorz

André Gorz (b. 1924) argues that "*the ecological movement is not an end in itself but a stage in the larger struggle.*"[8] That larger struggle is the one against capitalism. Gorz is a Marxist who rejects the centralism of the dominant Marxist tradition and uses Marx's philosophy to argue for a way of life that is no longer dominated by work. He wants a simpler lifestyle for all based on production limited to socially necessary goods. Everyone would work, but people would work less and at more satisfying jobs. To the extent possible, necessary but repetitive work would be replaced by automated machinery, a position that many environmentalists reject.

Gorz also contends that ecology cannot produce an ethic, another argument that is widely rejected by environmentalists. With the existence of journals like *Environmental Ethics,* it would seem that Gorz has lost part of the argument. Gorz contends that ecology should be seen as a "purely scientific discipline" that "does not necessarily imply the rejection of authoritarian technological solutions."[9]

Most environmentalists argue that ecology does produce an ethic, one that requires the rejection of "authoritarian technological solutions." But Gorz's argument is based on the fact that many environmentalists accept the possibility

---

6. Robert C. Paehlke, *Environmentalism and the Future of Progressive Politics* (New Haven, Conn.: Yale University Press, 1989), 144–45.

7. "Green Values" (Denver: Denver Region Greens, 1989).

8. André Gorz, *Ecology as Politics,* trans. Patsy Vigderman and Jonathan Cloud (Boston: South End Press, 1980), 3. Emphasis in the original.

9. Ibid., 17.

of using highly technological means to solve some of the world's pollution problems. Thus, while the left wing of the Green Movement rejects his position and argues for an ethic that is antitechnological, those to Gorz's right generally accept his conclusion and support the use of technology to solve problems brought about by technology.

Murray Bookchin

Murray Bookchin (b. 1921) is best described as an anarchist, but he also fits under the label of ecosocialism. Bookchin described what he calls "an ecological society" in the following terms: "An ecological society would fully recognize that the human animal is biologically structured to live with its kind, and to care for and love its own kind within a broadly and freely defined social group." [10] In the last part of his *Ecology of Freedom* (1982) and in his *Toward an Ecological Society* (1980), Bookchin describes a society that seems to be based on many of the principles outlined by Milbrath, Paehlke, and the Denver Greens. It is radically decentralized, participatory, and has overcome hierarchy, replacing it with a society that respects each individual and the planet on which we live.

ECOFEMINISM

The set of ideas called *ecofeminism* is a combination of feminism, the peace movement, and environmentalism.[11] It springs mostly from the part of feminism that views women as more in tune with nature than men, but it begins with the assertion that our ecological problems stem from the male notion of dominance as applied to nature and other human beings. Thus, it explicitly rejects the sort of technological solution accepted by Gorz. An interesting example of this sensibility can be found in Ursula K. Le Guin's short story "She Unnames Them" (1985), in which Eve is depicted as freeing the animals from Adam's domination by unnaming them—that is, giving them back their own identity rather than the identity imposed on them through Adam's names.

Ecofeminism tends to accept what is called the *Gaia hypothesis,* which sees the earth as a living being that must be nourished and protected rather than exploited. Many ecofeminists see this as part of a revived belief in what they call the Goddess, a revived religion that in some ways is close to nature worship. It should be noted that not all self-described ecofeminists are women and that parts of their beliefs, like the Gaia hypothesis, are widely accepted by other environmentalists.

Ecofeminists are thus using age-old traditions combined with new understandings contributed by feminism and environmentalism to give birth to a dif-

---

10. Murray Bookchin, *The Ecology of Freedom: The Emergence and Dissolution of Hierarchy* (Palo Alto, Calif.: Cheshire Books, 1982), 318.

11. The best statement of ecofeminism is *Reweaving the World: The Emergence of Ecofeminism,* eds. Irene Diamond and Gloria Feman Orenstein (San Francisco: Sierra Club Books, 1990).

ferent way of viewing the relationship between the human race and the rest of the natural world. They argue that technological solutions to environmental problems are male solutions that simply cause different problems in the future without correcting the current ones. Ecofeminists are close to the most controversial movement found in the Green Movement, Deep Ecology, but they contend that Deep Ecology has missed the point that our problems stem from the masculine worldview of domination rather than from the more general human-centeredness that Deep Ecology identifies as the source of our environmental problems.[12]

DEEP ECOLOGY

The single most controversial movement found within environmentalism today is Deep Ecology (a term coined in 1972 by Arne Naess [b. 1912]), sometimes called *biocentrism*. It is controversial because it places the rest of nature above humans. In other words, it is all right to damage human interests and even human beings in order to protect nature. One of its popularizers, Dave Foreman (b. 1946), the founder of Earth First!, puts it as follows: "This philosophy states simply and essentially that all living creatures and communities possess intrinsic value, inherent worth. Natural things live for their own sake, which is another way of saying they have value. Other beings (both animal and plant) and even so-called 'inanimate' objects such as rivers and mountains are not placed here for the convenience of human beings."[13]

The "deepness" of Deep Ecology lies in its rejection of the emphasis on human beings found in most of the Green Movement. There are "deeper" values that emphasize the entire biosphere, as opposed to just human beings. For Deep Ecology, nature is not for human use; it has value in and of itself. Nature has rights that need to be protected against human beings. Nature is the standard, and human beings are the problem.

Clearly such a position is not acceptable to many environmentalists. Murray Bookchin, for example, has attacked Deep Ecology in his *Remaking Society* (1989). Bookchin argues that the whole approach of biocentrism is wrongheaded. He contends that it simply reverses the domination of nature by humanity to the domination of humanity by nature. He says that the goal should be balance, not domination.

In 1984 Naess and George Sessions (b. 1938) spelled out eight principles to form a Platform of Deep Ecology.

1. The flourishing of human and non-human life on Earth has intrinsic value. The value of non-human life forms is independent of the usefulness these may have for narrow human purposes.

12. See Rik Scarce, *Eco-Warriors: Understanding the Radical Environmental Movement* (Chicago: Noble Press, 1990), 39.

13. Dave Foreman, *Confessions of an Eco-Warrior* (New York: Harmony Books, 1991), 26–27.

2. Richness and diversity of life forms are values in themselves and contribute to the flourishing of human and non–human life on Earth.

3. Humans have no right to reduce this richness and diversity except to satisfy vital needs.

4. Present human interference with the non–human world is excessive, and the situation is rapidly worsening.

5. The flourishing of human life and cultures is compatible with a substantial decrease of the human population. The flourishing of non–human life requires such a decrease.

6. Significant change of life conditions for the better requires change in policies. These affect basic economic, technological, and ideological structures.

7. The ideological change is mainly that of appreciating *life quality* (dwelling in situations of intrinsic value) rather than adhering to a high standard of living. There will be a profound awareness of the differences between big and great.

8. Those who subscribe to the foregoing points have an obligation directly or indirectly to participate in the attempt to implement the necessary changes.[14]

CURRENT TRENDS

Most of the current issues within environmentalism are concerned with how to get environmental concerns taken seriously within the political arena.

The Problem of Animal Rights

Closely related to Deep Ecology is a problem that has interested both philosophers and activists, the question of the rights of animals. The first question is, of course, do animals have rights? The second question is, if so, what are they?

On the whole, environmentalists accept the notion that animals have rights at roughly the same level as human beings—that is, at a minimum they have the right to be treated in the way that humans call humane. Others argue that animals have more rights, including the right to not be exploited by human beings. This position translates into vegetarianism and the rejection of the use of animals in scientific experimentation.

Animal rights are controversial among environmentalists. On the one hand, because most people do not want animals to be mistreated but also do not think that animals have rights, there are those who think the issue detracts from what they consider more important, such as reducing the actual degradation of the environment. On the other hand, groups like the Animal Liberation Front

---

14. See Arne Naess, *Ecology, Community, and Lifestyle: Outline of an Ecosophy,* trans. and ed. David Rothenberg (Cambridge: Cambridge University Press, 1989), 29. Reprinted by permission. Emphasis in the original.

(most active in the United Kingdom) and the Earth Liberation Front believe that animals have rights in exactly the same way as human beings and are willing to use violence against humans to further their position.

Most environmentalists take a middle ground where animals are concerned, wanting to protect species deemed endangered (a rapidly growing list worldwide), encouraging the reintroduction of species to traditional habitats where they no longer exist, and recognizing that the effects of humans on animal species regularly upsets any balance among species so that some species increase rapidly in numbers to the detriment of other species. Many environmentalists believe that this latter problem requires human intervention to reestablish the balance, while deep ecologists point out that it simply demonstrates that humans are the problem and cannot therefore be the solution. Law in the United States has generally followed the more conservative approach.[15] Specific laws of importance where animals are concerned include the National Environmental Policy Act of 1969 (83 Stat. 852), the Marine Mammal Protection Act of 1972 (86 Stat. 1027), and the Endangered Species Act of 1973 (87 Stat. 884).

Neo-Luddites and the Unabomber

In April 1996 Theodore J. Kaczynski (b. 1942) was arrested and identified as the so-called Unabomber who had assembled a number of bombs that had killed or injured leading figures in industry and technology. During the bombing campaign, the Unabomber published a manifesto justifying his actions and calling for a return to a more natural, less technological way of life. He and others like him have sometimes been called "neo-Luddites" after Ned Lud (or Ludd), a workman who broke stocking frames in 1779 because he was convinced that the newly introduced machines were taking away jobs. In the early nineteenth century a group of workmen calling themselves Luddites broke up textile machinery for the same reason, and the contemporary neo-Luddites like the Unabomber are also taking direct action against the forces that they see destroying the environment.

"Monkeywrenching"

In the Green Movement in the United States, civil disobedience or direct action is frequently called *monkeywrenching* after Edward Abbey's (1927–90) novels *The Monkey Wrench Gang* (1975) and *Hayduke Lives!* (1990), which describe a group of environmental activists who destroy things that they believe are damaging the environment. The Deep Ecology group called Earth First! follows the precepts of Abbey's novels, as do those who free animals from experiments or from battery farms (farms where animals are kept closely penned for life).

The people who are now being called *ecowarriors* contend that they are trying to break down the wall between the human and the nonhuman. It is their aim to protect biodiversity through direct action, particularly direct action that will play well to the media. There is no central organization in any of the

---

15. For the main laws, see http://www.epa.gov/epahome/laws.htm

groups that practice monkeywrenching; monkeywrenchers act either individually or in small groups. A number of ecowarriors practice what they preach by living in voluntary poverty.[16] Many in the Green Movement respect the ecowarriors and monkeywrenching while not believing monkeywrenching to be a good tactic politically.

A particularly famous case is that of Butterfly (Julia Hill) who lived in a tree she called Luna for 738 days (over two years) to protest logging. This act of monkeywrenching was at least partially successful in that she saved Luna and some other old-growth forest.[17]

The Eco-Village Movement

A worldwide movement has recently developed to establish small settlements that integrate human life into the natural environment. Such villages already exist throughout the world. The movement stresses learning from the ways that peoples throughout the world have successfully adapted to their environments.

"An eco-village is a human scale, full-featured settlement which integrates human activities harmlessly into the natural environment, supports healthy human development, and can be continued into the indefinite future."[18] They can be urban or rural, although so far most are rural. Urban eco-villages tend to be neighborhoods that have either collectively decided to transform themselves into a sustainable community or were purposely built to do so. Most rural eco-villages have resulted from changes made to existing villages, but a few have been built from scratch.

Green Political Parties

Germany has the most successful Green party (Die Grünen). It is part of the ruling coalition government with the Social Democratic Party and holds a number of cabinet posts, but its representatives have found it almost as difficult to be effective advocates for the environment with power as they did without it. Partially this comes from being the minor party in the coalition and partially it comes from the standard political problem of how one balances competing interests.

In the United States in the 2000 election, the Green Party drew national attention for the first time because its presidential candidate was Ralph Nader, who had long been a national figure. Nader did very poorly in the election, not even gaining enough votes to qualify the Green Party for federal election dollars in 2004. On the other hand, Nader almost certainly drew enough votes in Florida to affect the outcome of the election.

The U.S. Green Party platform stated that the "Green Key Values" are

---

16. See Scarce, *Eco-Warriors*, 5–6.

17. See Julia Butterfly Hill, *The Legacy of Luna: The Story of a Tree, a Woman, and the Struggle to Save the Redwoods* (New York: HarperCollins, 2000).

18. http://www.gaia.org/

1. Grassroots democracy
2. Social justice and equal opportunity
3. Ecological wisdom
4. Non-violence
5. Decentralization
6. Community-based economics and economic justice
7. Feminism and gender equity
8. Respect for diversity
9. Personal and global responsibility
10. Future focus and sustainability
11. Quality of life[19]

Although some of these key values are designed to appeal to hoped-for supporters, they are much the same as the statements by Milbrath, Paehlke, and the Denver Greens cited earlier.

Sustainability

A theme that appears throughout the Green Party platform is the central issue for most North American environmentalists—sustainability. One focus of sustainability is energy policy. The Green Party advocates the elimination of nuclear power and the development of renewable energy sources like solar and wind power. The party also advocates the "reduce-reuse-recycle" ethic so that fewer natural resources are destroyed and the development of alternative transport, "including natural gas vehicles, solar and electric vehicles, bicycles and bikeways, and MASS TRANSIT."[20]

Bioregionalism and Biodiversity

Another significant issue is what is called bioregionalism, which refers to the recognition that no single policy is appropriate to any political area. Each ecological region has its own, unique relationship among land, flora, fauna, and the human inhabitants, and this unique relationship needs to be respected.

In addition, each bioregion is biologically diverse, and environmentalists argue that such diversity must be maintained and fostered. The particular target of this concern is monoculture agriculture, the tendency to replace diversity with one cash crop like wheat or corn. The classic depiction of a bioregion is Aldo Leopold's (1886–1948) *A Sand County Almanac* (1949). A more recent look at bioregionalism is William Least Heat-Moon's (b. 1939) *PrairyErth* (1991), which examines the history and ecology of Chase County, Kansas (an area of 744 square miles) in great depth.[21]

---

19. http://gp.org/platform/
20. http://gp.org/platform/ Emphasis in the original.
21. William Least Heat-Moon, *PrairyErth: (a deep map)* (Boston: Houghton Mifflin, 1991).

Genetically Modified Foods

One of the most controversial issues today is the problem of genetically modified foods. Advocates say that the food produced is identical to natural foods, that horticulturalists and farmers have used genetic modification through selective breeding for centuries, and that genetic modification has the ability to radically increase food production and solve the problem of world hunger. Opponents argue that the scientific evidence is not yet established for any of these claims and that until it is, genetically modified crops should be grown only in very carefully controlled experiments or not at all. Particularly in the United Kingdom, groups have been destroying such crops when they can be identified. Proponents argue that Americans have been eating genetically modified foods for over ten years (few Americans know this) with no known side effects. For the last few years, most large European supermarket chains have required their suppliers to certify that no product contains any GM product and post large signs in their stores saying that everything is, to the extent possible, GM free. Such actions are much less common in the United States.

Radical environmentalism represents the beginning of an entirely new way of conceptualizing the world, a way that moves human beings off center stage and puts the biosphere, of which humanity is only a small part, at the center.

But for most people the impact of environmentalism is not found in a radical rethinking of the place of human beings in the biosphere but in smaller things like recycling, buying canned tuna certified as having been caught using methods that do not harm dolphins, eating more organic foods, and greater awareness of the importance of clean air and water. Others, of course, focus much more on specific issues such as the treatment of animals, genetically modified foods, or the protection of whales, and the environmental movement has certainly changed their lives significantly, as it has the lives of the activists who devote their entire lives to some aspect of the movement.

SUGGESTED READINGS

Some Classic Works

Abbey, Edward. *The Monkey Wrench Gang.* Philadelphia: J.B. Lippincott, 1975.

Bookchin, Murray. *Toward an Ecological Society.* Montreal: Black Rose Books, 1980.

Callenbach, Ernest. *Ecotopia: The Notebooks and Reports of William Weston.* Berkeley, Calif.: Banyan Tree Books, 1975.

Carson, Rachel. *Silent Spring.* Boston: Houghton Mifflin, 1962.

Club of Rome. *The Limits to Growth.* New York: Universe Books, 1972.

Ehrlich, Paul. *The Population Bomb.* New York: Ballantine, 1968.

Foreman, Dave. *Confessions of an Eco-Warrior.* New York: Harmony Books, 1991.

Gorz, André. *Ecology as Politics.* Translated by Patsy Vigderman and Jonathan Cloud. Boston: South End Press, 1980.

Ilich, Ivan. *Energy and Equity.* London: Calder & Boyars, 1974.

Leopold, Aldo. *A Sand County Almanac, and Sketches Here and There.* New York: Oxford University Press, 1949.

Muir, John. *The Velvet Monkey Wrench.* Santa Fe, N.Mex.: John Muir Publications, 1975.

Naess, Arne. *Ecology, Community, and Lifestyle: Outline of an Ecosophy.* Translated and edited by David Rothenberg. Cambridge: Cambridge University Press, 1989.

Singer, Peter. *Animal Liberation.* 2d ed. New York: New York Review of Books, 1990.

———. *In Defense of Animals.* Oxford: Oxford University Press, 1985.

Books and Articles

Abbey, Edward. *Hayduke Lives!* Boston: Little, Brown, 1990.

Alaimo, Stacy. *Undomesticated Ground: Recasting Nature as Feminist Space.* Ithaca, N.Y.: Cornell University Press, 2000.

Barry, John. *Rethinking Green Politics: Nature, Virtue, and Progress.* London: Sage, 1999.

Barry, John, and Marcel Wissenburg, eds. *Sustaining Liberal Democracy: Ecological Challenges and Opportunities.* Basingstoke, England: Palgrave, 2001.

Baxter, Brian. *Ecologism: An Introduction.* Washington, D.C.: Georgetown University Press, 1999.

Bryner, Gary C. *Gaia's Wager: Environmental Movements and the Challenge of Sustainability.* Lanham, Md.: Rowman & Littlefield, 2001.

Callenbach, Ernest. *Ecotopia Emerging.* Berkeley, Calif.: Banyan Tree Books, 1981.

Cavalieri, Paola, and Peter Singer, eds. *The Great Ape Project: Equality beyond Humanity.* New York: St. Martin's Press, 1994.

Coleman, Daniel. *Ecopolitics: Building a Green Society.* New Brunswick, N.J.: Rutgers University Press, 1994.

Davis, John, ed. *The Earth First! Reader: Ten Years of Environmental Radicalism.* Salt Lake City: Gibbs Smith, 1991.

Deep Ecology & Anarchism: A Polemic, with Contributions by Murray Bookchin, Brian Morris, Rodney Aitchtey, Graham Pur-chase, Robert Hart, Chris Wilbert. London: Freedom Press, 1993.

Defending the Earth: A Debate between Murray Bookchin and Dave Foreman. Montreal: Black Rose Books, 1991.

Desai, Uday, ed. *Ecological Policy and Politics in Developing Countries: Economic Growth, Democracy, and Environment.* Albany: State University of New York Press, 1998.

de-Shalit, Avner. *The Environment between Theory and Practice.* Oxford: Oxford University Press, 2000.

Devall, Bill, and George Sessions. *Deep Ecology.* Salt Lake City: Peregrine Books, 1985.

Diamond, Irene, and Gloria Feman Orenstein, eds. *Reweaving the World: The Emergence of Ecofeminism.* San Francisco: Sierra Club Books, 1990.

Dobson, Andrew, ed. *Fairness and Futurity: Essays on Environmental Sustainability and Social Justice.* Oxford: Oxford University Press, 1999.

———. *Green Political Thought.* 3d ed. London: Routledge, 2000.

———. *Justice and the Environment: Conceptions of Environmental Sustainability and Theories of Distributive Justice.* Oxford: Oxford University Press, 1998.

Doherty, Brian, and Marius de Geus, eds. *Democracy and Green Political Thought: Sustainability, Rights, and Citizenship.* London: Routledge, 1996.

Eckersley, Robyn. *Environmentalism and Political Theory: Toward an Ecocentric Approach.* Albany: State University of New York Press, 1992.

Environmental Ethics 1, no. 1–present (founded 1979).

Faber, Daniel, ed. *The Struggle for Ecological Democracy: Environmental Justice Movements in the United States. A Project of the Boston "Capitalism, Nature, Socialism" Editorial Group.* New York: Guilford Press, 1998.

Foltz, Richard. "Is There an Islamic Environmentalism? *Environmental Ethics* vol. 22, no. 1 (spring 2000): 63–72.

Francione, Gary L. *Introduction to Animal Rights: Your Child or Your Dog?* Philadelphia: Temple University Press, 2000.

———. *Rain without Thunder: The Ideology of the Animal Rights Movement.* Philadelphia: Temple University Press, 1996.

Guither, Harold D. *Animal Rights: History and Scope of a Radical Social Movement.* Carbondale: Southern Illinois University Press, 1998.

Haraway, Donna. *Simians, Cyborgs, and Women: The Reinvention of Nature.* New York: Routledge, 1991. First published London: Free Association, 1991.

Hayward, Tim. *Ecological Thought: An Introduction.* Cambridge, England: Polity Press, 1995.

———. *Political Theory and Ecological Values.* New York: St. Martin's Press, 1998.

Hill, Julia Butterfly. *The Legacy of Luna: The Story of a Tree, A Woman, and the Struggle to Save the Redwoods.* New York: HarperCollins, 2000.

Katz, Eric, Andrew Light, and David Rosenberg, eds. *Beneath the Surface: Critical Essays of Deep Ecology.* Cambridge: MIT Press, 2000.

Luke, Timothy W. *Capitalism, Democracy, and Ecology: Departing from Marx.* Urbana: University of Illinois Press, 1999.

Milbrath, Lester W. *Envisioning a Sustainable Society: Learning Our Way Out.* Albany: State University of New York Press, 1989.

O'Connor, James. *Natural Causes: Essays in Ecological Marxism.* New York: Guilford Press, 1998.

Paehlke, Robert C. *Environmentalism and the Future of Progressive Politics.* New Haven, Conn.: Yale University Press, 1991.

Peritore, N. Patrick. *Third World Environmentalism: Case Studies from the Global South.* Gainesville: University Press of Florida, 1999.

Prugh, Thomas, Robert Costanza, and Herman Daly. *The Local Politics of Global Sustainability.* Washington, D.C.: Island Press, 2000.

Purdue, Derrick A. *Anti-GenetiX: The Emergence of the Anti-GM Movement.* Aldershot, England: Ashgate, 2000.

Radcliffe, James. *Green Politics: Dictatorship or Democracy.* Basingstoke, England: Palgrave, 2000.

Schlosberg, David. *Environmental Justice and the New Pluralism: The Challenge of Difference for Environmentalism.* Oxford: Oxford University Press, 1999.

Shutkin, William A. *The Land That Could Be: Environmentalism and Democracy in the Twenty-First Century.* Cambridge: MIT Press, 2001.

Singer, Peter. *The Animal Liberation Movement: Its Philosophy, Its Achievements, and Its Future.* Nottingham, England: Old Hammond, [2000].

———. *Ethics into Action: Henry Spira and the Animal Rights Movement.* Lanham, Md.: Rowman & Littlefield, 1998.

Smith, Mark J. *Ecologism: Towards Ecological Citizenship.* Minneapolis: University of Minnesota Press, 1998.

Sturgeon, Noël. *Ecofeminist Natures: Race, Gender, Feminist Theory, and Political Action.* New York: Routledge, 1997.

Taylor, Angus. "Animal Rights and Human Needs." *Environmental Ethics* 18, no. 3 (fall 1996): 249–84.

Taylor, Bron. "Religion, Violence, and Radical Environmentalism: From Earth First! to the Unabomber to the Earth Liberation Front." *Terrorism and Political Violence* 10, no. 4 (winter 1998): 1–42.

Torgerson, Douglas. *The Promise of Green Politics: Environmentalism and the Public Space.* Durham, N.C.: Duke University Press, 1999.

Warren, Karen J. *Ecofeminist Philosophy: A Western Perspective on What It Is and Why It Matters.* Lanham, Md.: Rowman & Littlefield, 2000.

Worple, Ken, ed. *Richer Futures: Fashioning a New Politics.* London: Earthscan, 1999.

Web Sites

http://gp.org/ Green Party

http://solstice.crest.org/environment/renew_america/ Renew America

http://www.cnie.org/ National Council for Science and the Environment

http://www.earthisland.org/ Earth Island Institute

http://www.earthtimes.org/ The Earth Times

http://www.earthvision.net/ Earthvision

http://www.gaia.org/ Global Ecovillage Network

http://www.globalfutures.org/ Global Futures Foundation

http://www.gp.org/platform_index.htm Green Party Platform

http://www.greenparties.org/ Green Parties Worldwide

http://www.sierraclub.org Sierra Club

http://www.stopwhalekill.org/ Stop Whaling

http://www.social-ecology.org/ Institute for Social Ecology

"Selected Web Sites for Environmental Issues." In Gary C. Bryner, *Gaia's Wager: Environmental Movements and the Challenge of Sustainability* (Lanham, Md.: Rowman & Littlefield, 2001), 237–39.

Glossary

This glossary provides a short definition of certain terms used in the text to help the reader better understand the discussion. Many of the terms are discussed at some length in the text; the reader is referred to the index to locate that discussion. An asterisk identifies these terms. Because some words have different meanings in different ideologies, it is important, in using the index, to follow the word throughout the text.

Alienation   Estrangement or being cut off.

Al Qaeda   Islamic guerrilla group in Afghanistan that is enforcing a very strict interpretation of the *Shari'a* in the areas it controls.

*Anarchism   A system of social order achieved without government.

Aristocracy   Originally meaning rule by the few best, it now means rule by the few, usually with the implication of a hereditary few.

Authority   Legitimate power (*see* Power).

Ayatollah   A Shiite title meaning "sign of God."

Biocentrism   A theory that argues that the biosphere should be the focus of value as opposed to human beings being the focus (called anthropocentrism).

Bourgeoisie   In Marxism, refers to the owners of the means of production as contrasted to the proletariat (*see* Proletariat), who have only their labor power to sell. More generally used to refer to the property-owning middle class.

Bureaucracy   The set of nonelected public officials or administrators in any political system.

Burqa   Clothing, required for women by the Taliban in Afghanistan and in some ethnic groups, that covers the body from the top to the head to the ground with only a mesh opening over the eyes.

Caliph   Successor (Sunni).

*Capitalism   Private ownership of the means of production and the organization of production for profit.

Caste   An exclusive, hereditary class. Most often refers to the system found in

Hinduism in which people who are members of specific occupations are separated from other occupations through rigid social divisions that prohibit any kind of contact.

Charismatic leader   A person who is able to gain followers through the force of her or his personality.

Civil disobedience   The belief that disobedience to the law (*see* Law) is an appropriate means of forcing a political system to change the law.

Civil society   The set of largely voluntary associations and interactions found in the family, clubs, neighborhood associations, and so forth that operate outside the formal political system.

Class   A way of ranking or ordering society. In Marxism the ranking is based on the relationship to the means of production. Other ideologies rank on the basis of wealth, education, racial purity, service to the state, or some other criterion.

*Class struggle   In Marxism, used to describe the fundamental relationship between or among classes and the driving force of social change.

Cohousing   A modern version of co-operative housing in which a group of people own individual houses or apartments and collectively own the land and common buildings.

Colonialism   A system in which one state (*see* State) controls another state for the benefit of the former (*see also* Neo-colonialism).

Communal living   A group of people living together in an intentional community. Such communities have a wide range of forms from charismatic or authoritarian leadership to consensual democracy and from complete income sharing to complete private ownership.

*Communism   A social and economic system characterized by an authoritarian political system and a state socialist economic system. Originally meant community of goods or goods publicly held (*see also* Full Communism).

Communitarianism   Focus on the community rather than on the individual.

*Community   A sense of common interest.

*Conservatism   The belief that social change should take place slowly with a due account taken of tradition.

Consociational democracy   A system of power sharing in which each significant group in a country is guaranteed a place in the governing bodies and has a veto on some issues.

Cooperation   An economic theory in which people join together to form an economic unit from which they will all benefit.

*Corporatism   Sometimes called *neo-corporatism*. The arrangement of political and economic relationships so that power groups in society are actively involved with government in making public policy.

Cosmopolitanism   *See* Internationalism.

Critical theory   A general theory that views society from the point of view of the need to change it.

Decentralization   A system in which power is moved from a central organization to regional centers or from a large group to small groups composing it.

Deep Ecology   A movement that stresses the importance of the entire biosphere as opposed to human beings.

*Democracy   A political system characterized by direct or indirect rule by the people (*see also* Participatory democracy; Representation; *and* Consociational democracy).

Democratic centralism   A system developed by Vladimir Ilyich Lenin in which discussion within an organization is completely free until a decision is made, at which time all must support the decision.

Democratization   The process of developing democratic institutions in societies in which they did not previously exist.

Developmental socialism   A theory that proposes to use socialist economic policies to assist the economic development of a country.

Diaspora   From a Greek word meaning dispersion, diaspora originally was used to refer to Jews living outside the Holy Land but is now used to refer to any group with large numbers living outside their traditional homeland.

*Dictatorship of the proletariat   In Marxism, the transitional stage after a successful revolution in which society is gradually transformed.

Direct democracy   Democracy by citizens rather than by representatives.

Ecofeminism   A movement that argues that women are closer to nature than men and that the Green Movement fails to recognize the male bias of environmentalism.

Ecosocialism   A movement that combines environmentalism and socialism.

Elitism   The belief that society is and/or should be ruled by a small group of powerful people.

*Equality   Sameness in some defined way.

*Equality of opportunity   The situation that exists when an individual has the possibility of succeeding or failing on the basis of his or her own ability and effort with no artificial barriers to that success or failure.

Essentially contested concepts   Concepts over which there are fundamental, irreconcilable differences.

Ethnic group   A group of people united by race or national origin.

Extremism   The far right and the far left.

False consciousness   A phrase within Marxism referring to the results of the class-based socialization process in which an individual gains an incorrect view of the world. Similar to the concept of ideology (*see* Ideology).

*Fascism   Originally referring to the principles of the 1922 Italian anti-Communist revolution. Now a general term referring to authoritarian political systems characterized by extreme nationalism (*see also* National Socialism).

Federalism   The division of political power between a central government and governments representing defined territories within the country. These latter units, called states in the United States, may be further divided into smaller units, but these smaller units do not have the same standing as the other two levels of government.

*Feminism   An ideology centered on eliminating oppression of all human beings while stressing the importance of women.

Fourth World   There are two very different meanings in use today. In this book the phrase refers to indigenous peoples; it is also sometimes used to refer to the poorest of the developing countries.

Frankfurt School   The school of Marxist thought that developed critical theory (*see* Critical theory).

*Freedom   The ability to act without constraint (*see also* Liberty *and* Rights).

Führer   German word for leader. Used in National Socialism.

*Full Communism   The final stage of the Marxist theory of history.

General strike   A strike in which all workers engage at the same time. Generally believed to be a major tactic in a revolution or to put pressure on a government.

Government   *See* Political system.

Hajj   The pilgrimage to Mecca required at least once of every Muslim.

Hegemony   A word used by Antonio Gramsci and others to refer to the intellectual and cultural dominance of a class.

*Human nature   The essential characteristics of all human beings.

Idea of Progress   The belief that the world is getting continually better. May or may not include a role for human action.

Ideologue   A true believer or one who has an extremely limited view of the world based on an ideology. An unusually strong believer in an ideology.

*Ideology   A value system or belief system accepted as fact or truth by some group. It is composed of sets of attitudes toward the various institutions and processes of society.

Imam   Leader (Shiite).

*Immigration   Moving to a new country with the intent of establishing permanent residence.

Impeachment   A method of removing a public official from office that involves a hearing of charges before a body of public officials, most often a legislature.

Initiative   A method of bringing a proposed piece of legislation to a vote of the citizenry through a petition signed by citizens.

Internationalism   A belief in the need to unify the entire world in some way; a love of the world.

Jahiliyya   In Islam the period of "ignorance" or "barbarism" before Muhammad preached in Arabia. Used by Sayyid Qutb to refer to the present day.

Jihad   The struggle to follow Islam. Holy war.

Jingoism   Extreme nationalism.

*Justice   Fairness.

*Law   A rule established through an accepted procedure within a community that permits or prohibits certain actions. The system of rules so established.

Levellers   A seventeenth-century British movement favoring political equality.

*Liberalism   A general tendency to accept the ability of human beings to use their reason to reform the social system. A general tendency accepting change as inevitable but controllable. The advocacy of liberty.

*Liberation Theology   The combination of Marxism and theology in opposition to the oppression of the poor.

*Libertarianism   An ideology related to anarchism (*see* Anarchism) that advocates a radically reduced role for government. Also known as *minimalism*.

*Liberty   Freedom (*see* Freedom). Generally used to refer to legally established freedoms (e.g., civil liberty) (*see also* Rights).

Luddites   Men who broke up textile machinery in the early nineteenth century because they believed the machines were taking away jobs. *See also* Neo-Luddites.

Lumpenproletariat   The lowest class in the Marxist class analysis.

Majority rule   An electoral system in which 50 percent plus 1 or more of those voting win.

Maori   The minority population of New Zealand. The Maori settled New Zealand, probably from Polynesia, about one thousand years ago.

Market socialism   Socialism that accepts some aspects of the free market.

*Materialism   The belief that matter or the material (as opposed to spirit, the spiritual, or the ideal) is the determining factor in human life.

Minimalism   *See* Libertarianism.

Monetarism   The belief that the control of the money supply is the most important tool for manipulating a national economy and avoiding inflation.

Monkeywrenching   Direct action or civil disobedience to protect the biosphere.

Monopoly   An organization that controls trade in some commodity or a sector of the economy of a country.

Mosque   A building for Islamic worship.

Muslim   An adherent of Islam.

Nation   A people or race with common descent, language, history, and/or political institutions.

Nationalism   An ideology based on love for the nation (*see* Nation) or patriotism (*see* Patriotism) together with demands for action.

Nationalization of industries   Taking industries into public ownership.

*National Socialism   An ideology developed in Germany under the leadership of Adolf Hitler emphasizing an authoritarian political system, extreme nationalism, and racism (*see also* Fascism).

Naturalization   A process by which a citizen of one country becomes a citizen of another country.

Negative liberty   Liberty achieved by limitations on government activity.

*Neocolonialism   A system of economic dominance over a former colony by an industrialized nation (*see also* Colonialism).

*Neoconservatism   The position held by former liberals in the United States who have become fiscal and foreign policy conservatives.

Neo-corporatism   *See* Corporatism.

Neofascism   Contemporary versions of fascism found throughout the world but particularly common in France, Germany, and the United States.

*Neoliberalism   The position taken by liberals in the United States who have tried to modify the welfare-state image of liberalism.

Neo-Luddites   Contemporary opponents of technology. *See also* Luddites.

Neutralism   *See* Nonalignment.

New Left   The phenomenon of the so-called Sixties (1965–75) that tried to revitalize the old left while not making the same mistakes it had.

*New Right   The most conservative wing in U.S. politics.

Nonalignment   A stance taken in the Third World in which such nations refuse to identify themselves with either of the major power blocs—hence the name Third World.

Ombudsman   A Swedish word that has been adopted into English to refer to a public official whose duties are to protect the rights (*see* Rights) of citizens against government, particularly bureaucracies.

Participation   In democracy, to be actively involved in the political system.

*Participatory democracy   A form of democracy in which individuals who are to be affected by a decision make the decision collectively.

Patriarchy   The system of male dominance that affects all social institutions.

*Patriotism   Love of country (*see also* Nationalism).

Petite bourgeoisie   In Marxist class analysis, the class of small shopkeepers, artisans, and the like who are being pushed down into the proletariat (*see* Proletariat).

Pluralism   In the United States the political system seen as composed of competing groups.

*Political obligation   The duty to obey the dictates of the political system (*see* Political system).

*Political system   Those parts of the social system that have the ability to make authoritative or binding decisions for a territory.

Popular sovereignty   The belief, central to democracy, that ultimate political authority rests with the people.

Positive liberty   Liberty achieved through government support.

Postcolonialism   A contested concept concerned with the social, economic, political, cultural, and psychological conditions created by colonialism and the resistance to it.

*Postmodernism   A contested concept that rejects universals and emphasizes the multiplicity of viewpoints through which people view the world.

*Power   The ability to compel others to act in the way one wishes (*see also* Authority).

PR   *See* Proportional representation.

Privatization   The movement of activities from public control to private control.

*Proletariat   That class in Marxism that has only its labor power to sell (*see also* Bourgeoisie).

Property   Something owned or possessed. Private property: something owned by an individual. Public property: something owned collectively.

Proportional representation   A system of election in which individuals are elected on the basis of the proportion of the votes received rather than the majority as under majority rule (*see* Majority rule).

Qur'an   The holy book for Muslims.

Ramadan   The ninth month of the Muslim year. A month of fasting.

Reapportionment   The process of realigning the boundaries of electoral districts to bring them more in balance in population.

Recall   A mechanism by which an elected official may be removed from office during his or her term through a vote of the electors in the area he or she represents.

Referendum   A process of deciding political questions by the direct vote of the electorate.

Regionalism   The tendency that exists in a number of parts of the world to form economic and sometimes political agreements among states (*see* State) to form larger and more powerful units.

*Representation   A system in which voters choose other individuals to act in their place in making political decisions.

Republic   A state (*see* State) in which political decisions are made by elected representatives.

*Revolution   The process of bringing about radical political and social change, usually violently.

*Rights   Legally defined and enforceable freedoms (*see* Freedom). More generally, something to which a person is entitled. Traditionally divided into natural rights, or rights that are due a person just because of his or her existence as a human being, and civil rights, or rights that are guaranteed by government (*see also* Liberty).

Rochdale Society of Equitable Pioneers or Rochdale Pioneers   The mid-nineteenth-century founders of the cooperative movement.

Self-governing socialism   *See* Self-management.

*Self-management   A type of socialism (*see* Socialism) sometimes known as self-governing socialism in which workers' control (*see* Workers' control) operates in industry and decentralized democracy works in government.

Shari'a   Islamic law.

Sikh   An adherent of a monotheistic religion founded in India around 1500.

Social construction of reality   A phrase used in Marxism to refer to the socialization process. It means that an individual gains a view of the world based on her or his place in society.

Social Darwinism   The belief that relations among human beings are characterized by a struggle for survival.

*Socialism   Public ownership of the means of production and distribution. May be highly centralized as in communism (*see* Communism) or very decentralized as in self-management (*see* Self-management).

*Socialization   The process by which a society transmits its values from generation to generation.

*Social mobility   The process by which individuals move up or down in a society's social stratification system (*see* Social stratification).

Social stratification   The system by which a society ranks the people within it (*see also* Caste, Class, Equality of opportunity, *and* Social mobility).

*State   An organized community (*see* Community) with its own political system (*see* Political system) and law (*see* Law).

Sufi   A believer in Sufism, an ascetic and mystical movement within Islam.

Sunna   Exemplary behavior of Muhammad.

*Superstructure   In Marxism, all those parts of life that are produced by the basic economic relations of society.

*Surplus value   In Marxism, the value of goods produced above and beyond that needed to support labor.

Syndicalism   A system in which the means of production and distribution are under the control of a federation of trade unions.

Taliban   The former rulers of Afghanistan who were a small, extremely conservative sect within Islam.

Terrorism   A form of killing for political purposes. It differs from assassination in that it is frequently directed at nonpolitical targets and groups of people rather than individuals. Its purpose, as implied by the word, is to terrorize the people in a country.

Theocracy   Literally, rule by God. Usually refers to a government in which religious leaders rule directly or indirectly based on their claim of divine authority.

Toleration   The recognition and acceptance of differing belief systems, particularly the acceptance of beliefs believed to be wrong.

Totalitarianism   An authoritarian government, which involves itself in all aspects of society, including the private lives of citizens. The word initially developed to refer to Germany under Hitler and the Soviet Union under Stalin.

Ulama   Muslim religious scholar.

Utopia   Literally means "no place." Term invented by Thomas More (1478–

1535) that now refers to all representations of much better societies.

Utopian socialism   Refers to the ideas of a number of nineteenth-century thinkers who proposed ways of changing the world. Phrase was first used by Friedrich Engels (1820–95) and was meant as a criticism.

Welfare   The system of contributory and noncontributory pension, health, unemployment, and other benefits and social services funded and regulated by government.

Workers' control   Power (*see* Power) in the workplace in the hands of workers rather than management. The industrial system produced by such an arrangement.

Workplace democracy   Democracy within the working environment.

Biographical Notes

Edward Abbey (1927–90) is revered by radical environmentalists for his fictional portrayals of environmental direct action.

Abigail Adams (1744–1818) was an early advocate of women's rights in the United States and wife of John Adams, the second president.

John Adams (1735–1826) was the second president of the United States.

Jane Addams (1860–1935) was a social settlement worker and peace advocate. She ran Hull House in Chicago from 1889 to 1935. She was awarded the Nobel Peace Prize in 1931.

Theodor Adorno (1903–69) was one of the founders of the Frankfurt School.

Michel Aflaq (1910–89) was a founder of the Baath Party.

Ahn Byung-mu (1922–96) was the leading theologian of Minjung Theology.

Mullah Mohammad Omar Akhund (b. 1961) was the founder and head of the Taliban movement in Afghanistan.

Benedict Anderson (b. 1936) is the Aaron L. Binenkorb Professor of International Relations and director of the Modern Indonesia Program at Cornell University.

Susan B. Anthony (1820–1906) was one of the leaders of the women's suffrage movement.

Yasir Arafat (b. 1929) is the leader of the PLO (Palestinian Liberation Organization).

John Ashcroft (b. 1942) is attorney general of the United States.

Mary Astell (1668–1731) was an English author who proposed a separate community of women in her *A Serious Proposal to the Ladies* (1694).

Margaret Atwood (b. 1939) is the author of *The Handmaid's Tale* (1985), a picture of a future society in which women are suppressed.

Daw Aung San Suu Kyi (b. 1945) won the Nobel Peace Prize in 1991 for her efforts to reestablish democracy in Myanmar (formerly Burma), where she was under house arrest from 1989 to 2002.

Mikhail Bakunin (1814–76) was a leading Russian anarchist theorist who spent most of his life in western Europe.

Hasan al-Banna (1906–49) was the founder of the Muslim Brotherhood.

Salah al-Din Baytar (1911–80) was a founder of the Baath Party.

Simone de Beauvoir (1908–86) was a French author best known for her reflections on the status of women, *La Deuxième Sexe* (1949, in English as *The Second Sex* in 1952).

Samuel Beckett (1906–89) was an Irish playwright who lived and wrote mostly in France, is famous for his depictions of alienation, particularly in *Waiting for Godot*.

Edward Bellamy (1850–98), a U.S. author, is remembered for his best-selling utopian novel *Looking Backward 2000–1887* (1888). A movement for social change was founded to promote Bellamy's ideas and was influential both in the United States and abroad.

Alexander Berkman (1870–1936) was a friend of Emma Goldman and an activist in the American anarchist movement who spent many years in prison in the United States.

Isaiah Berlin (1909–97) was a British historian of ideas and social theorist.

Marie Louise Berneri (1918–49) was an Italian-born British anarchist.

Eduard Bernstein (1850–1932) was a follower of Marx who rejected revolutionary socialism. He was a major Marxist revisionist, arguing for evolutionary socialism and political activity.

Hakim Bey is a pseudonym of Peter Lamborn Wilson, who is coeditor of *Autonomedia* and *Semiotext(e)* and has written extensively on Sufism, Persian poetry, and Irish literature. As Bey he is known as one of the foremost theorists of contemporary anarchism.

Homi K. Bhabha (b. 1949) is an Indian-born professor at Harvard University and a major theorist of post-colonialism.

Vinobha Bhave (1895–1982) was an Indian spiritual leader.

Benazir Bhutto (b. 1953) has twice served as prime minister of Pakistan.

Osama bin Laden (b. 1957) is the leader of a worldwide terrorist network called Al Qaeda.

Ernst Bloch (1885–1977) was a German Marxist philosopher best known for his book *Das Prinzip Hoffnung (The Principle of Hope)* (1959).

Allan Aubrey Boesak (b. 1946) is a South African minister, theologian, and activist. He was found guilty of fraud in his use of funds intended for the victims of apartheid and served a year in prison before being released on parole.

Clodovis Boff (b. 1944) is a Servite priest and a professor of theology at the Catholic University of São Paulo. He is the brother of Leonardo Boff.

Leonardo Boff (b. 1938) is a Franciscan priest and professor of systematic theology at the Institute for Philosophy and Theology in Petrópolis, Brazil. He is one of the best-known theologians of Liberation Theology.

Murray Bookchin (b. 1921) is a major anarchist theorist who has recently been a major contributor to environmentalism in the United States.

Bernard Bosanquet (1848–1932) was an English conservative philosopher.

Willy Brandt (1913–92) was active in German politics throughout the post-war period. He was best known for his period as governing mayor of Berlin (1957–66) and as chancellor of the Federal Republic of Germany.

André Breton (1896–1966) was a French poet and a founder of the surrealist movement.

John J. Breuilly (b. 1946) is a professor of modern history at the University of Birmingham in the United Kingdom.

William F. Buckley (b. 1925) founded *The National Review* (1955–present) and has been a leader of American conservatism.

Edmund Burke (1729–97) is best known as the founder of conservatism.

George W. Bush (b. 1946) is the forty-third president of the United States.

Richard Girnt Butler (b. ca. 1919/20) was the leader of Aryan Nations, which is currently undergoing a struggle over its future leadership.

Étienne Cabet (1788–1856) was a French utopian socialist and founder of the Icarian movement that established a number of communities in the United States.

Ernest Callenbach (b. 1929) is the author of a series of books describing a fictional society emphasizing ecology.

Albert Camus (1913–60) was an Algerian-born French novelist and exponent of existentialism who won the Nobel Prize in literature in 1957.

Margaret Canovan is professor of political thought at Keele University, in the United Kingdom.

Rachel Carson (1907–64) was an early writer on environmental issues.

Whittaker Chambers (1901–61) is revered on the right for his anticommunist leadership.

Judy Chicago (b. 1939) is a feminist artist.

Winston Churchill (1874–1965) was prime minister of Great Britain from 1940 to 1945 and 1951 to 1955.

Robert Coles (b. 1929) is a child psychiatrist and professor of psychiatry and medical humanities at Harvard University.

Alex Comfort (1920–2000) is best known for his books on sexual technique, but his career has ranged through fiction, poetry, anarchist theory, and geriatric psychology.

James H. Cone (b. 1938) is the leading exponent of Black Theology and is Charles A. Briggs Distinguished Professor of Systematic Theology at Union Theological Seminary, New York.

Robert A. Dahl (b. 1915) is professor of political science at Yale University.

Dante Alighieri (1265–1321) was an Italian poet best known as the author of the *Divine Comedy* who also contributed to political theory.

Charles Darwin (1809–82) was a famous English naturalist who put forth a number of important theses about evolution.

Dorothy Day (1897–1980) was a founder of the Catholic Worker Movement.

Guy Debord (1931–94) was the self-proclaimed leader of the Situationist International.

Voltairine de Cleyre (1866–1912) was an American anarchist.

Milovan Djilas (1911–95) was a Yugoslav politician and social theorist best known for developing the theory of the "new class" within Marxism.

Andrea Dworkin (b. 1946) is a feminist writer.

Ronald Dworkin (b. 1931) is a legal philosopher.

Terry Eagleton (b. 1943) is an English scholar who has written on ideology.

Paul Ehrlich (b. 1932) was one of the first people in the twentieth century to write about the problems of overpopulation.

Jon Elster is professor of political science at Columbia University.

Friedrich Engels (1820–95) was a friend of and coauthor with Karl Marx.

Louis Farrakhan (originally Louis Eugene Walkott, b. 1933) is the current head of the Nation of Islam.

Shulamith Firestone (b. 1944) is a feminist writer.

Dave Foreman (b. 1946) is an active environmentalist and founder of Earth First!.

Charles Fourier (1772–1837) was a French utopian socialist.

Francis of Assisi (born Giovanni Francesco Bernardone, 1182–1226) was the radical founder of the Franciscan movement and is now recognized in Liberation Theology as an early advocate of the poor.

Michael Freeden (b. 1944) is the editor of the *Journal of Political Ideologies*.

Paulo Freire (1921–97) was a Brazilian social theorist best known for his book *The Pedagogy of the Oppressed*

(1972) and seen as a theorist of both anarchism and Liberation Theology.

Sigmund Freud (1856–1939) was the Austrian founder of psychoanalysis.

Betty Friedan (b. 1921) is a feminist author and lecturer.

Milton Friedman (b. 1912) won the Nobel Prize in economics for his work on monetary theory. He is the best-known conservative economist in the United States and taught economics at the University of Chicago for many years.

Francis Fukuyama (b. 1952) restarted the "end of ideology" debate in 1989.

Margaret Fuller (1810–50) was a teacher and writer struggling against the limited roles allowed women during her lifetime.

Muammur Gadhafi or Qaddafi (b. 1942) is the leader of Libya.

Mohandas K. Gandhi (1869–1948) was a leader of the anticolonial movement in India who used nonviolence as a means of bringing about social change. He had been influenced by Henry David Thoreau and influenced Martin Luther King, Jr.

Roger Garaudy (b. 1913) is a French Marxist philosopher who converted to Islam.

Clifford Geertz (b. 1913) is professor in the School of Social Science at the Institute for Advanced Study, Princeton, New Jersey.

Henry George (1839–97) was an American economic theorist who developed a theory based on land taxation, known as the single tax, as a means of redistributing wealth.

Charlotte Perkins Gilman (1860–1935) was a feminist writer, lecturer, and activist. She is now best known for her novel *Herland* (1915).

William Godwin (1756–1836) was the earliest British anarchist theorist.

Joseph Goebbels (1897–1945) was Germany's minister for propaganda and national enlightenment under Adolf Hitler.

Emma Goldman (1869–1940) was known as "Red Emma" and was a leading anarchist, lecturer, popularizer of the arts, and agitator for birth control, women's rights, and free speech.

André Gorz (b. 1924) is a French social theorist.

Antonio Gramsci (1891–1937) was an Italian social theorist and is considered one of the most original Marxist theorists.

Thomas H. Green (1836–82) was a professor of philosophy at Oxford University.

Alan Greenspan (b. 1926) is chairman of the Federal Reserve, a position he has held since 1988, and is generally considered the most powerful unelected official in Washington, D.C.

Angelina E. Grimké (1805–79) was an abolitionist and women's rights pioneer.

Sarah Moore Grimké (1792–1873) was an abolitionist and women's rights pioneer.

Gustavo Gutíerrez (b. 1928) is a Peruvian theologian and professor of theology at the Catholic University of Lima.

Jürgen Habermas (b. 1929) is one of the most important contemporary thinkers influenced by Marxism and the Frankfurt School.

Jörg Haider (b. 1950) was the leader of the Freedom Party (FPO) of Austria, a right-wing party that became part of the ruling coalition in Austria in 2000. Because of controversy over his stated beliefs, he resigned from the leadership of the party, but he remains a powerful force within the party and the country.

Matt Hale (b. 1971) is the Pontifex Maximus of the World Church of the Creator, a white supremacist church.

Michael Hardt is associate professor of literature and Romance studies at Duke University.

Michael Harrington (1928–89) was co-chair of the Democratic Socialists of America and a professor of political science at Queens College of the City University of New York.

Nancy C. M. Hartsock (b. 1943) is professor of political science and women's studies at the University of Washington in Seattle.

F. A. Hayek (1899–1992) was one of the most important conservative thinkers of the twentieth century. His *The Road to Serfdom* (1944) provided an ethical defense of free markets.

William Least Heat-Moon (b. 1939) is the author of *Blue Highways* (1982), *PrairyErth* (1991), and *River-horse* (1999). The name is often seen without the hyphen.

Ammon Hennacy (1893–1970) was an important American anarchist.

Adolf Hitler (1889–1945) was founder and leader of the National German Workers' Party, chancellor (1933–45), and head of state (1934–45) of Germany. He was the leading figure of the Nazi movement and is still venerated by Nazis and neo-Nazis everywhere.

Julia "Butterfly" Hill sat in a tree she called Luna for 738 days to protest logging.

Bonnie Honig is professor of political science and director of the Center for Law, Culture, and Social Thought (CLCST) at Northwestern University and senior research fellow at the American Bar Foundation in Chicago.

bell hooks is the pseudonym of Gloria Watkins, under which she has written a number of important works of African American feminism.

Ivan Illich (b. 1926) is the Austrian-born cofounder of the Center for Intercultural Documentation (CIDOC) in Cuernavaca, Mexico. He is a radical priest who has written extensively about contemporary society.

Alison M. Jaggar is professor of women's studies at the University of Colorado, Boulder.

Thomas Jefferson (1743–1826) was the third president of the United States. Of all the things he accomplished, Jefferson thought his three most important actions were writing the Declaration of Independence and the Virginia Act for Establishing Religious Freedom and founding the University of Virginia.

John Paul II (born 1920 as Karol Joseph Wojtyla), the first pope from Poland, was elected pope in 1978.

Lyndon Baines Johnson (1908–73), president from 1963 to 1969, presided over a period of great change in US social policy, particularly the beginnings of the extension of civil rights to African Americans and the war on poverty. He is still best known for his failure to solve the Vietnam crisis.

Theodore Kaczynski (b. 1942) is the Unabomber, who assembled and mailed bombs that injured or killed individuals who worked in the fields of technology and industry. He published a manifesto calling for a return to a less technology-based life and direct action to achieve that goal. He is currently serving time in prison for his actions.

John Maynard Keynes (1883–1946) was an English economist who argued for the use of government spending to stimulate the economy.

Ayatollah Ruhollah Khomeini (1900–1989) was the religious leader of Iran after the Shiite overthrow of the Shah. He was one of the intellectual fathers of Islamic revivalism.

Russell Kirk (1918–94) was an important modern conservative. His *The Conservative Mind* (1953) provided an intellectual basis for modern conservatism. He founded the journals *Modern Age* in 1957 and *University Bookman* in 1960; both served as outlets for conservative writing.

Peter Kropotkin (1842–1921) was born into the Russian aristocracy but became the most important anarchist thinker of all time.

Will Kymlicka is Queen's National Scholar and professor of philosophy at Queen's University, Canada, and one of the foremost theorists of multiculturalism.

Ernesto Laclau is a professor of government at the University of Essex in the United Kingdom.

Emma Lazarus (1849–87) was an American poet and essayist best known for her poem "The New Colossus," which appears on a plaque on the Statue of Liberty.

Ursula K. Le Guin (b. 1929) is a major science fiction, fantasy, and children's author whose novel *The Dispossessed* (1974) is a contribution to anarchist theory.

Vladimir Ilyich Lenin (born Vladimir Ilyich Ulyanov, 1870–1924) was the leader of the Russian Revolution of 1917 and ruled the Soviet Union from the revolution to his death.

Aldo Leopold (1886–1949) was the author of *A Sand County Almanac* (1949) and an early environmentalist.

Jean-Marie Le Pen (b. 1928) is the leader of the National Front in France.

Abraham Lincoln (1808–65) was the sixteenth president of the United States.

John Locke (1632–1704) was an important British philosopher and political thinker. His most important works were *Essay Concerning Human Understanding* (1689), and, in political thought, *Two Treatises of Government* (published in 1690 but written earlier). The U.S. Declaration of Independence was based on the *Second Treatise of Government*.

Ned Lud (or Ludd) (fl. 1779) provided the name for the Luddites. He broke up machinery (stocking frames) around 1799 because he believed the machines would take over his job.

Rosa Luxemburg (1871–1919) was a Polish Marxist revolutionary who opposed both Lenin's centralism and Bernstein's gradualism.

Jean-François Lyotard (1924–98) was a French philosopher best known for his exposition of postmodernism.

Catharine A. MacKinnon (b. 1946) is the most important feminist legal theorist.

James Madison (1751–1836) was secretary of state (1801–09) during the presidency of Thomas Jefferson and then the fourth president of the United States (1809–17). Madison is now mostly remembered as one of the authors of *The Federalist Papers* (1787–88) and as a major contributor to the drafting of the U.S. Constitution.

Errico Malatesta (1850–1932) was a leading Italian anarchist theorist.

Malcolm X (originally Malcolm Little, 1925–65) was a leader of the Nation of Islam, but split from it to form the Organization of Afro-American Unity before his assassination.

Karl Mannheim (1893–1947) was a Hungarian-born sociologist active in Germany until he fled the Nazis in 1933. He is best known as the major theorist of the sociology of knowledge.

Mao Zedong (1893–1976) was longtime leader of the People's Republic of China.

Subcomandante Marcos is the name used by the best-known leader of the Zapatista movement.

Herbert Marcuse (1898–1979) was a member of the Frankfurt School who stayed in the United States after the school returned to Germany following World War II. He was a major influence on the New Left.

Karl Marx (1818–83) was the founder of Communism.

Abu al-A'la al-Mawdudi (1903–79) of Pakistan was one of the intellectual founders of Islamic revivalism.

George McKay (b. 1950) is professor of cultural studies at the University of Central Lancashire, England.

Timothy McVeigh (1968–2001) was executed for bombing the Alfred P. Murrah Federal Office Building in Oklahoma City.

Lester Milbrath (b. 1925) is the director of the Research Program in Environment and Society at the State University of New York at Buffalo.

Angela Miles (b. 1946) is in the Department of Adult Education at the Ontario Institute for Studies in Education in Toronto.

John Stuart Mill (1806–73) was the most influential philosopher in the English-speaking world in the nineteenth century. He is best known today for his essay *On Liberty* (1859).

David Miller is Official Fellow of Politics at Nuffield College, Oxford University, England, and an important political theorist.

Charles de Secondat de La Brède et de Montesquieu (known as Montesquieu) (1689–1755) was a French political thinker whose book *De l'esprit des lois (The Spirit of the Laws)* (1748) influenced the writers of the U.S. Constitution, particularly his advocacy of a separation of powers.

Margaret Moore is an associate professor of political science at the University of Waterloo in Canada and author of The Ethics of Nationalism.

William Morris (1834–96) was the leader of the British arts and crafts movement who some label as an anarchist theorist. He considered himself a Marxist.

Chantal Mouffe is Quinton Hogg Senior Research Fellow at the Centre for the Study of Democracy at the University of Westminster (UK).

Muhammad (570–632) was the founder of Islam.

Elijah Muhammad (originally Elijah Poole, 1897–1975) was the spiritual leader of the Nation of Islam.

Warith Deen Muhammad (b. 1933) followed his father Elijah Muhammad as leader of the Nation of Islam and led his followers away from his father's separatist teachings and into traditional Islam.

Benito Mussolini (1883–1945) was the founder of the fascist movement and head of the Fascist Party in Italy.

Ralph Nader (b. 1934) was a leader for automobile safety and on various environmental and safety issues before becoming the presidential candidate of the Green Party in the 2000 election in the United States.

Arne Naess (b. 1912) is a Norwegian philosopher who coined the term "Deep Ecology."

Gamal Abdel Nasser (1918–70) was the leader of the Egyptian revolution and head of the country for many years.

Sergei Nechaev (1847–82) was an advocate of terrorism and the inspiration for the insane revolutionary in Fyodor Dostoevsky's *The Possessed* (1871).

Antonio Negri was a professor of political science at the University of Padua. He was arrested in connection with terrorist activities in Italy in the seventies, spent some years in exile in France, and is currently serving his sentence in Rome. Many believe that his arrest and conviction were without basis.

Jawaharlal Nehru (1889–1964) was a leader of the anticolonial movement in India and prime minister of India after independence.

Richard Milhous Nixon (1913–94) was president of the United States from 1969 to 1974 and is the only president who has been forced to resign from office to avoid impeachment. He presided over the largest expansion of social welfare programs in U.S. history, ended the war in Vietnam, and reestablished political relations with the People's Republic of China.

Kwame Nkrumah (1909–72) was the leader of Ghana from 1957, when it gained independence, to 1966.

Robert Nozick (1938–2002) was a professor of philosophy at Harvard University and author of Anarchy, State, and Utopia (1974), the best exposition of anarcho-capitalism.

U Nu (1907–95) was a leader of Burmese independence and secretary general of the United Nations.

Julius K. Nyerere (1922–99) was the first president of Tanganyika and then of Tanzania.

Susan Moller Okin is Martha Sutton Weeks Professor of Ethics in Society in the Department of Political Science at Stanford University.

Robert Owen (1771–1858) was a British utopian socialist who founded the New Harmony community in Indiana.

Robert C. Paehlke (b. 1941) is a writer on environmental issues.

Thomas Paine (1737–1809) was a political agitator, revolutionist, and political theorist.

Olof Palme (1927–86) was a Swedish leader of European democratic socialists.

Christobel Pankhurst (1880–1958) was a daughter of Emmeline Pankhurst and active in the British suffrage movement.

Emmeline Pankhurst (1858–1928) was a leader of the British suffrage movement.

Sylvia Pankhurst (1882–1960) was a leader of the British suffrage movement.

Anton Pannekoek (1873–1960) was the Dutch founder of Council Communism.

William J. Pierce (b. 1933) is the leader of the National Alliance.

Marge Piercy (b. 1936) is a writer whose novel *Woman on the Edge of Time* (1976) is a major feminist utopia.

Plato (427?–347 B.C.) was the founder of social philosophy in the West.

Pol Pot (1925–98) was until 1997 the leader of the Khmer Rouge guerrillas in Cambodia, which he renamed Kampuchea, and was responsible for genocide against its citizens.

Pierre-Joseph Proudhon (1809–65) was a leading French anarchist theorist.

Robert D. Putnam is the Peter and Isabel Malkin Professor of Public Policy at Harvard University and the author of *Bowling Alone* (2000).

Qaddafi, Muammur; see Gadhafi.

Sayyid Qutb (1906–66) was an Egyptian Sunni Muslim leader and one of the intellectual founders of Islamic revivalism. He was jailed from 1954 to 1964 and executed for his opposition to Egypt's leaders.

Thomas Rainsborough (d. 1648) was one of the leaders of the army who sided with the Levellers in the English Civil War.

Ayn Rand (1905–82) was a novelist, lecturer, and essayist who influenced the growth of libertarianism and minimalism in the United States.

John Rawls (b. 1921) is a professor of philosophy at Harvard University and has been the major liberal theorist of the twentieth century.

Ronald Reagan (b. 1911) was the fortieth president of the United States.

Élisée Réclus (1830–1905) was a Belgian geographer and an anarchist theorist.

Ernest Renan (1823–92) was a French philologist and historian.

Rudolf Rocker (1873–1958) was an anarchist theorist who was born in Germany and lived and wrote mostly in the United Kingdom and the United States.

George Lincoln Rockwell (1918–67) was the leader of the American Nazi Party until his assassination.

John Roemer is the Elizabeth S. and A. Varick Stout Professor of Political Science and Economics at Yale University.

Franklin D. Roosevelt (1882–1945) was the thirty-second president of the United States, serving in that office longer than any other president.

Murray Rothbard (1926–95) was a leading American anarcho-capitalist.

Jean-Jacques Rousseau (1712–78) is the best-known French political philosopher.

Claude-Henri Saint-Simon (1760–1825) was a French utopian socialist.

Margaret Sanger (1883–1966) was an early advocate of birth control and women's rights.

Jean-Paul Sartre (1905–80) was a French novelist and philosopher.

Albert Sauvy (1898–1990) was a French demographer who coined the term "Third World."

Sarah Scott (1723–95) was a British writer now considered an early feminist.

Amartya Sen (b. 1933) won the Nobel Prize in economics in 1998.

Léopold Senghor (1906–2001) was a leader of the anticolonial movement in Senegal, leader of the country after independence, and became known as a significant poet in French.

George Sessions (b. 1938) is one of the primary theorists of Deep Ecology.

Adam Smith (1723–90) is best known as the author of The Wealth of Nations (*An Inquiry into the Nature and Causes of the Wealth of Nations* [1776]).

Benjamin Nathaniel Smith (1978–99) was a member of the World Church of the Creator who, on July 3–4, 1999, in racially motivated attacks, killed two people, wounded eight people, and shot at numerous others before killing himself.

Georges Sorel (1847–1922) was a French journalist and political theorist.

Herbert Spencer (1820–1903) was an English philosopher and the major proponent of social Darwinism.

Lysander Spooner (1808–87) was a lawyer and abolitionist and an early American anarcho-capitalist.

Joseph Stalin (born Iosif Vissarionovich Dzhugashvili, 1879–1953) was the leader of the Soviet Union after Lenin.

Elizabeth Cady Stanton (1815–1902) was one of the founders of the first women's rights conventions in Seneca Falls, New York in 1848 and a leader of the nineteenth-century women's rights movement.

Max Stirner (pseud. of Johan Kasper Schmidt, 1806–50) was the founder of individualist anarchism.

Harriet Taylor (1808–58) wrote on women's rights and was the wife of John Stuart Mill, whom she influenced to write on the subject.

William Thompson (1775–1833) wrote on women's rights.

Henry David Thoreau (1817–62) was a naturalist, writer, and advocate of civil disobedience.

Leo Tolstoi (1828–1910) was a famous Russian novelist who is also known as an anarchist theorist.

Benjamin R. Tucker (1854–1939) was one of the most important American anarchist theorists.

Camilo Torres (1929–66) was a priest who joined the National Liberation Army (ELN) of Columbia and died in combat.

Sojourner Truth (1797–1883) was born a slave and became a noted lecturer and abolitionist.

Kwame Ture (Stokely Carmichael) (1941–1998) was a leader in the U.S. civil rights movement.

Unabomber; see Theodore Kaczynski.

Wilhelm Richard Wagner (1813–83) is best known for his operas expressing Teutonic mythology.

Alice Walker (b. 1944) is an African American author, best known for her novel The Color Purple (1982).

Nicholas Walter (1934–99) was a major British anarchist theorist.

Colin Ward (b. 1924) was one of the editors of the anarchist weekly *Freedom* from 1947 to 1960. He founded *Anarchy* and edited it from 1961 to 1970. An architect, teacher, lecturer, and freelance writer, Ward significantly advanced anarchist theory in the second half of the twentieth century.

Josiah Warren (1798?–1874) was an early American anarchist theorist.

Max Weber (1864–1920) was a German social theorist most remembered for his work on bureaucracy and his study of the social effects of Calvinism.

Mary Wollstonecraft (1759–97) was one of the earliest feminist theorists.

George Woodcock (1912–95) was a British anarchist theorist who settled in Canada.

Frances Wright (1795–1852) was a lecturer and writer concerned with women's rights, slavery, and the plight of workers.

Index